POWER, PRODUCTION, AND THE UNPROTECTED WORKER

THE POLITICAL ECONOMY OF INTERNATIONAL CHANGE
John Gerard Ruggie, General Editor

POWER PRODUCTION, AND THE UNPROTECTED WORKER

JEFFREY HARROD

Volume 2 in the four-volume series
Power and Production

New York • Columbia University Press • 1987

Columbia University Press
New York   Guildford, Surrey
Copyright © 1987 Columbia University Press
All rights reserved

Printed in the United States of America

Library of Congress Cataloging-in-Publication Data

Harrod, Jeffrey.
    Power, production, and the unprotected worker.

    (Power and production; v. 2) (The political economy
of international change)
    Includes bibliographies and index.
    1. Industrial relations.   2. Power (Social sciences)
3. Labor and laboring classes.   4. Peasantry.
5. Home labor.   6. Self-employed.   I. Title.
II. Series: Cox, Robert W., 1926–   . Power and
production; v. 2.   III. Series: Political economy
of international change.
HD6971.H287   1987   306'.36   86-26374
ISBN 0-231-05844-6

This book is Smyth-sewn and printed on permanent and durable
acid-free paper.
Book design by J. S. Roberts

THE POLITICAL ECONOMY
OF INTERNATIONAL CHANGE
John Gerard Ruggie, General Editor

Jeffrey Harrod, *Power, Production, and the Unprotected Worker*
1987

CONTENTS

ACKNOWLEDGMENTS

This book is one of a series of four that have been written as part of a collaborative effort between Robert Cox and myself. Two of the four are written by myself and two by Robert Cox. Each author is entirely responsible for the books which bear his name. The four books are a study of power and politics at the workplace, national and international levels.

The first steps towards writing these books were taken some fifteen years ago with the publication of an initial effort of Robert Cox to classify patterns of power relations surrounding production. This was soon followed by a publication building on the classification and written by both of us and some other colleagues.*

Since that time much has changed intellectually and substantively. We worked on the production of these four books for over ten years on a part-time basis via exchange of drafts, critiques, and working sessions in Europe during the summers. Although the books will be published at different times, all four have been in existence in various stages of drafts for some time. Each of us thus had each other's insights and analysis at hand and both of us have been seriously concerned and involved in much of the material found in each of the books.

It is perhaps almost unnecessary after having said all this to indicate the intellectual and supportive debt that I owe Robert Cox. It was his leadership and guidance that initially inspired

*Robert W. Cox, "Approaches to a Futurology of Industrial Relations," *International Institute of Labour Studies Bulletin* (1971), no. 8, pp. 139-64; Robert Cox, Jeffrey Harrod, and others, *Future Industrial Relations: An Interim Report*, Geneva: 1972 (International Institute for Labour Studies.

me and provided an approach to the questions of work, power, production, and politics. Without him of course, there would have been no study and no book of this nature. On the personal level it is necessary only to say that we are friends.

The other major intellectual debt I owe is to Paddy Summerfield for her penetrating destruction of any tendencies to lack of clarity that may have arisen from the language of social science (this is not to say she is responsible for those lapses that remain). Also, I recognize the importance of her constant supply of insights and information derived from a prodigious reading of creative literature arising from the cultural, ethnic, geographic, class, and gender divisions of the world.

This book is one in which a variety of experience and skills could be brought to bear, as I have attempted to explain in an appendix on research and citations. For this reason I mention and thank persons who may not find a place in the acknowledgments in other books or articles I may write. These are the following: George Schwarzenberger, whose unwavering devotion to a power analysis of international society struck a lasting chord in a late undergraduate already bruised by six years of being in the lowest ranks of power; Les Gilbert, who taught me presentational logic and investigatory techniques; Louis Chuard, who reminded me always that social science largely precipitates what any perceptive veteran of life and work knows anyway; the members of the New World Group in Jamaica of 1967 who, through their own search for a meaningful social science, helped me uncover and challenge the implicit assumptions of the values and procedures I was then following; Gerard Kester and Henk Thomas, who at different times and in different ways have supported the project and, in particular, took an initial interest in the earlier industrial relations systems approach and tested it in seminars and teaching in the third world; John Ruggie, as series editor at Columbia University Press, for a careful and critical review of the manuscript that yielded many valuable suggestions for improvements; numerous graduate professionals from the third world who have supplied me with information and comments in the context of educational programs in Geneva and The Hague. None of these persons, however, can in any way be directly blamed, associated with, or held responsible for what finally emerged.

ACKNOWLEDGMENTS

Intellectual products are social products that are indirectly supported by immediate family, colleagues, friends, associates, and contacts, together with those vast armies of working people who support contemporary, as well as past, European scholars exquisite privilege of having time to research, think, and write. To them goes both recognition and thanks.

I note with thanks the cooperation of Ms. Agnes Perrier of the International Labor Organization library; Kate Wittenberg and Leslie Bialler of Columbia University Press; and also Wendy Williams and Selma Noort who must serve as the symbol of all those many typists and others who are engaged in the physical production of this book.

This book, like my first, has been funded out of current earnings as a part-time academic and writer and has not been financially supported by any organization, university foundation, front, or conduit. The book was accepted for publication without any subsidy to the publisher, either financial or material. The Institute of Social Studies in The Hague, where I am a part-time faculty member, extended typing facilities for which I am grateful.

Petit Bornand-les-Glieres, France

INTRODUCTION

This book is one of four which present a study of power relations in societies and in world politics from the starting point of the power relations of production. To achieve this a classification of modes, or forms, of the power relations of production was made in an innovative manner. The study thus entails a demonstration of an approach with relevance and implications for most branches of social science.

Each of the books of the study is designed to be freestanding; that is, each may be read or resorted to without the need to have recourse to any of the other three. However, some aspects of the type and manner of presentation in the different books have been influenced by their position within the whole series. It is desirable, therefore, for any reader of a particular book to understand the nature and organization of all four books.

The objectives of the four books had two aspects: first to present the conceptual framework of the study with factual and historical illustrations; second, to demonstrate the viability and utility of a classification of the forms of social relations of production identified. This latter objective would require examination in some detail of the separate dynamics of the forms identified, the consciousness of producers within them, and the paths of growth, retraction, and transformation.

The first task of presenting the conceptual framework and providing an overview of the whole study was done by Robert Cox in *Production, Power, and World Order*: In this book the approach in the four books is subjected to theoretical and conceptual discussion, and applied to the broader questions arising in the last quarter of the twentieth century.

The second task—the presentation and analysis of the separate forms of social relations of production—required two decisions, namely, how the material was to be presented and how it was to be divided between the remaining books.

On the first issue, it was decided that each form of social relations of production would be presented as a monad—that is, as a self-contained structure that contains its own development and change potential. This has meant that priority has been given to the conditions, structure of power and dynamics of change as they appear from within the different forms. Consideration of the broader questions of change at the level of society or world economy arises by implication from the analysis of actions and consciousness of groups and classes within different social relations and from discussions of selected theoretical and contemporary issues related to social change.

As to the second necessary decision—the division of the work among the remaining books—two natural divisions within the classification were used. The first division was between those forms of social relations associated with societies following capitalist and noncapitalist paths of development. Thus those forms of social relations associated with noncapitalist development were separated and are to be considered by Robert Cox in *Redistributive Social Relations* (provisional title).

The second natural division in the classification was between those forms of social relations that in any specific circumstance were dominant and those that were subordinate. This dichotomy also corresponded to a division between those workers who are relatively more exploited and insecure—the nonestablished or unprotected worker—and those who enjoy more advantageous and stable conditions of work and income—the established worker. To some extent this division also corresponds to a division of the world labor force into those sections associated with third world countries and those associated with rich, industrialized countries. These divisions were then the basis for the two books, of which this is the first, by Jeffrey Harrod: *Power, Production and the Unprotected Worker*, which examines the subordinate forms and the unprotected workers most of whom are in the third world and *Power, Production and the Established Worker*, which examines the dominant forms and the established workers, most of whom are in the industrialized countries.

To assist in understanding the relationships between the various books the following abstracts of them may be used. The two books by Robert Cox:

Production, Power and World Order: Social Forces in the Making of History (New York, Columbia University Press, 1987)

This book deals with the intellectual origins of the conceptual framework used in all four books of the study. Discussions include an elaboration of the definition of a mode of social relations of production, social formations and forms of state. Dynamics at the level of the social formation and contemporary developments of the state at the international level show how the approach is crucial to an understanding of current and historical world developments.

Redistributive Production Relations, (Provisional title, forthcoming Columbia University Press)

Deals with two principal forms of social relations found in societies adopting a noncapitalist path to development. These forms are named as communalist and central planning. The description and analysis of the forms, and the internal relations are an important part of the work. As forms that have a society-wide coverage it has been possible to illustrate them basically from the experience of the Soviet Union and People's Republic of China

Power, Production and the Unprotected Worker: (New York, Columbia University Press, 1987)

Presents six forms of social relations as self-contained structures with their own developmental potential. Groups and classes within these forms are subordinate to groups in other structures within societies in which the dynamic of development is capitalist. The workers within them are the least protected in the world labor force and are often found in the conventional categories of subsistence farmers, peasants, urban marginals, unorganized wage workers, self-employed, and housewives. Each form is discussed from the standpoint of power relations within as, for example, those between peasant and landowner or self-employed and customers, and the dynamics and consciousness arising from

them. Finally, some consideration is made of how the results of these relations appear economically, politically and
in relation to social change at the national level.

The two books by Jeffrey Harrod:

Power, Production and the Established Worker: (forthcoming,
Columbia University Press)
Presents four forms of social relations as self-contained
structures with their own development potential. Groups
and classes within these are dominant in relation to groups
in other structures in societies following the capitalist development path. The four forms are named as enterprise
corporatist, bipartite, tripartite, and state corporatist. Workers within them have a relatively privileged status, can be
considered as 'established,' and are found in conventional
categories such as organized wage workers, civil servants,
military, police, and employees of large corporations. Each
form is discussed from the standpoint of power relations
within as, for example, those between the lower and higher
reaches of a bureaucracy, or those between unions, employees and state representatives. Transformational dynamics arising from these power relations and the role of
producers within the forms in extraction from, and political
control of, the wider society are also considered.

POWER, PRODUCTION,
AND THE UNPROTECTED WORKER

CHAPTER 1

POWER
AND PRODUCTION

In general this book, like the three others in the study, is about power. The approach to the study of power begins from the point where it is the most basic, continuing, and universal experience, that is, the power relationships surrounding work and the process of production.[1] This is the power that determines what is produced, controls production, and distributes the benefits; it is the basis for social, political, and world power and fundamental to all national and international change.

A refinement to the general approach of beginning the study of power at the level of production is to differentiate power relations within production on the basis of pattern, nature, and operation of power. The patterns of power relations that have been indentified in this study as existing in the contemporary world—twelve in number—are called modes or forms of social relations of production. The approach to power could then be termed the multiple social relations of production approach. As power relations are the crucial element in the various branches of social science such an approach has important applications especially in economics, sociology, political science and international relations.

Specifically this book is limited to exploring the relationships between dominant and subordinate groups and classes within six distinguishable patterns of power relations out of the twelve identified. The six forms of social relations of production discussed in this book cover the least powerful of producers within the world labor force—the unprotected workers. Their lack of power leaves them unprotected in face of opposing groups, unlike established workers where unions, corporations, or states have been the source of some protection and stability. The unprotected workers are subordinate workers within subordinate forms of social relations, because even the groups with the most immediate control or domination in the production process are themselves manipulated and controlled from elsewhere in the wider society.

In terms of individuals, or categories of workers within the world labor force, the book considers the power relations surrounding the subsistence farmer; the renting, indebted, or merchant-dominated peasant; the casual working urban marginal; the unorganized wage worker; the self-employed; and housewives. Together they represent more than 50 percent of the total world labor force. Also examined are the more powerful—landlords, moneylenders and merchants; purchasers of casual labor; entrepreneurs; employers, suppliers, buyers, competitors and regulators of the self-employed and male heads of household.

The book is divided into three parts of two chapters each. An introductory section to each part examines existing names and concepts applied to the bulk of the producers within the following two chapters, the manner in which these conventional categories would have to be viewed if they were to be disaggregated by using a multiple social relations of production approach and, finally, what has been the origin and nature of contemporary interest in specific groups of workers within the world labor force.

The six chapters in which the six separate forms of social relations of production are presented consider, in turn and in each case, the contemporary origins of the form, the proximate relationships with groups and classes within other forms, the internal relations of domination and subordination, the power relations with groups elsewhere, the role the form plays in the social and economic formation, the consciousness of groups and classes involved, and possible dynamics of transformation based upon the preceding factors.

There are a number of points to be made about this approach before explaining in more detail the concepts and the forms of social relations identified. The first is that in adopting the position that power in production is the fundamental source of power everywhere the approach could be called materialist. But to do so does not mean that it is a variety of "vulgar materialism" producing the "wonderful nonsense"[2] of those who wish to relegate questions of religion, social prestige, love, traditional thought structures, and ideologies to the limbo of a superstructure composed of the unacceptable categories of indirect and non-material forces. These are important, if not crucial, aspects of power, although they may indeed be remnants of extinct forms of social relations of production found useful in the contemporary power struggle.

Nevertheless, there is a certain heuristic technique involved in highlighting the struggle for power within the production process—an emphasis that is necessary to correct tendencies in social science that have either ignored power or concentrated on specific and fragmented aspects of it. Even when it has not been ignored, the concentration has been on the question "who governs?" rather than on "what are the sources of power?", "how are they maintained?", and "what are its dynamics?". The approach used in this study considers all of these questions.[3]

The second note on the approach must be to signal that this book is not intended to be neutral in the sense of a traditional value-free social science. It is not neutral in two ways. The first is especially important to a book which is particularly concerned with the most wretched of the earth and with the concentrations of power that produce the most extremes of poverty, degradation, and inhumanity. It is not neutral in that the basic objective of such an analysis of power is that it will in some way be a contribution to processes that result in transformation of the conditions and power structures and that this will result in the liberation of individuals, groups, and classes from the links in the chains of power that enmesh them and cause their material and spiritual misery. In completing the research for this book it would be difficult for any contemporary, rationally minded person with even the most rudimentary sense of social justice and equipped with all the standard justifications and excuses for the extremes of world poverty to maintain a neutrality in the face of what investigation and knowledge produce—the horrors of child in-

dustrial labor; the obscenity of the very existence of a "going rate"
for the deflowering of twelve-year-old East Asian girls in the sex
tourism industry; the slow, agonizing deaths from untreated ill-
ness of slum dwellers and peasants; the predictable "burning
out" of human capacities of eyesight and dexterity of unprotected
workers in the electronics industry; the drug-induced pace of
work in textile factories; and the workplace isolation of the migrant workers.[4] These are conditions that do not directly arise
from political persecution of minorities or activists, from the
continuance of brutalizing customs, or from flood and disasters,
so much the favorite of the world press; rather, they arise from
the normal processes of power within production.

The belief that these conditions should be expunged forever from human experience may be a subjective deviation from
neutrality. But even if the aim was such neutrality, the impact of
such an approach and book could not be neutral if it lives up to
its aim of giving an accurate analysis of power. Any accurate
analysis of power made extant must, almost by definition, be
subversive to established power. Such an analysis must reveal
how those with power acquired and maintained it and why those
without it are without it. Theoretically then a correct analysis of
power could be used equally as a guide to repression or liberation—by both the general of the army of liberation and the general
of the junta of repression. In practice, however, those in power
usually have a greater insight into its foundations, origins, and
especially its use and, as part of the process of maintaining it,
hide and disguise it. Thus, any raising of the curtain of myth and
misinformation about power disproportionately assists those
who were not educated in the ways of the power holders and
must learn through bitter experience or intensive reflection and
analysis the reality behind the smokescreens of cant and
hypocrisy.

Neither of these subjective and objective departures from
neutrality, however, must be allowed to interfere with the rigor
of analysis. The analysis must be objective in the sense of being
realistic, for to be otherwise would be self-defeating—to instill,
promote, and propagate an inaccurate analysis of power is precisely the tried and true mechanism of its maintenance. The tears
of anguish engendered by the unsupportable conditions men-

tioned above must never be allowed to cloud the vision that seeks to identify precisely those responsible and the dynamics of their power that result in its maintenance or downfall. Such is the task of realism and why it is so unpopular both with the powerful and with those who wish to provoke only tears and not change.[5]

The third point to note about the multiple social relations of production approach is that, compared with other approaches, it takes the emphasis of occupation, gender, religion, nationality, and sometimes class as the basis for organization, consciousness, and dynamics of change and puts it on the power relations of production. In the first instance it disaggregates such conventional categories of mass, proletariat, women, poor, and peasants into the different patterns of power that govern different sections of these blanket categories. It argues that the power relations surrounding production, as the primary source of consciousness, organization and action, must first be understood before it can safely be said that people will respond to calls addressed to them, whether they be status quoist, reactionary, or revolutionary. Thus any poor, or mass, in a third-world city, even though united by habitat and material conditions, may be more strongly divided by the forms of social relations of production that govern their working lives and that range from the diffuse power associated with casual, own-account activity to the direct domination of employers in an enterprise.

It should not be thought that the objective is therefore to create new, separate, and separatable categories, because only by understanding potential divisions of populations can any effort be made to forge the alliances necessary for a broader support for change or its converse of divide and rule.

Finally, a note of warning must be made about the limitations of this book. The first, which has already been mentioned in the introduction, is the self-imposed limitation of considering the six forms of social relations of production as self-contained structures and examining them on the basis of origins, internal power relations, external power relations, consciousness, and transformation. Thus there is no attempt to fit the material presented here into a more ambitious review of the development of capitalist societies and their future. Of course, the basic position of the approach is that, equipped with the approach and its application, any reader will better be able to construct a more meaningful analysis of societal, state, and world power and the directions of change than is possible with most conventional intellectual tools.

It is also then, for a similar cause, not a book of theory. Thus, for example, in this book technology in production is seen to be a function rather than a source or cause of power within production: in other words it is the power relations that determine how and when a technology is developed and what existing options so produced are used. Although there are theoretical debates on this issue they are not discussed here.[6]

The second limitation is the nature of the research. The material presented cannot be fitted into the traditional positivist social science in the sense that it adds facts or data to existing fields and areas of knowledge. This was not the objective. Constructed from secondary sources the book represents an exercise in an approach that presents a substantial reordering of existing materials that have most often been precipitated by positivist social science. It is a work of reordering and synthesis within a social science suffering perhaps from excessive specialization and information overload. Thus it reorders and synthesizes across many structurally defined disciplines and areas of knowledge. Such a process may produce new insights and new perceptions but not new data.

Another limitation arises precisely from the existing body of secondary sources. To apply the social relations of production approach to the whole world labor force and to the world's work is an innovative task. It has not been done before in this fashion or with this approach. The conventional literature is, of course, not presented and written with such an approach in mind, and typologies and categorizations are rarely made on the basis of power within production. There are therefore many informational holes in the literature and sometimes the task of disaggregation has been difficult. To distinguish the different power relations of a land-owning, market-producing farmer from those of land-owning, market-producing, but moneylender-dominated farmer is rendered difficult when in the bulk of discussions they are both considered as "peasants"; likewise, there is difficulty in distinguishing the specific relations of power between an artisan and an increasingly dominant single buyer of the product when despite such dominance the artisan is considered as "self-employed"; or again it is difficult to distinguish the variety of social relations found within one country or within the world in an industry such as mining or transport when all the workers in them are merely referred to as miners or transport workers.

Finally, there are informational gaps of a more important type within the existing social science and political literature. These occur when, for a variety of reasons, a specific phenomenon has not been the target of research or has not attracted research funds or interest. Such a case is that of political, class, or social consciousness; whereas it is generally explicitly or implicitly considered to be of crucial importance and determinant of social action there is rarely any extensive or intensive discussion of it. This lack of discussion and information is compounded by the general assumption that consciousness arises from occupation and sector rather than from the social relations of production.

These limitations must be remembered in considering this book. This is not by way of excuse. This book may not please the expert consulting only his or her areas of specialization for new data and not interested in a different approach. But for others the book can be used as an introduction to any specific area that the incessant specialization of modern scholarship demands: such a reader will see what an approach yields, or might yield, that puts power at the center of discussion in contrast to studies and approaches that discover power relations after moving the seeker of truth or strategy backward through elaborate and jargon-filled discourses.

Perhaps of even more importance is the potential for the approach presented here to be used as both a conceptual and policy tool within the different branches of social science.[7] In reformist planning and policy, in revolutionary economic and social restructuring, and in the general observations of human society and action, the mind-sets of economists, political scientists, and sociologists that do not make provisions for the existence of the variety of forms of social relations in production are almost bound to be inappropriate. Narrow and erroneous assumptions relating to human economic and social behavior are often tidy, safe, and, moreover, have been ossified into the supportive institutional structures of professionals and practitioners. The presentation of a new approach always involves an invitation to reconsider mind-sets, world-views and the nature of existing intellectual structures and professional practices.

SOCIAL RELATIONS
OF PRODUCTION

It is possible to see power existing at four levels: power in production, manifested by dominant-subordinate relationships within the production process; social power, which has been accrued by groups and classes over time; political power; as expressed through organizations which have a potential to control distribution and states; world power; which is the ability to extend power on a world scale. Although these four levels can be separated analytically, in reality they are an interconnected part of a whole that is a constantly changing structure.

The approach to power in all four of the associated books of this study starts with power in production "it begins with the arena of production and looks out from it."[8] Thus this book is concerned initially with the details of the dynamics of power in production—the social relations of production. An understanding of power relations in production then provides the basis for a better comprehension and a subsequent discussion of social, political and world power.

Power expresses the ability of some people to control or influence the actions of others. Work is the expenditure of human energy in order to convert or transform material substances into other forms or to contribute to the convenience, comfort, or desires of others. Production is a social process through which goods or services are created. Thus, a farming family through planting, hoeing, and weeding joins with the biophysical process of plant growth to produce an edible commodity. A domestic servant, travel agent, or bureaucrat works to supply a service of comfort, organization, or convenience for master or customer. All work, all are in a social process of production, and all are subject to power and authority.

People then always work within a context of power relationships. The objective of power surrounding production is control of what is produced, the structure of authority within production, and the distribution of the rewards of production. Thus, those with power within production seek to control the what, how, and who-gets-what of production. Those with less power may resist all of these attempts. The exercise of power and resistance to it determine the outcomes. Thus power relations determine the return and conditions of work—usually the greater the dominance within production the lower the return and the worse the conditions for the subordinate producers. The power relations then account for differences in return and conditions of work given that they also determine the technology and capital used.

How the dominant groups or classes use the goods, money, or labor extracted is another matter. They may consume it all as quickly as possible, they may feel it prudent to invest some of it to maintain future extraction, or they may feel that accumulation of tools, techniques, and social structures is necessary to increase future extraction. It is entirely conceivable that extraction and accumulation is just. If, for the sake of argument, protection of the weak is considered just, then power within production may be used to extract for purposes of distribution to weaker persons or for the supply of a needed social or community good or service. Usually this is not the case, especially in extraction from the unprotected workers discussed in this book.

The exercise of this power within production takes many forms and is based upon many circumstances. The power that a male head of household has over the production of cooking, cleaning, and child care by women workers of the household stems from a long tradition and ideology of the subordination of women within the household and the structure of finance and social opportunities that it has created. Such power is clearly different in form, origin, and nature from that exercised by a landowner extracting rent from a tenant farming family or the power to dismiss that an employer has over unorganized employees, or the power a union has both over its members and in relation to corporate managers or enterprise owners. Power may be based on at least physical coercion, material reward, or psychological manipulation.

Not only are there these differences but also any one producer may have to face a different number of sources of power within the struggle of power surrounding production—whereas a wage worker in a small enterprise may think, with some reality, that the dominant source of power is vested in the boss, the self-employed artisan or farmer must juggle with the extant or potential power that rests in the suppliers, customers, competitors, or state regulators. To illustrate the difference or change in a pattern of power relations, consider the example of a self-employed person whose return to work is governed by a pattern of relations involving at least suppliers and customers. If this person employs another person, then the pattern has changed. Return and control of production now involves not only the relationships between suppliers and customers but also the relationship between the previously self-employed person and the person employed. The pattern has changed and the self-employed person has become an employer within another pattern. Further examples of such changes and distinctions between patterns are found in the introductions of parts 1 and 2 of this book.

Out of this complex, interlocking flux of power relations operating at the level of work and production different patterns may be discerned. If lines were drawn among individual groups, organizations, and classes indicating direct or indirect power relationships, and these lines were of varying thicknesses indicating strength of power and perhaps of different colors reflecting the different nature of power—coercive, material, or psychological—then a visual image of distinct patterns of thick, thin, colors, and clusters of lines would be invoked among the nearly two billion members of the world labor force. Such an overview based upon reviews of the existing information of power within production has identified twelve predominant patterns covering the whole of the world labor force.[9] These patterns of power relations surrounding production have been called modes, or forms, of social relations of production.

Social relations of production is synonomous in this book with power relations of production and production relations.[10] Social relations is preferred because it puts the emphasis on the social aspect of production and because when the word social is combined with the word production it is clear that the relationship is one of power rather than affection. Power relations is used when it is felt that there is a special need to emphasize the power aspect, usually because it is forgotten or ignored. Social is used in both the individual and collective sense. The individual, independent bag carrier at a third-world railway station has a social relationship, however brief, with the person whose bag is being carried, a fact that is amplified if the carrier should steal the bag or the owner refuse to pay for the service. At the same time there is a social relationship between a worker organization and management, between an association of self-employed and a credit-supplying bank. The power relationship is emphasized by the fact that the owner of the bag may refuse to have it carried, the worker organization may call a strike, or the bank may increase its interest rates for the self-employed—all in the continuing process of the struggle for power over the production process and its yields.

The patterns of power relations, or social relations of production may be called forms or modes. The conventional association of the term *mode of social relations of production* is that with the historical-stage modes of social relations of production identified by marxists in the 1930s, namely, those of primitive communism, feudalism, capitalism, socialism, and communism.[11] Occasionally other modes are referred to in marxist literature, such as the petty commodity mode, which is said to exist, in Russian doll style, within the larger mode of capitalism. It should be clear from what has already been said that these uses are excluded in this book; that is, the view of a mode of social relations of production as an all-encompassing historical stage that serves as an explanation for all phenomena or as a dividing line is excluded.[12] This means, for example, the distinction between "precapitalist" and "capitalist" modes of social relations is not used: modes of social relations have been shown to persist even if the dominant groups and classes of society change and the power relations surrounding all production are involved in the process of change regardless of their supposed position within one schema of the elaboration of history.

Marx, as is well known, was less than clear in his own usage of the term *mode of social relations of production,* having identified at least eight such modes based on entirely different criteria.[13] One of the ways Marx used the term—to describe the material manner of production and the labor process, or social relations within it—is close to the definition used in this study.

In this way, if it were necessary, it could be argued that the definition used in this study was at least consistent with one of the definitions used by Marx. But such an argument is not necessary. The task of the social analyst is not to be engaged in an incessant, ritualistic, and esoteric discussion of sacred texts but rather to take the lead offered, in this case by Marx, by grounding analysis in power and production and developing meaningful applications to the contemporary world. However, in deference to the established tradition of marxist scholarship, to distinguish the innovative effort of this book, and to avoid all confusion, the term used in this book is *form* rather than *mode* of social relations of production.[14]

Before considering the general and theoretical definition of a form of social relations of production it is useful to distinguish the concept from two others which are also used to refer to power relations surrounding production namely, "industrial relations systems" and "system of labor control." Industrial relations system has been used in two different ways, first to describe the tripartite relationship between trade unions, employers, and agencies of the state as a stable system of power relations which produces rules governing conditions of work and wages. The second use of the concept of industrial relations system is as a system of work and production which can be found in any branch of activity and in a variety of different forms. This latter use of the concept comes close to that of a form of social relations of production and the two concepts were used as synonomous in a earlier publication relating to the current study.[15] The use of the concept of industrial relations systems is, however, undesireable: "industrial relations" is a confusing term to describe a system found, for example, to be operating in the agricultural sector; in addition, "system" implies a stability of relationships over time and takes the emphasis off dynamics and change leading to transformation. The other concept of importance, a system of labor control, may be defined as a distinct set of ideologies, strategies, and technologies used by those who control production to extract surpluses and maintain or increase the productivity of labor. It has been used to describe control of labor at the work-place as well as broader globally operating systems. While a useful concept for specific purposes, a system of labor control implies a dominant group with a clear and direct ability to manipulate employees which means, for example, workers governed by more diffuse power relations, such as own-account or self-employed workers, are not easily caught by the concept; a more important criticism is that it takes emphasis of the varying degrees of intensity of employers' power, off the possible labor responses and off the general dynamics of power relations.[16] For these reasons the concept of a form of social relations of production is less limited than those mentioned above and more elegant in both theory and practice.

The fuller meaning of a form of social relations of production will emerge when the characteristics of the forms and specific existing examples of them are discussed in this book. The general and theoretical meaning of a form of social relations of production as described by Cox is that the universal activity of work in order to produce social and economic needs always involves social relationships which take different historical forms. A form, or mode, of social relations of production is then one of these concrete patterns of relations which endures for a significant period of time. These forms may be presented as a set of ideal types. Such types, however, are only conceptual tools used temporarily to crystalize a social practice, enabling it to be compared and contrasted with other practices and, even more important, making it easier to highlight its points of stress, conflict or contradiction which always lead to transformation.[17]

Forms of social relations of production have objective, subjective, and institutional aspects. Among the objective aspects of importance are the material means of production, accrued social power, political power, and the way the produce is distributed. Subjective aspects include the basic ethic governing the production process, which is principally that of extant physical or material coercion, contract, and cooperation or corporatism.[18] These roughly correspond to coercive material and normative motivations to work or the forms power takes in influencing and controlling actions of people.[19] Another subjective aspect is the rationality produced by groups in production that interprets the world in accordance with the social relations and is distinct from broader ideologies. The institutional aspects may be seen as those of direct domination; those of corporatism, where attempts are made to place power relations within a single structure without recognizing conflict; and those of bargaining, which create organizations intended to recognize and mediate conflict.[20] Some of these aspects are elaborated further, both in this introductory chapter and through the detailed examination of the forms. Because this book is, however, concerned only with six forms of social relations that are subordinate and found in societies following capitalist development, the aspects most discussed are social power, direct domination, coercion, and distribution through a diffuse power struggle rather than through a centralized redistribution as experienced in centrally planned socialism.

Types of Social Relations of Production
    In order to see what forms of social relations of production are most important in the contemporary world, either because the groups within them spread their power throughout the wider society or because the forms have increasing or decreasing numbers of producers within them, it is necessary to identify the existing patterns and assign them names.
    This was a process based on an overview of the totality of power relations within production of the whole world labor force as described earlier. An initial set identified by Cox was then modified, adjusted, and expanded through review, consultation, and research.[21]
    The result was an identification of twelve patterns of power relations or forms of social relations of production that cover almost the whole of the world labor force in the late twentieth century. These twelve forms could have been labeled from 1 to 12 or from A to L, for they are all variations of power relations in production. For purposes of debate and presentation, however, names were given that create images or invoke concepts. This last comment should serve as a serious warning to those readers who wish to stay at the level of nomenclature and insist on discussing the accuracy or inaccuracy of the label, not because of the existence or nonexistence of the basic pattern of power relations described, but because the label does not fit some preexisting notion of what it precisely means. Such a process collapses the multiple social relations of production approach into yet another categorization of workers and occupations. This is one

reason why the names chosen do not follow any particular criteria; thus one refers to the dominant and subordinate groups—peasant-lord—one to the source of power of one group—the enterprise labor market—and another to the locale and institution of production—the household.

These twelve forms of social relations are presented here, in the briefest of terms illuminating in a necessarily crude way only the dominant and subordinate groups within them and providing some guide to the workers within them. This listing is intended only as an overview; a more expanded overview of them is found in Cox, *World Order* and detailed examination of each in the different books. The volume numbers where extensive treatment of them are given is placed in parenthesis.

Subsistence (this volume: chapter 2)

There are no identifiable and distinct groups or classes struggling for control of the production of producers within the subsistence form of social relations of production. This is because they are either isolated communities or family farms that are not able to produce a surplus, which is extracted by those who control a market or those who control land, capital, or distribution. This means that social relations are indirect and rest rather with the past or current structures, which have resulted in peoples' consuming all they produce and rarely having enough to consume.

Peasant-Lord (this volume: chapter 3)

Peasants are the subordinate group within this form. Peasants are those whose production is controlled by three types of "lords"—moneylenders, merchants, or landowners. They are neither subsistence farmers nor market-producing self-employed farmers. They are faced usually by a class of landowners supported by moneylenders, merchants, and state. They render their surplus in the form of money, produce, or labor. The domination is direct and the extraction high.

Primitive Labor Market (this volume: chapter 4)

The power relations are diffuse and time-limited between the casual purchaser of labor and the casual laborer. Having left the land and its attachment, people offer their ability to work for sale but can find no regular, structured purchaser and are forced to "scavenge" employment or income whenever it occurs. The power relations of this kind are found mainly in third-world urban labor markets and are epitomized by the street vendors, beggars, casual gardeners, cleaners, and domestic servants.

Enterprise Labor Market (this volume: chapter 5)

The power relations are direct between employer and employee within a productive enterprise but the employment has some structure and stability. Employers' power is manifested essentially by the power of dismissal, that is, the granting or withholding of work, which is the workers' only source of income. There is no worker organization to temper this power of withholding work, which is used as an arbitrary punishment or system to secure docile labor. One of the common instances of this form is the small, nonunionized industrial enterprise.

Self-Employment (this volume: chapter 6)

The power relations that govern the production and return of a self-employed artisan, farmer, shopkeeper, or personal service supplier are those that exist between the self-employed individual or family and those who control supply of needed inputs to production, those who control markets for output, those who compete for customers, and those who control state regulation of such activities. In short, the relations are between a self-employed producer and the supplier, buyer, competitor, and regulator.

Household (this volume: chapter 7)

The power relations are within a household, usually a family in which a dominant head of household, usually male, secures the production of household and family services for consumption by the household from subordinate female producers. Within these relations household services, particularly food preparation and childrearing, are produced.

Bipartite (Harrod, *Established Worker*, [forthcoming])

The formation of worker organizations transforms the power relations based upon employer dominance to that of countervailing or bargaining power between organizations of workers and employers. The power relations are bipartite—between employers and worker organizations with little intervention from elsewhere.

Tripartite (Harrod, *Established Worker*, [forthcoming])
The intervention of the state within a bipartite power situation, regardless of which side is assisted or controlled, means that three constellations of power must be considered, those of the workers, those of the employers, and those of the state. This is the form that governs the production of the unionized workers in Western Europe and elsewhere.

Enterprise Corporatist (Harrod, *Established Worker*, [forthcoming])
Large organizations can sometimes reduce power relations internally to those within an established, unchallenged hierarchy by purchasing cooperation of the producers through granting lifetime guarantees of work and organization-linked benefits and inducing an overriding loyalty to the organization. Thus, the power relations between subordinates and officers in the military, civil service, and large commercial organizations are subsumed under hierarchy, loyalty, and privileged material benefits to produce a typical enclave enterprise corporatism. One of the better known examples of this form, apart from the civil service and military everywhere, is the large Japanese corporation.

State Corporatist (Harrod, *Established Worker*, [forthcoming])
In some cases the state intervenes to control conflict by legitimizing worker organizations and employer organizations but controlling both of them to different degrees. Power relations are between the official worker organizations, employers, and state agencies in which the state is almost always, in the last resort, dominant. State corporatism rarely covers the whole of a national labor force, although this is the nominal claim. It may be declared as in Franco Spain or Chile under the Pinoche regime and undeclared as in the Philippines after 1972.

Communalism (Cox, Redistributive Social Relations [forthcoming])

Under collective production a collectivity, at a level below the state, redistributes both product and labor. Power relations like those of the subsistence farming household are reduced to an accepted authority structure that is revised and organized by the collectivity. The most noticeable example of such communalism was the original Chinese rural communes and the various experiments found in religious communes.

Central Planning (Cox, Redistributive Social Relations [forthcoming])

The power relations within central planning gravitate around the society-wide plan developed and executed by a powerful bureaucracy. Political support is coordinated through a party that reaches into worker organizations, management, and bureaucracy. In terms of national labor force the form of social relations is greater in scope than tripartite and state corporatism. The outcomes of planning and central control are more sure as a result of a prior political discourse and struggle that secures a more certain compliance to policies pursued.

The twelve forms identified cover the entire labor force of the world. This does not mean that there may not be other forms in existence and even more that there are not other forms in the process of emerging. The forms are dynamic, they are not fixed, and therefore they are undergoing transformation into other forms at different rates and in different ways. This means that at the margins of transformation other forms may appear. This is discussed below in the section on transformation.

If this list of twelve forms is neither stable nor exhaustive, arguments may be properly considered for increasing or decreasing the number of forms. Three examples can be given. The family workers of self-employed artisans, farmers, merchants, and traders have been included within the discussion on the self-employment form of social relations on the grounds that the predominant social relations that affect their lives, work, and consciousness are those of self-employment. Yet the power relations governing their production are not precisely those of the head of the family engaged in a direct power struggle with suppliers, buyers, competitors, and regulators, but neither are they subjected to the domination of an employer based on a labor market. Because, under current world conditions, their numbers are increasing, it is open to discussion whether or not this body of workers can be seen as a subordinate group in an important different pattern of power relations. The case is similar with landless laborers in many Asian countries. Superficially the power relations surrounding their work seem to be either the diffuse type associated with the primitive labor market or the employer domination of wage workers in an enterprise. Yet the seasonal nature of the work and the dependence of the farmer on labor at a precise time mean that the social relations are not easily analogous with those of a casual purchaser of labor within an urban labor market or of an employer in an industrial enterprise. Again, landless labor may be the central point for the observation of another pattern.[22]

Finally, there are more esoteric forms of social relations that, although conditions within them may be extreme, have not been considered important enough to be included in a basic list. Such an example would be bonded labor. Although legally banned in almost all countries of the world, there are many instances in which bonded labor has been officially and unofficially recognized.[23] Clearly, if labor is tied to an employer in which the latter's power is expressed by the ability to enforce, in a structured manner, the extraction of the ability to work without fear of desertion or losing the labor to alternative work or income opportunities, then the form of social relations is distinct from that of the enterprise labor market. These examples are presented to show that the list is not closed and never should be, a point that will be made even clearer in the discussion of transformation below.

SOCIAL FORMATION, CLASS, AND FORMS OF STATE

The concept of a social formation corresponds to what is generally called a society. The use of the term *social formation* emphasizes that society is viewed here from the standpoint of the variety of forms of social relations of production. Thus a social formation is a combination of a number of forms of social relations of production.

In practice a social formation usually corresponds to the territorial boundaries of a country because over time these have resulted in a quantitative and qualitative change in the links between forms of social relations as a result of moving from the national to the international level. This may not always be the case, however; Singapore has a primitive labor market and an enterprise labor market across the border in Malaysia, and the South African social formation incorporates self-employed farmers and dominated peasants in neighboring countries and territories who supply labor for South African industry. In the early 1970s it was often remarked that to see Swiss unemployment one had to travel to Naples in Italy. This was because at that time Switzerland had 30 percent of its labor force as migrants from Italy who were the labor for the Swiss enterprise labor market form of social relations. When laid off, these migrants were forced by migration laws to return to a primitive labor market serving the Swiss social formation but which was located in territory of Italy.

Within any social formation there are dominant and subordinate forms of social relations of production; that is, there is a hierarchy of social relations. The relationship of dominance and subordination is expressed in several ways. Dominant groups in one form may also be dominant in other forms, or alternatively, have power over other dominant and subordinate groups. Thus employers and owners of large corporations within the enterprise corporatist form of social relations determine the directions, return, and areas of possible activity of the employers or entrepreneurs in the enterprise labor market. This is because in contemporary conditions the small enterprise is often subordinate to the large corporations. But unions in tripartite forms of social relations may also have indirect power over the wages and conditions of workers outside the unions. The actions of workers and employers covered by the state corporatist social relations affect the workers of the enterprise labor market and the primitive labor market, as well as the peasants in peasant-lord relations; the reverse case is fairly rare. The relationship of dominance and subordination in the hierarchy of social relations, as with other power relations, also means that the groups in one form knowingly or unknowingly extract from the groups in the subordinate forms.

Within the twelve forms of social relations identified above there are seven forms of social relations that can be considered as subordinate in any social formation and five that are dominant.

The dominant forms are enterprise corporatist, bipartite, tripartite, state corporatist, and redistributive. The subordinate forms are communalist, subsistence, peasant-lord, primitive labor market, enterprise labor market, and household. The position of dominance or subordination is not a fixed one currently and has not historically been so. Thus, many of the currently subordinate forms of social relations have at some time in history been dominant ones; in nineteenth century Europe, before the growth of large corporations and before the establishment of trade unions, the enterprise labor market was a dominant form and the entrepreneurs formed a dominant class. Landlords in Western Europe, between the collapse of feudalism and the rise of industrialization, were a dominant group. Subsistence farming at one time governed the activities of the largest proportion of the earth's population. When land was distributed in France at the beginning of the last century, the population became predominantly market-producing, self-employed farmers served by self-employed artisans, and the self-employment form of social relations was dominant.

Only the primitive labor market and household social relations have never assumed a dominant position in a social formation. Sometimes the dominant and subordinate position of any particular form depends upon the nature of the social formation. Communalist social relations may have been a dominant form in postrevolutionary China but elsewhere they have tended to be subordinate when they have appeared in religious or political enclave communities. There are still exceptional cases where usually subordinate forms are in dominant positions; for example, the enterprise labor market form is currently dominant in Hong Kong.

Subordinate does not mean politically irrelevant—the current unrest of the poor people of the urban primitive labor market in countries of the third world is causing serious concern among ruling classes and dominant groups. What the unorganized workers of the enterprise labor market do in Western European social conflict may be crucial to future changes; the self-employed when organized in political parties have shown that they can shake the foundations of the social formations. Some detailed discussion of the political potential in dynamics of change of subordinate forms is found in the separate chapters.

Before providing some examples of the dominant-subordinate relationship within a social formation, it is first necessary to distinguish between two basic types of social formation that correspond to what is generally referred to as market and centrally planned economies or capitalist and socialist societies. Here distinction is made between social formations that have a capitalist dynamic and those with a redistributive dynamic.[24] Capitalist dynamic indicates that power in the formations can be based upon dominant groups' ownership of means of production, and distribution is through a decentralized struggle for power. Redistributive mode of development occurs where power is based upon the strategic position of a group within a centrally determined dynamic and redistribution is by a more centralized power structure. This book is concerned with the six subordinate forms of social relations found within capitalist-dynamic social formations, and examples are drawn from that experience.

Within the capitalist social formations a distinction must be made between the rich, developed, industrialized or center countries and the poor, less developed, less industrialized, peripheral or third-world countries. In the discipline of international relations these are sometimes referred to as great, middle, and minor powers within a global struggle for power. The terminology of most study areas and disciplines is unsatisfactory. The popular center-periphery notion is too unilinear to describe a generalized struggle for power and tends to create the false impression that decisions and actions at the periphery will be peripheral—a circumstance brought into doubt by the effect on the center of such events as the Vietnamese communist victory in 1975 and the successful redistribution of international income secured by the oil-producing countries, all of which are or were at the periphery. For this reason the basic distinction in this book is made between the industrialized countries, whose labor force is predominantly found in forms of social relations associated with town and industry, and third-world countries, whose labor force is predominantly found in forms of social relations associated with agriculture and unstructured industrial work. These are respectively the countries of Western Europe, North America, Japan, Oceania, and the majority of the countries found on the continents of Asia, Latin America, and Africa.

The industrialized–third-world division is, of course, also a power division, the third-world countries being the most penetrated, dependent, and dominated but not thereby rendered to the periphery or margins of world history and concern. The designation of third-world countries is used in preference to the more accurate less industrialized, least powerful, or poorer countries only because of convenience and with respect to preferences expressed by third-world scholars themselves and not because of any attachment to the original idea of a world divided into three.

In industrialized country social formations following a capitalist dynamic, the dominant forms of social relations tend to be enterprise corporatist, bipartite, and tripartite, and the subordinate forms tend to be enterprise labor market, self-employment, and household. In third-world country social formations following a capitalist dynamic, the dominant forms of social relations tend to be state corporatist, tripartite, and enterprise corporatist, and the subordinate forms are subsistence, peasant-lord, primitive labor market, enterprise labor market, self-employment, and household.

Within the dominant-subordinate relationships of forms of social relations of production there are some that are usually found together. Thus, the minority of the labor force covered by state corporatism in third-world social formations is invariably associated with a large peasant labor force in peasant-lord relations. These two forms are almost symbiotic. Enterprise corporatism in industrialized countries in which dominant groups extract from the rest of the population is invariably accompanied by an extensive enterprise labor market that provides material support. Household social relations are almost a universal but appear in their purest form in industrialized countries associated with the professionals in bipartite social relations and enterprise corporatism in the civil service and military.

Some examples follow. Japan is characterized by approximately 30 percent of the labor force within the large corporations, and the workers have a privileged status associated with enterprise corporatist social relations. Surrounding the corporations are the mass of small enterprises in which employer domination over a less privileged labor force ensures the presence of the enterprise labor market. In the agricultural sector there is a large proportion of independent farmers in self-employment social relations, and the women workers of the household social relations service the labor in all other forms via the household family. In the Philippines the 25 percent of the labor force within the state corporatist umbrella of labor laws and grants of privilege are dominant, while a labor-surplus life-style is supported by a massive urban marginal population within the primitive labor market and a smaller, but important, industrial labor force in enterprise labor market relations. Both the dominant and subordinate groups in industrial employment are supported by a markedly coerced and dominated peasant within peasant-lord relations. In France the 20 percent of the labor force found in tripartite social relations is in a dominant position that it shares, to some extent, with the civil service in the enterprise corporatist form. The power relations between the managers and owners and the union confederations profoundly affect what happens elsewhere in the social formation. But the large numbers and powerful organizations of self-employed farmers and others often challenge policies emerging from these relations. Employers in the subordinate enterprise labor market began recently to extend their operations and, in response to pressures, increase extraction from the workers by operating illegally in the "black" economy to escape both state-and union-determined wages and conditions of work provisions.

In Colombia, dominant groups in tripartite social relations in coalition with those in enterprise corporatism maintain a hold in face of unrest from peasants in the peasant-lord relations. There are large numbers within the primitive labor market among whom operate relatively successful insurgents and guerrilla groups. The strain of populism within Colombian politics reflects the need, as in Argentina, to appease the consciousness of the primitive labor market workers.

In this manner, then, a map of social relations of production can be produced for any social formation; even if the map is identical in terms of having the same composition of named forms, the power configurations in the social formation will be different as the numbers within the forms are different and different groups create and dissolve alliances. Equipped with a view of the groups in different forms, the consciousness of the groups produced by social relations, and the class alliances such a consciousness may produce, a political analysis can be pursued that indicates the direction of change, the form of state, and state action precipitated by such power dynamics. Consciousness, class, and state are the three remaining dimensions of social formations that need to be considered in this section.

Class is used here to mean a relationship that has existed or that exists. Class is based upon a consciousness of being a class and of sharing common experiences, upon a common view of the distinctions and cleavages in societies and of opposition and support. Class emerges from the consciousness and power within the social relations of production. This view of class means that not all groups with power in production can be conceived of as a class, and it is for this reason that the term *dominant group* has been used. A dominant group within a form of social relations may become a class through increased awareness and outside developments. Usually, however, a class is an alliance of groups found within different social relations.

Some examples are given here. It may be that landlords, that is, renting landowners, may be a class within peasant-lord relations in that they see themselves as opposed to peasants and in alliance with industrially dominant groups. The position is less sure with the enterprise owners of the enterprise labor market. They may not be a class themselves, but more likely they will form a coalition with the self-employed and others to make a class, sometimes known as the petit bourgeoisie. From the standpoint of subordinate groups, whether or not peasants will form a class is the question that dominates political strategists from both sides of the status quo/change divide. Whether again they will develop a class consciousness of a type that merges with that of the industrial worker of the enterprise labor market or the casual worker of the primitive labor market to form a working class is even more problematic. The differences of consciousness that the form of social relations and its associated lifestyle, world view, developed rationalities, and ideologies precipitate are the obstacles to the development or building of classes and solidarity. These are the most imponderable and uncertain questions within social science, but they are fundamental to the understanding of change. The multiple social relations of production approach is then an approach that identifies the fundamental sources of differences between groups and classes; in doing so it provides the tools for analysis which can be used either in amplifying such differences, as in a divide-and-rule strategy, or in overcoming such differences, as in a solidarity-for-change strategy, which are two of the major strategies in the struggle for power both among dominant groups and between dominant and subordinate groups.

The final aspect of the social formation to be considered is that of the state. The state is considered as a place in the social formation where forces can be concentrated and directed either towards maintaining the existing order or towards bringing about a new order.[25] This conception of the state starts with the notion of civil society and the state. Civil society is to be considered the realm of individual and particular interests and needs; historically it was seen to be the arena of the market composed of freely operating and contracting individuals as in the ideal type of nineteenth-century capitalism. The state began to be conceived as the combination of two viewpoints, namely, that it was a bureaucracy charged with the functions of maintaining its own position and the internal order and of facing challenges from the outside and, alternatively, that it was the expression of the collective will. Marx reinterpreted these prevailing German and French conceptions of the state into the structure—the sum total of the social relations of production—and the superstructure—the laws, constitution, and political structure of the state.

The view of the state as an interaction between civil society and the state or that between the structure and the superstructure avoids the tendency to try to reduce one to another and to seek which is preponderant. Such an interaction takes several forms that may be identified. in the discussions in this book the state appears within the social relations of production as a power that assists one or other of the dominant or subordinate groups or mediates between them. The form of state will tend to determine what action is taken. What is of importance in this book concerned with the subordinate forms of social relations is to identify the various ways the state intervenes without necessarily making reference to the form from which it issues. For example, almost everywhere the state attempts to intervene in self-employment relations to extract taxes and to regulate production; in the household it intervenes only to create usually weakly enforceable marriage contracts relating to childbearing and childrearing; in peasant-lord it has usually intervened to support landowners' power, to extract taxes, and, on occasions, to attempt reforms; in the enterprise labor market the intervention has been an attempt to regulate the conditions of work, to create a labor market, to consolidate employer power, and so on. The differences of intervention are not traced backward in this book to forms of state, but for any broader analysis of a social formation than is attempted here such an exercise would be essential.[26]

Some Definitions

It is now possible to list some definitions of terms and phrases as used in this book. An effort has been made to avoid different definitions and to use mainstream or practical usages as much as possible. The definitions presented here are more of a selection of those that may depart from usages found in different parts of the literature of different disciplines.

Work—the expenditure of human energy to transform materials or provide services.

Production—a social process that combines the work of people to create goods and services.

Form of social relations of production—a distinct and basic pattern of power relations within production sometimes referred to as a mode of social relations of production or a set of production relations.

Worker—(a) one who works, that is, expends energy within production regardless of sector, commodity, or occupation. Thus a peasant is a worker just as much as a housewife or a busdriver; (b) the least powerful in any form of social relations.

Producer—all the people within a form of social relations of production regardless of their power position. Thus an employer in an enterprise and a worker are both producers within the enterprise labor market form of social relations of production.

Dominant group—a dominant group within one form of social relations that is not a class or its status as a class is in doubt.

Subordinate group—a subordinate group within a particular form of social relations, with class status as above.

The return from work—the total material and psychological sustenance yielded from work. The concept of return includes wage, income, and job satisfaction; it would also include conditions of work, that is, the levels of risk of injury or disease and therefore life expectancy.

Extraction—the process of dominant groups' removal of goods, services, and labor from subordinate groups.

Social formation—a combination of forms of social relations that usually corresponds to the territory or a country.

Class—what results when dominant or subordinate groups conceive of themselves as a group with distinct objectives and opponents.

Capitalist—a society or social formation in which there is a decentralized struggle for power among dominant groups and in which power may be based upon nonstate ownership of capital. Capitalist does not mean capitalist social relations.

DIFFERENT CHARACTERISTICS OF FORMS OF SOCIAL RELATIONS

Each form of social relations has different origins, different power relations between groups within the form, different relations to other forms of social relations in the social formation, different development of consciousness of dominant and subordinate groups, and different paths in which the forms are transformed. In this book the six subordinate forms of social relations are examined in a uniform way. Six characteristics of each form are examined in turn, first, contemporary origin; second, the most proximate forms within the social formation; third, the internal power relations; fourth, the power relations between the groups within the form and the rest of the social formation and any function the form plays at the level of the social formation; fifth, the consciousness the social relations precipitate within groups;

and finally, some possible paths of transformation. Examining in brief the basic content presented under the headings of origin, proximate forms, internal relations, external relations, consciousness, and transformations both illustrates the manner of examination of the forms and provides more information about the concept of a form of social relations of production.

Origin

In this book a discussion of the origin of the form of social relations concentrates on the contemporary aspects. The more historic origins of all the forms, beginning with the fourteenth century, are discussed by Cox in *World Order.*[27]

What, therefore, is meant by origin is the cause of the appearance of the form or the origin of some essential feature of it. Thus the origin of the primitive labor market form of social relations lies in the structure of contemporary third-world social formations following the capitalist path of development. The origins of more than 200 million people in the world who cannot find structured employment and are forced to sell their ability to work on a casual basis are found in the structure of the social formation that incorporates the use of large amounts of capital in industry, the power of worker organizations in dominant forms, and transformations occurring within the peasant-lord form.

To take an example of the principal feature of a form, the origin of the enterprise labor market form lies in the nineteenth-century development of capitalism and the notion of employer domination based upon an ability to grant or withhold work. In the case of each form the origins are then discussed in this manner, seeking to explain in brief why the pattern of power relations has continued to exist in the contemporary world.

Proximate Forms

In the discussion of proximate forms of social relations the migration between forms is given predominance. Thus people in the enterprise labor market form usually come from the primitive labor market form when they secure structured and more regular employment in an enterprise, and people in the primitive labor market usually come from the peasant-lord or are forced back to the primitive labor market after losing employment. Proximity then refers principally to a relationship expressed by the shifting of population and by the observation that upheavals in one form cause changes in the numbers and perhaps therefore in consciousness and details of power relations in another. An example of this latter point is that at times of declines in economic activity the forced return to the primitive labor market of people who have become accustomed to the relations of the enterprise labor market makes a qualitative difference in the consciousness and actions of the primitive labor market workers. Similarly the massive entry of women from the household form in the enterprise labor market, often replacing males, will make a difference in the social composition of the workers and consciousness in the enterprise labor market.

Internal Power Relations

Internal power relations are the principal criteria for identification of a form of social relations of production. Under this heading the questions of the existence of identifiable groups and constellations of power are paramount. Without refinement one could identify within the six subordinate forms of social relations such dominant and subordinate groups or individuals as landlord and peasant, husbands and wives, casual buyers and sellers of labor, customers and self-employed, and many other groups the relations between which make up the total pattern of power relations. The way in which power is exercised and some of its characteristics take the discussion into the realm of the nature of power. Thus landlords tend to use coercion in the form of physical force to ensure a surplus-rendering peasant, employers in small enterprises use a number of psychological practices to block the formation of worker organization, casual labor sellers form networks and organizations to deal with fluctuating income, heads of household rely on the prevailing ideology concerning the role of women to secure the continued production of household services, and self-employed use organizations and individual tactics in the sturggle for power over the control of their production.

Power in most forms of social relations is directly expressed in the sense that there are identifiable groups who have power over production. In two cases, that of the subsistence and primitive labor market, power is indirect in that there may be no identifiable group with power over production. In these cases the origin of the form and the basic power over return and income have essentially been set from outside the forms and there are no inside representatives of it. Thus return to subsistence farming households is determined by the amount and quality of land it has, which has been fixed by dominant groups outside the form. Unless the form is undergoing transformation, then subsistence farmers cannot easily identify a group that directly extracts from their work. The casual worker in the primitive labor market likewise can only identify individuals in a fleeting relationship. Significantly, in both cases, consciousness is often expressed in the form of adherence to abstract and dominating universal forces, gods, and millennialism, because there can be no immediate target for anger, injustice, and/or deference.

Outside forces intervene in the power relations of all the forms either directly or indirectly. The state frequently intervenes in peasant-lord relations, usually to back up the power of the landlords. Trade unions may attempt to organize the unorganized workers of the enterprise labor market, feminist groups may urge housewives to reconsider their roles, and churches seek to capture the force of despair in the primitive labor market workers. They all do so in opposition to, or in conjunction with, the basic power relations of the form. It is for this reason the multiple social relations of production approach illuminates the inadvisability of advocating any single policy, for either reformist and revolutionary objectives, that cuts across different forms of social relations.

External Power Relations

The relationship between one form of social relations and the whole hierarchy of forms within any single social formation constitutes the external power relations. The external relations for subordinate forms are ones of subordination and exploitation in that there are transfers between producers in one form of social relations to another. Exploitation is seen, not as being based upon any notion of absolute value, but as indicating different rewards to work emerging from the social relations of production. Workers in enterprise corporatist social relations, that is, those working for large dominant corporations, have better conditions of work and return than those in the small enterprises of the enterprise labor market and indeed may even live longer as a result. Yet they may be engaged in the same work and sector. The lack of privilege of one is the result of the transfers made to the other. Similarly the better conditions of industrial workers in third-world countries are connected with transfers from the exploitation within the peasant-lord form. Objectively this is the case but of course this may not be the intention of those involved.

Economic transfers are made through exchanges between forms in which the differential conditions are incorporated in the goods or services and may be expressed in such terms as inter-sectorial terms of trade and unequal exchange, although the measure of value is neither labor time nor scarcity.[28]

The other principal external relation concerns the way the form of social relations is used in the social formation by dominant groups and that may not be in an entirely material way. Thus in seeking to maintain their own power in face of the state, the managerial class of dominant corporations refers for political support to the idealized image of an entrepreneur in a small enterprise. Housewives are urged to supply psychological servicing, benefiting the smooth functioning of other social relations. Powerful political groups use the insecurity engendered by self-employment social relations to keep the self-employed as political allies, and the desperate conditions of the primitive labor market social relations are used as a threat in disciplining labor. The third external relation of importance is the linkage between groups in the process of forming or dissolving class alliances. This is connected with the question of consciousness and transformation.

Consciousness

It is inherent in the notion of a form of social relations of production and in the concept of social class as defined above that any individual's consciousness is largely determined by the form of social relations in which he or she works. While consciousness is a broad concept and would include all subjective perceptions of the person's position within the world, a study devoted to power must emphasize the more obviously power-linked aspects of consciousness.

The emergence of a distinct consciousness from the social relations of production is a difficult process to chart. Given that it is affected by religion, culture, and traditions that are often residues of past, transformed social relations, the ultimate form consciousness takes must remain an area of mystery and uncertainty. It is for this reason, more than any other, that social change, especially that released by revolution, has tended to be unpredictable—the forms of consciousness are not exactly known, and expression of them and changes in them are volatile.

This being said, it is clear that the effect of working constantly in an industrial enterprise under the watchful eye of the entrepreneur equipped with the power of instant dismissal, or of working in a field desperately trying to produce for rent payments under the threat of eviction or beating, or of begging work and money daily, or of arguing with suppliers over prices, produces a different basic consciousness of work, life, and society. This consciousness may be divided into two aspects, the material and the psychological.

The material aspect of consciousness is what appears in the literature broadly as "interest"; each producer may be aware of his or her material interest within a certain form of social relations, that is, what actions will increase or decrease power and thereby affect return. They are aware then of the social relations of production, aware that they are controlled or are controllers, influenced, or manipulated. When producers are unaware of social relations or refuse to accept they are part of a power flux, this is sometimes referred to as a false consciousness in that the lack of awareness enables those who are aware to further manipulate. Hegemony of a dominant group is to some extent based upon producing an ideology that disguises and retards awareness of power relations and therefore secures an acceptance of the unrecognized hierarchy.

Rationalities developed by dominant groups within specific forms of social relations also serve the same purpose of disguising or mitigating hierarchical power. Examples are the small enterprise entrepreneur rationality of the "working boss ethic," which is an explanation for differential returns to work, or a male head of household's explanation that household services are naturally "women's work," or the landowner's promotion of a divine right to deference.

The material aspect of consciousness may cause an unorganized wage worker to resist a union organizing drive because
it is clear that at the individual and the enterprise level, union
intervention may bring dismissal or reduce existing benefits; or
a renting peasant may not respond to a call to arms when the
leadership of the movement is ambivalent about land distribution
after the war is won; or marginals in urban slums may not support
social movements, because of their lack of protection against the
bulldozer ready to destroy their habitat in retaliation. They all
show an awareness of the power relations surrounding their
production. The bulk of substantive political discussion is based
upon the notion of a material consciousness inherent in individuals, groups, and classes arising from their position within the
social relations of production.

The other aspect of consciousness is, however, more vague
because it cannot easily be calculated from the objective material
position within social relations and may never be directly expressed. A material consciousness allowing a cost-benefit analysis of any considered action may be based on, or distinct from,
a deeper consciousness. This consciousness corresponds to a
social character developed from adjustment to social relations or
to the notion that the forms of social relations produce not only
goods and services but also types of people.[29]

Thus the unorganized worker mentioned above may not
join the union, because of a calculation of ultimate benefit, but
that does not mean that he/she does not hate the work, the su-
pervisor, or employer; it does not mean that he/she will not engage
in acts detrimental to maximum output or, when conditions are
right, will unleash the restrained hate and sense of injustice in
rapid and violent action. While casual workers of the primitive
labor market may avoid association with liberal or revolutionary
groups because of a calculation of final outcome, it does not mean
that they will not suddenly and with energy and passion follow
a populist leader whose promises may be objectively false, or
join a millennialist crusade that promises ultimate salvation, or
even themselves violently destroy their habitat. The self-employed artisanal family may calculate rationally whether it is
worth joining groups of self-employed but may well do so from
a base of psychological insecurity produced from the necessity
to maintain a delicate balance of power between predators in

order to secure income and occupation. The insecurity of the self-employed as a form of consciousness may also, however, be the basis of a class alliance in which the solution to insecurity appears to be offered. These latter are the deeper manifestations of consciousness emerging from social relations, and it is often on these that alliances are forged or classes created.

In one sense then class consciousness may transcend a consciousness of material benefit and power relations derived from a particular form of social relations. The material interests of different groups may have to be overridden by the satisfaction of a deeper element of consciousness. Often it is broader ideologies or the cross-cutting appeals to ethnicity, gender, nationality, and nationalism that assist in this process. Thus the ultimate goals of a peasant movement or an urban labor movement may appeal only differentially to renting or self-employed farmers or to casual workers and unorganized wage workers, but these differences may be subsumed under an ideology promising a better society, or individual salvation, or national liberation, or more power for ethnic groups or women. But such ideologies and emotional forces must still take cognizance of the deeper consciousness arising from the social relations of production—the outcome will be very different when there is a conjunction of broad appeals with consciousness than when there is conflict, even when this is not well expressed or obvious.[30] The awareness of these two levels of consciousness arising from different forms of social relations is the most necessary for understanding the process of social change but at the same time is the most difficult.

Transformation

A form of social relations of production as a pattern of power relations is by definition dynamic. Power is always in flux. Power relations between groups is the expression of the contradiction of the social relations of production. This is not to say that forms of social relations are not stable over long periods of time, but it does say that there are constant crises arising from the opposing groups' power struggle within production and that while these crises may be solved with traditional means within the form, the possibility is always present that the crises will be solved by transforming the form of social relations.

Contradictions between actions to increase power or reduce subordination and the effects of such actions are at the basis of all transformations of social relations. Thus in order to solve insecurity, a self-employed person may be tempted to accept the guarantees offered by a dominant purchaser of his or her output. The contradiction is that the more a single purchaser buys the output the more the producer becomes dependent upon the purchaser and the more independence and control over production is lost. The final outcome would be that the self-employed person becomes a de facto employee of a single buyer, and the power relations are transformed. An employer may wish to increase personal power and wealth by increasing the size of the enterprise but as he or she does so, the blocks to worker organizations inherent in a smaller enterprise become weaker. The contradiction of increasing power by economies of large scale is the development of countervailing worker power. A union in a bipartite relationship with employers may call on the state for assistance only to find that the state assumes a continuing dynamic role in the power relations and the bilateral relations between union and employer are destroyed to create a tripartite new pattern. The case is similar when landlords call on state support to protect their power in the ownership of land but find that the state then extracts taxes, paving the way for land redistribution and the transformation from peasant-lord social relations to self-employment.

Transformation from the inside arises when the dynamics of power produce crises and confrontation that are resolved by the change of the configuration of power and thus of the form of social relations. Transformations are the cause of the changes in the numbers of producers within any particular form or for the elimination of the form from the social formation entirely. A successful union organizing campaign within the enterprise labor market transforms social relations in the direction of bipartite or tripartite relations and reduces the numbers of workers in the enterprise labor market. Successful nonrevolutionary peasant movements may secure a limited redistribution of land or undermine the power of moneylenders and create or restore independent farming families within self-employment social relations. The mismanagement of enterprise corporatism may mean that the staff associations become more powerful and establish a bipartite power bargaining relationship, or unions may collapse into enterprise corporatism, or the official unions of state corporatism may not accept their role and transform social relations toward tripartitism. Some of these transformations are partial, but when the presence of the whole form or its dominance in the social formation is at issue, such transformations may change the composition of the social formation.

It is in the nature of the subordinate forms of social relations that transformation from the inside is not common. Transformations within dominant forms of social relations are more common, partly because the groups involved can expect their actions to have a direct impact in other forms and thus destroy the social isolation of the action of groups in subordinate forms. In general, however, any transformation that affects the social formation is a combination of outside intervention and alliances across forms of social relations.

Transformation occurring through intervention from outside the pattern of power relations and from alliances is the basic dynamic of social change. The interventions, usually by the state and dominant and subordinate groups in other forms, are interventions within an existing dynamic of power and cannot be considered as dominant or neutral to such a dynamic. Indeed the interventions will be successful, for whatever purpose, only if the power and consciousness context is understood. Some examples of transformation occurring from outside interventions are presented here. The increasing power of large corporations and of the state regulations are transforming self-employment social relations in industrialized countries to the point where the numbers are severely reduced. Liberal professionals, once the most privileged of self-employed, must now bargain in bipartite fashion with the state or employing corporations in order to maintain their return to work. The managers of enterprise corporatism destroy peasant-lord and subsistence relations when they introduce large-scale mechanized farming in third-world countries. The state intervenes to create market-producing, self-employed farmers or peasants in attempts to secure extraction from subsistence farmers. Both unions and corporations undermine the power relations of the enterprise labor market, women's organizations seek to eliminate household social relations, and ɔlitical parties, churches, and revolutionary and progressive organizations seek to create alliances between groups or classes to change social relations and social formations.

When alliances and class formation are successful to the point that the nature of the social formation changes and the development dynamic changes from that of capitalist to noncapitalist, then the new dominant groups transform many of the subordinate forms found within capitalist societies. Dominant groups within redistributive social relations under centrally planned socialism generally ban the enterprise labor market, outlaw self-employment of the artisanal type, eliminate the lords of the peasant-lord form, and so on. Communalist may replace peasant-lord relations, although invariably household social relations continue and, in third-world social formations, subsistence and primitive labor markets also remain. The role that dominant and subordinate groups play in social movements that have revolution and change of the social formation as an objective are considered at the end of each chapter in this book.

There remains to consider the paths or direction of transformation whether occurring from the inside or the outside. The dynamics of power may precipitate several different paths toward transformation. Thus peasant-lord relations may be transformed into the direction of self-employment, when peasants acquire land and produce for a market, or of communalist under revolutionary regimes; enterprise labor market relations may be transformed in the direction of either bipartite or tripartite; and subsistence may be transformed toward either peasant-lord or self-employment social relations. None of these paths is fixed, although the options are limited. The various transformational paths conclude the discussion of each of the subordinate forms of social relations discussed in this book.

THE UNPROTECTED WORKER

The term unprotected worker is one of convenience and is intended to indicate the nonestablished worker or the least powerful of producers in the world labor force. The division between the established and nonestablished worker emerged most significantly at the end of the last century in the then industrializing countries. But there had always been more privileged and less ✶ privileged workers throughout the history of work whether the division be seen between artisans and peasants or between field and house slaves.

In the industrial context of the last century the division between the established and nonestablished was between the high-skilled unionized and the lower skilled unorganized workers. The latter were disparaged by some marxists as the lumpenproletariat and pushed to the margins of theorizing and concern ✶ because of their supposed lack of revolutionary potential. Whereas this division is the basis of dividing the labor force in this study, and whereas the established worker may still correspond to the situation at the turn of the last century in Europe, the current nonestablished or unprotected worker category has been extended to encompass workers in forms of social relations that were already disappearing in Europe of the last century, such as the peasants of the peasant-lord relations and the marginals of the primitive labor market.

The unprotected workers are those workers in forms of social relations who have not been able to develop sufficient individual or social power to resist domination and secure a degree of protection. The division between the unprotected worker and the established worker, as with all relations based on power, is one of degree and is open to dispute. At the ends of the extreme, however, the situation is very clear. In the bipartite social relations of the auto industry in the United States in the 1970s or the enterprise corporatist relations of Japanese enterprises, the bulk of the workers were protected from dismissal for life, surrounded by laws, practices, and constraints against employer power, so much so that employers began to consider labor as a fixed rather than a variable cost (inasmuch as rates of pay, conditions, and employment could not be varied). The workers were established and protected. The details of the social relations of these workers are the subject of Harrod, *Power, Production, and the Established Worker* (forthcoming). At the other end of the scale is the casual worker in a third-world city who is at the mercy of the casual employer of labor and can never expect the state, union, or other worker organization to prevent the most economic and physical abuse. Between these extremes are the degrees of protection based upon different elements of power. Workers in an enterprise are more protected by the structure of employment, scarcities of labor, and the open social nature of production than the marginals of the primitive labor market. But they are exposed, in the ultimate, to instant dismissal by employers. Peasants are unprotected against extortionate interest rates from moneylenders or prices from merchants while self-employed farmers are more protected because their multiple power relations permit more options. Yet self-employed farmers are at the mercy, in the ultimate, of those who control the market, which is increasingly the state but also large corporations.

At the margin of the established-unprotected division exist those workers who have secured a protection under conditions where it is unusual or those who have only recently emerged from subordinate social relations. Thus it may, at first sight, seem unlikely that a Brazilian industrial worker within the state corporatist system of that country could be considered as established or protected given that the social rights and the distribution of income are so bad. Yet in comparison with the marginals of the *favelas* or the peasants and Indians of the rural hinterland, the industrial worker is afforded a measure of protection by the state-created official unions and regulatory agencies. Nevertheless, it is here that the dividing line between established and unprotected worker becomes indistinct.

Unprotected workers appear in all social formations within one or more of the six forms of subordinate social relations that cover them. In some third-world countries unprotected workers could comprise as much as 85 to 90 percent of the country's labor force (defined as people between 15 and 70 years of age) with only the police, armed services, and civil service comprising the established workers. There are some industrialized countries that have the reverse pattern with more than 90 percent of the labor force being established and protected by state, union, or corporate agreement.

On a world scale the task of assessing the proportions of the world labor force comprised by different workers in different forms of social relations is even more difficult. Available statistics are not based on the criteria of power relations, and estimates have to be made via indirect statistical routes or by surveys of expert opinions. In each chapter some indications of the statistical routes available for each form are provided. Adjusted and updated expert opinion surveys made originally in 1972 indicate the following proportions of the world labor force covered by the six forms of social relations covering unprotected workers: subsistence—between 4 and 7 percent; peasant-lord—between 16 and 19 percent; primitive labor market—between 9 and 12 percent; enterprise labor market—between 11 and 15 percent; self-employment—between 7 and 10 percent; household—between 2 and 3 percent.[31] The unprotected worker then certainly comprises more than 50 percent of the world labor force. Of the nonsocialist world labor force—and the People's Republic of China alone accounts for 25 percent of the world labor force—at least 75 percent is composed of unprotected workers, that is, approximately 1.2 billion people.

NOTES

1. Robert W. Cox, *Power and World Order: Social Forces in the Making of History* (See New York: Columbia University Press, 1987), Introduction to Part 1. (Hereafter cited as Cox, *World Order.*)

2. Frederick Engels, *The Correspondence of Karl Marx and Frederick Engels* (New York: International Publishers), pp. 475–77, as quoted in George Plekhanov *The Materialist Conception of History* (New York: International Publishers, 1964), p. 7.

3. These questions are considered in relation to the world level of power in Jeffrey Harrod, "Transnational Power," *Yearbook of World Affairs* (1976), 30:97–115.

4. On children's industrial labor, see for example, Anti-Slavery Society, *Child Labour in Morocco's Carpet Industry* (London: 1978); on children in the sex tourism industry, see Truong Thanh-dam, "The Dynamics of Sex Tourism: The Case of Southeast Asia," *Development and Change* (1983), 14:533–53; Linda Galley, "For Sale: Girls," *Southeast Asia Chronicle* (1983), no. 89; "Thailand: Lust City in the Far East, *Time,* May 10, 1982; on use of stimulants in industrial production, see, for example, Kim Chang Soo, "Marginalisation, Development, and Korea's Workers Movements," *AMPO* (1977), 9(3):20; on workplace isolation of migrants, see, for example, "A Modern Slavery Institution in Denmark," *Fagbladet* (Denmark) April

10, 1980. Most microlevel reports of slum and agricultural work refer to both the industrial and environmental diseases that result.

5. Discussions of realism related to this observation are found in Jeffrey Harrod, "International Relations, Perceptions and Neo-Realism," *Yearbook of World Affairs* (1977), 31:289–305; and Robert W. Cox, "Social Forces, States and World Orders: Beyond International Relations Theory," *Millennium Journal of International Studies* (1981), 10(2):126–55.

6. See, for example, the extensive treatment of the question of technological determinism in G. A. Cohen, *Karl Marx's Theory of History: A Defence* (Oxford: Clarendon Press, 1978).

7. See on the application of the approach, Jeffrey Harrod, "Informal Sector and Urban Mass: A Social Relations of Production Approach," (The Hague, mimeo, Institute of Social Studies, 1983).

8. Cox, *World Order*, p. x.

9. Robert W. Cox, "Approaches to a Futurology of Industrial Relations," *International Institute of Labour Studies Bulletin* (1971) no. 8. pp. 139-75: Robert W. Cox, Jeffrey Harrod and others, *Future Industrial Relations: An Interim Report* (Geneva; International Institute for Labour Studies, 1972); Cox, *World Order*, Chapters 2,3,4.

10. See, Cox, *World Order*, p. 12.

11. For a discussion that puts this "five-member" schema into a multiple social relations of production framework, see Attila Agh, "Labyrinth in the Mode of Production Controversy," *Studies on Developing Countries*, no. 105 (Budapest: Institute for World Economics, 1980).

12. Cox, *World Order*, pp. 11–15 and ch. 1; for a critique of the so-called "pre-capitalist" social relations, see Rod Aya, "Pre-capitalist Modes of Production," *Monthly Review* (January 1978), 29(8):37–45.

13. See, for example, the discussion in Eric R. Wolf, *Europe and the People Without History* (Los Angeles: University of California Press, 1982), pp. 73–77.

14. These two usages then depart slightly from Cox *World Order*, who uses "mode" and "production relations."

15. The concept of an "industrial relations system" is generally considered to have been most well developed by John Dunlop *Industrial Relations Systems* (New York, Holt, 1958); industrial relations systems was used as synonomous with a form or mode of social relations of production in Cox, Harrod and others *Future Industrial Relations:*

16. See Jeffrey Harrod, "Social Relations of Production, Systems of Labour Control and Third World Trade Unions," in R. Southall, ed., *The New International Division of Labour and Third World Trade Unions* (London, Zed Press, 1987b) for other uses and definitions of a concept of labour control see also Richard Scase, ed., *Industrial Society; Class Cleavage and Control* (London, Allen and Unwin, 1976). J. Crisp, *The Story of the African Working Class* (London, Zed Press, 1984); Robert W. Cox "World Systems of Labour and Production" (mimeo, IPSA Conference Paper, 1974).

17. See Cox, *World Order*, p. 4, "Thus there is no incompatibility between the use of ideal types and a dialectical view of history. Ideal types are a part of a tool kit of historical explanation".

18. Ibid., pp. 22–26.

19. See A. Etzioni, *Modern Organizations* (New York: Prentice-Hall, 1963) for a more extensive application of motivation and control; and Harrod, "Social Relations of Production, Systems of Labour Control".

20. Cox, *World Order*, pp. 26–29.

21. Cox, "Approaches to a Futurology of Industrial Relations," Cox, "World Systems of Labour and Production" (mimeo, 1973); Cox, Harrod, and others, *Future Industrial Relations*.

22. See, for example, the discussion in Jan Bremen, "Seasonal Migration and Co-operative Capitalism," in *Economic and Political Weekly* (1978), 8(31–33):1350; Pranab Bardhan and Ashok Rudra, "Types of Labour Attachment in Agriculture: Results of a Survey in West Bengal, 1979," *Economic and Political Weekly* (1980), 15(35):1477–85.

23. According to an Indian Ministry of Labour Report in 1978, there existed at least two million bonded laborers who were often unable to change employers. See *ICEF Collective Bargaining Bulletin* (Geneva, November 1980), no. 7/8, pp. 15–16.

24. See Cox, *World Order*, ch. 4.

25. Ibid., ch. 5.

26. An argument is made for disaggregating the view of state action in A. Hussain and K. Tribe, *Marxism and the Agrarian Question* (London: Macmillan, 1981), 2:148–49.

27. Part 1.

28. See, for example, John Kenneth Galbraith, *Economics of the Public Purpose* (London: Andre Deutsch, 1973); V. M. Dandekar, "Bourgeois Politics of the Working Class," *Economic and Political Weekly* (January 12, 1980), pp. 73–83.

29. See, for example, Erich Fromm and Michael Maccoby, *Social Character in a Mexican Village: A Sociopsychoanalytic Study* (Englewood Cliffs, N. J.: Prentice-Hall, 1970): "As individuals express their life, so they are. What they are, therefore, coincides with their production, both with what they produce and how they produce," Karl Marx and Frederick Engels, *The German Ideology*, as quoted in James Russell, *Marx-Engels Dictionary* (Sussex: Harvester, 1980), p. 734.

30. See, for example, the discussion in Ashok K. Upadhyaya, "Class Struggle in Rural Maharashtra (India): Towards a New Perspective," *Journal of Peasant Studies* (January 1980), 7(2):213–34; James C. Scott, "History According to Winners and Losers," in A. Turton and S. Tanabe, eds., *History and Peasant Consciousness in South East Asia* (Osaka: National Museum of Ethnology, 1984), pp. 161–210. For an application of the multiple social relations of production approach as presented in this study to the disaggregation of an occupational group, see Truong Thanh-Dam, *Virtue, Order, Health and Money: Towards a Comprehensive Perspective on Female Prostitution in Asia* (New York, United Nations, 1986).

31. See, Cox, Harrod and others *Future Industrial Relations*.

Part 1

Subsistence Farmers and Peasants

The two chapters in this part are devoted to two of the several forms of social relations of production found in agriculture. These two, subsistence and peasant-lord, govern the lives and production of the majority of the people in the world who spend the bulk of their lives cultivating the earth and husbanding animals. Such people have gained widespread contemporary attention because they endure the extremes of domination, oppression, and poverty and, moreover, because they have frequently joined revolutionary armies.

Very often such people have been lumped together with all others who work in the agricultural sector and have then been collectively referred to as "peasants." In this book, however, subsistence farmers and peasants are carefully distinguished from each other and from other agricultural workers found in other social relations. To do this each must be given definitions that are somewhat different from those in general use because the definitions must signify social relations rather than material circumstance, sector, or type of farming. Subsistence farmers are defined as those people, usually found in a household unit, who consume all that they produce and use the bulk of their working time to produce it; peasants are those whose production is controlled and whose surplus is extracted by landlords, moneylenders, or merchants or a combination of all three.

The objective of this part is not to consider in detail the ensemble and intricate interconnections of all the forms of social relations found in the agricultural sector. To do so would involve examination of the social relations surrounding the landowning, self-employed farmer; the marginalized landless laborer; the unorganized or unionized plantation or farm worker; and the rural woman household worker. But since the division of the material presented in this book is by social relations and not by sectors, the objective of this part, as all others, is to analyze separately—in monad style—two forms of social relations. Nor is there any significance in selecting these two forms for the first part of the book. It is for other writers, if they wish, to analyze by sector or social formation or to consider material, class, and consciousness linkages between forms of social relations to a greater extent than is presented here.

This being said, there are, nevertheless, a number of reasons why it is convenient to discuss in one part with a common introduction these two forms of social relations of production. First, subsistence and peasant-lord social relations are different from all other ten forms identified in that they are found only within the agricultural sector. For this reason these forms may be termed the social relations *of* agriculture rather than *in* agriculture. All other forms of social relations may be found in any of the economic sectors of agriculture, industry, or commerce and are never exclusive to one sector. Thus when a farm is organized as an enterprise on a wage-labor basis, the employer-employee power relations prevail just as they would if the product was plastic toys rather than sugar cane, cocoa, or vegetables.

The social relations that produce subsistence farmers and peasants are unique to agriculture for two basic reasons: first, life can be supported from farming, for the work directly produces food, clothing, and shelter—a factory laborer could never have subsistence relations because it is not possible to eat a plastic toy if that, for example, was what the worker was producing; second, peasants are the objects of a special type of power. This power has had many centuries in which to ossify into a unique structure of tradition, myth, and psychological domination associated exclusively with control over land and products from land. Such structures have not found their duplication in other spheres of property, such as industrial capital, and if ever they did, there is no reason why peasant-lord relations would not be found in the industrial sector.

Second, peasants and subsistence farmers are near the bottom of any hierarchy in rural power. It is perhaps only the marginalized, seasonal, landless laborer who may be reduced to a desperation lower than that of a subsistence farmer or peasant. Subordinate producers in other forms of social relations in agriculture all have greater room for maneuver in any attempt to redress power. For example, workers within enterprise-type farms and plantations have often had some success in creating countervailing worker organizations or unions, and self-employed farmers use a variety of tactics to manipulate markets and tax collectors. This position of being the least powerful of cultivators always raises the possibility that peasants and subsistence farmers will form a united social class in any movement against dominant groups or classes. Such potential unity may also be cemented by the proximity of the two forms of social relations; that is, subsistence farmers are frequently being transformed into peasants through land reform and technology introduced by dominant groups in the social formation.

Third, and of crucial importance to twentieth-century world history, is the role that these least powerful of cultivators of the third world have had in the major political and structural changes that have taken place in the past forty years. Peasants, uniting in revolutionary movements to escape from the oppression of the landlord class, whether indigenous or colonial, have made up the mass of fighters in the armies of revolution or national liberation. They participated in the overthrow of dominant power structures and classes in China in the 1940s, Cuba and Algeria in the 1950s, Indo-China in the 1960s, and Nicaragua and Mozambique in the 1970s,[1] and they continue to pressure regimes in the 1980s such as those in Peru, the Philippines, and the Sudan, and even when not actively participating they have provided the base and food for the more enthusiastic soldiers of the revolution. This is not to say that they have led the revolutionary armies, nor, as will be discussed later, have they necessarily been a determining force within them. At times they have refused the call to mobilize and have delivered to the opposing forces erstwhile revolutionary leaders. Furthermore, it may be that the epochs of revolution based on peasants and concerned directly with issues of land are drawing to a close as the numbers of landless laborers, casual workers, household, and enterprise workers in the cities increase and become more sophisticated in strategy and consciousness.

Fourth, and finally, at the time of writing there is another reason for considering subsistence farmers and peasants together: they constitute the largest proportion of the total agricultural labor force in third-world countries and produce the largest amounts of food. These latter characteristics become important when third-world countries are exhorted to adopt national austerity plans in order to pay interest and capital to capital-exporting countries and for increasingly more expensive oil and energy. Under such conditions the price of locally consumed and exported agricultural produce becomes of crucial importance; the locally consumed produce will substantially determine the income of workers producing industrial goods, for in these countries the largest proportion of wages goes for food, and the exported produce will help determine the level of foreign exchange earned. In turn, cheaper agricultural produce may mean the possibility of cutting the real income of industrial workers and increasing export crop sales. Austerity measures, then invariably mean a squeeze on peasants' income and more rapid and brutal intervention against subsistence farmers to make them produce a surplus. Promoted internationally by private and public financial institutions, such policies, in effect, become a generalized international squeeze on peasants and subsistence farmers but also, of course, on self-employed farmers and others producing in agriculture.[2]

The questions of what policies and strategies appeal to the subsistence, the renting, indebted, and merchant-dominated cultivator in the third world; what factors will undermine the apparent legitimacy of landlords' power; and what transformational paths can be encouraged will therefore continue to keep subsistence farmers and peasants at the near center of calculations in the minds of existing or aspiring generals of local and world power and their technocratic advisers.

Whereas these may be good reasons for discussing peasants and subsistence farmers within one part of this book, there are, however, equally important reasons that within the agricultural sector as a whole they must be seen as two distinct forms of social relations among the at least seven forms that may be found somewhere within the production of agricultural goods. Part of the objective of the approach adopted in this book is to provide a disaggregation of standard perceptions of large groups of people such as "the mass," "working class," "marginals," and "peasants." In the case of the agricultural sector the task is rendered even more necessary and difficult because of the dominating concept of the "peasant" and the "peasantry." Some discussion of these later concepts must be undertaken before our moving to the more specific consideration of the different forms of social relations in agriculture.

THE TRADITIONAL "PEASANT" CONCEPT

For centuries the basis for the prevailing perception of the people of the rural areas in both the third world and the now industrialized countries has been that they did not live in towns and that they worked on the land. The quintessence of this perception has been that the generalized concept of a "peasant" that has been used as a blanket categorization to encompass all those who work on the land without wage payments. The different forms of social relations in which they might be found have been disregarded. Although in specialist literature, and among experts on agricultural development, a more discriminating approach has recently been adopted, it is still the case that the "peasant" concept enjoys a continuing status as a meaningful category of producers.

The peasant concept is, of course, both attractive and ubiquitous; it is attractive because to the outsider it seems to satisfy the search for a categorization for all those who seemingly have similar social and attitudinal characteristics derived from the particular type of means of production used—land—and the particular type of work—cultivation—that is performed. It is ubiquitous because the concept of peasant invades descriptions of types of farmers, types of agriculture, and types of movements. Once such a widely accepted and pervasive categorization had been made, it was but a short step to formulate and apply a "typical peasant" cluster of characteristics and attitudes to all agricultural workers. Peasants were thus in the most recent past seen, at least in Western European and North American perceptual tradition, as ignorant, sullen, servile, inscrutable, and occasionally, but usually ineffectually, rebellious, while peasant agriculture was small-scale, primitive, and inefficient cultivation.

The origin of the peasant concept is associated with the two preoccupations that have dogged thought and policy about life in the rural areas and the social and political nature of the people who lived there, at least since the beginning of the nineteenth century. Both of these preoccupations stemmed in part from reactions to the social horrors of nineteenth-century European industrial towns and were attempts to find ways to mitigate the degradation, violence, and the lack of cooperation that the industrial town represented. One theme concerned the possibility of a social cohesion in rural life that had been "lost" in the transition to urban industrialized society. The other concerned the possible role the rural population could play in a total transformation of society that could eliminate both industrial and rural exploitation forever. These two themes are perhaps symbolized by the ideas about rural peoples found in the works of Ferdinand Tonnies and Karl Marx.

Tonnies, writing during the transition of North Germany from a predominantly rural and agricultural to a predominantly industrial society, thought he saw a cohesion in the rural population that was lacking in the urban counterparts.[3] He developed and counterposed the ideas of community (gemeinschaft) and association (gesellschaft). This dichotomy was essentially a comparision between an imagined organic cohesion of rural life and the more formal and contractual nature of social relations in the atomized conditions of urban society. Although the concepts of community and association have had widespread application as analytical categories in social sectors, there is little doubt that Tonnies expressed a value judgment and a regret for the loss of perceived community life in rural areas.[4] The loss of community has subsequently become a recurring theme within theories of, and prescriptions for, the problems of mass urban societies of the twentieth century. This theme has been reflected in movements as far apart in space, time, and objectives as the Narodnik movement in Russia before the 1917 revolution, where the Russian village—the mir—was believed to have a structure and a spirit of cooperation that put it in advance of urban social structure on any path toward a socialist society, and the "back-to-the-land" mid-twentieth-century idealization of rural life advocated principally by intellectuals in rich countries who sought refuge from corporate-dominated industrial society. Tonnies has contributed to a century of romanticizing about life in the rural areas.

In contrast, Marx was not inclined to view agricultural workers with any such romanticized admiration, but neither could he grant them the same effort of sympathetic understanding he gave to the urban worker. With Frederick Engels he argued in the *Communist Manifesto* that the bourgeois, in shifting social domination from countryside to town, had "rescued a considerable part of the population from the idiocy of rural life." This typical urban disdain was hardly conducive to understanding agricultural workers from within their own social relations.

Marx did, however, distinguish between landowning and land-renting peasants, arguing that the former were in a precapitalist mode of production, for through landownership, they owned the means of production.[5] Likewise, rural farmers of the non-European world were seen to be in another precapitalist mode—the Asiatic mode. These distinctions of social relations were not, however, sustained when the central concern of revolution in Europe was considered. Categorical statements were made about the whole of the rural populations regardless of possible differences in social relations within it. French peasant villages were, for Marx, like "sacks of potatoes"—individual units bound together by a relatively fragile social fabric.[6] This was indeed the prevailing situation in France and Germany, the two countries with large populations of landowning farmers with which Marx was familiar. But his opinion that such farmers were inert, conservative, or reactionary, based upon such evidence as the French peasant's support of Napoleon III, was then rather indiscriminately extended to "peasants" in general by other writers and activitists.[7] Despite the known rebelliousness of peasants manifested in the form of explosive violence, the view that they were marginal to any political movements was subsequently adopted by generations of European socialists and politicians who were, like Marx, from the towns and familiar with industrial rather than agricultural labor. They likewise accepted the prejudice that peasants were ignorant and hidebound by custom. Universally the rural producer, either at home or in overseas colonies, was relegated by writers and activists to the shadows of any political concern.

In the twentieth century it gradually became apparent that the romantic versions of rural life attributable to Tonnies' notion of *gemeinschaft* and also Marx's castigation of rural life were equally distorting lenses. Reconsideration of the nature and role of peasants developed, however, not because of serious examination of the logic of prevailing views, but because rural people began to make themselves heard to urban politicians and intellectuals, not by words but by actions.

In particular, the role of peasants in the colonial liberation struggles and revolutions following the 1939–1945 war awakened interest in all quarters—both revolutionary and reactionary—in the dimensions of agricultural existence. Industrializing and productivity-minded regimes in the third world also found that more information about the rural experience was needed for the purpose of imposing taxes and raising agricultural productivity. The result was an explosion of empirical and sociological information about the rural areas, particularly in third-world countries, during the 1960s.

These studies, regardless of their various objectives and the ultimate use to which they may have been put, began to reveal the diversity of forms of social relations in agriculture. They revealed that Tonnies' *gemeinschaft* was not necessarily based upon a positive cohesion derived from shared values but was often created as a defensive reaction to extraction from rural production by landlord, state, town, and industry: from this perspective rural life was one of individual desperation enclosed in a common ethic for purposes of mutual defense. Furthermore, the rural cultivators revealed themselves to be far from ignorant and passive in the organization of production, in the appreciation of ecological systems, and in the ability to mobilize and fight. The images of idiocy and tranquil passivity melted into those of militancy as the perception of the rural populations began to change in the minds of scholars, politicians, and political activists.

This inroad into the prevailing and disparaging belief held about cultivators and their consciousness has not, in general, ushered in a new era of a more discriminating examination of the social relations of production in rural areas, especially in discourses outside of specialist literature. But it provided at least, a starting point for a now increasingly aired argument that the term *peasant* should be abandoned completely or at least that it should be used more restrictively.[8]

The restrictive definition of peasant, used in this book is that of a rural cultivator whose production is governed and surplus removed as the result of a lack of power in the face of landlords, moneylenders, or merchants.[9] Such a definition clearly excludes a large proportion of those who work on the land who would be traditionally caught in the peasant concept. Thus, it does not include any landowning, self-employed farmers free from merchant or moneylender domination, because their power relations are more with those who control the larger market for the sale of their produce and those who supply inputs for their production; it does not include the subsistence farming household that does not have immediate power relations with any dominant groups or classes, and it does not include the employing farmers and their wage laborers, for the power relations issue from the existence of laborers within a labor market.

Any escape from the generality of the "peasant" and "peasantry" means that the social relations of production can, and must, become the determining criteria of any categories of the rural populations. The multiplicity of social relations of production in the rural areas must then be examined briefly before a detailed look at subsistence and peasant-lord relations.

SOCIAL RELATIONS
OF PRODUCTION IN AGRICULTURE

There have been many attempts to distinguish different groups of cultivators by criteria that approach or approximate those of social relations.[10] However, most of these have been seen as mere divisions within a "peasantry" rather than distinct social phenomena that produce different dynamics and consciousness. Awareness of such divisions as Lenin's rich, middle, and poor peasants or divisions made on the exclusive criteria of the legal relationship of cultivator to land, has not prevented interventions in the lives of cultivators from being made on the basis of their perceived homogeneity. To take one example from many available, it could be argued that the motto "Land or Death" adopted by the Peruvian revolutionary leader Hugo Blanco in the early 1970s to mobilize the rural population did not take sufficient account of the social relations that divided the population and that would make the acquisition of land appeal to only one group within one form of social relations. For renting cultivators the issue would be landownership, for the landowning it may have been the rigors of debt bondage. Perhaps then the slogan would be meaningful only for the landless. Yet Blanco had to write from detention in an attempt to persuade the land-renting farmers to even allow the landless into the movement.[11] Detailed analysis of the situation in Peru indeed revealed that there was in fact a vicious struggle going on between the land-renting farmers and the landless that no movement having land as its sole objective or symbol could overcome.[12] Because landless laborers and renting farmers are within two different forms of social relations, an approach emphasizing their potential difference is closer to reality than that classifying them even as distinct strata in a "peasant" class.

Similar problems may be observed with the introduction of higher yield seeds into third-world agriculture—the so-called green revolution. Increased yields through technology mean something entirely different in different patterns of power relations—in one it increased merchant power, in another it increased power for employers, and in another it increased power for those who control market prices. With an understanding of the multiplicity of patterns of power, of forms of social relations, it would have been more easily predictable that the introduction of this type of seed into many areas would, as it did, increase poverty, as well as wealth, and create new divisions and conflicts.[13]

The best known division of rural cultivators is that of

Lenin's categories of rich, middle, and poor peasants. The rich, middle, and poor peasants correspond respectively to farmers who own land and employ others, those who work their own land with family labor, and those who are tenant farmers or who are partially landless. Although the basis of this categorization, if interpreted in this way, approaches social relations of production criteria, it is far from satisfactory. Landowning farmers may lose control of their production through indebtedness or merchant domination of market distribution, in which case the power relations surrounding production have little to do with the fact that they own their land.[14] In addition the whole division is made more confusing by the names given, which are based exclusively on income criteria, although Lenin would normally be expected to be sensitive to power rather than income as an important indicator. Thus, it is possible that the so-called "middle peasant" who owns land may be poorer than the so-called "poor peasant" who rents, if, as suggested above, the level of extraction by moneylender or merchant or the size of the holding forces consumption down to very low levels.

In contrast, both in perception and outcome, Mao Zedong, for the purposes of formulating rural revolutionary strategy in China in the 1920s, abandoned Lenin's division of rich, middle, and poor peasants for a sophisticated multiple categorization of occupational structure in the rural areas.[15] Although the formal criterion was occupation, the categories made symbolized forms of social relations of production, many of which have been identified in the introductory chapter of this book. Mao apparently did this for the purpose of strategy while still using the "poor peasant" concept for mobilizing purposes. This insight enabled him to see that the landowning farmers could be used to oppose the hated, taxing warlords until both were so weakened by the engagement that they could be more easily eliminated by the poor peasants.

The recognition of the multiplicity of social relations of production in the contemporary rural areas brings into doubt the notion of a peasant class, the term being used here in its traditional general sense. The question of a peasant class is rendered complicated and confused not only by the blanket notion of peasant but also by the standard divisions and categories within a "peasantry" that have, through sheer force of reality, entered into the discussion. Thus some authors consider Lenin's division of rich, middle, and poor peasants as classes, others as strata, others as subsections, and so on.[16] Discussions at such a high level of abstraction as that relating to a "worker-peasant" alliance under the circumstance where there is a lack of agreement on what constitutes a class of cultivators becomes almost meaningless, as Mao Zedong realized, at least for the purpose of strategy.[17]

As will be discussed later, any of the subordinate producers within the different forms of social relations of production identified in chapter 1 may constitute a class, inasmuch as they may have similar material conditions of life and have developed similar rationalities. But whether there is a consciousness of an opposing class or group power or some organizational manifestations of class and whether such potential classes of subordinate producers can come together into one class with a unified consciousness and strategy is a question that can often be answered only in the specific case, by analysis of the sector or the specific social formation. This is the task that is deferred here in favor of first identifying the different forms of social relations of production, and second, looking closer at the subordiante producers, in the two principal forms found in the rural areas.

Seven different forms of social relations of production can be observed in agricultural production in the third world. Considered from the standpoint of subordinate producers these forms are seen when production and income is: (1) controlled within a household or collectivity, as in household or community subsistence farming; (2) dominated by a landlord, moneylender, or merchant who extracts from the cultivator rent, interest, and profit; (3) governed by those who control a "market" that is the source of return for production, as in the case of a self-employed farming family; (4) controlled directly by an employer to whom the agricultural worker is subordinated in a wage relationship; (5) determined by an employer whose power is counterbalanced by a trade union and/or constrained by government regulation; (6) determined by group decision based upon acceptance of society-wide goals, as in agricultural communes; and (7) controlled by a statewide planning structure. In terms of the named forms of social relations presented in chapter 1 of this book, these correspond to (1) subsistence, (2) peasant-lord, (3) self-employment, (4) enterprise labor market, (5) bipartite or tripartite, (6) communalist, and (7) central planning.

These seven forms govern all agricultural production in the third world but not necessarily all that is produced in the rural world. Household social relations are not included in the list, for they govern the production of household services, child-bearing, and childrearing; but of course, the existence of the household form of social relations and the subordination of women to this production would be essential, if not crucial, to any sectoral analysis. Also, outside the third world, it is possible, although unlikely, that some agricultural production could be governed by the enterprise corporatist form of social relations.

The distinction between these forms of social relations within agriculture can be illustrated by the following hypothetical case of movement of people from one form to another. If a subsistence farming family previously supporting the members of the household through direct consumption of what was grown on owned or controlled land is persuaded to grow a cash crop, then the return to work and production becomes governed by the relationship between the family production unit and the controllers of the market who determine the price of the crop, the family has moved from the subsistence form of social relations to that of the self-employed. If more land is acquired and the head of household starts to employ others, the return to the individual or household would then be partly governed by the amount paid to laborers, that is, by the power relations of a labor market. The self-employed farmer would have become an employer in the enterprise labor market. Meanwhile, if young women of the household acquired employment at a nearby plantation in which there was an embryonic workers' organization and the power relations between it and the employer govern the womens' conditions of work, they would be in the bipartite form of social relations. If things went badly on the farm and the land is seized to pay debts, the previously employing head of the household members have become peasants with production and return governed by the power relationship between them and the landlord.

Such individual movements from one form of social relations to another would not normally affect the continuing existence of any of the forms involved. If migrations reach such proportions that there are no producers left, as is happening with the subsistence form, then the form can be considered as transformed. If at any time on journeys through different forms of social relations the hypothetical household or some of its members join an effective and successful movement of cultivators to enforce demands against landlords and other dominant groups, then the power relations change toward the bipartite pattern even though landlords continue to exist and rent continues to be paid. If the movements have revolutionary objectives and are successful, the participants in them may find that they precipitate a change of the social formation and find themselves as producers on a collective, cooperative, or communal farm.

It is necessary here to inject a note of warning. It must be made clear that even this classification of social relations in the rural areas is not definitive and leaves much to be desired. Systems of rent payment, landholding and wage employment in rural areas are notoriously complex, embedded as they often are in centuries of cultural, religious, and traditional structures. In Latin America, for example, in one variety of the *latifundia-minifundia* system, large landowners secure their supply of cheap wage labor from the families cultivating the surrounding *minifundia* plots, which are not even large enough to provide the food support for a family. The produce from the plot must be augmented with the wages, in money or kind, from the *latifundia*. In this system several different forms of social relations of production appear to be mixed together. The cultivators seem to be partly in subsistence, partly in wage labor, and yet, when the question is posed about the nature of the power relations governing the total situation, it becomes clear that they live and work under the type of domination identified as the peasant-lord pattern of social relations. Furthermore, the production of household services and childrearing may well be performed within household social relations that exist parallel to others and cause household workers, usually women, to be in two forms of social relations at the same time (see ch. 7, Household Social Relations).

Even if pure examples of the forms of social relations existed in reality, the endless combinations of wage labor, seasonal employment, part-rented and part-owned farms, levels of indebtedness, state interventions, and individuals producing within two forms at the same time mean that there will always be a number of hybrid, marginal, and transitional situations. Nevertheless, given the objective of this book to examine the principal rather than the marginal constellations of power, consciousness, and transformational process among the world's unprotected workers, concentration on the two forms of subsistence and peasant-lord is both necessary and justifiable.

NOTES

1. See Eric Wolf, ed., *Peasant Wars of the Twentieth Century* (New York: Harper and Row, 1969); Gordon White, Robin Murray, and Christine White, eds., *Revolutionary Socialist Development in the Third World* (Sussex, England: Wheatsheaf, 1983); Jean Ziegler, *Les Rebelles: Contre l'ordre du Monde* (Paris: Seuil, 1983).

2. See, for example, the analysis in Harry Cleaver, "Internationalisation of Capital and Mode of Production in Agriculture," *Economic and Political Weekly Review of Agriculture* (March 1976), pp. A2–A16; E. Feder, "Monopoly Capital and Agricultural Employment in Third World," *Journal of Contemporary Asia* (1981), 2:135–68; Jean Kopans, "From Senegambia to Senegal: The Evolution of Peasantries," in Martin A. Klein, ed., *Peasants in Africa: Historical and Contemporary Perspectives* (London, Sage, 1980), pp. 77–105. This is, of course, not a new phenomenon; only the extent and depth of the worldwide integration of rural producers is new. For an account of an earlier integration and illumination of the deliberate policies of the process, see Bogamil Jewsiewicki, "African Peasants in the Totalitarian Society of the Belgian Congo," in Klein, *Peasants in Africa*.

3. F. Tonnies, *Community and Association* (East Lansing: Michigan State University Press, 1957, first published 1887).

4. See Mehmet Bequiraj, *Peasantry in Revolution* (Ithaca, N.Y., Center for International Studies, Cornell University, 1966) pp. 7–10.

5. See Karl Marx, "The Eighteenth Brumaire of Louis Bonaparte," in *Karl Marx and Frederich Engels: Selected Works*, vol. 1 (London: Lawrence and Wishart, 1950), pp. 302–3; see A. Hussain and K. Tribe, *Marxism and the Agrarian Question* (London, Macmillan, 1981), p. 141, where it is argued that Marx never developed the "peasantry" as a "definable category of population."

6. Marx, *Selected Works*, p. 415.

7. Hussain and Tribe,*Marxism*.

8. See, for example, Henry A. Landsberger, ed., *Rural Protest: Peasant Movements and Social Change* (London, Macmillan, 1974), pp. 10, 12; Sydel Silverman, "The Peasant Concept in Anthropology," *Journal of Peasant Studies* (October 1979), 7(1):49–85, argues that the definition of a peasantry should be restricted to political-

economic criteria; Hussain and Tribe, *Marxism,* where the implicit argument is that use of the "peasantry should be reconsidered by Marxists; Sidney Mintz, "Afterword: Peasantries and the Rural Sector: Notes on a Discovery," in R. P. Weller and S. E. Guggenheim, eds., *Power and Protest in the Countryside: Studies on Rural Unrest in Asia, Europe and Latin America* (Durham, N.C., Duke University Press, 1982), pp. 180–88, for a discussion of categorization of peasants and the inadequacy of the current concept.

9. This roughly corresponds to a well-known definition by Eric Wolf, *Peasants* (Englewood Cliffs, N.J.: Prentice-Hall, 1966), p. 10: "peasants are rural cultivators whose services are transferred to a dominant group of rulers that use the surplus to underwrite its own standard of living. . . . The peasant pays rent, that is, money, produce, or labor because of an asymmetrical power relationship." The importance for definitional purposes of peasant cultivators retaining control over the means of production is discussed in C. Sen, "Interregional variations in peasant differentiation; a comparison of Punjab and Maharashtra in the early 1970's." (Trivandrum India, Center for Development Studies, 1984).

10. See, for example, Keith Griffin, *The Green Revolution: An Economic Analysis* (Geneva, United Nations Research Institute for Social Development, 1972), pp. 15–17; Benno Galjart, "A Model of Local Systems for Understanding Rural Development Processes in the Third World," *Rural Sociology* (1975); 40(3):345–46; H. Friedmann, "Household Production and the National Economy: Concepts for the Analysis of Agrarian Formation," *Journal of Peasant Studies* (January 1980), 7(2):158–84; and Ajit Kumar Ghose, "Agrarian Reform in Developing Countries: Issues of Theory and Problems of Practice," in A. K. Ghose, ed., *Agrarian Reform in Contemporary Developing Countries* (London, Croom Helm, 1983); pp. 3–28. Even writers who begin their discourse with strict social relations criteria often lapse, however, into categorizations based on unknown criteria; see, for example, Yu. G. Alexandrov, "The Peasant Movements of Developing Countries in Asia and North Africa After the Second World War," in Landsberger, *Rural Protest,* who refers to "peasantry" (p. 360), "poorest peasants" (p. 356), and "sector of peasant movements" (p. 362).

11. Hugo Blanco, *Land or Death: The Peasant Struggle in Peru* (New York, Pathfinder Press, 1977), p. 157.

12. Tom Brass, "Class Formation and Class Struggle in La Convencion, Peru," *Journal of Peasant Studies* (January 1980), 7(4):427–57. For similar reasons small landowning farmers have sometimes resisted land reform programs; see, for example, D. Goodman and M. Redclift, *From Peasant to Proletarian; Capitalist Development in Agrarian Transitions* (Oxford, Blackwell, 1981), pp. 109–14.

13. For a discussion of the meaning of this process in terms of consciousness of the different subordinate producers within the rural areas, see James C. Scott, "History According to Winners and Losers," in A. Turton and S. Tanabe, eds., *History and Peasant Consciousness in South East Asia* (Osaka, National Museum of Ethnology, 1984), pp. 161–210.

14. Loss of control of production through indebtedness is discussed in chapter 3; for the argument that an analysis of power relations, including that of farmer/ moneylender, would eliminate the middle peasant category in India, see A. Rudra, "Class Relations in Indian Agriculture," *Economic and Political Weekly* (June 3, 1978), 13(22):916–23.

15. See Hamza Alavi, "Peasants and Revolution," *The Socialist Register 1965* (London, Merlin Press, 1965), pp. 252–262; Ralph Thaxton, "Mao Zedong, Red Miserables and the Moral Economy of Peasant in Modern China," in Weller and Guggenheim, *Power and Protest,* pp. 132–56.

16. See, for example, the use of the Lenin divisions as classes in Wan Hashim, "The Political Economy of Peasant Transformation: Theoretical Framework and Case Study," *The Journal of Social Studies* (Dacca, Bangladesh, October 1980), no. 10:47–79; for the historical data argument about the meaning of the division in its historical context, see Terry Cox, "Awkward Class or Awkward Classes? Class Relations in the Russian Peasantry Before Collectivisation," *Journal of Peasant Studies* (October 1979), (1):70–85; Scott, "Winners and Losers," changes the trichotomy into "rich farmers, poorer smallholders and landless labourers," each designated as a class.

17. Even an author who otherwise uses conventional marxists' categorizations and modes of production accepts that because of the lack of a single peasantry, abstract discussions of such issues as "revolutionary potential" of peasants are "basically misconceived." See Henry Bernstein, "Concepts in the Analysis of Contemporary Peasantries," in R. E. Galli, ed., *The Political Economy of Rural Development: Peasants, International Capital and the State; Case Studies in Colombia, Mexico, Tanzania and Bangladesh* (Albany, State University of New York Press, 1981), p. 24.

CHAPTER 2

SUBSISTENCE SOCIAL RELATIONS

In the forest region of Ghana, farm-
ers, using only machetes, hoes, and axes, slash and then burn an
area of bush to create a plot for growing their year's supply of
food. This slash-and-burn or *"swidden"* method of cultivation is
one of the methods typically used, especially in Africa and Latin
America, by a farming household that will rely exclusively on
the plot cleared for its basic food needs. There are only minimal,
if any at all, market sales, for the bulk of what is produced is
consumed directly.[1]

The household members consume all that is produced,
and lack of land, labor, or technology, and on rare occasions
inclination, means that any production over what is needed for
immediate consumption is not possible. Because there is no easily realizable surplus to extract, and land, or other means of
production, is owned or controlled by the farmer, neither the
state, nor the landlords, merchants, and moneylenders, intervene
in a structured way in the routine of production and consumption. Taxes, debts, profits, and losses do not enter the relatively
isolated economic lives of such farming households.

The form of social relations surrounding this type of subsistence production is then marked by an absence of groups and
powerful individuals—so much a feature of most other forms of
social relations—that are directly engaged in extraction and distribution over what is immediately produced. As already noted,

this is one form of social relations in which the relations are indirect. Power relations could be said to exist only between the household and dominant groups and classes in other forms of social relations whose actions are not normally directed specifically at subordination and extraction from the subsistence farmers; since there is no immediate surplus to be extracted, there is no immediate struggle for power to secure it. Any struggle that arises does so only in the context of an attempt to destroy subsistence relations, such as when subsistence farmers are driven off their land or provided with more land or capital to make them produce a surplus. It is the dominant groups of landlords in peasant-lord relations, and of employers in wage-labor plantations, farms, or industry that have forced people into a situation in which they do not have sufficient land to produce more than is necessary to sustain an often very short life.

It is at the level of the social formation also that the only real possibility of exploiting subsistence social relations exists. This occurs when subsistence relations produce a "surplus" of labor. If the subsistence household produces enough to raise an expanding family, then those who migrate to wage labor as adults become the "product" of the subsistence household. When they become laborers in different social relations then the costs of the unproductive years of childhood are borne by the subsistence families.

Within subsistence relations the household is a collective unit of production for all products and services for life support.[2] Allocation of work and distribution of product, then, remains at the individual level and is governed by tradition and custom within the community or household. Heads of households, tribal councils, and other collective regulating bodies have a certain authority concerning the details of production. This means that to a degree there exists dominant and subordinate members within the community or household who are allotted certain types of work and receive certain types of benefits from their work by virtue of their status, which is often based on age, sex, and kinship. Women, for example, are rarely heads of households and are rarely on an equal basis with men with regard to the work they do or the privileges received. But it makes no sense to conceive of heads of subsistence households and others as having a collective interest opposed to subordinate members, for those potential classes or dominant groups are subsumed under the collective nature of the work, the direct consumption of product, and the lack of linkages with classes or groups outside the immediate circumstances. Subsistence relations may have an authority structure but no structure of opposing interests. (For references to the community of tasks within subsistence households, see chapter 7.)

The term *subsistence* as used to describe social relations of production must be distinguished from other uses of the word. Clarity in usage is confused by disagreement concerning what constitutes subsistence farming. For some authors subsistence means that food grown on the farm is all consumed, but it may nevertheless represent only a part of total household income, other parts of which come from wage labor or other nonfarm activities; for other authors, it means that the farm supplies all the needs of the household through a combination of directly consumed food and cash income from market sales, or it is a level of consumption that is the minimum necessary for biological survival;[3] or, more statistically, it means all farms under a certain size.[4] Clearly all of these circumstances could arise within very different forms of social relations. The criteria adopted here must be associated, not with the quantity of production or consumption, but with the nature of the social relations.

It is simple to distinguish the most pure form of subsistence where there are no sales outside the household and no wage labor whatsoever—that is, no intervention of forces outside the household. Such pure cases are rare: in Africa almost all originally self-sufficient farmers and farming communities are now using some of their total time worked in order to produce for sale or to participate in wage work;[5] in Guatemala the farm absorbs less than one third of potential family labor time, making the search for wage labor predominant.[6] At what point such time worked for markets or employers changes the social relations to the extent that there is a substantial change in control over subsistence work and production is almost a matter of individual judgment in any particular case. It would seem that if a farmer worked no more than 15 to 20 percent of total time worked for market production or in wage labor, the social relations connected with total production would not be significantly altered. As a rough guide then, it can be said that when more than 80 percent of total time worked is for direct comsumption, subsistence relations prevail. Such a definition reduces drastically the numbers of "subsistence" producers in the world labor force as calculated by using the conventional and often contradictory definitions.

Between 4 and 7 percent of the world's labor force is estimated to be found in subsistence agriculture. The actual crop and manner of cultivation is extremely varied—the marginal rice farmer of Thailand, the vegetable garden cultivators of Haiti, the communal agriculture of tribal Africa, and the independent fishermen of tropical islands all have subsistence production relations. Africa is the region most usually associated with subsistence farming because of the predominance of tribal agriculture in some areas, but in fact this pattern is also found in varying proportions in most third-world countries.

The living conditions of people in subsistence agriculture are generally poor although not always so. Of course, they lack manufactured goods and health services but the seasonal nature of the agricultural production may mean that only a few months per year are taken up with intensive work. When sufficient land is available then it may be possible to satisfy basic nutritional needs with minimal work inputs compared with the amount of hours usually required from other workers to satisfy the same needs. These latter conditions, which are mainly confined to the remoter regions of Asia and Africa, are fairly rare and are disappearing rapidly.

TYPES OF SUBSISTENCE RELATIONS: COMMUNAL AND INDIVIDUAL

Two different types of such subsistence relations are noticeable in the world today. The first type can be regarded as a survival of the so-called "natural" or "primitive" economy of fairly small tribes and communities that have somehow escaped the expanding impact of national and global political and economic forces. These are now very rare and probably still exist in a precarious state only in Papua New Guinea, the tropical forests of Brazil, and in Botswana and Namibia in Africa.[7]

These communities are, however, of some historic importance because of the sharp contrast their social relations make with those found in other rural areas of the third world, which are characterized by the domination of the production process, by an identifiable group or class and the power struggle that surrounds such control. Self-sufficient production based upon the tribe, clan, and groupings of families has been in existence since the beginning of settled agriculture and, generally preceded rather than followed any production for exchange, participation in markets, or the use of money.

This type of subsistence relations is usually found in fairly small and self-contained communities and has been investigated most extensively by economic anthropologists. While the objective of their work has often been to prove or disprove already existing theories of the nature of humankind and its development, two aspects of findings of the anthropological literature about which there is some agreement are important for social relations of production. The first is that economic activity must be complementary to, or compatible with, goals and values that arise in other spheres of social life. The second, which follows from the first, is that there are "leveling practices" in relation to wealth and accumulation that help preserve the overall balance of the community.

The complementarity of society and economy became apparent to anthropologists who, in studying such communities, sought to distinguish persons and groups who were rich and powerful. It became clear that status and power were equally dependent upon social factors such as age, kinship, wisdom, and social skills, as it was on the accumulation of material wealth.[8] Further, it was observed that economic activity would have to be compatible with other roles and functions that prevented production from becoming paramount as a determinant of status and power.

The leveling practices seemed to function to prevent the development of a differentiation based on wealth, which might have produced a propertied class or group and so destroyed the balance of the community—in other words, would have changed the social relations. Thus the Northwest Coast Indians of what is now the United States had a periodic "potlach" in which large amounts of material goods were deliberately burned by "rich" men to achieve status, but also, of course, to destroy the means for any divisions in the community based on wealth. A very different mechanism, but with the same result, occurred in some African tribes where envy was considered an evil force. If possession of goods made the possessor an object of envy, then he could avoid the evil force only by reducing the possibility of being enviable, namely, through the dissipation by gift or destruction of material goods amassed. Such practices have been recorded throughout the world, and vestiges of them are still found in villages in which the original communities have long been destroyed.[9]

The destruction of the residual-historical type of subsistence agriculture often occurred through the development of the second type of subsistence relations—the subsistence household operating as a unit without strong communal values or practices governing production. This second type of subsistence relations is of more recent origin. Typically these relations are found when a family farms a plot that it owns or controls and that must provide the bulk of the household's needs. Where this type of subsistence differs from the first is that there are no overriding social obligations or leveling practices relating to surpluses, for any surpluses available would certainly be extracted through the intervention of a merchant, moneylender, or taxcollector. Distribution and allocation within this type takes place within the household according to its variety of forms and practices; the African polygamous household in which the male has more than one wife and distributes work and food between two nuclear families based on wives differs from the Hindu tradition of the joint family based on patrilineal property rights.

In many areas of the world the subsistence plots of land owned or controlled are in fact insufficient to support a family at the prevailing standard. These subfamily plots, as they are called, proliferate throughout the world with the highest concentration in Africa and Asia; if a subfamily plot is a holding below 5 hectares, then mid-1970s estimates indicate that in Latin America 50 percent of total holdings were less than 5 hectares while in Asia and Africa it was well over 80 percent.[10] Although production from such farms varies enormously with climate, terrain, and especially the factor of whether the land is irrigated or rain fed (irrigated producing more than rain fed), these figures indicate the extent to which a viable household subsistence plot has been eroded.

Under these circumstances it is normal for members of the family to secure "off-farm" income in wage labor, trading, or artisanal work.[11] They then supplement the subfamily farm plot with income derived from elsewhere in an attempt to raise the total income to a family level; as they do so the self-sufficiency and subsistence social relations of the household are transformed as the social relations that determine return shift toward being governed by wage labor and own-account activities.

The increasingly smaller number of households that farm family-size plots and sustain a living without substantive recourse to other activities but also without a surplus are in such an economic position because of a general scarcity of land; in general, although not always, as noted above, if more land were available, subsistence farmers would move to create some surplus to immediate family subsistence needs. The origin of such shortages of land lies in the general historical events and processes that have crowded large numbers of people onto small amounts of land. Although some of these processes continue and people still enter subsistence farming, for most of the cultivators these processes are past. They work a fixed amount of land, and further reduction or expropriation of it would mean they would become virtually landless laborers. Expropriation and reduction of land are not continuing issues in social relations but rather a violent transformational attempt coming from the outside. Current subsistence families are the successors of those who lost past battles in which sufficient and suitable land was the prize on offer.

Three factors have assisted the concentration of land in the hands of the few and left others with insufficient land. The first, and most important, is the process and means by which individuals or groups were able to concentrate land into their own hands and develop sufficient power to prevent others from appropriating it. This involves the question of the general power of landowners and will be discussed later in connection with the evolution of the peasant-lord form of social relations. The second factor is the occasional physical decline in the amount of land available through natural causes such as earthquakes, floods, or erosion caused by misuse of land. The desert encroaching into previously viable arable land in the Sahel in Africa is such an example.

The third factor, which is more directly relevant to the origins of this type of subsistence relations, concerns the fragmentation of existing land holdings through rapid increases in population. For a variety of reasons, not least of which has been the introduction of industrial Western medical practices and philosophy, there has been developed a pattern of high surviving birth rates, particularly in rural areas. In India, for example, the growth of the agricultural population between 1951 and 1966 was about 100 million or about a 33 percent absolute increase, and the predictions for Latin American rural population to year 2000 indicate a 2.7 increase per annum or more than double the current population.[12]

Without land reform this increase in population often means that previously self-employed farmers producing a surplus for the market are reduced to subsistence farmers through subdivision of land. Such was the case with Mexican land reforms, which began in 1911 and in which land was redistributed to create viable, surplus-creating plots. Population pressure was, however, a major factor in causing the plots to be subdivided until more than three quarters of private farms in 1960 were subsistence size.[13]

TRANSFORMATION: CREATION
OF SURPLUS AND SUPPLY OF LABOR

For dominant groups subsistence relations are unproductive— they yield no surplus and therefore cannot be a source of wealth or profit to those outside. Merchants seeking profit, colonialists seeking land and labor for export crop production, governments trying to tax—in short, any individual, class, or group that wishes to extract labor or produce from subsistence farmers—must first destroy or transform subsistence social relations. Subsistence cultivators are seen from the outside as either a marginal nuisance, or a reserve of labor or as occupying a reserve of land.

For these reasons subsistence farmers, when established, have historically been subject to purposeful destructive interventions from the outside in order to force them to yield land, labor, or surplus products. The subsistence communities, representing the first type of subsistence relations, have experienced external interventions by colonialists, established landlords, and governments that have now almost entirely modified or destroyed their economy and way of life. Although these communities had complex and subtle internal mechanisms to maintain internal cohesion and prevent destructive conflicts, they were unable to deal with the variety of material attractions, technologies, and forms of coercion of the societies that impinged upon them.

The type of instrument used to destroy such communities depended upon the type of extraction attempted. When control over land or securing wage labor was the objective, then economic or physical forced eviction from traditionally held lands was the instrument used. This had the double advantage of securing the land for large farms or plantations and acquiring a pool of virtually landless labor to work on the newly created enterprises. In Zimbabwe (formerly Rhodesia), for example, successive colonial regimes used a range of tactics to secure labor from subsistence communities, including heavy taxation, expropriation, and cattle destocking; these, coupled with population increases, produced such a surfeit of labor that by 1951 an attempt was made to restore the previous self-sufficiency of subsistence farmers.[14] Indian communities in North and South America were and still are particularly affected by such actions: in the Mato Grosso area of Brazil, indigenous subsistence populations are still being displaced by companies that create *fazendas* (ranches) by burning forests to grow grass and raise beef. One of these *fazendas* covers 570,000 hectares,[15] the equivalent of about 335,000 subsistence holdings of average Latin American size. Deliberate or accidental genocide has also on occasions produced the same effect—the ravages that foreigner-carried influenza viruses and other alien microorganisms wrought in Latin America and the islands of the Pacific are well known.

Eviction or forced changes in the control various persons

and groups had over land were the principal mechanisms used when the objective was not to secure use of occupied land but to create rent-paying farmers dominated by landlords. But land sufficient to produce a surplus that could be extracted by landlords as rent was not always available for every family or group of the preexisting subsistence community or population. Those for whom surplus-producing land was not available became landless laborers or isolated subsistence farmers. Thus the destruction of traditional agriculture created at the same time isolated subsistence farming families, rent-paying peasants, and laborers.

Other methods of intervention did not directly appropriate the land or labor of subsistence communities but rather exploited internal tendencies in these communities in order to extract a surplus from them. The attraction of distilled alcohol such as whisky to the North American Indians, for example, was so great that in order to pay for it they produced a surplus for exchange and plunged themselves into degradation and virtual extinction as they lost control of their production and found their social structure undermined by alcoholism; the so-called "bushmen" of South Africa are, in 1985, also unable to deal socially with alcohol, which is being sold in officially organized shops on army camps, where they are being recruited by the South African army from their previous subsistence life. In similar fashion European traders used the existing social power of African tribal chiefs in inducing them to assume the role of brokers and exploiters of their own and neighboring peoples.[16]

Currently, however, interventions are directed mostly against the second type—the subsistence family working owned or controlled land—and are intended to create a farm unit producing a surplus that can be extracted via a market or taxing mechanism and perhaps, at the same time, release labor for local wage employment. These attempts take two basic forms: the first is to increase production through a combination of increased work for the farming household plus different, more efficient, agricultural techniques; and the other is to increase the amount of land and labor used. In both cases the usual stated objective is to increase material welfare of the producers and to transform the social relations into the direction of those associated with a self-employed, farming family producing for the market and for the state. Thus through the mechanisms of profits of merchants, cheap food for urban populations, and taxes, at least part of the extra production would be transferred to other sections of the population.[17]

The policies associated with the first method of attempted transformation include the application of high technology and creation of agricultural extension services, cooperatives, marketing boards, and other state-created organizations for marketing purposes. Application of technology is supposed to make subsistence farming more efficient through the use of higher yield seeds, fertilizer inputs, better irrigation, some mechanization, and what is believed to be better knowledge of agricultural techniques. Experience to date with applied technology has brought about some change for subsistence farmers—but in the direction of an indebted peasant rather than toward self-employed small farmers because they have had to surrender a substantial proportion of their increased production to moneylenders and merchants.

Cooperative and marketing boards encourage the growing of a surplus by providing marketing facilities and some collective capital or services. This approach is particularly prevalent when subsistence farmers, as in some parts of Africa, can acquire more land. Marketing boards, state enterprises, and cooperatives have encouraged them to grow a proportion of commercial crops (cocoa, oil-seed, groundnuts), which the boards and cooperatives then market. In most of these interventions the net effect is to increase the time worked by the subsistence family in return for extra, usually monetary, income and to extend state control over subsistence agriculture.[18]

Subsistence social relations are then currently severely under attack. Because they produce no surplus, they are seen as a danger or as useless by those who determine public policy. It is unlikely that even those few remote communities that have not yet experienced outside intervention will for long be left alone.

The response of subsistence farmers to these onslaughts has been mixed. There has often been reference in technocratic discussions to a "subsistence mentality," which is supposed to include passivity, reluctance to innovate, ignorance, and resistance to the outside.[19] Government officials, technical assistance experts, and agricultural marketing managers complain of the passivity or resistance toward their efforts to transform subsistence social relations. In some cases this is merely a reluctance on the part of subsistence farmers to work harder when their own basic needs are already satisfied, in others it is that the risks of innovation are greater than perceived benefit or that the benefits will go to others, not to the subsistence household.[20] The precarious ecological balance of subsistence farming means that a full or partial failure to produce the annual crop may result in starvation, sickness, or death for some of the household. Under such circumstances it is not surprising, and quite rational, that subsistence farmers would require overwhelming and positive proof before being voluntarily prepared to make changes in accustomed patterns of work and production. Subsistence farmers, even more than peasants and self-employed farmers, have therefore had good reason to suspect outsiders and outside intervention.

By the nature of their activity, subsistence farmers are fairly isolated. No merchant or marketplace joins them together and provides information and patterns of social interaction and possible solidarity. The absence of class lines within the social relations means that negative cohesion against a widely perceived enemy is less likely to appear than would be the case, for example, of peasants confronting landlords or tax collectors. The perceived enemies of the subsistence farmer tend to be weather and natural disasters, and it is usually only in the wake of natural calamity that mass dislocations or innovations in productive activities take place. The main immediate social demand of subsistence farmers would be for more land, since shortage of suitable land and excessive subdivision are the principal causes of their poverty. Yet not paying rent and only rarely working elsewhere means that consciousness of the possibility of land redistribution and a sense of how access to land is controlled by dominant groups in the social formation comes only when producers within other relations have started to act to change their own situation.

When subsistence relations have been destroyed and subsistence farmers made landless wage laborers or dominated peasants, it has been argued that the preexisting consciousness of self-sufficiency and independence contradict the new situation of

domination and oppression, creating a base for rebellion or revolution.[21] The restoration of a more equitable and independent
life as supposed to be found in subsistence relations has been
said to be the objective of rebellions and revolutions in Southeast
Asia and Latin America in particular. Thus it has been suggested
that the subsistence farmers forced off their land by sugar production in the 1920s provided the base for the Castro movement
in Cuba in the 1950s.[22] But such actions and consciousness have
been developed through experience in other social relations in
which class structures are more apparent. It then appears that it
is the dominated peasants and landless laborers who have
emerged from subsistence who become involved in movements
for change rather than subsistence farmers themselves.

NOTES

1. The literature relevant to subsistence social relations of production is
divided between the subjects of economic anthropology and agricultural development. The former generally deals with the remnants of "communual" subsistence
and usually concentrates on a holistic approach to the community, investigating
attitudes, customs, and practice. Agricultural development accounts, which have
proliferated since the mid-1950s, provide details of subsistence farming families
within an orientation of examining, or promoting, a process of change that has
ended, or would end, subsistence relations. The latter sources do not usually discuss
social relations of production but do provide an empirical base for discovering the
effects of changes in social relations.

2. See, for example, the description in G. Dahl, *Suffering Grass: Subsistence
Society of Waso Borana* (Stockholm, Department of Social Anthropology, University
of Stockholm, 1979).

3. For a discussion of the quantitative criteria for subsistence, see J. Rou-
veyran, *Logique des Agricultures de Transition: L'example des societies Paysannes
Malgaches* (Tananarive, Malagasy Republic, Editions G.P., 1972), p. 120, and for a
definition of subsistence farming that implies subsistence social relations, see M.
Naseem, "Small Farmers and Agricultural Transformation in Pakistan," (thesis,
University of California, 1970), p. 38, viz,

subsistence implies 1) dependence of the household upon the output of the farm to
maintain family and animal labour and 2) dependence of the farm upon the household for its labour requirements. A self-sufficing relationship between the farm and
the household, with limited sales in the market.

4. See, for example, T. L. Sankar, "India," in M. S. Wionczek, ed. *Energy in the Transition from Rural Subsistence* (Boulder, Colorado, Westview Press, 1982), p. 179.

5. See John H. Cleave, *African Farmers: Labour Use in the Development of Smallholder Agriculture* (New York, Praeger, 1974).

6. See, Robert Caceres, "Guatemala," in Wionczek, *Energy in Transition*, pp. 67–88.

7. For examples of a discussion on the well-being of some subsistence farmers, see the arguments of Colin Clark and Margaret Muswell, *The Economics of Subsistence Agriculture* (London, Macmillan, 1964), pp. 1–2, and see R. T. Shand and W. Straatmans, "Transition from Subsistence; Cash Crop Development in Papua New Guinea," *New Guinea Research Bulletin* (Canberra) 54:(1975), 1–198.

8. For example, "All observations of primitive peoples teaches us that the social motive, the desire for an exceptional position in the group, has outweighed the economic motive," R. Thurnwald, *Economics in Primitive Communities* (Oxford, Oxford University Press 1965–first published 1932) p. 179.

9. Examples of these practices are found in Ruth Benedict, *Patterns of Culture* (London, Routledge, Kegan Paul, 1935); G. M. Foster, "The Anatomy of Envy: A Study in Symbolic Behaviour," *Current Anthropology* (1972), 13(2):165–202; Benno Galjart, "Incentives, Levelling Mechanisms and Rural Development," *Sociologia Ruralis* (Special Issue, 1974), pp. 65–71. For a discussion of the effects of destroying traditional mechanisms of land distribution, see Homa Katanzian, "The Agrarian Question in Iran," in A. K. Ghose, ed., *Agrarian Reform in Contemporary Developing Countries* (London, Croom Helm, 1983), pp. 309–57; in areas there are still strong remmants of such practices, according to Keith Hart, *The Political Economy of West African Agriculture* (New York, Cambridge, 1982), pp. 148–49.

10. As quoted in E. Clayton, *Agriculture, Poverty and Freedom in Developing Countries* (London, MacMillan, 1983), p. 16–17.

11. For examples of "off-farm" earnings as a proportion of total "income," see, for example, Rufigio I. Rochin, *Responsiveness of Subsistence Farmers to New Ideas: Dwarf Wheat on Unirrigated Small Holdings in Pakistan* (University of Wisconsin-Madison, reprint No. 88, 1972); J. R. V. Daane, *Responses of Peasant Paddy Growers to Farmers Organisations in West Malaysia* (Wageningen, Netherlands, Landbouwhogeschool, 1982); Caceres, "Guatemala."

12. Albert F. E. Binsbergen, "The Contribution of Small Farmers and Rural Workers Towards Food Production and Development in Latin America," *Land Reform, Land Settlement and Cooperatives* (1977), no. 1, p. 17.

13. Gerrit Huizer and Rodolfo Stavenhagen, "Peasant Movements and Land Reform in Latin America: Mexico and Bolivia," in Henry D. Landsberger, ed., *Rural Protest: Peasant Movements and Social Change* (London, MacMillan, 1974), pp. 383–92.

14. S. Mahlahla, *The Economic Transformation of Indigenous Agriculture in Zimbabwe, 1900–1964* (Ann Arbor, Mich., University Microfilms International, 1983).

15. Charles Vanhecke, "Mato-Grosso, Western Bresilien Terres en Transe," *Le Monde* (February 8, 1975), pp. 1 and 5, and R. J Wesche, "Amazonic Colonization: A Solution for Brazil's Land Tenure Problems's," in L. R. Alschuler, ed., *Dependent Agricultural Development and Agrarian Reform in Latin America* (Ottawa, University of Ottawa Press, 1981), pp. 135–45.

16. See, for example, Lars Sandstrom, The Exchange Economy of Pre-Colonial Tropical Africa (London, C. Hurst, 1974), and discussion in Yu. G. Alexandrov, "The Peasant Movements of Developing Countries in Asia and North Africa after the Second World War," in Henry A. Landsberger, Rural Protest: Peasant Movements and Social Change (London, MacMillan, 1974), pp. 358–67.

17. See Kenneth Post, "Peasantisation and Rural Political Movements in Western Africa," European Journal of Sociology 23(2):(1972), 13–44; for accounts showing how intervention is used to supply labor for agri-industry, see, for example, Stophan Gudeman, The Demise of a Rural Economy: From Subsistence to Capitalism in a Latin American Village (London, Routledge, 1978), and R. Londono, Economic Analysis of Subsistence Agriculture in Garcia Rovira, Colombia (Ann Arbor, Mich., University Microfilms International, 1975); for commercialization, see, for example, Bogamil Jewsiewicki, "African Peasants in the Totalitarian Control Colonial Society of the Belgian Congo," in Martin A. Klein, ed., Peasants in Africa; Historical and Contemporary Perspectives (London, Sage, 1980), H. O. Sano, The Political Economy of Food in Nigeria 1960–1982; A Discussion of Peasants, State and World Economy (Uppsala, Scandinavian Institute of African Studies, 1983) and L. S. Grossman, Peasants, Subsistence Ecology and Development in the Highlands of Papua New Guinea (Princeton, N.J., Princeton University Press, 1984).

18. See, for example, the discussion in Shand and Straatmans, "Transition from Subsistence," pp. 188–90, and on government use of cooperatives to control and extract from farmers, see Lionel Cliffe, "Rural Political Economy in Africa," in Bernard Magubane, ed., The Political Economy of Contemporary Africa, 1976, pp. 121–24; Hart, West African Agriculture; Cristobal Kay, "The Agrarian Reform in Peru: An Assessment," in A. D. Ghose, ed., Agrarian Reform in Contemporary Developing Countries (London, Croom Helm, 1983), pp. 185–235.

19. See, for example, A. I. Richards, F. Sturroch, and J. M. Fortt, Subsistence to Commercial Farming in Present-Day Buganda (Cambridge, England, Cambridge University Press, 1973).

20. Thus many reports deny a nonrational resistance to interventions; see, for example, T. L. Sankar, "India," p. 180.

21. This is inherent in the "moral economy" writers, especially J C. Scott, The Moral Economy of the Peasant Rebellion and Subsistence in Southeast Asia (New Haven, Conn., Yale University Press, 1976). A similar argument is made for the organization of wage workers into trade unions, that is, unions as an attempt to recapture lost rural security; see chapter 5. Enterprise Labor Market Social Relations.

22. Barent Landstreet, "Urbanisation and Ruralism in Cuba," in Alschuler, Dependent Agricultural Development, pp. 147–68.

CHAPTER 3

PEASANT-LORD SOCIAL RELATIONS

The greatest majority of the people
in the world who work on the land are forced to surrender either
a large part of what they produce or a large part of their own
labor to those who control land, the access to markets, or loans
needed for production. The power relations surrounding production are essentially between the farming households—the
peasants—and the landowners, merchants, or moneylenders,
who collectively and for convenience are called the lords.

The peasants are the victims of an extremely lopsided
power situation; the peasant household has no real power to
force restraint upon those who extract from its work. It has no
effective organization to protect its interests and to temper the
more excessive demands of the lord, nor is it able to manipulate
the market, undercut merchants or moneylenders, or withhold
labor without risking starvation, harassment, or both. The domination exercised over peasants is direct, and they deliver produce, labor, and/or money as rent directly to the landlords,
moneylenders, and merchants.[1]

Those who have control in peasant-lord social relations
may constitute a class in the sense discussed in the introductory
chapter. The control of land, money, and markets is largely based,
however, upon the residue of social prestige of landownership
and, more important, the ability to secure military and police
assistance, or at least acquiescence, in violent repression of protest or other attempts to change or transform the situation.

The result of all these factors is that peasant-lord social relations are universally associated with three features. The first is an extraordinarily high level of extraction; the proportion of production removed from the peasant household reaches as high as 90 percent in some cases and is rarely less than 50 percent.[2] In fact, many rents, interest, or merchant prices are set in such a manner as to leave just enough for the peasant family to survive in order to continue agricultural production and biological reproduction.[3] The second factor is the poverty and despair that such levels of extraction create. The third is that peasant revolts, violent repressions, and revolutionary armies have characterized societies in which peasant-lord social relations have had a dominant position. Mass murders, imprisonments, and evictions often await those peasants who protest their domination while poverty continues for most of the others.

Peasants in peasant-lord social relations are estimated to be at least 15 percent of the world labor force. Some 30 percent of the world population is directly dependent on the food and commercial crops they produce. Peasants, subsistence farmers, and landless laborers make up the bulk of what is known as the "rural poor," which has been the stated contemporary concern of policies aimed at maintaining political stability or securing a semblance of social justice or increased welfare for the populations of the poorer countries.[4]

Peasant-lord social relations often have deep roots in tradition and have been institutionalized in complex ways by religion, law, and culture. Superficially they manifest themselves in a bewildering variety of tenure systems, rent systems, and social patterns. In Latin America, for example, there are peasants who are called *inguilinos* because they rent land "inside" large farms—*latifundias*—and must render labor and crops to the landlord as their rent. Outside, their fellow peasants are often *medieros* sharecroppers, so-called because they must "share" 50 percent of the crop with the landlords.[5] In India the complexity of the caste system is entwined with the high-caste landowners' taking money and rent and service from lower caste or casteless tenants.

Even concepts at the highest level of abstraction are rendered difficult to disentangle in practice. "Rent" is a generic term for that part of peasant production passed by peasants to those who dominate production, but it comes in many forms and disguises. For landlords resident in rural areas the rent may be paid in kind, as with the rice payments in India, for immediate consumption or sale on a market, or it may be a form of sharecropping. When landlords are absent and live in the town, it may be paid in money, leaving the peasant to deal with the conversion of his produce into money and so raising the prospect of the two-tiered extraction of merchant's profit and the landlord's rent. Sometimes it is in the form of labor or a service performed without wage by the peasant family—in Latin America this is called *pongo, begar* in parts of India, and *kasanvu* in Buganda in Africa. Rent then assumes many disguises and is called many names, a situation complicated by the fact that many receivers of substitute rent, when reporting to outsiders, reduce its importance and even sometimes deny its existence.[6]

The intricacies of rent-paying systems, the cultural diversity, and the extreme complexity, subtlety, and unseen aspects of rural society in general—all stumbling blocks for would-be rural economists and planners—must be a constant reservation to any generalizations made about peasant-lord social relations from a world perspective.

In the very broadest of terms, then, there are continental patterns of peasant-lord relations that are important to the understanding of both the prevailing images and the more detailed aspects of peasant production. Latin America is the continent where the form of domination of the peasant is more visible because of the juxtaposition of large landholdings and the small plots of rent-paying and labor-supplying peasants—a landholding structure now often referred to as the "bimodal" structure. It has been estimated that in Latin America as a whole 2 percent of the population owns 50 percent of the land. In the imagery of Europeans, and even more in that of North Americans, the Latin American bimodal variation of peasant-lord relations is sometimes inaccurately perceived to be a general world model. In Africa, however, prevailing patterns are different. There are fewer large landowners than in Latin America, and these are often either large government or foreign-owned corporations or are found in countries in which colonial or racist patterns of landholdings have persisted, as was the case in Rhodesia and South Africa. Peasant-lord social relations in Africa occur more between medium-size landowners and their tenants and merchants and marketing authorities of commercial crops, such as cocoa and tobacco.

In Asia residues of land reforms have, in many countries, resulted in a less concentrated landownership pattern than in Latin America and, therefore, in larger numbers of small-scale landowners and tenants—the so-called unimodal landholding structure. But this apparently greater equality of power over land and therefore production in Asia is controverted by the prevalent power of moneylenders and merchants to whom independent farmers, through overextended indebtedness, have often been forced to surrender control of production.

The trinity of extractors from peasant households—landowners, moneylenders, and merchants—is present in Latin America, Africa, and Asia. But the roles of these landowners, moneylenders, and merchants have different weights in these different regions and their respective powers vary. The nature of these different types of dominant groups and the origin and basis of their domination are central to the understanding of the persistence of peasant-lord relations.

THE LORDS AND THEIR ORIGINS

As with all the forms of social relations identified in this book the nomenclature is intended not to add precision to the definition but merely to provide a label. In the case of the power relations of the peasant-lord type a difficulty arises in finding a suitable designation for the dominant group or class composed mainly of landowners, moneylenders, and merchants. It is clear that only a small proportion of these could even qualify for the imagery of a feudal lord. The combination of the various holders of power over rural producers, however, certainly results in a domination and material conditions, if not psychological orientation, similar to that resulting from the power of feudal lords. The designation "lord" then will be used, despite its shortcomings and essentially narrow applicability, to all those who are in a position of power and are able thereby to extract from rural producers.

In two of the three basic categories of lords on the dominant side of the peasant-lord power relations further subdivision into types may be made.

Within the first category of lords—the landowners—there are two basic types. The first are landowners who control large concentrations of land, are often absent or at least distant from the work and production on the land, and rent to peasants in return for money, produce, or labor—this is indeed the "manorial" type of landowner. The second type of landowner controls much less land, rents to peasants for money or produce, and is often involved in the day-to-day operation of the farm.

The archetype of the manorial landowner is the absentee landowner or the resident rural lord of traditional imagery who is master of all he surveys and receives extreme deference, respect, and loyalty from "his" peasants.

Often such concentrations of land and personal authority have been derived from past regimes such as the agrarian bureaucracies of Asia or the ecomienda of colonial times in Latin America. In Western Europe such concentrations of land and authority were shaken by the French Revolution and its extension, although they continued in Eastern Europe until much later. High concentration of ownership of land coupled with a high level of agricultural tenancy are rough indicators of the presence of this type of lord. Latin America, as already noted, is the region where this pattern is now most prevalent and the landlord-tenant relationship is the most common expression of peasant-lord social relations.

The other type of landowner differs from the first in that the holdings of land are smaller and he often plays an active role in production, sometimes working alongside the tenants or farming part of the land himself. Such landlords are sometimes referred to as "kulaks," after the Russian landowning and renting farmer who had an important social and economic position in prerevolutionary Russian agricultural villages. For Lenin these were the "rich" peasants, and they became a major obstacle in the Russian revolutionary government's attempt to collectivize and extract from the agricultural sector. Currently they can be considered as within peasant-lord relations only if their basic relationship with peasants is one of renting via money, labor service, or sharecropping; that is, they have not become farmer-entrepreneurs basing their extraction on surpluses from wage laborers.

Kulak-type landlords, unlike the manorial type, are increasing rather than decreasing on a world scale. The introduction of commercial crops to be grown by small farmers, partial or incomplete land reforms, and the impact of some agricultural technologies that create the need for more capital and larger contiguous units of land have meant that, through purchase and inheritance, some peasants have been able to increase their landholding to a point where they are able to rent out excess land. A classic example of this process was the introduction of smaller scale cocoa production in Ghana, which resulted in increased disparities in rural landholdings as successful farmers started new farms and rented their original holdings to sharecroppers.[7] Such development has now been duplicated in many African countries.[8] Introduction of new technologies in Malaysia, Philippines, Indonesia, and other Asian rice-growing countries, as well as in some African countries, has caused land values to rise faster than the incomes of tenants, meaning that it is more difficult for tenants to become landowners but conversely easier for existing landowners to increase their holdings until they reach kulak status[9]. In Peru the creation of kulak-type landlords came as the result of a land reform that constrained and reduced the manorial type of large landowners.[10]

All these processes that are at the origin of the kulak-type landowner also convert kulak landowners into farmer-entrepreneurs organizing their holdings and extractions, not by renting or sharecropping, but by hiring labor for a farm enterprise. Landowners take back their rented land from tenants in order to manage it themselves and to reap the benefits of new technology. This increase in "capitalist" agriculture, as it is often called, is a major third-world rural event of the past decade that will be discussed later in this chapter; here it is sufficient to note that the same process may both create and destroy peasant-lord social relations.

Because in some cases kulak-type landlords often both lease land and employ labor they directly bridge two forms of social relations of production—those associated with peasants of the peasant-lord form and those of the wage labor of the enterprise labor market form. It was this latter factor that caused the Soviet authorities in the 1920s to consider kulaks as capitalists because they took surplus value from wage laborers. In the context of peasant-lord social relations this category of landowners is important as a group that exerts power over peasants purely by virtue of landownership rather than with the larger landowners, where there may be a concurrent ability to manage, market, and employ.

Landowners rent out their land, which means that the concept and practice of land tenancy is a crucial aspect of peasant-lord social relations, just as is the socially established apparent legitimacy of private ownership of land upon which the tenancy structures are based. In the poorer countries of the world, tenancy therefore, almost always indicates the presence of the peasant-lord social relations. It is rare that within such countries the tenant and peasant have been able to resist the power of landlords to the point that relations have changed, as in the case of the Western European tenant farmer. Outside of Western Europe only perhaps in Taiwan, South Korea, and Japan has the condition of tenancy been separated from the condition of subordination of tenants; the complex of reasons and developments that led in these countries to less than dominated tenant farmers is discussed below in the section on transformation.

Though tenancy is perhaps the most characteristic form of peasant-lord relations, it is not the only one. Tenancy does not arise in a formal way in the case of the second and third categories of lords, namely, the moneylenders and merchants.

Moneylenders, the second category of lords within peasant-lord relations, are found throughout the world, although their power differs greatly, being greatest in Asia and lowest in Africa. They are called different names, ranging from "credit suppliers" to "usurers," but their importance is their initiating role in creating "indebted peasants" who surrender a large part of their production as interest.

One reason why moneylenders may achieve a dominant position within the peasant-lord social relations is that cultivation requires a continual restriction of current consumption for benefit of future production, as in the case of seed, which must be retained out of each year's crops or, alternatively, purchased from elsewhere for the next planting. To eat, in the current season, next seasons' seed is to invite starvation or the intervention in production of those from whom the needed seed, or money to buy it, is borrowed. Likewise, with more recent agricultural techniques, money has had to be borrowed to buy fertilizer in order to use seeds that increase yields. Yet cultivation makes no guarantee of a level of return out of which the money and the interest can definitely be repaid—weather particularly affects the yields. To borrow for a future production that never materializes means an even further descent into indebtedness.

Under such circumstances those who supply credit when yields are bad, when seed or money for fertilizer was not saved, or when social obligation (such as the marriage of a daughter in some cultures) calls for unusual expenditure acquire considerable power over the cultivators' final product. In Sri Lanka "patrons" loaned rice seed but demanded a 50 percent "traditional" interest every six months; in Indonesia loan rates are 30 to 50 percent every four months; in Bangladesh moneylenders will loan in return for buying the rice produced at half the market price; in Central Luzon in the Philippines it is between 100 and 150 percent per year; in Thailand moneylenders from the ethnic minority of Chinese are known in the Thai language to the peasants as "god with a fat purse."[11]

Indebtedness makes peasants out of potentially self-employed farmers; the control over distribution, and sometimes the details of production, are lost to the power of the moneylender; and peasant-lord relations prevail.[12]

The third category of lords—the merchants—has both a "trader" and a "state" manifestation. At the trader level they operate between a farmer and the buyer. The trader's power usually lies in a monopoly of local transport or storage facilities, social and economic links with markets that the peasant is unable to make, and possession of commercial and legal skills. When a combination of these factors enables the trader to acquire sufficient power to fix unilaterally the price paid for produce, then the farmer may lose control over the results of production to the trader. Not all traders then can be considered as lords in the peasant-lord relationship, but in many parts of the world, particularily in Latin America and increasingly in Asia since the introduction of modern agricultural techniques, traders do in fact exercise such power.[13]

Traders' power is usually based upon a monopoly of marketing, but even when such a monopoly is not easily apparent, traders may secure a monopoly in practice by establishing a client relationship with a particular farmer; this is a practice by which a trader establishes an exclusive trading relationship with certain farmers that, by tacit agreement or arrangement, other traders will not try to break. Because traders sometimes supply services of a personal kind to farmers, the relations can approach a "patron-client" relationship in which the social relations that yield surpluses are cemented by a set of mutual, though unequal, obligations between dominant and subordinate parties. Such relationships are found wherever farmers are dependent on delivery of produce to a distant or complicated market. The trader then, whether in the pure merchant guise or with patron overtones, can be found as the dominant party in peasant-lord power relations.[14]

More recently the growth of state intervention and involvement in commercial and large-scale agriculture has led to the situation where the state physically organizes the collection of produce at prices fixed by its agencies. Whether or not such a monopoly over marketing and prices results in peasant-lord relations depends upon the level and the use of the surpluses extracted, if the earlier definition of a peasant is sustained, namely, one who is forced to surrender the bulk of production in order to underwrite the privileges of others. Thus a state that extracts purely to provide consumption income for urban-based elites becomes a merchant state, and farmers are reduced to dominated peasants in much the same way as large landowners might have done.[15] If the state reduces its level of extraction through a redistribution of benefits and infrastructure to farmers, then the power relations are mediated by a redistributional ideology or mechanism.[16] Note, however, that state agencies, unlike moneylenders and traders, are not subjected to an essential dynamic that makes them gravitate toward the maximum extraction and thus to the impoverishment and domination of the farmers. The development of a merchant-state is not then inevitable.[17]

The landlord class may include all these categories of lords, although there may also be different roles played by the same individuals; landowners, for example, are also moneylenders and merchants. Each disturbance in the rural social relations of production changes their roles. Sometimes moneylenders increasingly become landowners renting to tenants, as currently in Thailand. Sometimes the introduction of commercial crops brings forth a new class of merchants who control access to the market, and sometimes a partial land reform alters the structure of landholding so as to strengthen the kulak landlords at the expense of both larger landowners and self-employed farmers.

Peasant-lord social relations continue to prevail, partly because a resilient class has been formed conscious of its own interests and intent upon maintaining peasant-lord relations. Although more powerful landowners may be joined in any particular social formation by the smaller kulak type landowners and by merchants and moneylenders to form a powerful coalition, it is usually the owners of the larger amounts of land who are able to call upon state force when needed or to forge relationships with dominant groups in industry. Some discussion is now needed of the basis of such resilience.

BASIS FOR DOMINATION: SOCIAL POWER, ALLIANCES, VIOLENCE, AND SURPLUSES

The power of the various lords to dominate rests on two foundations, first, accumulated social power and, second, alliances with other dominant groups and classes that supply the means of political authority and physical coercion.[18]

The social power of those who controlled the land no doubt began to accumulate from the time of the earliest fixed agrarian activities. As a result, peasant-lord relations, more than any other form of social relations of production, have been surrounded with an elaborate carapace of ideology, psychology, and tradition. European feudalism, as a sophisticated elaboration of a control structure based upon land, bequeathed its status, mystique, and residual laws to the capitalist societies that succeeded it. Feudalism gave landownership a prestige and social power beyond that of money alone. As a result successful industrial entrepreneurs used the newly acquired money to purchase security for their new position by making alliances with the landed interests. In the imperial expansion of Europe into Asia, the new rulers, especially the British, often perceived a similar structure of ancient rights in a local landed class. They used this class as a relay of imperial rule and thereby strengthened the traditional authority of landowners and conserved or strengthened their social power.[19]

So it is that in contemporary Latin America landlords and tenants may not merely be in an economic relationship but together constitute a total social structure with a stability that has persisted for more than 200 years since colonial times. The landowner has power over all aspects of the life of peasants and expects (and often receives) deference from those ruled. Domination, rent, and exploitation are as if in the natural order of things.

The church and other religious influences, usually strong in rural areas, have often supported the authority of the landowner, encouraged humility on the part of the peasant, and posited the extraterrestrial cause of, and solution for, existing misery.[20] In India, caste supplements the power of the landowner by fragmenting society and obstructing any cohesion among the exploited.[21] In some countries, such as Bolivia, Rhodesia (Zimbabwe), Guatemala, South Africa, and others, the various landlords and moneylenders are of different racial and ethnic origin from the peasants. Therefore, domination is assisted by promoted notions of racial superiority and any internalized belief in inferiority or self-denigration on the part of the peasants.

The accrued social power of landlords results in the widely observed apparent servility, docility, and deferential attitudes on the part of the peasants, and when such characteristics can still be seen, then the landlords' power is most likely intact. But contemporary developments have been eroding the legitimacy of the landlords' social power and have thereby made the conditions more favorable for transformation of peasant-lord relations through collective action of the peasants, land reform, or development of employing enterprise farms.

The history surrounding the second pillar of the lords' power, that of alliance with other groups and classes, has been an uneven one. There are few states today in which the landlord class is politically dominant, though it may conserve considerable social power. Current landlord support from more powerful groups, particularly those associated with industry and commerce, is assisted by two factors—the ideology of private property rights and the economic function which agricultural production plays in maintaining an urban-industrial sector.

Landowners, moneylenders, and merchants symbolize a cluster of ideas that are also supportive of the existence of other dominant groups or classes. In particular, these ideas are the inviolability of property, the obligation of debt service, and the concept of a free market. Any attack or attempt to undermine any of these principles of social organization tends to be seen as a generalized attack upon the social system. Thus even though landlords may not wield great influence in the state and may be regarded by other dominant groups as vaguely reactionary and obstructive of modernization of the economy, these groups will often support the lords against peasant revolt, because such revolts are seen as a challenge to virtually every interest vested in the existing structure.[22]

The economic function of peasant-lord relations in the social formation has likewise helped to cement landlord alliances with other groups or has at least created general interest in the maintenance of peasant-lord relations. When peasants deliver rent to the landlord class, they are in effect delivering produce that is surplus to their subsistence needs. This surplus becomes the basis of the landlord's higher standard of living and also finds its way into the urban industrial sector, either in the form of investments by the landlords when the surplus is exported or as food for the urban population.

Peasant-lord relations may not be technically the most efficient in terms of maximum output from available land and labor, but their coercive nature is apparently efficient in extracting surpluses. Less coercive and voluntaristic social relations may not be as efficient at extracting surpluses; self-employed farmers, and sometimes subsistence farmers, can potentially choose a slower pace, or even leisure, after they have ensured minimum family food requirements. Their surplus would then be smaller. The techniques of unmechanized agricultural production also play a role, because the slightest lack of motivation or application in performing farming work substantially affects production. A centimeter's difference in the depth of hoeing or planting, a slight decline in the diligence in weeding, a lack of interest in the margins of cultivation may mean a precipitous decline in eventual yields. Fear, or close supervision, then appears the only means of maintaining highest levels of productivity among agricultural workers. Close supervision requires a restructuring of agriculture and even then, as in collectivization, may not always produce the results required. Thus, for example, sharecropping may be used to extract even by landowners who in other areas of business use "modern" methods involving wage labor, because they are unable to "buy" supervision and do not wish to do it themselves.[23]

The fear and coercion of the peasant-lord relations are thus accepted, in some cases reluctantly, by those who see them as the only way to continue to extract surpluses from peasants. Those who are allowed to continue to extract benefit from the two basic problems that regimes, governments, and dominant groups have experienced in almost every geographic and cultural circumstance; the first is how to enable small farmers to create a surplus and the second is how to remove it from them.

There are also indirect beneficiaries of peasant-lord relations. The surplus food of peasants is cheaper than that produced by cultivators enjoying social relations that permit greater returns for their labor. Cheap food benefits industrial employers who may have to pay higher wages if food prices increased, as well as industrial workers if such pay increases were difficult or impossible to obtain. When surpluses enter export markets, a whole range of commercial, administrative, and transport-based groups acquire a vested interest in the agricultural status quo.

Latin American *dependencia* theorists have represented peasant-lord social relations as the innermost of a series of concentric circles of exploitation that, moving outward, pass through rural lords, urban-based commercial and industrial groups, the export industry, and importers in rich countries and ultimately end with the rich country consumers. All such beneficiaries of peasant-lord relations are potential allies in the upholding of the lord's power at the national and international levels. Peasants, perhaps more than any other subordinate workers in any form of social relations, are the subjects of a truly globally supported system of domination.[24] As a consequence of its supportive role in both ideological and economic terms the landlord class has usually had sufficient power to command or call upon the state and other groups in maintaining its social relations. Landlords have often been able to resist encroachments of state wide systems; the landlords in Spain during the Franco regime, for example, were able to prevent the extension of corporate state structure in the rural areas.[25]

When peasants revolt, then they have invariably met with state-supplied troops, armies, and police that inflict imprisonment, murder, and physical brutality[26] The use of violence is not, however, confined to institutionalized or state-organized violence. Kulak-type landlords have been particularly prone to execute their own direct violence with the probable knowledge that they would be likely to escape the nominal penalties of the law administered by an inadequate or acquiescent state. The murder of hundreds of thousands of peasants in Indonesia after the fall of the Sukarno regime was partly the work of small landowners acting against the landless and tenants who had responded to the call of the Indonesian Communist Party to attempt to change their status.[27] The landlord class, where it continues to exist as an important component of the dominant groups in social formations—and this is the case in many parts of the third world—cannot remain secure without these ideological and economic supports.

Despite this appearance of inviolability of the landlord class there are now, as will be discussed in the next two sections, many indications that the relative power of landlords is declining. The state has often tempered the power of the landlord class. The state has fielded two armies: one was of a conventional military sort, which coupled with the police helped the lord to suppress the sporadic violent protest of peasants; the other was an army of tax collectors, which directly competed with the lord for a share of peasant products. The cost to the lord of the repressive army was the extraction by the other army of tax collectors, and the price was high, for not only did the lord have to share his spoils, but also the state entered the scene as a potential rival to the authority of the lord.

For the past thirty years unequivocal state support for the lords in peasant-lord relations has been less certain for two reasons. First, there was a doubt among governments and industrialists that peasant-lord relations permit the most efficient use of available resources, at least in the technical economic sense. For example, in countries where landownership is highly concentrated, much land is not used intensively, and some may not be cultivated at all. The second reason for the uncertainty of state and other groups' support of the landlords was the fear that the harshness of the peasant-lord relationship, the violent and crushing nature of rural poverty, the increasing number of totally landless rural workers, and generalized unemployment will spark a fire that could destroy the existing social formation. Although fear of revolution and revolt in the countryside can thus bring increased repression on behalf of the landlords, it can also cause uncertainty about the advisability of continuing support for peasant-lord relations. These are the basic reasons that have caused, in the last thirty years, a series of state interventions in peasant-lord relations with the stated objective of transforming them.

INTERVENTION IN PEASANT-LORD RELATIONS: LAND REFORM, TECHNOLOGY, AND AGRIBUSINESS

Intervention in peasant-lord relations has come mainly from groups in control of the state. These interventions manifest themselves primarily in the programs of land reform, through the application of new technology in agriculture commonly known as the Green Revolution, and in attempts to create producer marketing and financing cooperatives.

Interventions from outside peasant-lord social relations, which were not directly under state control, although always with some sort of official approval or acquiescence, have been made by corporations or industrial groups intent on creating large-scale farming, sometimes referred to as agribusiness.

Many of these interventions claim to be for the purpose of replacing old-fashioned peasant-lord relations by something more modern and efficient. Thus land reform has often had the stated objective of converting peasants into independent, self-employed farmers. Cooperatives providing marketing and credit facilities were to have been set up with state support for the express purpose of freeing peasants from merchant and money-lender domination. On the other hand, large-scale farming requiring the amalgamation of peasant-owned or rented land transforms peasants and subsistence farmers into wage laborers. All these attempts have made changes, sometimes material and sometimes in the consciousness of peasants, and they are thus important factors in the dynamics of peasant-lord social relations.

Land reform was a policy pursued by many governments from the end of the second world war until at least the mid-1960s, especially in countries that had recently obtained their formal independence. Its announced aims were to increase production and taxation, reduce rural poverty, and improve social justice by redistribution of land and/or the granting of ownership rights over rented land.[28] In some respects this policy represented the abandonment of the belief developed in the industrializing countries of Europe throughout the nineteenth century and supported by economic thinkers as disparate as Karl Marx, Adam Smith, Friedrich Engels, and David Ricardo, that owing to economies of scale, large-scale agriculture was more efficient than small-scale agriculture.

In the conditions of some less industrialized countries in the middle of the twentieth century, the question of agricultural production was viewed differently. In the absence of massive investments in mechanization, high concentrations of land, either farmed as large farms or rented to peasants, were not considered to be the most efficient from the standpoint of the total production from available land and labor. Yields per hectare from larger farms were lower than yields from small farms farmed by independent farmers, such as those in Japan. Conversely, smaller farms with large amounts of available labor were often very low in productivity per person although high in yield per hectare. In Latin America the *minifundia* sector contains the manpower and *latifundia* sector the land, but the more efficient and socially just combination of the land and labor has been obstructed by the existence of peasant-lord social relations based on large, concentrated landownership.

For governments such as the Nehru government of India, which came to power in 1947, immediately after granting of formal independence, the object of land reform was based on the concern of urban and liberal intelligentsia for rural poverty. Other governments seem to have initiated land reform as a preemptive strike aimed to divert the possibility of a peasant-based revolution. The "preemptive" motivation received impetus from the example provided by the Cuban revolution in 1959, which, like those of China in 1949 and Algeria in 1958, was based upon the help and acceptance of revolutionary aims by peasants, farmers, and agricultural wage laborers. Land reform was written into the United States-supported international program for assistance to Latin American governments—the Alliance for Progress—and found its way into the bilateral aid programs of rich countries and the multilateral programs of the United Nations and its specialized agencies.

The 1960s was a decade in which land reform was endorsed officially by many governments and international organizations as a key development policy. In the Alliance for Progress program, receipt of United States' finance was made conditional upon commitments to land reform; this type of pressure meant that hardly a country in which extensive peasant-lord relations exist could afford to *overtly* defend the status quo in land distribution or to be without a nominal land reform law.

In most cases, however, land reform attempts were to be made within the existing power structure of the social formation and did not bring about a fundamental modification of peasant-lord relations. The typical land reform package was a two-stage policy of (1) compensation to landowners designed to convert them into capital holders who would invest in, and support, industrialization programs and (2) the conversion of peasants into independent farmers producing for a market who, motivated by their new power and wealth, would likewise contribute through taxes and by more efficient production of food supplies to the process of industrialization. Yet there was little historical precedent to suggest that such a policy could be easily put into practice. The major previous widespread land reforms had all come about either as the consequence of revolutions (as in France 1789, Mexico 1911, Cuba 1961), or following the unseating of a colonial power (as in Egypt 1952), or after an international war and its consequential shift of populations and social turbulence (as in Taiwan in 1952, South Korea 1955, and, to a lesser extent, in the Japan of 1946).[29]

The special nature of these examples was borne out by the fate of the land reform measures undertaken in a number of third-world countries from 1950 onward. Some partial reforms involving changes in land tenancy laws, or intended redistribution without sufficient power or determination of enforcement, made it simple for large landowners to circumvent or evade reforms supposed to reduce their power and privilege. Such half-hearted measures resulted often from the fact that the government or the legislature that drafted the reform laws was in fact dominated by landlords. In Latin America, governments anxious to acquire United States' grants passed land reform laws that became known as "flowerpot" laws because they were intended to have a high visibility, like a flowerpot in a window, but to have no substance that would seriously affect the landlords' rural power.

Many laws provided ceilings on the number of hectares any one person or family could hold. One common way of circumventing this kind of provision (in Egypt, for example) was that owners transferred land to friends and relatives in whose name it was formally registered, leaving the basic holding intact under the de facto control of the original owner. Elsewhere small farmer beneficiaries of land reforms fell quickly into debt and sold or mortgaged their land to moneylenders or ex-landlords, so that a new concentration of landholding emerged. In parts of India, kulak-type farmers fiercely opposed and sabotaged any agreements made on the distribution of land to tenant farmers and landless rural workers and in fact became net beneficiaries of land reform as the larger landowners took their compensation and left the rural areas in order to become investors in industry. Likewise, in Peru the aftermath of the agrarian reform of 1969–1975 has been the emergence of a new privileged class of entrepreneur-farmers and kulak landlords with peasants benefiting unevenly or not at all.[30]

In 1978, after two decades of discussion, programs, and internationally promoted reform measures, in Latin America, for example, 90 percent of cultivatable land still remained in the hands of less than a quarter of the agricultural population. In general, and throughout the world, no considerable or widespread improvement in the conditions of peasants resulted from all this discussion and experimentation with nonrevolutionary land reforms.[31]

The general failure of land reforms in the 1950s and 1960s can be attributed to a failure to recognize or, more likely, to accept how the peasant-lord form of social relations is supported in the political and economic structures of social formations in which this form is prevalent. Subsequent realization that effective land reform is, by its very nature, a challenge to established power as a whole and not merely to that of the landlord class may have indeed provided some of the enthusiasm for the attempt to raise agricultural productivity by technology and solve unrest and poverty problems of the rural areas. This attempt, commonly known as the Green Revolution, sought to avoid any confrontation with established power by increasing production through the use of technology.[32]

In 1961, scientists working on agricultural productivity produced new seeds, which under certain conditions were able to yield two or three times more than traditional varieties under similar conditions.

Increased yields from land might mean increased consumption for peasants, but it would not if the extra production merely accrued to a landlord as part of the rent; to a moneylender for interest on loans for seed, fertilizer, or irrigation; or to a merchant who had remained in control of the market for the production. Three features inherent in the Green Revolution technology reinforced, rather than diminished, the contradictions within peasant-lord social relations.

First, the new seeds required greater capital inputs in the

form of fertilizer and agrochemicals in general and irrigation than the existing agricultural techniques did. Second, the increased yields and intensified cropping meant the requirement of large amounts of labor for short and infrequent intervals. Third, greater know-how was needed by the cultivator in the use of seed and fertilizer and in marketing.

These features have had various effects. The increased capital requirements sometimes resulted in increased indebtedness through which farmers lost control of production to moneylenders. This could have the effect of extending the scope of peasant-lord relations as previously independent farmers lost their status. At an early stage the fragility of the seeds sometimes meant disastrous crop failures and the abandonment of land, which then passed cheaply to the already richer farmers and thereby increased the hold and power of the kulak-type landlord. Finally, the need for a large amount of seasonal labor created an incentive for the development of a reserve of partially employed landless laborers. In the Punjab region of both India and Pakistan this development ruptured the traditional system in which the landlord class was economically interested in the survival of the peasants and resulted in the landlords' having a minimum concern for the peasants' welfare. This interest had never been extended to seasonal wage laborers; peasants displaced by the dynamics of the Green Revolution into this category found that even the minimum provisions of the peasant-lord relations were no longer available.[33]

The Green Revolution has had different effects in different countries, but the most general finding on its social consequences is that it has increased the numbers and power of the kulak-type landlord, created farmer-entrepreneurs using landless laborers, helped consolidate the positions of middlemen and moneylenders, and caused accelerated disruption of the overall structure of rural societies.[34] Thus while not transforming peasant-lord relations, the Green Revolution has introduced new uncertainty, increased social tensions, and produced new rural-based power groups, all of which will ultimately have profound effects upon the prospects for transformation of the form of social relations whether from within or from without.

Attempts to transform peasant-lord relations into community-based farming cooperatives have, like the Green Revolution, produced changes without fundamentally transforming social relations. Perhaps the most famous of these attempts has been the Tanzanian experiment with Ujamaa villages. The basic objective of this program was to create farming villages in which the villagers would farm communal land while continuing to live within individual joint families. In accordance with the socialist philosophy of the government this program was intended to prevent the emergence of peasant-lord relations where they did not exist and curtail them where they did. This project encompassed subsistence farmers, self-employed farmers, and occasionally kulak-type lords and their peasants. The program is now, however, considered as having failed, having ever covered only 8 percent of the agricultural labor force. Significantly, the areas of least success and greatest problems were where cash cropping on a self-employed farmer basis or where kulak landlords prevailed. Established peasant-lord relations proved too difficult to transform, though the scheme made some headway in areas of subsistence farming.[35]

Cooperatives, in general, have been based upon improvements in marketing, financing, or sharing of expensive equipment, rather than, as in the Ujamaa experiment, the introduction of a collective form of production. Whereas they represent an intrusion in peasant-lord relations, their transformational possibilities are of a long-term nature related more to changes they may provoke in peasant consciousness than to any direct and immediate impact.[36]

This is not the case with agribusiness, which is one thrust from outside peasant-lord relations that has had a direct transformational effect. Agribusiness is the name given to a phenomenon that unites farm input industries and produce fertilizers, machinery and seeds, the farm itself, and the food- processing industry. In the agribusiness complex the demands of the first and third components, input and processing, determine the nature of the second—the farm. The nature of the input industry is such that it supplies expensive machinery and fertilizers that, for financial and technical reasons, can be used only in capital-intensive, large-scale farming. Furthermore, the tendency to concentration of farms is enhanced by the processing industry, which yields economies of scale by mass processing of food and commercial products grown to as near standard shape and quality as possible. Agribusiness is organized internationally and involves the highest reaches of corporate power in the most powerful of states; for operations in Central America, for example, fifteen corporations from the United States have created a Latin American Agribusiness Development Corporation (LAAD) that is diversified in the production of beef, vegetables, cut flowers, and wood.[37]

When agribusiness enters the farming sector, peasant-lord relations have usually been destroyed. Corporations buy land from the former owners, whether they be large or small, expel tenants, and introduce highly mechanized farming using a smaller labor force of wage employees. Some of the previous tenants thus may become landless wage laborers, and the rest have little recourse but to migrate toward the slums of the cities. In Chile and Brazil, the advent of agribusiness has meant that peasants have been told in effect to "reap your crop, sow grass for cattle and leave."

Multinational agribusiness is increasing its scope rapidly in both rich and poor countries. In the United States it displaces small family farms, whereas in Kenya, Philippines, and Dominican Republic it displaces peasants and replaces erstwhile peasant-lord social relations. Agribusiness represents a threat to peasants from outside peasant-lord relations—it compensates landlords and evicts peasants and is the reverse of the formal objectives of land reform, which were to expropriate landlords and provide peasants with land.

It is clear from the extent and nature of these intrusions over the past thirty years that peasant-lord social relations are under attack from a variety of sources. It is also clear that such attacks have disturbed rather than transformed them. Perhaps the most crucial development for future transformations and for the precise nature of the relations among peasants, landowner, moneylenders, and merchants has been the appearance in greater numbers and with greater power of the kulak-type landowners and moreover, of the farmer-entrepreneurs.[38] These latter represent an accelerated intrusion into the rural areas and agricultural production of enterprise labor market social relations in which landless rural workers sell their labor to commercially organized farmer-entrepreneurs. This development of "capitalist" agriculture, as it is frequently called, intensifies the presence of landless rural laborers whose social relations and therefore consciousness are distinct from that of peasants and, at the same time, perhaps adds a larger faction—farmer-entrepreneurs—to the landlord class. Peasant-lord social relations thus begin to lose their dominant position within agricultural production, the effect of which is to call further into doubt blanket considerations of rural producers as peasants and create the even greater necessity to distinguish consciousness and action arising from the specific forms of domination inherent in peasant-lord relations.

PEASANT ACTION: REVOLT OR REVOLUTION

Perhaps the most hotly debated issue surrounding peasant-lord social relations concerns the attitudes peasants may have toward collective action for the improvement of their conditions, that is, transformation of their social relations. In short, what are peasant attitudes toward revolt, rebellion, and revolution? Opinions on this issue range from that of Marx, which was that peasants were rarely a revolutionary force, to the more contemporary viewpoint symbolized by Franz Fanon, that peasants are the only revolutionary section of the population, at least in less industrialized and colonized countries.[39] To some extent this polarization of opinion arises from the failure to make a distinction between different forms of social relations of production in agriculture; self-employed farmers may not be as willing to resort to violence or revolution to redress grievances as peasants or landless laborers may be. They cannot all be described as peasants and be assigned a uniform attitude toward revolution. Certainly the interplay between categories of rural workers found within different forms of social relations will determine the outcome of any peasant movement, whether it be moderate or revolutionary, but here the basic discussion is confined to the potential action and role of peasants as defined throughout this chapter, namely, within peasant-lord social relations.

Peasant attitudes will vary in accordance with the nature of the collective action. The term *revolt*, as used here, is confined to local outbursts of protest and violence that can usually be solved or suppressed at the local level. Rebellions are regional or national uprisings, usually having an identifiable and specific cause and seeking a change in peasant-lord relations but not involved with a leadership or organization that has broader based and far-reaching objectives. Revolution implies action of a coordinated nature with long-term objectives and seeking more fundamental changes not only in peasant-lord relations but also within the whole social formation.

Despite the enormous geographic, cultural, and agricultural diversity of the peasant condition, peasant-lord relations have resulted in at least three aspects of peasant consciousness and behavior that have been observed throughout the world. These are a generalized hostility toward outsiders, a tendency for discontent to be manifested by short outbursts of violence, and a total, or holistic, view of existing social relations and the causes of poverty or immediate difficulties.

The first aspect, that of hostility toward outsiders, has been one of the sources of the stereotyped image of peasants. The implacable hostility or animosity with which peasants have greeted reformers, revolutionaries, and technicians alike has helped to amplify the sullen, conservative, and uncooperative image of peasants. There are, of course, good reasons for such hostility, as already noted; the objective of most outsiders in the rural areas is further extraction from the peasants, be it in taxes, produce, or labor. In modern India it is reported that, for peasants, outsiders are people who come on bicycles or jeeps, and never on foot, that they must always be outwitted, and that the gifts they offer are nothing but bait for even further traps.[40]

If peasants had a universal knowledge of history, their worst suspicions of outsiders might well be confirmed, for rarely have outsiders brought the satisfaction of peasants' most immediate needs. Without a wider consciousness, peasants will see the objective of any revolt or revolution in which they are urged to participate usually in terms of acquiring more land or becoming landowners. Yet after peasants have fought revolutionary battles and installed revolutionary regimes, the new governors of society may not redistribute land or provide peasants with their most cherished wish. On the contrary, many such regimes in the past have preferred the concentration of land and the expropriation of peasants in favor of collective farms or cooperatives.[41] More cautious land reforms under radical or revolutionary regimes in which land is distributed to peasant occupiers are now appearing, as in Nicaragua,[42] for example. Nevertheless, reticence and lack of trust may be part of a necessary defense mechanism even against revolutionary well-wishers.

The second aspect of peasant behavior is the tendency for social protest or exasperation to be manifested by short outbursts of violence that are enclosed by long periods of apparent docility and servility. Peasant rebellions and revolts have been numerous throughout the long history of peasant- lord relations, but they have rarely been instrumental in transforming social relations, even though the anger and violence have usually been directed at the landlord class.[43] This *jacquerie* type of violence, as it was called in medieval France when the French cultivator was nick-named *"Jacques,"* is more a symptom of the general violent nature of peasant-lord relations than an event in a process by which relations are permanently transformed. There are several important reasons for the short-lived nature of peasant revolts or at least for why revolts do not easily grow into rebellions and revolutions.

The first reason is found within the nature of cultivation or animal husbandry. Peasants and cultivators in general have a fairly subtle and delicate relationship with the elements of farming—earth, weather, labor, animals, etc.—that permits them to satisfy the demands of the lords, as well as their own needs. Under such conditions the smallest disturbance, such as a decline in labor input at a certain point in the cultivating season or the absence of the most skilled and knowledgeable person, may have disastrous effects on production. Successful animal husbandry, for example, requires the constant presence of the farmer, for even short absences may mean decreased milk yields, sickness or death of the animal, or loss of valuable animal offspring through lack of proper attention. The time available for any long-term and consistent organization requiring long or regular absences is limited and almost noexistent if the peasant family is to continue to cultivate normally. Absences mean either there is less food, given that rent is extracted as normal, or a double burden of labor is placed upon those who stay, usually women, the old, and the young; these latter comprise the hidden shadow army of support workers for the visible army of revolutionary glory. These "dictates of the harvest and the herd"[44] mean that only when the individual cultivator decides to risk life-supporting production and disrupt the work balance of the household can peasant armies be created. Personal revolutionary decisions must be taken by peasants before time can be devoted to a movement that has revolution as its objective.

A second reason for the short duration of peasant action lies in the specific, local, and immediate causes of revolts. A landlord's demand for increased rent or service, the failure of a crop attributable to causes other than climate, or the usurpation of what are considered as "traditional" rights of way, marketing facilities, or grazing and water rights upsets the precarious balance of cultivation and the conditions of life arising from it. The result may be an immediate and violent action in an attempt to restore the preexisting conditions. Under these circumstances the action is easily contained by the landlord class and its allies; it enters into local history as a "revolt" or "disturbance." An improvement, usually temporary, in conditions may be granted and the possibility of the revolt's spreading is minimized. Only when the specific grievance is duplicated nationally or regionally do revolts become more widespread and earn the designation of rebellions.[45]

The final reason for short-lived peasant revolts is simply that they are often crushed with brutal efficiency, which prevents them from spreading or being of a longer duration. There is little chance of longer term action if leaders of peasant revolts are imprisoned, or murdered or disappear.

Returning to the general discussion of the behavior of peasants, the third widely observed characteristic is that, once aroused, they seem to demonstrate a lack of moderation or selection in their objectives or the destruction that results from their violence. Once a revolt breaks out, it manifests itself in a seemingly total and indiscriminate attempt to destroy all vestiges and symbols of repressive social relations, even if, as in the case mentioned above, the cause of the revolt was specific and any rational objective may be to merely restore the status quo ante. Here again, it is believed that the nature of the peasants' work of cultivation plays a role in producing this characteristic. Effective cultivation requires a holistic view of phenomena, a reluctance to disturb, and an appreciation of interrelatedness in what is now called the ecological system. These views and orientations may be transferred to the social order; if it works, however badly, it should be left alone, but if it is perceived not to work, then just absolutely as it was maintained it must be destroyed.[46] There is then a reluctance of peasants to examine any individual aspect of a situation or adopt a partial solution but in contrast a readiness, when revolt does break out, to proceed to complete and total attack on the whole of their immediate social structure and relations.

These three aspects of peasant consciousness provide some clues to the possibility of transformation of peasant-lord social relations, but the full picture can be seen only when other dynamics in the relations are taken into account. One of the most crucial of these has been the gradual weakening of landlord social power already mentioned in discussing the nature of those who extract from peasants.

Under feudalism the lord's right to extract from peasants was supposed to be justified by the protection they afforded the serfs. By analogy, in more modern times, supporters of the continued existence of peasant-lord relations have often emphasized the "service" function of the lords. In this view gifts from lords on feast days or to newborn children, or the lords' provision of "employment," capital, rides to hospitals in jeeps, grace in bad harvest years, deferment of debts, money income through marketing, and so on, are seen as meaningful aspects of a lord's service function. Likewise, some moneylenders, and occasionally smaller landlords and merchants, may acquire some local prestige and acceptance by offering such services.

When compared with the level of rent paid by the peasants, however, such services and gifts are but easily afforded and insignificant largesse, whose purpose may be to provide symbolic, rather than material, justification for the general harshness of social relations.[47] Increasingly the lords' power now lacks the binding force of being seen as based upon mutual, if unequal, advantage to both peasant and lord.[48] The social prestige of the lords is also becoming incompatible with ideas and images invading rural life as transistor radios and village television centers become more commonplace, as sons and daughters leave for formal education and return with different perceptions, and roads, trucks, and buses provide peasants with wider market and social linkages.[49]

In Latin America another factor is that the church has lost some of its power in upholding peasant deference to large landowners and the general status quo[50]; indeed the development of "liberation theology," in which it is argued that the church must "switch sides" and support peasant movements can be seen as an attempt to recoup a following lost under the impact of the developments outlined earlier. These latter have also weakened landlords and other extractors in favor of entrepreneur-farmers; land reforms in Peru, Chile, and Venezuela, for example, and the Green Revolution in Asia have often profoundly shaken the established power structures and eliminated or weakened the traditional landlord class. Thus the pace of change in rural areas, the failure of the contemporary extractors from peasants to have little other function than maintaining domination, must now be considered as an important factor in any discussions of transformations arising from peasant actions.

Peasant-lord social relations in their current form are not destined to survive as an important form. On a world scale the transformation of such relations has increased rapidly since the middle of the century. The elimination of peasant-lord relations in China alone has made an important impact on the numbers of persons within the form. Algeria, Cuba, Cambodia, Vietnam, Mozambique, and Nicaragua are examples of countries where the destruction of peasant-lord relations have been secured or are being attempted while nonrevolutionary processes in Japan, Taiwan, and to some extent South Korea have also reduced the numbers of peasants in these countries. The question is not whether the form can be sustained by the landlord class and any allies in the face of these encroachments but rather the manner in which the transformation will be effected. The answer to this question in turn depends upon the consciousness and attitudes of peasants toward specific attempts to transform their social relations.

There are two transformational processes that are based upon peasant action. The first is when changes in peasant-lord relations are the result of the role of so-called moderate peasant organizations; the second involves peasant participation in revolutionary action that eliminates peasant-lord social relations and most likely changes the configuration of the whole of the social formation.

Moderate peasant movements are those that have an organization of peasants—such as a union or association—with an objective of achieving specific and partial improvements in peasant conditions through long-term pressure on the landlord class. The methods of applying such pressure are, at least in the first instance, nonviolent and involve petitions, strikes, and demands on governments and other groups that may have power to influence the policies of landlords. Such organizations have not had a great success in achieving their objectives, especially if they have not been assisted or supported by other, more powerful groups and organizations.[51]

Elements of peasant consciousness, particularly the short-term and holistic bias, make long-term and moderate organizations with partial objectives difficult to sustain. In addition, peasants often lack the organizational skills and knowledge of the wider social formation necessary for efficient pressure and bargaining. Yet persons who might have such skills come from the outside and are likely to be treated with suspicion. Landlords unused to any sort of assertiveness by peasants treat peasant organizations as a potential for revolt or revolution and, especially in Latin America, repress them with just as much force as the more violent, less moderate outbursts. The result is that peasant social action that might lead to the formation of stable organizations is met with violence by the landlords, and when peasants respond in like manner, the action soon becomes a short-lived and crushed revolt.[52]

The only occasions when moderate peasant organizations

have proved to be instrumental in achieving rapid changes in peasant- lord relations have been when they have been used by powerful groups opposed to landlords' short-term interests. Thus the United States occupying administration in Japan in 1946 used existing peasant and farmer organizations to force a land reform that finally destroyed landlords' power and rapidly reduced the number of renting farmers.[53] In the invasion and control of Taiwan by the mainland Chinese forces of Chiang Kai-shek, peasant organizations were used to change social relations in agriculture in favor of the new rulers, whose interests were more urban and industrial.[54]

Current dynamics in peasant-lord relations may, however, provide peasant organizations with more powerful outside help than has previously been the case. Declining legitimacy of the role of landlords makes it easier to recruit peasants to organizations. Groups opposed to continued peasant-lord relations on the outside may see moderate peasant organizations as a better alternative than a possible revolutionary army. It is perhaps for this latter reason that moderate peasant organizations have been promoted internationally by development assistance programs and international agencies.[55]

Transformation of the social relations through a gradual weakening of landlord power under the two-pronged thrust of peasant organization within and withdrawal of support from traditional allies may be too slow for the pace of changes already arising from the dynamics of peasant-lord relations. The combinations of the partial interventions from outside, the growing consciousness of peasants of the wider social formation, the economic conditions of other workers, and the growth of landless laborers may outrun any concessions that can be squeezed from the landlords. In this case peasants may well still provide one of the bases for revolutionary action.

It is perhaps an impossible task to attempt to generalize about the relationships of peasants to revolution.[56] It has now been realized that the mix of peasant consciousness, the material conditions of the country and area concerned, and leadership policies create so many variables in any particular case that predictions become very hazardous. All that can be considered is the modern historical record of revolutions and revolutionary movements and the role of peasants in them, given that most accounts do not adapt the restrictive definition of peasant as used here. It is fairly clear that peasants alone have not taken the initiative in the revolutions of the twentieth century. As already noted, in China the independent farmers and the kulak landlords played a crucial role in the installation of the revolutionary regime of Mao Zedong by leading the opposition against larger landlords.[57] This was partly because landowning farmers suffered more at the hands of the regional warlords of the 1920s and 1930s than peasants, who were partially protected by the alliance between the warlords and the larger landowners. In addition it has now become evident that Mao's Red Army had a core adherence of landless laborers for whom the appeal of the movement was both a restoration of dignity and an indefinite future state of well-being rather than concrete material objectives such as land, lower rents, or less taxation.[58] In India it has been the self-employed farmers and the Communist party, often led by urban intellectuals, that were important elements in the principal revolutionary rural-based movements after 1940.[59] In Burma before independence it was the self-employed farmers who led the battle against the British colonial authorities, for they were angered at the regimes failure to maintain prices on the market.[60] Often the picture of the precise role of peasants is not clear; in both Yemen and Mozambique struggles between peasants and lords have been merged with urban actions of urban workers.[61]

This lack of a clear and decisive role within a general revolutionary situation implies that peasant- lord relations do not create a broader class consciousness among peasants that is strong enough to thrust them into the leadership of revolutionary movements or even strong enough to provide the cohesion among themselves necessary to overcome landlord coercion against so-called moderate organizations.[62] Conversely, however, the consciousness produced by their extreme power relations makes education and mobilization easier and may provide a substantive base from which to forge coalitions and create broader class-based action.

Peasants have then been ambivalent toward the adoption of drastic long-term action. Although their holistic bias provides a ready-made consciousness for revolutionary action, the short-term demands of cultivation and the hostility to outsiders, who are likely to be active in the formation, if not in the leadership, of peasant armies, takes time to overcome. Successful revolutions with peasant assistance have had a leadership that has acquired loyalty and knowledge through living, working, and fighting with peasants—such as Mao in China and Castro in Cuba. Peasants have tended to follow rather than lead. They have supplied the soldiers to fight revolutionary battles but only after it has been well demonstrated that there is a chance of winning and that the revolutionary army of organizations can in fact withstand the power available to the landlord class.

Long-term alliances with other revolutionaries are then difficult. It is difficult for industrial workers, radical army officers, or religious leaders to demonstrate in advance of action that they have the power to free the peasants from the most immediate results of the domination of the landlord class. As the turbulence resulting from the external interventions in peasant-lord relations increases, the possibilities of new alliances and combinations occur. Rural wage workers, both within enterprise farms and industrial enterprises, and the partially employed landless laborers bring enterprise labor market and primitive labor market social relations into close proximity with peasant-lord relations.[63] The social relations, and the consciousness produced by them, mean rural wage workers and landless laborers may emerge as potential allies for peasants perhaps in a more meaningful way than urban-based workers.

This particular discussion of the revolutionary potential of peasants, as they are defined here, only emphasizes the consideration of the transformation of social relations cannot be successfully considered in an isolated or separated fashion.[64] Yet peasant consciousness is real, and the social relations are distinct and must be understood with precision before embarking on broader social analysis of dynamics and direction of change.[65] This has been the limited objective of the latter part of this chapter. In conclusion it can be said that it is the intricate combination of the type of outside interventions and the attitudes of other agricultural producers and industrial workers that will determine the nature of the reaction of peasants and the subsequent speed and nature of the transformation of peasant-lord relations.

These combinations will certainly be made and will be different in each national case; success will depend to a considerable extent upon how well the various groups involved understand the nature and dynamics of the basic social relations of the peasant-lord variety and their interrelationships with those that govern the lives of other unprotected workers.

NOTES

1. The details of peasant-lord social relations have been drawn basically from three types of sources: (1) articles and studies of various regions, villages, and farms; (2) structured and unstructured interviews with professionals from the third world (a high proportion of those interviewed were originally from the rural areas, although they were mainly sons and daughters of small landlords or self-employed farmers); (3) participant observation and investigation among small self-employed dairy farmers and cultivators in France. This latter source provided technical and economic details of cultivation and animal husbandry that, although not within peasant-lord relations, nevertheless have some universal applicability and helped in the interpretation of technical and economic data on rural production.

2. Estimates of the total amounts extracted from peasant households via rents, interest, and prices are found mainly in detailed "household survey" studies; see, for example, Akma Takahashi, Land and Peasants in Central Luzon: Socio-Economic Structure of a Philippine Village (Honolulu: East-West Center Press, 1969); Ben Kiernan and Chanthou Boa, Peasants and Politics in Kampuchea, 1942–1981 (London, Zed Press, 1982), p. 58; J. R. V. Daane, Responses of Peasant Paddy Growers to Farmers Organisations in West Malaysia (Wageningen, Landbouwhogeschool, 1982).

3. See, for example, the discussion in E. Feder, The Rape of the Peasantry: Latin America's Landholding System (New York, Anchor Books, 1971), p. 130; and B. Hartman and J. K. Boyce, A Quiet Violence: View from a Bangladesh Village (London: Zed Press, 1983), p. 163.

4. See, for example, Dharam Ghai and Samir Radwan, Agrarian Policies and Rural Poverty in Africa (Geneva, International Labor Office, 1983), and for a critical account of such policies, see Ernest Feder, "The World Bank—FIRA Scheme in Action in Temporal, Veracruz," in R. E. Gali, ed., The Political Economy of Rural Development: Peasants, International Capital and the State; Case Studies in Colombia, Mexico, Tanzania and Bangladesh (Albany, State University of New York Press, 1981), pp. 159–73.

5. For an illustration of the complexity of the single rent- paying system of sharecropping, see the essays on the subject in T. J. Byres, ed., Sharecropping and Sharecroppers (London, Cass, 1983).

112   SUBSISTENCE FARMERS AND PEASANTS

6. On the general unreliability of information provided by landlords and the reasons for it, see, for example Kusum Nair, *Blossoms in the Dust: The Human Element in Indian Development* (London, Duckworth, 1961); Michel Launey, *Paysan Algerien; La terre, la vigne et les hommes* (Paris, Editions Seuil, 1963), p. 61; Robert Chambers, *Rural Development: Putting the Last First* (London, Longman, 1984), pp. 48–75, and for an example of a landlord's false denial of rent payments, see the incident recorded in W. and C. Derman, *Serfs, Peasants and Socialism: A Former Serf Village in the Republic of Guinea* (Berkley, University of California Press, 1973), p. 238.

7. See Polly Hill, *The Migrant Cocoa Farmer in Ghana; a Study in Rural Capitalism* (Cambridge, England, Cambridge University Press, 1963).

8. See Michael D. Levin, "Export Crops and Peasantisation: The Bakasi of Cameroun," in Martin A. Klein, ed., *Peasants in Africa: Historical and Contemporary Perspectives* (London, Sage, 1980), pp. 221–41.

9. Although this is certainly more associated with Asia, it is also happening in some African countries; for a detailed account of the process, see, for example, H. O. Sano, *The Political Economy of Food in Nigeria 1960–1982; a Discussion on Peasants, State and World Economy* (Uppsala, Scandinavian Institute of African Studies, 1983).

10. See T. Alberts, *The Agrarian Reform in Peru 1969–1975* (Lund, Sweden, University of Lund, 1976—Research Policy Program Paper No. 103).

11. See, on Sri Lanka, Rene Dumont, *Paysanneries aux abois, Ceylon, tunisie Senegal* (Paris, Editions Seuil, 1972); on Indonesia, F. Kasryno, *Land Tenure and Labour Relations in West Java, Indonesia: A Case Study in Four Villages* (The Hague: Institute of Social Studies, 1981), p. 46; on Bangladesh, Hartman and Boyce, *A Quiet Violence*, p. 162; on Philippines, W. Wolters, *Politics, Patronage, and Class Conflict in Central Luzon* (The Hague: Institute of Social Studies, Research Report 14, 1983), p. 137; on Thailand, interviews, see note 1.

12. Most references above indicate this process. For a detailed account, see, for example, tom Brass, "Class Formation and Class Struggle in La Convencion, Peru," *Journal of Peasant Studies* January 1980, 7(4):427–57.

13. See, for example, discussions in Christopher J. Baker, "Frogs and Farmers: The Green Revolution in India, and Its Murky Past," in T. P. Bayliss-Smith and S. Wanmali, *Understanding Green Revolutions: Agrarian Change and Development Planning South Asia* (Cambridge, England, Cambridge University Press, 1984), p. 50; and in Ethiopia, Alula Abate and Fassil G. Kiros, "Agrarian Development, Structural Changes and Rural Development in Ethiopia," in A. K. Ghose, *Agrarian Reform in Contemporary Developing Countries* (London, Croom Helm, 1983), pp. 143–44; Hartman and Boyce, *A Quite Violence*, p. 189.

14. For a discussion of the patronage system, see Wolters, *Politics, Patronage.*

15. See, for example, the discussion in Barbara Harriss, "Agrarian Change and the Merchant States in Tamil Nadu," in Bayliss-Smith and Wanmali, *Understanding Green Revolutions*, pp. 53–58.

16. See R. W. Cox, *Redistributive Social Relations* (provisional title) (New York, Columbia University Press, forthcoming.)

17. See the discussion for the need to analyze separately state agencies and the critique on the state-equals-monolith school in A. Hussain and K. Tribe, *Marxism and the Agarian Question*, vol. 2 (London, Macmillan, 1981), pp. 148–49.

18. For a general historical account of alliances, see Barrington Moore, Jr., *Social Origins of Dictatorship and Democracy; Lord and Peasant in the Making of the Modern World* (Boston, Beacon Press, 1966). And for a discussion of alliances in

Latin America, see Rodolfo Stavenhagen and Francisco Zapata, *Future Industrial Relations: Latin America* (Geneva, International Institute for Labor Studies, 1972), p. 28; and Teodoro Buarque de Hollanda, "The Structural-Historical Background of the Agrarian Problem . . . in Latin America," in L. R. Alschuler, ed., *Dependent Agricultural Development in and Agrarian Reform in Latin America* (Ottawa, University of Ottawa Press, 1981), pp. 147–68. See also Homa Katanzian, "The Agrarian Question in Iran," in Ghose, *Agrarian Reform*, pp. 309–57.

19. This was especially the case in India. See the discussion of the Indian landholding system dominated by the Zamindar, who controlled but did not own land, in D. Warriner, *Land Reform in Principle and Practice* (Oxford, Clarendon Press, 1969), p. 158–67.

20. See Moore, *Social Origins*, pp. 455–57.

21. See, for example, the condition of "untouchability" detailed in D. von der Weid and G. Poitevin, *Roots of a Peasant Movement* (Pune, India, Shubhada-Sarswat, 1981).

22. See, for example, E. Malefakkis, *Agrarian Reform and Peasant Revolution in Spain: Origins of the Civil War* (New Haven, Conn., Yale University Press, 1970), and the statements of radical peasant leader Hugo Blanco in Hugo Blanco, *Land or Death: The Peasant Struggles in Peru* (New York, Pathfinder Press, 1977), pp. 158–60; and for argued statement opposing liberal and socialist agrarian reforms in preference for "free market" agriculture, see E. Clayton, *Agriculture, Poverty and Freedom in Developing Countries* (London, MacMillan, 1983).

23. See Jose-Maria Caballero, "Sharecropping as an Efficient System; Further Answers to an Old Puzzle," in Byres, *Sharecropping and Sharecroppers.*

24. For a review of the dependentist arguments, see Lawrence R. Alschuler "Introduction," in Alschuler, *Dependent Agricultral Development*, (1981), pp. 1–10; for a review of the integration of African peasant into the world economy of colonial times, see Martin A. Klein, "Introduction," in Klein, *Peasants in Africa*, pp. 9–43.

25. See J. Martinez Alier, *Labourers and Landowners in Southern Spain* (London, Allen and Unwin, 1971).

26. See the discussion in Gerrit Huizer, "Peasant Organisations and Their Potential for Change in Latin America," in *Land Reform, Land Settlements and Cooperatives*, (Rome, UN Food and Agricultural Organization, 1971), No. 2, pp. 1–8.

27. The origins of these events are discussed in Antonie C. A. Dake, *In the Spirit of the Red Banteng: Indonesian Communist between Moscow and Peking* (The Hague, Mounton, 1973), pp. 241–49.

28. for general discussions of the question of land reform, see Warriner, *Land Reform*; for a review of the developments during the 1960s, see Anon, "Land Reform its Reasons and Meaning," *Civilisations*, (1970), 20(3); for a review of the record of the 1970s, see E. H. Jacoby, "Has Land Reform Become Obsolete?" in E J. Hobsbawm, W. Kula, and A. Mitra, eds., *Peasants in History: Essays in Honour of Daniel Thorner* (Calcutta, Oxford University Press, 1980), pp. 296–305.

29. Some discussions of this point are, for example, found in E. H. Jcoby, *Agrarian Unrest in Southeast Asia* (New York, Columbia University Press, 1948), p. 258; and Eric Wolf, ed., *Peasant Wars of the Twentieth Century* (New York, Harper and Row, 1969).

30. See Alberts, *Agrarian Reform*, and Cristobal Kay, "The Agrarian Reform in Peru: An Assessment," in Ghose, *Agrarian Reform*, pp. 185–235.

31. For a critical account of land reform in India, see P. C. Joshi, "Land

Reform and Agrarian Change in India and Pakistan Since 1947," *Journal of Peasant Studies*, (1974), 1(2):164–85; K. Finkler, "From Sharecroppers to Entrepreneurs: Peasant Household Production Under the Ejido System in Mexico," *Economic Development and Cultural Change*, (1978), 27(1):103–20; and for overviews by country, see the collections of Ghose, *Agrarian Reform*, and S. Jones, P. C. Joshi, and M. Murmis, eds., *Rural Poverty and Agrarian Reform* (New Delhi, Allied Publishers, 1982).

32. The objective of avoiding confrontation with landlords through use of technology is made explicit in, for example, Theodore W. Schultz, *Transforming Traditional Agriculture* (New Haven, Conn., Yale University Press, 1964), p. 206, and *Puebla Project: Seven Years Experience (1967–1973: Analysis of Progress in a Rainfed Area of Mexico* (Mexico City, International Maize and Wheat Improvement Center, 1974), pp. viii and ix.

33. See F. R. Frankel and K. Von Vorys, *The Political Challenge of the Green Revolution: Shifting Patterns of Peasant Participation in India and Pakistan* (Princeton, Princeton University Press, 1972), pp. 37–39.

34. These findings are discussed in most writings on agrarian reform; see, for example, Ho Kwon Ping, "Victims of the Green Revolution," *Far Eastern Economic Review* (June 13, 1980), pp. 103–6; Baker, "Frogs and Farmers"; Clifford F. Smith, "Land Reform as a Pre-condition for Green Revolution in Latin America," in Bayliss-Smith and Wanmali, *Understanding Green Revolutions*, pp. 18–35; Robert W. Bradock, "Agricultural Development in Tamil Nadu; Two Decades of Land Use Change at Village Level." in Bayliss-Smith and Wanmali, *Understanding Green Revolutions*, pp. 136–72; for an example in Africa, see Sano, *Political Economy of Food*.

35. Michaela Von Freyhold, *Ujamaa Villages in Tanzania: Analysis of a Social Experiment* (London, Heinman, 1979).

36. See, for example, the discussion in Sano, *Political Economy of Food*, and the description of the experience with a "cooperative land reform" in Peru 1969–1975 in Alberts, *Agrarian Reform*, and Kay, "Agrarian Reform in Peru."

37. Radha Sinha, "Agribusiness a Nuisance in Every Respect?" *Mazingira* (1977), 3/4:16–23; for general discussions of agribusiness, see, for example, E. H. Jacoby, "Transnational Corporations and Third World Agriculture," *Development and Change* (July 1975), 6(3):90–97; for specific examples, see Sano, *Political Economy of Food*; Leonardo Castillo and David Lehman, "Agrarian Reform and Structural Change in Chile 1965–1969," in Ghose, *Agrarian Reform*, pp. 240–70; Buarque de Hollanda, in Alschuler, *Dependent Agricultural Development*; Gary A. Hawes, "Southeast Asian Agribusiness: The New International Division of Labour," *Bulletin of Concerned Asian Scholars* (October–December 1982), 14(4):20–30.

38. See, for example, Gail Amvelt, "Capitalist Agriculture and Rural Classes in India," *Bulletin of Concerned Asian Scholars* (July–August 1983), 15(3):30–55; Anthony Wilson, "The Formation of Capitalist Agriculture in Latin America and Its Relationship to Political Power and State," *Comparative Studies in Society and History* (January 1983), 25(1):83–104.

39. Franz Fanon, *The Wretched of the Earth* (New York, Grove Press, 1968), p. 48; for an overview of the contemporary debates, see Theda Skocpol, "What Makes Peasants Revolutionary?" in Robert P. Weller and Scott E. Guggenheim, eds., *Power and Protest in Asia, Europe, and Latin America* (Durham, North Carolina, Duke University Press, 1982), pp. 157–79.

40. Frederich Baily, *The Peasant View of the Bad Life* (Institute of Development Studies, Brighton, England) Communication No. 30, (p. 23; and Ashok K.

Upadhyaya, "Class Struggle in Rural Maharashtra: Towards a New Perspective," *Journal of Peasant Studies* (January 1980), 7(2):213–34.

41. See, for example, Fidel Castro, "Why We Didn't Divide the Latifundios," in M. Kenner and J. Petras, eds., *Fidel Castro Speaks* (Harmondsworth, England, Penguin Books, 1972), pp. 70–73. see also the comments in the conclusion of Wolfe, *Peasant Wars*, pp. 301–4; and for the difficulty of securing peasant support for "noncapitalist transformation," see the discussion in the conclusions of Klaus Ernst, *Tradition and Progress in the African Village: The Non-capitalist Transformation of Rural Communities in Mali* (London, Hurst, 1976).

42. See Peter Peek, "Agrarian Reform and Rural Development in Nicaragua, 1979–1981," in Ghose, *Agrarian Reform*, pp. 273–302.

43. See, for example, Roland Mousnier, *Furerus Paysannes: Les Paysannes dans les revoltes du XVIIIe siecle: France, Russia, China* (Paris, Calman Levy, 1967), p. 354.

44. William Beinart and Colin Bundy, "State Intervention and Rural Resistance," in Klein, *Peasants in Africa*, p. 313.

45. See the definitional discussion in Kathleen Gough, "Indian Peasant Uprisings," *Bulletin of Concerned Asian Scholars* (July–September 1976), 8(3):2–18.

46. Mehmet Beqiraj, *Peasantry in Revolution* (Ithaca, N. Y., Center for International Studies, Cornell University, 1966).

47. See, for example, Nair, *Blossoms in the Dust*.

48. For a narrative and actual historical account of the decline of social power of a kulak landlord in Bangladesh, see "Hafis, the Landlord," in Hartman and Boyce, *A Quiet Violence*, pp. 125–34.

49. For an analysis that gives this phenomenon a central place in the factors promoting change, see F. L. Tullis, *Lord and Peasant in Peru: A Paradigm of Political and Social Change* (Cambridge, Mass., Harvard University Press, 1970), p. 224. This point was also made by many Africans interviewed; see also Arnoldo Ventura, "Jamaica," in M. S. Wionczek, G. Foly, and A. van Buren, eds., *Energy in the Transition from Rural Subsistence* (Boulder, Colorado, Westview Press, 1982), pp. 109–30.

50. See, for example, Stephan Gudman, *The Demise of a Rural Economy: From Subsistence to Capitalism in a Latin American Village* (London, Routledge, 1978), especially pp. 160–63.

51. For comments of a peasant activist on the failure of peasant organization, see Frances Moore Lappe and Hannes Lorenzen, *Land Reform: Is It the Answer? A Venezuelan Peasant Speaks* (San Francisco, Institute for Food and Development Policy, 1981).

52. Huizer, "Peasant Organisations," p. 8; and, for example, Peter Singelmann, *Structures of Domination and Peasant Movements in Latin America* (London, University of Missouri Press, 1981), especially pp. 208–9.

53. See Roland Dore, *Land Reform in Japan* (Oxford, Oxford University Press, 1959); and Laurence I. Hewes, *Japan—Land and Men: An Account of the Japanese Land Reform Programme 1945–51* (Ames, Iowa, Iowa State College Press, 1955).

54. See, Russell King, *Land Reform: A World Survey* (London, Bell, 1977), p. 209.

55. International Labor Organization, the Food and Agricultural Organization, and the World Bank have all had policies encouraging the formation and operation of moderate peasant organizations; see, for example, Ghai and Radwan, *Agrarian Policies*.

116 SUBSISTENCE FARMERS AND PEASANTS

56. Many of the works already cited consider the question of peasant participation in moderate or revolutionary organizations; see Hamza Alavi, "Peasants
and Revolution," in The Socialist Register 1965 (London, Merlin Press, 1965); Wolf,
Peasant Wars; Moore, Social Origins of Dictatorship. These provide broad discussions, the cases of China, India, Russia, and Cuba being most frequently cited; for
more recent case studies, G. White, R. Murray, and C. White, eds. Revolutionary
Socialist Development in the Third World (Brighton, England, Wheat Sheaf Books,
1983).

57. Alavi, "Peasants and Revolution," pp. 314–15.

58. See Ralph Thaxton, "Mao Zedong, Red Miserables and the Moral Economy
of Peasant Rebellion in Modern China," in Weller and Guggenhiem, Power and
Protest, pp. 132–56.

59. Gough, "Indian Peasant Uprisings"; Alavi, "Peasants and Revolution."

60. Michael Adas, "Bandits, Monks, and Pretender Kings: Patterns of Peasant
Resistance and Protest in Colonial Burma: 1826–1941," in Weller and Guggenheim,
Power and Protest, pp. 75–105.

61. See Fred Halliday, "The Peoples Republic of Yemen: The Cuban Path in
Arabia," in White, Murray, and White, Revolutionary Socialist Development, pp.
25–74; and David Wield, "Mozambique—Late Colonialism and Early Problems of
Transition," in White, Murray, and White, Revolutionary Socialist Development,
pp. 75–113.

62. Some writers attribute this to the idea that aspects of peasant-lord relations produce politically conservative attitudes as, for example, the case of indebtedness; see the discussion of this latter issue in Brass, "Class Formation"; see also
the discussion of the relationship between political perspective and the economic
aspects of peasant production in Samuel L. Popkin, The Rational Peasant: The
Political Economy of Rural Society in Vietnam (Berkeley, University of California
Press, 1979).

63. See,for example, the account of the arrival of wage labor to agricultural
community in Gudman, Demise of a Rural Economy.

64. This is the concluding argument of Skocpol, "What Makes Peasants
Revolutionary?"

65. See, for example, the discussion of the different consciousness via interpretation of the same event (the Green Revolution) of "poorer peasants" and landless laborers in James C. Scott, "History According to the Winners and Losers," in
A. Turton and S. Tababe, History and Peasant Consciousness in South East Asia
(Osaka, National Museum of Ethnology, 1984), pp. 161–210; many of the works
already cited examine aspects of peasant political consciousness and attitudes in a
manner that allows for distinction between the various subordinate workers in the
social relations of production found in agriculture; see, for example, Gudman,
Demise of a Rural Economy; Hartmann and Boyce, A Quiet Violence; Adas, "Bandits,
Monks"; Lappe and Lorenzen, Land Reform.

Part 2

Urban Marginals and Unorganized Wage Workers

The two forms of social relations of production discussed in the two chapters of this part cover a variety of workers ranging from those in sporadic employment or own-account activities to those with regular work in small enterprises or workshops. In most discussions, studies, and accounts all these workers are considered within one category or at least intermingled in a variety of concepts and schemes. The purpose of this brief introduction is to consider such concepts and categorizations, distinguish them from the approach adopted here, and examine the possibility of making a more meaningful and, it is hoped, perceptually more accurate disaggregation based on a multiple social relations of production approach.

The subordinate producers within the two forms of social relations discussed in this part are subjected to the power of the casual and irregular purchaser of labor and the employer paying wages for continuing work performed within the framework of an enterprise. For reasons discussed later the workers in the first form of social relations—the primitive labor market—may be called urban marginals, and those in the second—the enterprise labor market—the unorganized wage workers.

The bulk of the producers within these social relations are in the countries of the third world that are pursuing the dependent capitalist path of development and industrialization. But enterprise labor market relations are found almost everywhere and are assuming an even greater importance in industrialized countries in the contemporary period.

Like people working in the rural areas, those working in urban and industrial circumstances (which is the case of most producers within these two forms of social relations of production) have been subjected to blanket appellations that create a false impression of homogeneity among the populations concerned and therefore represent distortions of reality.[1] Because such appellations have often been derived from the historical experiences of the currently industrialized countries, it is the third-world urban populations that have been more subjected to categorizations and countercategorizations emerging from both marxist and nonmarxist perceptions.

Disaggregation of the urban poor (to select for the moment one of the many names used) has often been attempted but more on the basis of material, occupational, spatial, or class criteria. These attempts have usually emerged either from the positivist search for concreteness, to be able to count or objectify, or merely from an ethnocentric transposition of categories derived from different social circumstances at different points in historical development. Such would be the case, for example, of the description of "unemployed" or the "lumpenproletariat" to describe the urban poor; both the traditional marxist and nonmarxist approaches to the urban poor can then be faulted for attempting to fit current third-world urban populations into preexisting categories.

URBAN MASSES

Within marxist-oriented literature at least the following appellations for the urban poor can be found—masses, urban masses, marginal masses, broad masses, laboring poor, urban peasants, urban marginals, subproletarians, subpopulations, protoproletarians, and lumpenproletariat. The reason for the development of so many names for the same section of the population stems largely from the problem of trying to fit the existing social reality of a third-world city into an almost ideal-type two-class model. Marx's implied transition from "rural idiocy" to that of "wage slave" has not occurred so smoothly in the contemporary third world as it did in the last century in Western Europe, and hence the appellations listed here are conceptual dustbins created for those people perceived to be stuck between peasant and worker.

There are basically three marxist attempts at disaggregation that need to be discussed in more detail: petty commodity production, industrial reserve army, and marginality.

Petty commodity production is the marxist transitional mode of production found between feudalism and capitalism and corresponds in essence to the production of goods on a small scale, that is, artisanal or workshop-type industrial production. It therefore has little room for the production of services and, in consequence, for the individual, such as a domestic servant, who forms such a large part of the labor force of any contemporary labor-surplus social formation. Nor, for the same reason, is there a place in the petty commodity production mode for the inactives, partially employed, or women producing household services within a family.

For these latter reasons and others the concept has had to be refined, defined, expanded, and contracted in order to try and make it fit the contemporary third world. It has been said, for example, that the petty commodity mode encompasses, at the same time, wage and salary workers for small-scale operations, self-employed owners of capital, unpaid family laborers, casual workers in wage sector employment, and quasi-wage-earning journeymen.[2] Such a definition still excludes own-account activities, inactives, and household service production, and yet at the same time it includes such disparate workers as a wage employee in a small enterprise and a child helping in a shop. Hence, any possibility of discussion of consciousness and dynamics emerging from the mode is rendered impossible.

The residual marxist category between that of the capitalist mode and the petty commodity mode would be the "industrial reserve army." While a reserve of unemployed labor, the presence of which depressed general wage rates and to which employers could resort for further labor, was a factor in the industrializing process in the United Kingdom in the nineteenth century, its importance is more doubtful in the contemporary third-world situation—a point that will be discussed in the next chapter.

Furthermore, almost any current definition of reserve army would have to include the inactives; the partially employed; casually employed service workers, such as prostitutes and domestic servants; and women workers in household production. Thus the workers within the industrial reserve army would have such a teeming variety of power relations surrounding their production that the concept could serve only as a mechanistic labor market concept in which labor is seen to be a homogeneous factor of production.

Finally, there is is the concept of marginality, which was developed by marxists but has also been used more widely.[3] Marginality may be seen as a concept derived from the inadequacy of the petty commodity mode and the industrial reserve army to describe the desperately poor engaged in a wide variety of actives and concentrated within third-world cities. Derived from a description of marx in which "margin" had a material connotation—the poor were at "the margins of existence"—it has been extended to include a marginality to politics and economics of the social formation, as well as to a marginal psychic condition. The more extreme positions, which redefiped marginality as irrelevant and the psychic condition as an internalized acceptance of poverty and subjugation, have been subjected to widespread criticism and rejected.[4] Furthermore, when marginals are said or implied to be a combination of the industrial reserve army and those in petty commodity production, then the description "urban marginals" is as misleading as all other such aggregations. If, however, the term is used narrowly and descriptively to indicate those people without, or at the margins of, more regular employment and who thereby often live equally at the margins of legality as defined by the wider society and at the margins of habitable urban space, then the term, although not the concept, can be retained.[5] The people caught by the narrow use of this term are indeed those who wold normally be within the primitive labor market form of social relations.

The marxist concepts in general and as traditionally developed in relation to the third-world urban poor then offer little potential for disaggregation. Breaking free from this tradition, but still using the concept of social relations of production in one of its several meanings adopted by Marx, is one way to produce a more meaningful appreciation of the power dynamics and consciousness among the urban poor.

INFORMAL SECTOR

Conventional nonmarxist designations for the unprotected workers of industry and town are no better than the traditional marxist concepts. Inasmuch as the conventional nonmarxist paradigms are often able to ignore the questions of power and class entirely, then the possibility of analyzing change arising from the dynamics of power relations surrounding production is normally completely excluded.

For some years the urban poor were described either as "unemployed" or "service sector" workers. The first description was a direct transposition of a category from the industrialized countries; in the third world it had little meaningful applicability, there being so little structured employment from which to become unemployed, while, in contrast, there were a vast range of activities that fell between structured regular employment and total inactivity. The "service sector" idea served as a neoclassical economists' dustbin for all those who could not be included in the statistics of·employment in the industrial or agricultural sectors. It was for some time almost a euphemism for the crushing poverty and service-rendering conditions of the people who lived in third-world slums.[6] Toward the end of the 1960s it became apparent that these categories did not adequately describe the conditions for positivist research. Thus, although a sectoral analysis was not abandoned, there were discussions of such concepts as the "invisible" or "murky" sectors.[7] Such blocks of populations were, however, invisible or indistinct only to those who viewed the teeming slums through the three-sector binoculars of the neoclassical economists and peered at the service sector from the elevated vantage point of the "modern," "monetary," or industrial sector.

It is not surprising then that by the early 1970s another sector, other than the service sector, had to be invented in order to keep a sectoral analysis alive. Thus the informal sector was introduced and promoted by international agencies.[8] The informal sector tended to be defined in terms of employment structures; all those people who were not formally, structurally employed were in the informal sector. In physical production terms the informal sector covered production that occurred outside of visible, formal organizations subjected to the laws and policies of the state. In some earlier discussions the informal sector covered all so-called informal activities, from occasional street trading to artisanal production. But after its use in policy discussions it has increasingly come to mean an informal manufacturing sector—the production of goods in small enterprises or artisanal workshops. In this restricted sense the informal sector covers workers within the enterprise labor market form of social relations, that is, workers within an enterprise, employed, subject to the power of employers but not in unions or otherwise easily protected by state legislation—the unorganized wage worker.

As the informal sector gravitated toward being a description of the production, and occasionally the conditions, of the unorganized wage worker, other concepts had to be launched in order to deal with the persistent residue of irregular nonwage workers. One of these was the notion of the "casual poor." Although the concept mixes a material criterion "poor" and a work structure "casual" it nevertheless comes close to the marginal concept, or the workers of the primitive labor market.[9]

Like the marxist concepts devised to describe the activities observed among the urban poor in the third world, the informal sector has been subjected to much criticism, especially for a misplaced emphasis on the lack of organization of production and for its being seen as a distinct, rather than an integral part of a national economy.[10] The criticism here is in addition that, despite redefinitions and attempts to restrict its scope, it still covers a multiplicity of social relations of production,[11] policies applied to the informal sector will always then fall differentially on the self-employed, the urban marginals, and the unorganized wage workers who are normally trapped within it.[12]

SOCIAL RELATIONS
OF PRODUCTION
IN TOWN AND INDUSTRY

There have been some attempts at disaggregation of the urban poor and the unprotected worker in town and industry in the third world that imply social relations of production. One author using class criteria identifies three classes—petty bourgeoisie, subproletariat, and paupers—that may well correspond to producers within three distinct social relations.[13] Others have identified types of casual work, segments of the labor force, or forms of labor power that have social relations of production implications.[14] The problem with most such attempts is that they go either backward from class to social relations or forward from work structures or labor force segments to social relations. They cannot then make power relations surrounding production the source of dominant and subordinate groups, of consciousness, contradictions, and dynamics that produce change.

In adopting the multiple social relations of production approach of this study, it can be noted that of the twelve forms or modes of social relations identified, eight are found in urban and industrial situations within capitalist social formations. Workers within them have different degrees of power over their production, conditions of work, and distribution of the product. At the upper end of the power scale are the workers in powerful unions, within corporations, state employment, or under state protection—namely the established workers of the corporate forms of bipartite, tripartite, enterprise corporatist, or state corporatist social relations. At the lower end of the power scale are the unprotected workers associated with four different forms of social relations, two of which are the subject of the two chapters in this part.

These workers are, first, the mass of unskilled, partially or totally unemployed people usually living in an urban slum.

When such people find work it is of a casual, temporary kind, and employers are individual purchasers of services or goods. Social relations are diffuse and fragmented, and any purchaser of labor has absolute power based on the overabundant supply of persons competing for the sale of labor. Such workers have their counterparts in the rural areas as casual or seasonal laborers. Second, are those employed in the small-to-medium industrial enterprises who have no job security and little collective power. The power relations within such enterprises are characterized by a preponderant employer power over employment, conditions of work, and wages. Employer power is, however, tempered by the more restricted labor market for the skills necessary for the enterprise and the need for a stability of employment to achieve higher productivity. Third, are the self-employed, defined as those who have achieved some stability and regularly produce for a market. Finally women producing household services and engaged in childbearing and childbearing; power relations are within a household (However that may be culturally defined), and women are usually subordinate in their production to the men in the household.

The social relations sketched above have been called the primitive labor market, enterprise labor market, self-employment, and household forms. To illustrate vividly the juxtaposition of these social relations and the possible movement of individuals between them, an example may be used that takes actual elements of existing conditions to make a composite case history. Such an example would be a woman and her family in North India who are forced to leave the countryside through the pressures of peasant-lord relations in order to settle and seek work in the city. Upon their entry to the town they are supported to some extent by relatives, and the woman finds work as a domestic servant. She has become a partially or casually employed person within the primitive labor market. Any buyer of her labor as a domestic servant or casual laborer on construction has virtually absolute power over the terms and conditions of her work, for there are so many other women, permanently or transiently in the city, anxious to sell their labor. A friend of a cousin starts a small sewing shop and occasionally employs her as a cleaner after she has finished her work as a servant and satisfied the demands of her children and husband. The proximity to sewing machines, the possibility of practice on a friend's machine, and submission to the sexual demands of the entrepreneur eventually result in her getting a job in the expanding enterprise. She has become a worker in the enterprise labor market receiving a regular wage but under threat of uncompensated dismissal at any time. After the first few days at work her production equals or surpasses that of some of the others, and the employer has an interest in keeping her regularly employed; he does not want the bother of finding or training another worker and fears that any replacement may not be such a fast or cooperative worker. His power is thus tempered by the labor market for the more scarce skill of sewing. For purposes of further illustration an improbable event may be assumed in that she acquires her own sewing machine and starts making clothes for children of richer persons. Her style is distinctive and a friend of an aunt can supply cheap cloth. She develops a market for a single dress, she keeps her production methods secret, and refuses to employ anyone to help her. She has thus become self-employed, and her social relations of production are between those who buy her clothes and those who supply the cloth. Her skill in balancing these in order to acquire the maximum power and therefore the maximum return for her work is what keeps her self-employed. During the whole of these developments she has borne and cared for her children and yielded to her husband's demands for a large family and the traditional services of women within the household form of social relations.[15]

Each of these different circumstances and different forms of social relations of production produces different material conditions and different levels and types of consciousness, but they all have a common element; in each the woman in question is basically unprotected against the power of employers, customers, controllers of markets, husbands, or family. No organization, state agency, or group of individuals intervenes effectively on her behalf to protect her from even the harshest and most arbitrary exercises of power. She has little chance of altering the conditions of work within any of the patterns of power relations although she may, as has been shown, move from one to another and acquire some positive change in material benefits.

PRIMITIVE AND ENTERPRISE
LABOR MARKET
SOCIAL RELATIONS

In this part on the urban marginal and unorganized wage worker only the first two forms of social relations, corresponding to the Indian woman's work as a casual construction worker and a seamstress in the garment enterprise, are considered. These two forms can be subjected to some general remarks.

First, and by far the most important, is that the workers in them are in a labor market in the sense that they individually offer their ability to work either to other individuals, as is often the case in the primitive labor market, or to enterprises, as in the enterprise labor market. They also sell their labor directly in the form of services and occasionally as goods when there is irregular individual production—for example, when food is prepared within the household for sale but the sales are not regular or structure enough to give rise to self-employment social relations. The detailed nature of these labor markets and the reason for their names are found in the following separate chapters.

Second, these two forms are spatially proximate. The enterprises of the enterprise labor market are found within, and the workers often dwell within, the principal habitat of the primitive labor market workers. Thus any urban slum in the third world is populated by both the marginals of the primitive labor market and the unorganized workers of the enterprise labor market as well as the self-employed and women household workers.

Third, they are proximate in the social formation. The poverty and conditions of the marginals in the primitive labor market serves as a disciplining force for the workers of the enterprise labor market, ant the marginals occasionally supply personal services to both workers and employees, and the enterprise labor market represents the most immediate goal of the marginals in the search for more stable wage employment.

Further similarities and linkages are less clear. Class linkages are especially problematic; the employers of the enterprise labor market may also be the users of the casual labor of the primitive labor market, but so are civil servants and occasionally the higher paid workers within large enterprises or in highly skilled work. Unorganized wage workers may be considered as part of an industrial proletariat, whereas such a designation for urban marginals is less certain. In the final analysis, urban marginals and unorganized wage workers are in two different forms of social relations producing different consciousness of their situation, and any unity is achieved in the process of creating alliances rather than out of a similarity of consciousness, as will be discussed more extensively in both of the following chapters.

One important difference between the two forms that should be noted is that the primitive labor market is a phenomenon of the third world, of dependent capitalist development, whereas unorganized wage workers are found in both the industrialized and third-world countries and even in some centrally planned socialist countries.

The workers and dynamics of these two forms of social relations have acquired some contemporary importance. In the case of the primitive labor market the growth of urban centers in the third world and the raw conditions of people who live in them have meant that the future of the urban poor and the viability of the cities themselves have begun to preoccupy publics and policymakers alike. Further, political attention has switched to some extent from peasants as carriers of revolutionary change to that of the urban poor as potential supporters and determinants of the success of revolutions or, conversly, as the greatest threat to the international status quo.[16]

For the enterprise labor market two issues are of current concern. First is the role that the enterprise labor market social relations, especially the variant associated with the small enterprise, can play in the industrialization process in the third-world countries. Subsumed under discussions of the "informal sector," the power relations between enterpreneurs and unorganized wage workers in small enterprises become the policy focus of industrialization within the framework of capitalist development. Second, as union membership has declined in the already industrialized countries, more and more industrial workers are finding themselves in enterprises without unions, subject directly to employers' power. In the case of illegal or underground activities by enterprises, the state may also be excluded from monitoring the conditions of work. These developments herald the reemergence of the unprotected worker in large numbers in social formations in which there had been a progressive decline in the numbers of such workers over the past half century.[17]

NOTES

1. Inasmuch as such distortions impede the efficiency of reformist change or revolutionary strategy, the author has labeled them elsewhere as "concepts against change." See Jeffrey Harrod, "Informal Sector and Urban Masses; a Social Relations of Production Approach' (The Hague, Institute of Social Studies, 1980), mimeo.

2. Caroline O. N. Moser, "Informal Sector or Petty Commodity Production: Dualism or Dependence in Urban Development," World Development (1978), 6(9/10):1041−64. Some rethinking of the use of the concept is evidenced by Jacques M. Chevalier, "There is Nothing Simple about Simple Commodity Production," Journal of Peasant Studies (July 1983), 10(4):153−86.

3. See, for an example of the original use of the concept, Rodolfo Stavenhage, "Marginality, Participation and Agrarian Structure in Latin America," Bulletin of International Institute for Labour Studies (June 1970), No. 7:57−92.

4. For a critique of the use of the concept to exclude marginals from processes of exploitation, see Janice E. Perlman, The Myth of Marginality Urban Poverty and Politics in Rio de Janeiro (Berkeley, University of California Press, 1976); for a review of the criticisms but the retention of the use of "urban marginal," see Manuel Castells, "Squatters and Politics in Latin America:A Comparative Analysis of Urban Social Movements in Chile, Peru, and Mexico," in Helen Safa, ed. Towards a Political Economy of Urbanisation in Third World Countries (Delhi, Oxford University Press, 1982), pp. 250−80.

5. See this definition in, for example, Gino Germani, Marginality (New Brunswick, New Jersey, Transaction Books, 1980), and Colin Murray, "Struggle ffrom the Margins: Rural Slums in the Orange Free State," in Frederick Cooper, ed., Struggle for the City: Migrant Labor, Capital, and the State in Urban Africa (Beverly Hills, Calif. Sage, 1983), pp. 275−315.

6. See, for example, R. S. Mathur, "Economic Development and the Tertiary Sector," Indian Journal of Industrial Relations (July 1972), 8(1):31−45.

7. See, on the "murky" sector, G. S. Fields, Rural-Urban Migration, Urban Unemployment and Underemployment and Job Search Activities in Less Developed Countries (New Haven, Conn., Yale University Economic Growth Center, 1972), p. 11.

8. See, for example, Employment, Incomes and Equality: A Strategy for Increasing Productive Employment in Kenya (Geneva, International Labor Office, 1972).

9. See R. Bromley and C. Gerry, eds., Casual Work and Proverty in Third World Cities (New York, Wiley, 1979).

10. See, for example, Gerard Salem, "De la Calabasse a la Production en Serie: Les Reseaux Commerciaux Laobe au Senegal et en France," in Cooper, Struggle for the City, pp. 245–6.

11. For an example of the all-inclusive use of the informal sector for the urban poor, see Nirmala Banerjee, "Survival of the Poor," in Safa, Towards a Political Economy, pp. 195–246 and for a critique of the concept for its lack of precision see Harrod, "Informal Sector and Urban Masses" and Priscilla Connolly, "The Politics of the Informal Sector: A Critique," in Nanneke Redclift and Enzo Mingione, Beyond Employment: Household, Gender and Subsistence (London, Blackwell, 1985), pp. 55–91.

12. For a similar argument in relation to the blanket concepts within agricultural sector, see discussions in James C. Scott, "History According to Winners and Loser," in A. Turton and S. Tanabe, eds., History and Peasant Consciousness in South East Asia (Osaka, National Museum of Ethnology, 1984), pp. 161–210.

13. Jan Bremen, "A Dualistic Labour System? A Critique of the 'Informal Sector' Concept," Economic and Political Weekly (November-December 1976), 11(48, 49, 50).

14. Bromley and Gerry, Casual Work and Poverty; John Friedman and Flora Sullivan, "The Absorption of Labour in the Urban Economy; the Case of Developing Countries," Economic Development and Cultural Change (April 1974), 2(3):385–413; see also the attempt to arrive at social relations via analogies to conventional industrial relations in Chris Birkbeck; "Self-Employed Proletarians in an Informal Factory: The Case of Cali's Garbage Dump," World Development (1978), 6(9/10):1173–85; see also an attempt to use the distinction between the selling of labor power and the selling of one's body to highlight the social relations in Castells, "Squatters and Politics," pp. 234–35.

15. This account was constructed from academic and journalist reports and confirmed by scholars from the area.

16. See, for example, "An Age of Nightmare Cities," Newsweek (Oct. 31, 1983), pp. 26–33; David Drakakis-Smith, Urbanisation, Housing and the Development Process (London, Croom Helm, 1981); on stability and status quo, see Henry Bienen, "Urbanization and Third World Stability," World Development (July 1984), 12(7):661–92.

17. See, for example, M. Harper, Small Business in the Third World: Guidelines for Practical Assistance, (Chichester, England, Wiley, 1984); on increasing numbers of unprotected workers in an industrialized economy, see for example, Robert Taylor, Workers and the New Depression (London, Macmillan, 1982).

CHAPTER 4

PRIMITIVE LABOR MARKET SOCIAL RELATIONS

In most large urban areas of the third world many hundreds of thousands of people scour the city in search of income derived from an immense variety of activities such as car washing, car minding, shoe cleaning, hawking, number running, domestic service, casual prostitution, gardening, tire repairing, and casual laboring, to name but a few from the total range. There are others who live by theft, extortion, or begging and those who have no basic work activity at all, are sick, disabled, and supported by networks of relatives or households.

These people are typical of those whose lives are governed by the primitive labor market form of social relations of production. They have no continuous or stable structure of power surrounding their work, they are at the mercy of the individual purchaser of labor who has virtually absolute power; no state agency or worker organization intervenes on their behalf. They are impoverished, exploited, dominated, and subordinate without there being an immediately distinguishable group that controls production and distributes surplus, as for example, the landlords do in peasant-lord relations or employers in enterprise labor market relations.

There are perhaps more than 250 million people in the world whose lives and work are governed by such relations. They are found in almost every country of the third world following a capitalist developmental path and also even in some countries that have adopted socialist development. *Favelas, villas miserias, barrios, bidonvilles,* shantytowns, and dungles are some of the names that have been given to the symbol of their existence— the urban slum; these names and others like them stand in testimony to the diversity of cultural and geographic circumstances in which the primitive labor market worker is found. Thus those trapped within these social relations usually have to contend not only with the personal aspects of material poverty but also with the polluted and degrading conditions of modern city slums.

Because such people are at the fringes of regular employment, often live at the periphery of normally habitable urban areas, frequently engage in activities on the borders of what is considered to be legal, and are always near the physical margins of existence, they have been called the urban marginals.[1] Perhaps even more than the peasant they have become the world symbol of absolute poverty.

The central focus of this chapter on the primitive labor market social relations is that of the urban marginal who represents the core condition of a worker in this form of social relations. However, a rural version of the urban primitive labor market is developing rapidly with landless laborers as the subordinate workers. The past decades of changes in third-world agriculture and the destruction of peasant-lord relations in favor of enterprise-farms employing wage laborers has led to the large increases in the numbers of landless laborers.[2] Many of these migrate to the cities, as they have done in the past, and enter the primitive labor market, but increasingly many now stay in the rural areas, while yet others oscillate between urban casual work and casual wage labor on farms, some even from an urban rather than a rural base.[3] In this chapter any consideration of landless laborers is based on their condition as embryonic urban marginals, but this does not preclude the possibility that a new form of social relations of production is forming or already in existence surrounding the special nature of power relations between employing farmers on enterprise farms and their seasonal, casual laborers.[4]

The interest in such urban marginals, as represented by the degree of attention they have received in written accounts and in the policy discussions of globally operating organizations, shows a pattern in the second half of the twentieth century similar to that relating to peasants: it has tended to change in apparent accordance with the importance placed upon the perceived role of this section of the population in the fermentation of social unrest. Toward the end of the 1970s the image of revolutionary demonology changed in the centers of world power. The rapid growth of third-world urbanization, the 1968 ghetto-based violence of the black poor in the United States, the cult of the urban guerrilla in Western Europe, and the activity of third-world urban-based revolutionary groups, particularly in Latin America, changed the imagery of the revolutionary from the peasant-under-arms attacking cities from without to the urban guerrilla boring and bombing from within.

Partly as a consequence of this shift in attention, the writing on slums and the politics and economies of slum dwellers has greatly expanded. Prescription, in analogy to land reform for the peasant, began to be developed for the workers of the primitive labor market. The International Labor Organization's launching of the "informal sector" concept around 1972, for example, precipitated a large number of data-oriented studies of the social conditions of primitive labor market workers, as did the World Bank's (IBRD) policy concerned with the so-called self-employed entrepreneur of the slums.[5]

Whereas the basic power relations of the primitive labor market (as is discussed later in this chapter) have long been in existence, the more recent attention given to the material conditions of, and planner policies for, the slum areas revealed many of the details necessary for a clearer picture of the dynamics and consciousness of this form of social relations. Such details are especially necessary in an examination of the primitive labor market social relations because they are invariably confined to the individual level, although they are still social inasmuch as they concern production and work that takes place in a social circumstance.

The purchaser of labor has almost absolute power, first, to purchase the labor offered or not and, second, to set the conditions of work and the price paid for labor used. This power rests partly on the absence of permanent organizational structure in which production takes place (which prevents any state intervention or the growth of worker organization) and, above all, on the ability of employers to secure other workers prepared to supply the goods and services at lower cost or under less stringent conditions.

The primitive labor market is then a buyers' market. The epitome of work here is that performed by a small boy in Mexico selling chewing gum to traffic-bound car drivers, the crowd of would-be bag carriers in India's railway stations, the men in Egypt fighting over who should watch over a parked car and secure a guardian's fee, the beggars in Guatemala displaying their sores, or the itinerant *sampaquita* flower sellers in the Philippines. These latter have a high public visibility and are familiar figures in all images of third-world poverty, but primitive labor market social relations exist outside of the public view and govern casual laborers and domestic servants, as well as gangs engaged in illegal activities such as procuring and distributing stolen goods or running protection rackets. Casual labor begins to be institutionalized; in India women may work as casual laborers on and off for more than twenty years interspersed with domestic service.[6] In the oil-rich countries of the Arab world, migrants for construction company occupy slums or are camped to facilitate what one writer has described as a "rent-a-slave" system since the status of the worker is close to that of a "temporary chattel."[7]

The conventional distinguishing characteristics of those within the primitive labor market relations compared with other urban workers in other forms is that they have no regular wage employment or any stable or guaranteed income derived from their activities. The broadest conventional categorization of primitive labor market workers is "casual workers." But there are also a number of activities that cannot easily be conventionally described as work and in which work is separated from production. Thus theft and begging are work, that is, expenditure of energy for the individuals concerned, and beggars or thieves can therefore be considered as workers, yet no direct commodity or service results except perhaps that of income redistribution. There are also those who are permanently or temporarily between casual work who are supported by friends and family and neither work nor produce—in the transposed terminology of other times and societies these would be the "unemployed."[8]

There are then essentially three groups of workers within primitive labor market relations—the inactives, the casually or partially employed, and the casual "own-account" worker. Each of these categories departs from conventional definitions and official statistics, and for the purpose of further discussion some explanation is needed.

Inactives is the term preferred for those people, although they are few, who are in receipt of support and do not work and produce. Inactives appear everywhere in the social formation as dependents—the very young, very old, or infirm—but they are numerically more important within the primitive labor market, for they can include healthy individuals who are unable to find any employment at all. The casually or partially employed are the more typical of the primitive labor market, and their definition here is close to conventional usage.

The designation "casual own-account workers" is used to describe the casual, unstructured, irregular, and time-limited relationships such as those surrounding the work of gum sellers, bag carriers, and car guardians mentioned earlier. The term is needed in order to depart from the sometimes conventional designation of such people as "self-employed." The description of self-employed in this book is reserved for those people who have regular, stable, and longer term relations, particularly with the suppliers of needs for their production and the buyers of the good or service. These relations are distinct enough to be a separate form of social relations and are discussed in a later chapter. But because the distinction between own-account workers in the primitive labor market and the self-employment relations is one of the degree of power the individual can acquire over supplier or buyer, only detailed analysis of each case can indicate the stage to which the power relations have evolved.

The proximate forms of social relations to the primitive labor market are the peasant-lord, from which the casual worker has usually migrated; the enterprise labor market, to which the worker migrates on finding wage labor (unless he/she is lucky enough to secure establishment worker status within enterprise corporatist or tripartite relations); and self-employment. As with the case of the transition from own-account to self-employed, the line between them is indistinct. Thus, a casual worker of the primitive labor market working temporarily and briefly within an enterprise is at the mercy of the employer because of the latter's ability, at no cost or inconvenience, to replace one casual worker with another more desperate for employment; the development of an individual or collective power in which the employer finds it a more costly process to sustain a high rate of labor turnover implied by casual work may be a slow and incremental process. The enterprise use of new technology, external changes in the availability of labor, or the personal acquisition of skill by a worker may begin to undermine the employer's absolute power over casual workers and so change the power relations toward the enterprise labor market pattern. The individual, unstructured nature of primitive labor market power relations means that there are more workers than in other forms who are at the margins of different patterns of power relations—a characteristic that has made such power relations and people to be the most difficult to study, classify, and incorporate into theories of state or society.

The workers in the primitive labor market are within a labor market in the sense that any preexisting attachment to the land has been dissolved or is in the process of dissolution—they now have only their labor to sell.[9] The labor market is "primitive" in several ways. First, the relationship between buyer and seller of labor is unaffected by any meaningful intervention of law, formal organization, or individual bargaining power based on a marketable skill. There are no trade unions, cooperatives, or powerful associations that enter the employment relationship. State labor legislation may exist but is either deliberately not enforced or is unenforceable in the conditions of diffuse, individual, and casual labor. Any such intervention or regulation would normally create a more complicated and sophisticated labor market—without them the market remains primitive.

Second, it is primitive in the sense that any production of goods and services that does take place is achieved with the most rudimentary of technology and virtually no capital. Third, it is primitive because, at least from the industrial standpoint, workers generally sell muscle power rather than a skill.

From the viewpoint of employers and others with wealth and power the primitive labor market workers are considered as unskilled, undifferentiated, and interchangeable units of labor.

Skills do exist, however, but they are more in relation to the way an individual copes with the conditions of dire poverty. Employers do differentiate between workers but use physical rather than skill criteria, as for example, when younger persons are preferred for casual work or prostitution, or people of a certain race as servants, because of their claimed aesthetic appearance, such as the Nubians from Upper Egypt and Sudan as domestics in Egypt, or children for street vending because of their supposed poignant appeal. Nevertheless, relative to most urban-industrial employment the primitive labor market worker is the least skilled, and any acquisition of a marketable skill (such as the Indian woman learning to be a seamstress in the earlier example) would mean an individual migration to different forms of social relations of production.

The people left within the primitive labor market area are, then, those who are unable to migrate, or who are prevented from migrating, to more skilled and better paid work. Thus the primitive labor market is maintained partly by a discriminatory process based on race, ethnicity, physique, and social characteristics that prevents people from securing regular work. Within it are found a disproportionate number of the physically infirm, the mentally retarded, the social outcasts, and worker-children. People of the primitive labor market are often distinguishable from the rest of the population by race, tribe, ethnicity, or language: the Amerindians in Mexico, Bolivia, and other Latin American cities; the southerners in the Philippines; the Malays in Singapore; the untouchables in India; and the Yoruba of Lagos, Nigeria, are typical examples.[10] Whenever a primitive labor market has begun to develop at the fringes of state regulation in contemporary Western Europe or North America it has been peopled by racial or ethnic minorities: the black minority and illegal Mexican migrants in the United States, new Commonwealth and southern European migrants in the United Kingdom, Algerians in France, Turkish and Italian migrants in Germany and Switzerland—in short, all those without full legal rights or who are in other ways sufficiently socially or physically disabled as to be easily excluded from state regulation and regular employment.

Sometimes social or physical disability sustains primitive labor market relations in circumstances that would normally give rise to different social relations. Children who are regularly employed in industrial enterprises would, if they were adults, normally be able to develop individual or collective power based upon their acquirement of skills and the regularity of their production. It is possible to keep them on a casual basis and with no power mainly because they are children. The entrepreneur employing them, as in the case of the widespread use of girls between the age of eight and twelve in the Moroccan carpet industry, secures primitive labor market wages in circumstances that would normally give rise to the more costly enterprise labor market wages and conditions.[11]

The migrations from peasant-lord relations, transformations in the rural areas, high birth rates, and structural blocks to other social relations and employment mean that the primitive labor market is in chronic disequilibrium stemming from an oversupply and underdemand for the type of labor available. As a result there is no downward limit to prices for the goods, services, and labor offered by those so anxious to sell to too few buyers. Income can be well depressed below that necessary to sustain the lives of the worker or children of the workers— sometimes known as the state of superexploitation; in the Tondo slum area of Manila in the Philippines, 80 percent of families or more than 150,000 persons had income below the subsistence level in the mid 1970s;[12] in Enugu in Nigeria the services rendered by the urban marginals are paid for at "less than the historical subsistence level living conditions" and the high death rate due to the unsanitary conditions is matched by the inflow of migrants from the rural area.[13]

Primitive labor market social relations are principally a phenomenon of the third world. The instances and analogies that exist in the industrialized countries are minor compared with the vast and growing numbers in the third world.[14]

By basing estimates on official statistics of unemployed, inactives, urban poor, and other such designations it can be said that regionally, Latin America and the Caribbean have the highest proportion, approaching 20 percent of the total regional labor force with at least 30 million people involved. In Asian and Arab countries the primitive labor market as a proportion of the labor force is lower than in Latin America, ranging from 12 to 16 percent, but the larger population means that the numbers involved reach well into the 200 millions. In Africa the percentage is lowest of the three continents but is growing faster. Some idea of the growth of the primitive labor market may also be indicated by the growth of urban slums in the world, for as the principal habitats of the lowest and most desperate of urban-based workers these are also concentrations of primitive labor market workers. There are now 1.8 billion people living in third-world cities of which at least 300 million are "squatters." If the number of third-world urban dwellers increases, as projected by United Nation's estimates, to 2.5 billion and structured employment continues to be scarce, then the numbers within primitive labor market social relations will as much as double within the next 25 years.[15]

Currently between 9 and 12 percent of the world labor force is estimated as being within primitive labor market relations. While that proportion may not seem large, it is at least twice as large as the total number of established workers.

ORIGINS AND DEVELOPMENT OF THE PRIMITIVE LABOR MARKET

In mid-nineteenth-century France, Marx observed that there were "five million who hover on the margin of existence and either have their haunts in the countryside itself, or with their rags and their children, continually desert the countryside for the towns and the towns for the countryside."[16] Observations such as this and the well-known poverty, degradation, and slums of other European countries at the time seemingly provide a historical analogy with the primitive labor market in poor countries today.[17] Europe was then, just as many poor countries are now, passing through a period of rapid population growth, of vast restructuring of urban-rural political and economic relations, and of enormous internal migrations.

The nineteenth-century European experience, however, incorporated a number of unique historical factors. During the period of the growth of the primitive labor market, Europe was able to export at least 40 million of its population increase of 100 million to the Americas.[18] Industry was labor-intensive and required large amounts of regularly employed but unskilled labor; imperialism meant captive markets for exports from these new industries. New industrial production was, in a fairly short period of time, able to absorb the inflow of population from the rural areas into regular industrial and service employment. The European poverty against which Marx, Dickens, and Zola reacted was essentially a transitional occurrence within a process of industrialization and global expansionism and a primitive labor market on the scale, and particularly with such a persistence, that is found in the third world today but was not experienced during the European industrialization process. This transitory nature of absolute poverty in the European experience encouraged some theorists of contemporary economic development to believe that the primitive labor market would disappear of its own accord as soon as industrialization took off into self-sustained growth. This model of development, so respected by the modernization theorists of the 1950s and 1960s, meant that economic development policy was directed toward rapid industrialization, regardless of the emergence of a mass of impoverished would-be workers, on the grounds that their gray and dismal conditions would be eclipsed by the glittering statistics of rapidly rising industrial output. When in many cases the output was not so glittering and in almost every case the primitive labor market did not disappear, the argument shifted from its being an unfortunate byproduct of industrialization to a not essential but nevertheless useful appendage securing a disciplined labor force and a supply of cheaper labor for labor-intensive industrialization.

In contrast, theorists who sought to apply Marx's analysis of nineteenth-century European conditions to the twentieth-century third world believed that the primitive labor market would be destroyed only by a structural change of the social formation. For them the primitive labor market was Marx's "reserve army of labor" and was an essential and integral part of economic development under capitalism. Marx originally believed that the nineteenth-century unemployed and partially employed performed three basic functions for the development of capitalism: first, they ensured a cheap reproduction of labor, as unemployed women gave birth to babies who as adults were destined to be unemployed; second, they constituted a type of "buffer stock" of labor that enabled employers to immediately expand the use of labor in response to fluctuations in product demand; and third, they ensured that labor was never scarce and therefore avoided a situation that, under pure market conditions, would have meant a rise in general wages. This latter depressant effect on general wage rates was an important part of Marx's prediction of pauperization of the mass and the downfall of capitalism through the consequent development of revolutionary consciousness of those pauperized. Marx's analysis of the causes of the primitive labor market—exodus from the rural areas, increased birth rate, and a decreasing ratio of labor to capital—certainly applies today, just as the labor reproduction function does. The labor supply and general wage depressant effect has, however, been brought into doubt. The reasons for these doubts are ironically similar to those that challenged the accuracy of the prediction of the modernization theorists that the primitive labor market would at least show signs of dissolution as industrialization advanced.

The persistence and size of the primitive labor market in third-world countries today, which confounds both traditional marxist and modernization theories, is the result of the absence of the special conditions that eventually eliminated its apparent historical analogy. In the first place, migratory possibilities, so much part of the nineteenth-century scene, have dried up. The closing of European doors to the non-European migrant workers that began in the mid-1960s had been completed by the late 1970s. Further, it is clear that total *permanent* migration from the countries of the third world to the industrialized countries of Europe and North America has never reached the scale of the nineteenth-century European migration to the Americas.

Second, rather than following industrialization, as in the case of Europe of the last century, trade unions and important levels of state employment within certain sections of the labor force have accompanied, or even preceded, the onset of industrialization in countries that currently have large primitive labor markets. This has arisen partly from the transfer of models of trade unions, established laws, procedures, and state institutions from already industrialized countries to those that were colonies or near-colonies and that were not industrialized.[19] Thus, for example, in ex-British colonies, trade unions were permitted and promoted by the British imperial administration before political parties were allowed. This policy was based on the belief that if trade unions were permitted for a minority of workers, they could be suitably steered toward a narrow nonpolitical posture and would be less subversive to the empire than political organizations.[20] These countries often started their formal independence and industrialization processes with well-established trade unions associated with political parties.[21] After independence such unions often adopted a "job protection" policy in an attempt to preserve the limited amount of regular and stable industrial employment for their members.[22] Employers sometimes concurred and encouraged this policy: in Bogota and in Cali in Colombia, union and nonunion rates for the same work are not substantially different but employers use union membership as a positive "screening" process to secure stable workers.[23]

At the same time as the establishment of trade unions the state became a major employer—another stark difference between third_orld and European industrialization. This reinforced the group of established workers with regular employment; in the cities of Malaysia public sector employment involves nearly 40 percent of the labor force and is accompanied by rigid pay scales based on educational credentials.[24] In Zaria, Nigeria, in the early 1970s road gangs permanently employed by the state earned two to three times more for the same work as the casual workers of the primitive labor market.[25]

The effect of these developments meant that an established worker protected by union and state was created early in the industrialization process, and this in turn resulted in distinct policies by both national and international dominant groups and classes. Many employers and controllers of capital did not attempt to use labor-intensive manufacturing techniques that would create the most employment but on the contrary sought to use capital-intensive processes.

All these factors created blocks to the use of the "reserve army of labor," not to mention the income distribution effects of important wage differentials for urban industrial workers for the same work.[26] The urban marginals were not then absorbed into a growing industrial employment nor were wage rates forced down to casual levels to make all seeking work available at similar rates and under equal economic conditions.[27] The primitive labor market form of social relations became established as a permanent feature of third-world capitalist social formations.

The third factor accounting for the longevity and size of the current primitive labor market stems from the integration of the industrialized sectors of third-world countries with the world market economy, which has its centers in Western Europe and North America. Arguments are made that the nature of the integration results in the preservation of urban poor in the third world as part of a global reserve army of labor to be used to depress prices of exports from such countries and increase return on investment and loans.[28] The centers of the world economy are rich in capital and technology, and the industries they have allowed to develop within the poor countries have tended to be based upon capital-intensive industrial techniques that require only a few highly skilled workers—at least when compared with the techniques used at the beginnings of industrialization at the center.[29]

Marx and others believed that the reserve army of unemployed in the nineteenth century would remain in proportion to the regularly employed labor force and that the latter would expand as capitalism and industrialism increased, even though labor used would be in declining proportion to the amount of capital. In the contemporary situation in the third world, however, capital has been substituted for labor at the beginning of the process rather than through the gradual development of labor-saving techniques, and industry has not developed in such a way as to decrease the proportionate numbers of primitive labor market workers.[30] On the contrary, the hope of work that the presence of industry induces sustains the migration from the countryside and the oversupply of workers unskilled in industrial occupations to such an extent that in some countries the numbers within the primitive labor market exceed those who have regular industrial employment.

Workers in the primitive labor market find themselves there as a result of the mixture of hope and despair that brought them, or their parents, to the urban centers in a fruitless search for regular industrial employment. They have been expelled from, or surplus to, peasant-lord relations and blocked from regular employment; they belong neither to the structured world of industrial employment nor to peasant production. From the outside they are often considered as unessential, a disposable, throwaway labor force whose best possible collective action would be to disappear. From the inside it is a question of survival in spite of the daunting social and environmental conditions.

THE SOCIAL RELATIONS
OF SURVIVAL

The individual social relations between a beggar and a kind-hearted or conscience-stricken almsgiver, between the prostitutes and client, between sweet-seller and customer, or householder and casual gardener are so disparate that they permit no structured or collective relationship uniting either subordinate or dominant individuals against each other. Yet among the subordinate primitive labor market workers there exists a wide range of social relations and structured, if informal, organizations. Most of these emerge from the overriding problems of people surviving without regular income or from the cooperation necessary to organize various income-generating activities—in short the social relations of survival.

Collective defensive reaction to a hostile environment is manifested in the variety of informal organizations that exist among primitive labor market workers. The organizations are informal in that they have no written structure or any legal personality in the larger society; they are of three distinct types— organizations that sustain or create the possibility of acquiring some income, those that establish and maintain systems of mutual self-help, and those that are for the defense or improvement of living conditions.

Examples of the organizations of the first type are the complex arrangements found in Calcutta, Mexico City, and other cities that provide designated pitches and necessary materials for shoeshine boys[31]—the loose associations of traders which determine areas of operation and, when trading is illegal, provide early warning systems against approaching police raids.[32] A particularly prevalent form for income generation are the gangs that organize theft or the sale of stolen property or run protection and extortion rackets. In Manila the collection of protection payments by transport jeep drivers is precisely organized, and drivers must display garlands of flowers (purchased from other primitive labor market workers) to demonstrate which gang is protecting them and that the money has been paid[33]; in Nigeria casual workers employed on farms and daily transported from the city established a boycott system and a name—"*daringa* men"—for farmers who cheated by lowering the casual worker rates once they were in the fields and were dependent upon the farmer's transport back to town.[34]

Another example is the youth street gang found in some slum areas. These gangs create loyalty and group cohesion by adherence to rituals, symbols, styles, and names which represent and distinguish their members.[35] They protect their members, fight skirmishes with state authority, engage in petty theft and street robbery, and have been known to force employers to allocate casual work to gang members. When these and other more sophisticated organizations rob from the rich they are providing income through an informal, violent, and minor form of income redistribution. When they are organized from the outside, as with some of the more sophisticated protection arrangements, they represent merely another type of dangerous, casual, and underpaid work typical of the primitive labor market.

The second type of organizations are those that create an informal social security system through work sharing, income sharing, or mutual help. Such organizations are usually based upon immediate family or kinship networks, although some have a social, ethnic, or religious basis. The simplest form is found where the earning member of a large or extended family or simply a household is collectively supported and encouraged in her/his activity by the others. Thus, in Lima, Peru, children between eight and twelve provide for a family through preparing and marketing of food,[36] and likewise in Bangkok child flower sellers are supported and serviced by other family members[37]; in India a household requires three earning members in the primitive labor market to support it compared with one in regular employment[38]; and Mexican women combine childbearing and child rearing with the sole provision of family income through trading.[39] But family activities of this type are often part of broader networks of relatives, that is, kin-based networks. In almost all the slums of the world researchers and observers reported such extensive kin-based networks; in Nairobi and Lagos, for example, inactive male rural migrants circulated first from one relative to another and then moved to other networks based on social contacts and friends; in Lebanon the family is the organizing base from which casual work is sought.[40]

These organizations of the second type, as well as others such as the street gangs, have been evolved to suit the needs of a population in which income from casual work and other activities shifts constantly from one person to another. Life expectancy and conditions would certainly be worse if, instead of some form of income sharing, it was the prevailing practice to return and dispense income received on an individual or narrow family base.

The third organizational form is one in which the primitive labor market worker has an unknown role, although it would be logical to assume that he or she plays an important part. These are the "civic" organizations that aim at the improvement of a particular slum or sometimes its enlargement. Squatters' movements in which new migrants from the countryside or existing slum dwellers occupy land and build their shelter in a deliberate organized fashion are worldwide phenomena. In Chile in 1970, before the election of the marxist Allende government, movements and settlements of slum dwellers were organized by political parties and trade unions and showed a high degree of efficiency in achieving their basic objective of resisting government attempts to contain the slum population.[41] Other organizations of slum dwellers emerge from a particular action, such as the occupation and protests in Mexico City in 1973 for improvement of conditions.[42] In the slums and squatters' areas of Bombay a paramilitary "civic" organization has flourished which, led by a populist figure, has organized committees in the slums with civic objectives such as waste collection, supervision of sweepers, and so forth.[43]

As urbanization increases so have the numbers of organizations whose basic objective is improvement of amenities and environment, but none of these organizations enters into social relations of production in the sense that it has meaningful impacts on power relations and therefore on the return for work performed. Although it can be argued that informal social security networks function as income distribution mechanisms making wages and payment for work more acceptable and that gangs may, on occasions, force a higher rate of pay for a particular job, such examples are minor compared with the overwhelming power of the purchaser of labor. The organizations are for the survival of the individuals in the primitive labor market and, while ameliorating their conditions, at the same time they help ensure the survival of the primitive labor market and its service to the social formation. For some commentators the promotion of such community action groups is yet another mechanism for legitimization and social control of the urban poor.[44] It is only when such organizations merge or are incorporated in a broader protest or social movement that the possibility of transforming the social relations of the primitive labor market is at stake. This latter issue is taken up in the subsequent section on transformation.

The relations between the seller and purchaser of labor within the primitive labor market thus remain fixed at the individual level, and the almost absolute power of the purchaser of labor to substitute one seller of labor with another, or not to buy the labor offered at all, remains intact. Even when there is a supposed "going rate" in money wage terms for a particular job or service, such as in the case with domestic servants, users of primitive labor market workers can usually increase working time without extra pay.[45]

The price paid for an often unessential service or good is frequently as much dependent on the sense of charity or guilt of the purchaser as on any market-or economic-cost-based price— a situation exemplified in the case of beggars. Thus the amounts demanded and received by prostitutes, bag carriers, car watchers, door openers, sweet sellers, and others vary according to the immediate situation and the nature of the purchaser, and in the case of an unrequested service, the possibility that the provider will receive nothing at all is always present. Casual labor rates bear some relationship to the general structure of wages, but primitive labor market workers are always, for one reason or another, discriminated against and receive substantially lower rates than any acceptable minimum among regular wage workers.[46]

While it might seem self-evident that an oversupply of cheaper and easily dominated labor may be desirable for those who have the wealth and power to use it, there are a number of costs that must be borne by the wider society for the perpetuation of such conditions of exploitation and poverty. Economists tend to see these costs as an underutilization of potentially productive labor while political scientists and urban sociologists see them as the development of insecure and politically unstable countries increasingly dominated by "primate," ungovernable cities. Such costs and benefits become clearer by considering the rose and place of the primitive labor market social relations within the social formation.

BENEFIT: A LABOR SURPLUS LIFE-STYLE

Dominant groups within the social formation use the primitive labor market worker in three distinct ways: as casual workers in enterprises, as cheap reproducers of labor, and as performers of individual services. First, within enterprises; some enterprises have adapted their organization of work and use of labor to maximize the use of casual labor. In adapting to a high labor turnover they avoid the costs inherent in a regular work force. In Nairobi there is a dual system of car-body repair work shops, one using established workers in a "safe" area of the city and the other situated on the fringes of the slums and using the casual labor of its inhabitants.[47] The construction industry in India also has an extensive system for the use of casual, women's labor and specifically seeks out new migrants from the countryside because they are considered "more reliable, disciplined and hardworking."[48] The construction industry in general has the highest use of casual, primitive labor market workers, for it is one of the few industries that has continued to be able to use large amounts of industrially unskilled labor.

Sometimes enterprises also use typical own-account workers rather than casual labor; in Mexico City manufacturers have used networks of street vendors to break supermarket distributive monopolies,[49] but, as with other vendors employed by enterprises, their social relations are really closer to those of the structured employment of the enterprise labor market. These are exceptions—in general, enterprise owners and managers prefer a more stable labor force sifted to exclude "troublemakers." They need workers employed on a regular basis so that productivity is enhanced from gradually developed skills and habitual integration into the process of production. Thus it is that, in Bombay, employers seek out workers with families and pay a higher rate to them because of their greater reliability, even though there is a plentiful supply of itinerant males from the primitive labor market who could do the same work at a lower rate.[50] Enterprise use of the primitive labor market is not quantitatively important.

The second use of the primitive labor market worker is more important. As long as there is some migration from the primitive labor market into industrial employment, such employers benefit by not having had to pay a contribution toward the nonproductive years of childhood. The wages of established or enterprise labor market workers usually have a "family" component in that the wage is set sufficiently high so as to support unproductive children, as well as the adult wage earner. When an adult from the primitive labor market is employed, however, the cost of his or her upbringing has often been borne by parents, relations, and members of social networks and not by the employer through the wage of the father, mother, or relative. Because the survival needs of a child are at the expense of health and shortened life of those who care for it, production is at the expense of years of life lost. Superexploitation occurs, for income is not sufficient to reproduce the labor force with reasonable life expectancy. Thus the men, and particularly the women, of the primitive labor market are, to some extent, the economic reproducers of cheap labor to be used elsewhere.[51]

The third use of the workers of the primitive labor market may be the most important; they are the suppliers of a myriad of personal services at exceptionally low cost. Thus a person with even a moderate income can afford domestic servants in countries where a primitive labor market exists, and the same applies for gardeners, prostitutes, car washers, and so on. In countries without a large labor surplus even the wealthiest citizens must perform many of these services themselves or secure them through the surrender of a large proportion of their income.

Overall, these three types of production may be "marginal" when compared with the essential nature of the production of peasants, self-employed farmers, or industrial workers; a refusal by peasants to deliver produce to a market, or by railway workers to run the trains, will produce a political crisis that would not be the case in withdrawal of the services of the primitive labor market workers. However, the importance of the primitive labor market to the social formation lies, not only directly in production, but also indirectly, in the realm of social psychology.

The benefits and services that can be derived by richer people from a proximate and overabundant labor surplus creates a distinct life-style that is revered by them for the comfort, privilege, status, and well-being it produces. In such labor-surplus countries the components of wealth are disproportionately the result of direct use of large amounts of cheap labor—servants, luxurious gardens, restaurants and hotels, domestics, cooks, nursemaids are all available at very low cost. Without these, however, a sense of wealth would be more difficult to acquire because in social formations where a primitive labor market is found, there is usually neither sufficient capital—or technology—to change the components of wealth in the direction of greater *material*, rather than *service*, consumption, at least for all except the very rich.

The services derived from labor abundance acquire psychological importance far beyond any value that would be assigned to them in national accounting statistics. The joy of a foreigner from high-cost and labor-short societies at having the privilege of the rich of labor-abundant societies is expressed in a pamphlet for American newcomers to Bombay issued by the American Womens' Club "Be a Queen for Your Stay"; it states, "your dream of having servants is about to come true."[52] To remove the services of the primitive labor market would reduce the quality of life of the richer urban dwellers to such an extent that it would shake the confidence and foundations of the social formation of which the primitive labor market is an integral part.

The primitive labor market is also an important psychological disciplining force affecting workers in other forms of social relations. The physical presence of the marginal population and the precarious conditions of life are constant reminders of the benefits of having escaped from among them. Urban marginals are a permanent negative reference group demonstrating, in stark reality, the possible penalties of losing employment. Their presence is a psychological coercion against potential organizers, political agitators, and protesters among employed workers, for to lose favor of an employer, become unemployed, and return to casual, own-account work can almost be measured in terms of numbers of years of life expectancy lost and certainly in terms of the degree of deterioration in the health of the children in the worker's family. The fear of such a drastic downward movement then disciplines labor and cements the status quo in other parts of the social formation.[53] This fear is also a part of the explanation for the established workers' desperate search for job security in order that existing poverty cannot actually be used (rather than be used psychologically) in this way; ironically, the greater the degree of their success in protecting themselves from a descent to casual work, the more rigid the divisions between workers in different social relations and the more permanent the primitive labor market.

These are some of the benefits that groups and individuals reap from the workers in, and the presence of, the primitive labor market. These benefits also show why dominant groups are less opposed to the continued presence of the slums and primitive labor market than the generalized antipoverty rhetoric would imply. But the form of social relations also produces grinding poverty and degradation for those within it that is manifested in violence and theft. The rich fear the poor of the primitive labor market because of the individual violence and sometimes the expectation of mass violence. Fear and its counterpart, repression of the object feared, thus become the hallmark of those social formations that create, permit, and/or sustain the presence of the marginal people of the slums and barrios.

COSTS: THE GARRISON SOCIETY, VIOLENCE AND REPRESSION

On the way from the airport of Manila in the direction of the center of the city the traveler can see a white-painted wooden fence of narrow planks that stands at least five meters high. It was built at the time of a Miss World contest to hide from the visiting spectators the teeming slums of the outskirts of Manila. Subsequently it served the same purpose for other visitors, including those discussing the problems of third-world poverty at the 1979 UNCTAD IV conference held in the luxurious international convention center. A similar structure, only this time in concrete, stands a few yards from the originally resplendent sports stadium in Kingston, Jamaica. It was built in the 1960s to hide, from the eyes of dignitaries visiting to the Commonwealth games, the "dungle," as it is locally known; that is, the cross between a jungle and a dungheap that is the slum of West Kingston.

In two ways these structures are symbolic of the dominant group's attitudes to the workers of the primitive labor market and other inhabitants of slums. They are symbolic, first of the fear with which slum dwellers are contemplated and, second, of the policies of rejection and repression or, occasionally, elimination.

Fear is generated by the acts of individual violence that in turn are generated by the desperate conditions of the primitive labor market workers and others.[54] The informal and individual attempts of the poor to redistribute income and wealth through violence make ownership of money or property a danger in itself. For such owners individual violence is perceived as holding out the possibility of generalized violence. For the rich this threat is, unlike that arising from peasant-lord relations, within minutes or meters of their comfortable enclaves.

One historic and traditional mechanism of alleviating fear and satisfying guilt has been the development of a self-satisfying ideology that legitimizes and excuses the existing conditions. In the nineteenth century, social Darwinism, or the ideology of the survival of the fittest, not only legitimized the presence of the urban poor but also led to their punishment for their lack of success. Poverty was the punishment for voluntary indolence, and the urban poor were accepted as inevitable by economists, church, and state; each of these latter contributed to elaborate explanations and ideologies to mitigate the fear that was felt and the moral affront that the continued presence of the poor implied. Such ideologies have not emerged in relation to the primitive labor market of the third world today. At best, reference is made to the "law of the jungle" or to the belief that, under current conditions, "someone must be poor in order that others can live properly"; at worst, explanations are racist and refer to the usually racial or ethnic distinctiveness of the very poor as compared with the rich.

As already noted, in the contemporary period, only economic theory has attempted to rationalize the presence of the primitive labor market as a necessary stage of economic development. Elsewhere the primitive labor market is said to be illegitimate, undesirable, unnecessary, and dangerous; although it is used in the ways already outlined, it is nevertheless best unmentioned and ignored, and when it impinges too heavily, it is screened with walls or attempts are made to destroy it by force or starvation. Thus, in Brazil, it is reported that government bureaucrats, with grim irony, unofficially named one of their policies "Operation Euthanasia," for its effect was to starve to death those groups (of which the primitive labor market workers of the *favelas* was only one) that were marginal to the prevailing ideas of national industrial development and modernization.[55]

The more immediate response of dominant groups to the individual violence stemming from the primitive labor market is the creation of a garrison society. In it sections of society live in fortified houses protected by guns, dogs, police, bodyguards, security guards, barbed wire, and booby traps. The walls and fences create a sense of security and hide the fact that the sometimes modern, resplendent, and apparently rich areas of the cities in the third world are but islands in a sea of poverty, both urban and rural; a labor surplus life-style precipitates a garrison living mode.[56]

The political implication of the foregoing is that those who have property and privilege to protect, be it even minor, call for a "strongman government" and support the police or any other person or organization able to "deal with" or "clean up" the violence of the streets and the seemingly fearful wave of the unwashed who, in the eyes of the privileged, may at any moment quit their shacks with the intent of violently invading the bastions of privilege.

Governments have occasionally resisted such demands in favor of reformist measures designed to limit, if not eliminate, the primitive labor market. These attempts usually founder because, in the ultimate, they require a restructuring of the social formation through changes in other forms of social relations. Thus if urban migration is to be reduced by increasing the relative well-being of the rural workers, then peasant-lord relations would have to be changed,[57] and this is very difficult without making a fundamental challenge to power structures in rural areas. If work were to be created for the unemployed or partially employed, then the nature and technology of imported industry would have to be controlled, or any existing trade unions would have to be checked in an attempt to dissolve the division between established and unprotected workers.[58]

All of these policies point to drastic changes that those who control government are either not willing or are not powerful enough to make. These difficulties demonstrate that the primitive labor market is a byproduct of other established forms of social relations too integrated in the social formation to yield to specific and particular policies of reform. So, more often than not, resort is made to the bulldozer against the settlement and to the police and the army against any recalcitrant individuals and groups.[59]

As the level of street violence rises, governments declare states of emergency and institute widespread state political control and repression; this pattern is particularly obvious in the Philippines' suspension of political rights after the state of emergency declared by the Marcos government in 1972, in the more temporary state of emergency in India in 1974, in Turkey in 1980, and in many other coups and countercoups in Latin America and Africa. Government action is often partial, physical, and sporadic, for it is essentially designed to contain the peaks of violence and ensure the safety of those who enjoy more amiable social relations.

These actions, of course, are not directed only at primitive labor market workers. Unrest and labor protest in the town or the countryside merely provide increased opportunities for the workers of the primitive labor market to redress their grievances and acquire income through street violence. Nor is it only such workers who engage in petty violence. But the perception of dominant groups is that it is among the inactives and own-account workers that some of the roots of turbulence and collective opposition lie, and although this may be a misperception, policies are still based upon it.

Successful repression of the violence is usually achieved by military or similar authoritarian governments. Single-party or single-person governments that succeed in bringing "peace to the streets" do so usually through corporatist policies. Such governments restrict social movements and politics throughout the whole society and use police and army terror to secure submission of marginal populations. Frequently, the established-unprotected worker dichotomy is formalized by bringing the politically strategic industrial worker under the umbrella of labor laws, minimum wages, and other protective legislation while, in contrast, no attempt is made to change primitive labor market and peasant-lord relations. Note then that the primitive labor market is both a cause and a characteristic of state corporatism.[60]

It now remains to examine the social responses of the primitive labor market workers to these conditions and policies, the forms of consciousness on which such responses may be based, and some existing examples of transformations.

CONSCIOUSNESS: MILLENNIALISM AND POPULISM

In attempting to provide some indications of the consciousness that arises from the contradictions and dynamics of the primitive labor market social relations of production, the problem of information and disaggregation becomes particularly acute. Neither empirical scholars nor social revolutionaries distinguish precisely the various attitudes and roles of different occupational groups and certainly do not recognize distinctions arising from different forms of social relations of production. In the analysis of movements, events, consciousness, or actions, the composition of those who make up millennialist churches, support popular leaders, occupy land, or riot is rarely considered, beyond the conventional blanket categories of working class, urban workers, masses, or unemployed. It must be remembered, therefore, that there is not sufficient information at the moment to determine the nature of consciousness and extent of participation of the primitive labor market workers in broader movements and actions. All that can be done is to consider those forms of consciousness and action that have a known historic association with primitive labor market workers as they appear in their conventional disguises—particularly as marginals, paupers, subclasses, and lumpenproletariat.

Two principal social expressions of basic consciousness associated with uprooted, rejected, low-status, desperately poor, and marginalized populations are millennialism and populism. Both of these involve vague promises of a future salvation from the existing conditions, both are associated with individual leaders and persons, and both address themselves to the lowest status and poorest sections of any society. The social-psychological aspects of these movements correspond to what is known of the world-view emerging from primitive labor market workers and what indeed might be expected from the immediate social experience of such people.

The vague and diffuse nature of the targets or causes of poverty in both millennialism and populism corresponds to the fragmented nature of primitive labor market social relations; the social relations of production do not precipitate a collective consciousness that is immediately directed toward redressing power within production or securing an immediate amelioration of conditions of work. The absence of an immediately identifiable target has already been mentioned, and the socially fragmented way in which work is done prevents a continuous relationship of solidarity or companionship based on the workplace.

There are, however, three important psychological and physical aspects of the primitive labor market worker that find expression in millennialism and populism, and these must be discussed before looking more closely at the movements themselves. First, and one rarely given sufficient emphasis, is the impact of physical conditions on action and apparent psychological attitudes. The conditions of life in slums are such that the inhabitants invariably suffer from malnutrition, irregular eating, and lack of medical facilities and sanitary services. Disease of all kinds is widespread. These conditions produce the lassitude and fatalism that observers have noted among such populations and have attributed entirely to psychological origins.[61] Infectious meningitis—a brain stem disease that is partly result of slum-type overcrowding—leaves children mentally impaired, if they recover at all; some types of undernourishment can also have detrimental mental effects. Increasingly, as industrialization proceeds, slum populations are in the highest polluted areas of cities and are at high risk to suffer the well-known mental and physical effects resulting from airborne lead pollution and environmental, water, and food contamination from industrial effluents.

The second aspect as the base of consciousness of the primitive labor market worker is the situational and psychological condition of uprootedness and marginality. Many of the workers are migrants from the countryside. They are uprooted from one life-style and plunged into another to which it bears little resemblance. Even under the best of economic circumstances, displaced and uprooted people suffer the anomie of psychological cultural conflicts, malaise, and identity crisis, that is, a feeling of a lack of belonginess, a confusion of what one is or is supposed to be, and an unfamiliarity with values and social signs of the new social circumstance.[62] In the case of the primitive labor market workers such malaise is compounded by the fact that their racial or ethnic origins are different from those of the dominant groups in the urban context. In their activities they find themselves selling their labor, their bodies, or their services to richer people who are, almost by definition, of different race. Thus the urban marginals for the Chinese in Malaya are the Malays; for the rich "brown-skins" of the Caribbean, the black people; for the Mestizo-Spanish of Latin America, the Indians; for the Arab-Egyptians, the black Nubians.[63]

The third aspect of importance in consciousness formation is more directly associated with the immediate power relations. The relationship of individual dominance and subordination is psychological, and sometimes institutionally, manifested by a prevailing master-servant relationship. The low social status of the work of the primitive labor market apparently provides confirmation of the racially promoted notion that there are persons who are fit only to be dominated and to serve. One of the principal activities of primitive labor market workers is to work as domestics, especially in the case of women. Significantly, domestic service is considered as one of the lowest forms of activity, and many are ashamed at ever having done it. In one survey in Surinam, former domestic servants who by chance had briefly acquired regular wage labor and then lost it declared that they would rather starve than return to the indignity of domestic service;[64] in South Africa maids invoke the slave image of domestic service—"we are like slaves" they frequently report.[65] The effect of a lifetime of low status, of racial discrimination, of constantly serving and never being served, of being the lowest in almost any scale of social status produces anomie, negative self-image, and lack of self-respect and self-esteem. The types of consciousness that arise from these factors can, to some extent, be seen as a psychological mechanism for the restoration of a measure of equilibrium and self-esteem to the personality.

These social and psychological aspects may be reinforced by dominant groups that use them to ensure the continued subjugation of the primitive labor market workers. At every contact those at the bottom of the hierarchy of status and wealth are encouraged to believe that they are there by force of genetics, health, competence, or ethnic background and so are in their rightful place. That the people of the primitive labor market should accept—internalize in the language of social psychology—these notions is desired and promoted by those who either fear, or profit from, the primitive labor market. The objective, which has achieved some success, is that any consciousness that emerges should be one in which the status quo is accepted.

It is not surprising, therefore, that populations composed primarily of primitive labor market workers have been widely observed as having fatalistic and despairing attitudes. They tend to give the impression that there is no hope, that fate decrees their condition, and that no action on their part will change it. The most famous concept derived from these observations has been that people with such attitudes suffer from a self-reinforcing "culture of poverty."[66] Those accepting the concept have argued that fatalism is itself the cause of poverty, which has meant that the poor can be blamed for their own poverty, as in the nineteenth-century rationalizations of poverty. The attractiveness of this doctrine to those who wish to believe that relative poverty does not arise from social domination has meant that the fatalistic attitudes of marginal populations have been much overstated.[67]

The primitive labor market workers, on the contrary, have shown energy, creativity, and ingenuity when dealing with the material problems of poverty. Furthermore, as will be discussed in following sections, their social actions in recent times have been anything but fatalistic and despair-ridden. What was probably being observed within the culture of poverty was the contrast between consciousness emerging from social relations of production, which provide an easily identifiable enemy and a consequential target for immediate improvement, and the impossibility of such mental and social developments' emerging from the social relations surrounding urban marginal work activities. Nevertheless, some elements of fatalism and despair, as well as the physical conditions affecting energy and mental attitudes, anomie, and social identity problems, are directly related to a consciousness supportive of the millennialist and populist movements.

Millennialist and other popular religious movements may indeed be seen as precisely the psychological palliatives for the social, material, and mental conditions discussed above.[68] They offer total, imminent, and collective salvation from the horrors of the existing world. These movements and the churches, which are the institutional expression of them, offer to those who follow them hope for the coming of a millennium—a vaguely defined golden age of a thousand years. Natural disasters, oppression, and especially marginality are the roots of the millennialist movements that have inevitably flourished in times of widespread social disruption or on the exclusion of a section of the population from the mainstream of change. In the period of economic and social decay of the Roman Empire the proles accepted Christianity with its promise of a second coming of its prophet and millennium of peace and happiness.

So it is that the current urban marginals of the primitive labor market tend to support established churches with millennialist overtones such as the Jehovah's Witnesses, Seventh Day Adventists, Fundamental Baptists, Revivalists, and other lesser known denominations of different religions.[69] A high proportion of them are also found in messianic movements—those movements led by a "divine messenger" in whom all the hopes and visions of a better future are vested. Messianic movements sometimes create physical "cities" within cities in which the faithful are in fact relieved of the burdens of the life of poverty and subordination: In Brazil a movement led by a prophet, a former airline pilot, established the City of the Brazilian Universal Brotherhood—Eclectic City—in which believers practiced a religion based upon elements of the Catholic, Jewish, Protestant, and other religions. The city achieved a high degree of economic organization and increased wealth.[70]

In Manila, the millennialist church of the Sangra Christi established its own well-protected city, including a "university." More recently "popular" religious movements have had an impact upon marginal populations—that is, a religious following based upon a fundamental or selected aspect of the world's major religions—Islam, Christianity, and Buddhism. The appeal of Islam to the dispossessed population is, for example, expressed in a term meaning that at least the religion provides a "little blessing" in an otherwise desperate condition.

In addition to providing a "little blessing," millennialist, messianic, and popular religious movements restore a sense of identity, a touchstone for the psyche, and a spiritual reason for living.[71] Significantly the elements of the doctrines are usually a fierce rejection of the prevailing life-style of nonadherents, the damnation of the established society, and exhortation to clean, uncorrupted living. The moral degradation and corruption of the human spirit among the marginals and the dominant groups are a recurring theme of preachers, prophets, and tracts, coupled with the offer of "salvation" and "cleansing" through acceptance of the belief. Objectively these movements channel energies of their adherents away from transforming social relations while at the same time correctly identifying some of the ills of the existing situation.[72] To some extent they are the safety valves of social discontent—something approaching the opiate of the mass that Marx assigned to religion. Yet they are a form of collective con-

sciousness of the primitive labor market worker—they do gal-
vanize energies of numbers of people and so provide the possibility of being a tool for manipulation.

The importance of such movements was particularly recognized in the anticolonial struggles when religions could be
joined with nationalism, allowing nationalist leaders to use them
for nationalist ends. In India, Bengali nationalists tried to unite
the image of Mother India with the Hindu goddess Kali; in Algeria
and Indonesia "popular" Muslim sects were created for the anticolonial effort.[73]

In Latin America the "liberation theology" movement associated with radical Catholic priests and nuns has used the basic
appeal of religious movements among the urban poor for mobilization purposes. In Argentina the Third World Priest Movement
(Tercenumdistas) attempted to use popular Catholicism to organize acts of protest by the underemployed against local companies
"as they lacked any form of unionization."[74] In similar manner
Paulo Friere, a Brazilian priest, also made an attempt to use
religious consciousness as a base for a process of social "conscien-
cisation."[75] In Nicaragua radical Catholic priests not only supported the socialist Sandinista revolution but also took political
office in the revolutionary government.

Such attempts to mobilize the urban poor by religious
appeal to achieve social change have never succeeded in transforming the social relations of the primitive labor market except
for the small number of individuals who live in the church-
established enclaves. But the potential of such movements to be
used in the context of broader based and revolutionary attempts
to change the structure of the social formation cannot be excluded
and the suspicion and repression with which they have been
treated by dominant groups and classes are perhaps testimony to
that potential.

The second major form of consciousness affecting the primitive labor market worker and arising from the condition of
social rejection and despair is populism. Populism is closely
aligned to millennialism, and even more to messianic movements, for whereas these latter promise the imminent coming of
a prophet, a holy person, or an event, after which all will change
for the better, populism associates these promised events with a

living political figure. Sometimes the distinction between the prophet and populist political leader becomes blurred; Nkrumah in Ghana, for example, called himself "The Redeemer," and some of his followers assigned him divine characteristics.[76] At the level of the social formation, populism is a political movement, associated with a charismatic individual, that develops an organizing power spread over a number of groups and classes. Although such populist regimes have a special role and importance in general political developments, what is of concern here is the extent to which workers in the primitive labor market accept populist personalities and movements and support them as an expression of their consciousness. In fact, evidence from Latin America indicates widespread support from marginal populations, rural migrants, unemployed, and others in the conventional categories who are normally within primitive labor market relations.[77] In Africa ethnic divisions among recent urban arrivals are considered to be a source for support of personal and populist rule.[78]

Populist and charismatic leaders, according to Max Weber, are those who present on the public stage the core of any particular distinct culture or subculture.[79] Thus populist leaders not only promise improved material conditions but also revalue the image of self-denigration held by marginal populations; they promote at the highest status level in society the image of a group of people who, almost by definition, are studiously ignored and rejected by established political leaders and who are treated as nonpersons within social relations of production. Perón in Argentina exalted the *"descamisados*—the shirtless ones," although they were generally known as *"cabecitas negras"* (black heads): Bustamente in Jamaica promoted the *kwashi* (worker) and the "little man"; and Ghandi turned caste on its head by recognizing the *harijan*—the untouchables. Most of such leaders are rewarded with a fanatic and virtually inextinguishable loyalty.

Populism provides a *collective* restoration of identity and self-respect to the primitive labor market workers, whereas millennialist movements supply an *individual* revaluation of identity for those who adhere to them.[80] Millennialism arises more from the material conditions that the primitive labor market produces, but populism is directly connected to the social relations in that it provides a political force and expression for those whose social relations prevent or exclude the development of other forms of consciousness and their resultant organizations, such as labor movements, unions, political parties, and informal pressure groups.[81] It has been suggested, for example, that the apparent intense appeal of the Perónist movement in Argentina to women arose from social relations of the household and primitive labor market precisely because workers within those social relations, particularly the household, could not easily find identity and appeal in exhortations of the "working class," "higher wages," and other slogans inapplicable to their social reality. The emergence of Evita Perón—General Perón's wife—as a populist figure is connected to the disproportionate numbers of women in the primitive labor market in Argentina compared with other countries at that time.[82] Populism is the type of consciousness that the primitive labor market form of social relations of production generates, although it also has intimate connections with the dynamics of other social relations elsewhere.

The importance of the primitive labor market workers to the strength of populist movements has meant that when populist leaders have acquired power it has been necessary to repay them by improving the material conditions of their followers. Thus apart from the social and psychological benefits of restored identity, populist movements have invariably resulted in some improvements in material conditions; the populist government of Getulio Vargas in Brazil until 1945 saw increased benefits for all urban groups largely at the expense of the countryside. Even the most ardent opponents of Peronism admit that material benefits were achieved for the "shirtless ones," and this was an important aspect of acquiring continuous support. Imitations of populism, such as that of the Marcos regime in the Philippines, also brought changes for a small section of the primitive labor market. Occasionally subnational populist leaders with a local and specific following within the slum population are able to strike bargains with authorities in the established society by virtue of their ability to offer some promise of restraint on the level of individual violence, deliver votes, and provide other fear-mitigating assurances for the fear-ridden. In this manner minor concessions for the urban marginal population can be gained. Such gains, however are often of a type that reinforces the general conditions associated with the primitive labor market. Thus an agreement by government authorities to refrain from destroying a section of a shanty town and to allow some of the inhabitants to retain the cardboard, tin, plastic, palm, or reed that covers them nevertheless formalizes the existence of such habitats.

In most cases, however, populist leaders lack the intention of changing social relations, and such regimes have never transformed the primitive labor market. Populist governments, in the ultimate, become dependent upon power holders in dominant social relations within industry and agriculture.[83] These groups provide support in return for the manipulative power of the populist government in what are seen as volatile groups in the social formation. Ultimately, the contradiction between populist appeal and promises and the lack of action to change social relations results in the downfall of the governments while the primitive labor market stays in place or even increases in size. Nevertheless, the consciousness-raising nature of populist movements makes them less reliable tools for the maintenance of the status quo and provides the primitive labor market workers with a model of a hero or heroine—a figure for which they will continue to search in order to find a symbolic repository of hope and renewed identity.

The appeal of millennialism and populism can be considered as a product of social relations of the primitive labor market form; such movements are always likely to manifest in social formations where primitive labor market social relations cover significant sections of the populations. How, or if, such basic consciousness is used to change or sustain the structure of the social formation will be determined by local social variations and personages. What is apparent, however, is that, unlike some other forms of social relations, the consciousness and dynamics of the primitive labor market do not lead to a transformation of the social relations arising from the social action of the workers themselves. Transformations come from the outside in the context of substantive changes in the economic and social structure of the wider society. The two remaining sections deal with two existing situations in which primitive labor market social rela-

tions have been basically eliminated from the social formation—
the industrial dependency and the revolutionary examples.

TRANSFORMATION: DEPENDENCY AND INDUSTRIALIZATION

Despite the general rule that industrialization of third-world social formations has not allowed the pattern of the earlier indus-
trializations of Western Europe in which the primitive labor
market social relations were a temporary part of a transition, there
have been a number of cases where at least the size of the primitive labor market has been kept in check. Two such examples
are Taiwan and Singapore.

In these two countries direct foreign investment producing
for export has resulted in a rapid and continuous expansion of
industrial employment. This development has reduced the primitive labor market to almost nothing in favor of the unorganized
regular industrial employment of the enterprise labor market. It
follows that there has been a marked improvement in the share
of the national income for the poorest group, where the primitive
labor market worker would normally be found.[84] However, in the
global context, these countries cannot be confidently cited as
models to emulate, nor can they be seen as quantitatively important, for the following reasons.

First, in both cases heavy direct investment has come
principally from the United States, which throughout the process
of industrialization had a strategic interest in the countries. The
levels of direct foreign investment in these countries have been
exceptional, and there is little possibility that the experience
could be repeated on a global scale. Second, both Taiwan and
Singapore had special circumstances in the rural areas that have
reduced the numbers seeking employment in the town. In the
case of Taiwan a relatively successful land reform—initiated
essentially by the invaders from mainland China who were able
to resist and ignore pressures from the local landlord class—
stemmed the pace and size of the urban-rural migration sufficiently for industry to absorb any displaced labor.[85] Singapore is
a city-state with no rural production or peasant-lord relations and

therefore no such migration. Furthermore, and particularly significant, 30 percent of the Singaporean labor force are daily border migrants from Malaysia—primitive labor market relations are between Singapore nationals and nonnational Malays. Primitive labor market social relations exist then in Singapore, but the material and physical results are transposed into neighboring Malaysian urban appendages.[86] If the national boundary is ignored it could be said that a primitive labor market exists within the Singapore social formation.

These two countries have been dependent upon foreign capital, foreign markets, and on a foreign-enforced land reform in the case of Taiwan and on foreign labor in the case of Singapore. They have therefore been most dependent upon outside linkages for industrialization, which is why they may be called the dependency model of transformation. The unusual aspects of the foreign investment pattern and the rural-urban relationship make these countries special cases that are unlikely to be repeated. Similar policies of dependent industrialization, notably in Colombia, South Korea, and Kenya, have, in fact, produced, rather than avoided, the development of a massive primitive labor market.[87]

TRANSFORMATION: AT THE MARGINS OF REVOLUTION?

Primitive labor market workers or urban marginals are the poorest section of any modern urban society and are considered to be one of the most highly exploited groups of people. This has meant that revolutionary thinkers and activists have viewed the primitive labor market social relations in two ways: first, that it should be high on the list of priorities for elimination in postrevolution restructuring and, second, that primitive labor market workers could or should have a role in supporting movements whose state objective is to restructure society in their favor. This latter issue—the actual or potential role of urban marginals within general revolutionary movements—has been one that has preoccupied social scientists, politicians of the status quo and revolutionary activists for more than two centuries.

When dealing first with the ability of revolutionary regimes to eliminate, or transform, primitive labor market social
relations—it is apparent that the process is neither rapid nor
necessarily automatic. Perhaps the most successful experiences
in eliminating such relations have been in Cuba and China and
to a lesser extent Vietnam, to take some better known examples.
In China it was not until some ten years after the revolution of
1949 that casual work in small enterprises was eliminated; in
Vietnam the rural resettlement program, in which people were
returned to the countryside to farm individual plots, relieved
pressures on urban unemployment.[88] The government of Cuba
(and Chile under the brief marxist leadership of Allende) adopted
policies directed at changing attitudes, ambitions, and work hab-
its of existing urban marginals through the establishment of gov-
ernment- and party-promoted organizations.[89] Urban employment creation and agrarian reform have meant that the primitive
labor market in Cuba has declined over a period of time. However,
the experience of Algeria shows that despite an ideological an-
tipathy to such social relations, planning imbalances may easily
result in the emergence of such social relations within a nomi-
nally socialist social formation. The Algerian government's emphasis on heavy industry with imported capital-intensive technology plus high birth rates has begun to produce a level of
unemployment and a pool of urban casual and migrant workers
typical of a primitive labor market as found elsewhere.[90]

The uncertainty of how to deal with people whose demands are more likely to be for work than for a transformation
of authority at, and increased returns from, structured work could
well be at the source of confusion within the discussions on the
second issue relating to urban marginals and revolution, namely,
their potential for revolutionary action.

Until very recently there appeared to be a general agreement among both marxists and nonmarxists that any positive role
for groups that correspond to urban marginals was highly unlikely. In 1926, for example, Mao Zedong thought that the urban
unemployed were difficult to handle and "apt to be destructive,"
although they were susceptible to becoming a revolutionary force
if given proper guidance.[91] Not even this potential was allowed
by the contemporary black revolutionary writer Eldridge Cleaver,

who was of the opinion that they "are absolutely unstable and follow those who provide a livelihood."[92] Franz Fanon, despite a belief in the exclusive revolutionary role of the urban workers, was ambivalent about the marginals. Earlier revolutionaries, including Lenin and Bakunin, challenged the conventional marxists' view of the lumpenproletariat, but the original bias has persisted.

Empirical and behavorist studies, which have very different ideological biases, have tended to confirm the lack of revolutionary or even disruptive activities among modern marginal populations. For example, a sociologist, writing in a military journal, divided the "political' activities of the lowest income groups in Peru into three sections and found that "all three (sections) involve non-disruptive activities."[93] Likewise, a political scientist researching in two Latin American cities found that among the urban poor there was a deferential approach to authority, that rural migrants were even less demanding than other groups in the city, and that, in total, the urban marginals were "a very low threat to political and social systems."[94] Similar reports are made about Africa and Asia.[95]

If then, the urban marginals were thought unlikely to play an active and positive role in revolutionary situations, would it be that they would play at least a passive role and provide refuge for more active urban guerrillas—to provide an urban sea in which the guerrilla fish would swim (to paraphrase Mao Zedong)?[96]

Until the late 1960s there was no serious attempt to base armed revolutionary struggles on the slums and to substantially involve the primitive labor market worker. The idea of a noncolonial urban guerrilla was thus new to revolutionary theory and practice in the contemporary period. The failure of Che Guevara to fulfill the rural version of the guerrilla "foco" theory, which argued that a guerrilla alone could create conditions for a general revolution, brought the cities into theory of revolution. Not only did this contradict the prevailing theories on the need for revolutions to be peasant based, which were derived from Mao Zedong, Giap, and others, but it also ran counter to the negative aspects of urban actions, which were most vividly expressed in Castro's words that cities "were the graveyards of revolutions."[97]

Revolutionary strategists and theorists began to take the urban guerrilla seriously, and, particularly in Latin America, many such groups were formed. The Tupamaros in Uruguay; the group led by Carlos Marighela in Brazil; similar groups in Venezuela, Argentina, and Central America; and the Naxalites in India began to practice kidnapping, bombings, sabotage, police ambush, and other aspects or urban guerrilla warfare.

Yet, as if to prove Castro's words, within seven to ten years of formation of these groups—even the most successful and powerful, the Tupamaros and Naxalites—had been eliminated; their leaders assassinated, both in and out of prison; their organizations wiped out, infiltrated, and destroyed. The failure of these attempts could be taken as proof of the individualist, opportunist, and unreliable nature of workers from the primitive labor market. On the other hand none of the analyses made by the revolutionary groups themselves or the social scientists gives any clear indication of the relative participation of urban occupational groupings, not to speak of workers in different forms of social relations. Only in the case of the Naxalites is it clear that the urban guerrillas were supported by the primitive labor market workers.[98] The Naxalites were a rural guerrilla movement that, after suffering defeats in the countryside of West Bengal, took to the slums of Calcutta. There they found support from the most recent rural migrants—the most recent recruits to the primitive labor market. In other cases it is difficult to ascertain whether it was the urban marginals who provided shelter for guerrillas; or whether is was those in self-employment who cooperated most closely with the police; or whether the infiltrators were employed, unemployed, or women; or whether women in household social relations either supported, with their services, relatives involved or actively participated in the groups themselves. In short, the relationship between the consciousness and dynamics of social relations and active support for revolutionaries was not adequately examined.

Part of the reason for this was that revolutionaries were generally from the middle class, often students or ex-students, and were essentially wedded to the undifferentiated marxist two-class model of society. In Latin America this meant the feudal, aristocratic, landowning class was the principal target, and the cities, seen as the playground of the multinationals, were secondary to that struggle. The urban struggle was only complementary to the rural struggle—the marginals remained marginal even in revolutionary strategy.[99] The most successful group—the Tupameros—was based, not upon the slum dweller and primitive labor market, but on the widespread connections with political parties, sympathetic professionals, and trade unions.[100] The lack of information and the apparent absence of attempts to raise the consciousness of the urban marginals based upon their social relations mean that their role in these events remains uncertain.

One widely accepted strategy of guerrilla warfare, however, would certainly alienate, in material terms, the primitive labor market worker. Most of the theorists see guerrilla activity as the first step to achieving a repressive response from the dominant power that in turn will force those against whom it is directed to respond. In the formulation of Brazilian urban guerrilla Carlos Marighela, who was shot by police in 1967, guerrilla activity was necessary to turn a political crisis into an armed conflict by performing violent actions that will force those in power to transform the political situation in the country into a military situation. This will alienate the masses, who, from then on, will revolt against the army and police and thus blame them for this state of things.[101] This might certainly apply to and have an effect on the workers in forms of social relations based on bargaining or even those in regular employment or self-employment, but those in the primitive labor market are already the target of physically repressive techniques. What would be an intolerable intrusion or restriction for an established worker is a daily occurrence and fact of life for the primitive labor market worker who, being the weakest, would in any case suffer the most in any further increase of police activities in the slums. Logically this particular tactic is unlikely to appeal to the primitive labor market worker.

The combination of the class background of the revolutionaries, the ideological perspective derived from nineteenth-century marxist analysis, and the nature of the revolutionary cases considered, which were mainly anticolonial—all of these contributed to assign to the urban marginals a place at the very margins of revolution.

But apparently this was not a place that either the marginals themselves or analysts closer to the shantytowns were prepared to accept, and as a result there has been substantial rethinking and reconsideration of the general ideas about the political role of urban marginals.[102] This has issued from five interconnected intellectual and historical developments. First, the sheer size and rapid growth of the third-world "urban problem"; second, the abandonment of the culture of poverty and passive-poor thesis; third, the action and organization of the urban poor in relation to their living, rather than working, conditions; fourth, the arrival of very different examples of revolutionary processes to study, in particular, Nicaragua, Mozambique, and Iran; and fifth, the rediscovery of urban people and elements of consciousness derived from industrial and urban social relations within past, supposedly peasant-based, revolutions.

The growth of the urban population and the reconsideration of the culture of poverty thesis have already been mentioned in this chapter. Together they resulted in more resources for the study of urban populations and perceptions of researchers less biased toward seeing lassitude and fatalism among the subjects of study. Interlocked with these first two developments was the third, that of the actual political actions taken by the poor, especially in Latin America.[103]

Throughout the last decade there occurred impressive actions of the urban poor to seize land and generally exert political pressure in order to improve their living conditions. Although these occurred mainly in Latin America, there were also examples on other continents; in Turkey night seizures of land and establishment of squatter settlements were known as "parachute" settlements because of their sudden appearance.[104] These actions contributed to "new social movements" based on issues such as urban ecology and living conditions rather than on the traditional mobilizing causes of the conditions and return to work or national liberations.[105] These movements in turn raised the possibility of alliances between urban marginals and other groups and classes.

Within the traditional analysis, alliances of urban marginals with other classes would be difficult because of their supposed inability to supply goods or actions in support of the "leaders" of the revolution, the peasants, or organized workers. Compared with groups of workers within strategic industries, or peasants already under arms, the possibility of the urban marginals' supplying anything but crowds in the streets to welcome the victors seemed meager. But the new social movements and the actions of the urban poor seemed to provide an unexpected asset—issues that could capture under the "common banner" of improvement of living conditions all the various groups of urban workers.[106] Although this has yet to happen and, as already noted, the organizations are also possible instruments for preventing, rather than instituting, change,[107] there can be no doubt that the actions and movements of the urban poor have provided an organizational base and an experience that may well emerge, in different forms, in any given social conjunction.[108]

The third element in the reconsideration of the political potential of urban marginals was the involvement of urban population in the more recent revolutions. In these cases there remain problems of disaggregation because analysts still refer to such blanket or normative categories of "progressive workers" or "urban mass."[109] Nevertheless, there are some indications of the role of primitive labor market workers in, for example, the coming to power of nationalist and socialist governments in both Mozambique and Nicaragua. In Mozambique many of the recruits to the revolutionary movement were recent migrants to the towns who had felt the "trauma of socio-economic transition" and suffered from status resentment and economic injustice.[110] In Nicaragua the revolutionary Sandinist organization established "mass" organizations that paid specific attention to the urban marginals, with the result that the fighters were eventually received and operated in the urban areas in a manner that would not have been predicted by the earlier theories of passivity and docility of the urban poor.[111] In Iran, evidence is accumulating indicating that important support for the actions that brought down the regime of the Shah and installed a fundamentalist religious government using millennialist rhetoric was precisely from the recent migrants from the dislocations of the countryside. Driven out from social relations in the areas that had incorporated religious and social traditions and precipitated into primitive labor market social relations within a city—Tehran—which was intent on "modernization," that is, denying a large part of the social experience with which the migrants were familiar, the migrants found solace in fundamentalist religion and its promise of structural and moral change.[112]

The final element in the reconsideration of the political role of the urban marginals is the reexamination of past revolutions, which reveals that there were perhaps more urban connections than theory, or even the revolutionary leaders themselves, would admit. Thus a review of previously less well-known cases reveals an "urban bias" of revolutions. In Bolivia in 1952 the urban marginals certainly played a role, whose extent is not fully known, in a revolution that started in the city and then spread to involve the rural areas through providing arms for the peasants.[113] The initiation of the revolution in Algeria against French rule in 1954 via a series of bombings in the cities, the "ghetto" branch of the Algerian revolutionary organization, and the fact that it was the shoeshine boys and laundry men who paced out distances to allow for precise targeting of Viet Cong mortars in Vietnam stress the previously underemphasized supportive role that urban marginals have played.[114]

Not even the Cuban revolution, high in the imagery of a peasant-based revolution, is free from a suspicion that the urban poor played a greater role than is admitted. From 60 to 80 percent of the rural guerrilla army was recruited from the urban areas, and in the two years that preceded the taking of Havana, there were more than 5000 urban bombings.[115] A revised view would then be of a symbiotic relationship between a small rural-based army supported both actively and passively by large segments of the urban population, which at that time would have been heavily composed of primitive labor market workers.

Although any reconsideration of the Chinese 1949 revolution could not reset it within an urban framework, it is becoming clear that the Red Army and the mobilizing doctrine of its leadership had more connections with the "rootless" poor of existing and future primitive labor markets than had previously been allowed. Not only was a large part of the Red Army composed of landless and uprooted vagabonds but also the major source of recruits was defections from the opposing army, which had earlier been recruited from the unemployed, ex-employed, and urban marginals.[116] It is not surprising then that one scholar notes that the Red Army embraced the "millennial vision of a poor people's kingdom" and that cadres, themselves from the urban marginals, were prepared "to organize and lead a lumpen armed counterforce both to support the peasant movement and liberate the nation."[117]

Perhaps these reconsiderations only indicate that little is precisely known of the roles of various workers from different social relations of production within political movements, simply because of an adherence to inadequate traditional categorizations or the use of those not based in social relations of production; perhaps it is a more fundamental restoration of the world's urban very poor to the center of the stage of both cause and action in social change. Whether this latter is the case or not, it is clear that if third-world landless people increase, cities expand, and employment stagnates or fluctuates, the primitive labor market social relations of production and the consciousness they produce will assume a political importance in spite of their previously marginal place in economic and social structures and discourses about them.

NOTES

1. The notion of "marginality" was discussed in the introduction to part 2. Six types of sources have been used in the writing of the chapter on the primitive labor market form of social relations of production: (1) anthropological studies concerning the social and cultural structure of the urban poor—these studies often use a participant observation technique; (2) urban planning and housing studies—this literature has proliferated since the mid-1960s as a result of the growth of urban areas and housing problems in the third world; (3) microeconomic studies of occupations among the urban poor—these provide the most important collection of substantive data on the details of the social relations of production for the occupation of groups studies; (4) behavioral science and sociological studies of politics, social movements, and voting patterns in urban areas of the third world; (5) fictional, autobiographical, journalistic reports, and film accounts of slum life that provide insights and add illustrations to technical literature; (6) nonparticipant observation

and interviews. During visits and residence in third-world countries the author made a special effort to visit and interview people of the urban areas about their life and work. Some of the material presented in this chapter was also discussed with professionals from the third world, including social workers, labor ministry officials, and others attending higher education courses in Europe.

2. See, for example, Kedan N. Baidya, "The Landless Poor—India's Growing Problem," *Mazingira* (1985), 8(4):22–28.

3. See, for example, Nicholas Van Hear, "By-Day Boys and Daringa Men," *Review of African Political Economy* (December 1984), No. 31, 44–57.

4. See chapter 1 p. 19.

5. See *Employment, Incomes and Equality: A Strategy for Increasing Productive Employment in Kenya* (Geneva, International Labor Office 1972); for examples of the studies the informal concept initiated, see the special issue of *World Development* (1978) (September/October), 6(9/10).

6. See the life history of an Indian casual construction worker in L. Gulati, *Profiles in Female Poverty: A Study of Five Poor Working Women in Kerala* (Oxford, Pergamon Press, 1982).

7. See Janet Abu-Lughod, "Urbanisation and Social Change in the Arab World," in John Walton, ed., *Capital and Labour in the Urbanized World* (London, Sage, 1985), p. 141.

8. The terms *unemployed* and *underemployment* have only a limited applicability in countries where regular wage labor represents as little as 5 percent of the labor force. The term *inactive* is also less than sympathetic to those whose inactivity is a result of disease, malnutrition, and depression as a direct result of the lack of employment. Here the term *inactive* applies only to those who are totally dependent upon support from relatives and family for their basic needs and contribute in only a minor way to any productive activity.

9. For a general description of the process of severance from the land and settlement in urban slums, see, for example, W. Mangin, "Tales from the Barriadas," in W. Mangin, ed., *Peasants in Cities* (Boston, Houghton Mifflin, 1970). For two national examples, see P. Phongpaichit, *Rural Women of Thailand: From Peasant Girls to Bangkok Masseuses* (Geneva, International Labor Office, 1980).

10. The most extreme example of this phenomenon is described in Philip Mayer, "From Tribe to City in South Africa," in Gino Germian, ed., *Modernization, Urbanization and the Urban Crisis* (Boston, Little Brown, 1973), pp. 174–93. For this aspect of segmented labor markets, see Dipak Mazumdar, *The Urban Labour Market and Income Distribution: A Study of Malaysia* (Oxford, World Bank/Oxford University Press, 1981).

11. See *Child Labour in Morocco's Carpet Industry* (London, Anti-Slavery Society, 1978), pp. 71.

12. See Philippine National Housing Authority, *The Tondo Foreshore and Dagat-Dagatan Development Project* (Manila, Philippines, 1979), pp. 7–8.

13. See E. M. Gbanite, *Third World Urbanization: Enugu, Nigeria* (Ann Arbor, Mich., University Microfilms, 1981), pp. 4–5.

14. Casual and illegal work outside of structures created by the state, enterprise, or union has been increasing in the past decade in industrialized countries. The majority of such work ultimately centers, however, around the small, often illegal enterprises, and social relations are of the enterprise labor market pattern (See chapter 5, pp. 218–219.) See, for example, Juliette A. Thorpe, *The Informal Economy: Non-Market Service Provision in an Urban Setting* (Ann Arbor, Mich., University Microfilms, 1979).

15. *Estimates and Projections of Urban, Rural and City Populations 1950–2025* (New York, United Nations, 1985). For breakdowns referring to employment and labor markets, see S. Kannappan, *Employment Problems and the Urban Labour Market in Developing Nations* (Ann Arbor, Mich., University of Michigan Press, 1983), especially chapter 2.

16. Karl Marx, "The Eighteenth Brumaire of Louis Bonaparte," in *Karl Marx and Frederich Engels: Selected Works*, vol. 1 (London, Lawrence and Wishart, 1950).

17. One of the most pertinent among the numerous descriptions of the British urban poor of the eighteenth and nineteenth century is found in J. L. and Barbara Hammond, *The Town Labourer 1970–1832: The New Civilization* (London, Longmans Green, 1920). The phenomenon of displaced rural dwellers' becoming roaming marginals in the cities predates the industrial revolution; see the descriptions in Christopher Hill, *The World Turned Upside Down* (Harmondsworth, England, Penguin, 1975), pp. 39–56.

18. Geoffrey Barraclough, *Introduction to Contemporary History* (London 1964), pp. 8 and 272.

19. For a discussion of these transfers in relation to trade unions, see Jeffrey Harrod, *Trade Union Foreign Policy* (London, Macmillan, 1972), pp. 207–28.

20. This policy was stated explicitly by Sidney Webb as British Labor government Minister of Labor in 1929; see *ibid.*, p. 208.

21. The international political economy reasons for this development are examined in Jeffrey Harrod, "Social Relations of Production, Systems of Labour Control and Third World Trade Unions," in R. Southall, ed., *The New International Division of Labour and Third World Trade Unions* (London, Zed Press, 1986).

22. See, for example, Dorothy Weeks, "Adaptive Strategies of Men and Women in Zaria, Nigeria: Industrial Workers and Their Wives (Ann Arbor, Mich., University Microfilms, 1973), p. 77. This was essentially the finding of an International Labor Organization mission to advise on the creation of employment in Colombia. See Dudley Seers, "New Approaches Suggested by the Colombia Employment Program," *International Labor Review* (October 1970), 102(4):377–91; see also Kannappan, *Employment Problems*, pp. 197–208.

23. See R. Mohan, *The Determinants of Labor Earnings in Developing Metropoli; Estimates from Bogata and Cali* (Washington, D.C., World Bank, 1981).

24. See Mazumdar, *The Urban Labour Market*, p. 361.

25. See Dorothy Remy, "Formal and Informal Sectors of the Zaria, Nigeria, Economy: Analytical Framework with Empirical Content," in Helen I. Safa, *Towards a Political Economy of Urbanization in Third World Cities* (Delhi, India, Oxford University Press, 1982), pp. 233–46.

26. Wage rates fluctuate and are sometimes widely different for different countries. Whereas such differentials between various groups of workers is the general case, there may be notable exceptions, as, for example, noted above in Mohan, *Determinants of Labor Earnings;* likewise in Brazil, at certain periods, enterprise wage rates have been depressed to near primitive labor market levels; see B. R. Roberts, *Cities of Peasants: The Political Economy of Urbanization in Third World* (London, Edward/Arnold, 1978).

27. "Employed labour . . . may be overpaid" as the result of the defense of the market wage through "strong labor union activity and minimum wage laws," Orville John McDiarmid, *Unskilled Labor for Development: Its Economic Cost* (A World Bank Publication Summary) (Washington D.C., International Bank for Reconstruction and Development, 1977), p. 2.; for examples of scholars who have

argued against the reserve-army–wage-depressant thesis, see Jose Nun, *Superpoblacion Relative, Ejercito Industrial de Reserva y Masa Marginal* (Geneva, International Institute of Labor Studies, 1969), and Rodolfo Stavenhagen, "Marginality, Participation and Agrarian Structure in Latin America," *Bulletin of International Institute for Labor Studies* (June 1970), no. 7, pp. 51–92; see also the structural argument of Terence McGee, "Conservation and Dissolution in the Third World City: The Shanty Town as an Element of Conservation," in Noel Iverson, ed., *Urbanism and Urbanisation: Views, Aspects, and Dimensions* (Leiden, Netherlands, Brill, 1984), pp. 107–21.

28. See, for example, Christopher Chase-Dunn, "Urbanization in the World System: New Directions for Research," in David Drakis-Smith, ed., *Urbanisation, Housing and the Development Process* (London, Croom Helm, 1981), pp. 111–37; McGee, "Conservation and Dissolution"; Alejandro Portes and John Walton, *Labor, Class, and the International System* (London, Academic Press, 1983).

29. See, for example, the analysis in Vittorio Corba and Patricia Meller, "Trade and Employment: Chile in the 1960s," *The American Economic Review* (1979), 69(2):196–201; this issue is taken up further in chapter 4 on the enterprise labor market.

30. The gradual realization of this situation was one reason for the launching of official policies for increasing employment based on labor-intensive processes. Such policies were especially promoted by the International Labor Organization (ILO) in its World Employment Programs. Examples of reports advocating such policies are *Sharing in Development: A Programme of employment, equity and growth for the Philippines* (Geneva, ILO, 1974), in which labor-intensive industrial exports are advocated, and *Roads and Redistribution: Social Cost Benefits of Labour-Intensive Road Construction in Iran* (Geneva, ILO, 1975), where is was proposed that subsidies be paid to contractors who used labor instead of machines; see a review of such policies in Asian countries in R. Amjad, *The Development of Labour-Intensive Industry in ASEAN Countries* (Bangkok, ILO/ARTEP, 1981). For an example of the original basic arguments of economists on the issues, see R. S. Mathur, "Economic Development and the Tertiary Sector," *Indian Journal of Industrial Relations* (July 1972), 8(1):31–45.

31. See, for example, S. S. Bhattacharya, "The Shoe Shiners of Patna," *Sociological Bulletin* (India) (1969), 18:167–74, as quoted in Jan Breman, "A Dualistic Labour System? A Critique of the 'Informal Sector Concept,' " *Economic and Political Weekly* (November-December 1976), 11(48/49/50).

32. See Andrew Hake, *African Metropolis* (Sussex, England, Sussex University Press, 1977), p. 191.

33. See, for example, F. Lana Jocana, *Slums as a Way of Life* (Quezon City, Philippines, University of Philippines Press, 1974), pp. 121–22.

34. See Van Hear, "By-Day Boys."

35. Examples of such groups are found in Hake *African Metropolis*; Jocana, *Slums*; Harrod, *Trade Union Foreign Policy*, p. 166.

36. See Ximena Bunster, "Talking Pictures: Field Method and Visual Mode," *Signs* (Autumn 1977), 3(1):278–93.

37. See S. and D. Morell, *Six Slums in Bangkok* (Bangkok, UNICEF, 1972).

38. Nirmala Banerjee, "Survival of the Poor," in Safa, *Towards a Political Economy*, pp. 178–79.

39. See Lourdes Arizpe, "Women in the Informal Sector—Mexico City," *Signs* (Autumn 1977), 3(1):25–27; and Lourdes Arizpe, "Relay Migration and the Survival of the Peasant Household," in Safa, *Towards a Political Economy*, pp. 20–46.

40. See Suad Joseph, "Family as Security and Bondage: A Political Strategy of the Lebanese Urban Working Class," in Safa, *Towards a Political Economy*, pp. 151–71; for an earlier and pioneering account of social networks in Africa, see Peter C. Gutkind, "The Energy of Despair—Social Organization of Unemployed in Two African Cities, Lagos and Nairobi: A Preliminary Account," *Civilisations* (Brussels), 14(3):186–214 and (4):380–405; an overview of ethnic based networks is found in Kannappan, *Employment Problems*, pp. 189–96.

41. Manuel Castells, *Luttes Urbains* (Paris, Maspero, 1977), pp. 92–119.

42. See Arizpe, "Women in the Informal Sector."

43. V. S. Naipaul, *India: A Wounded Civilization* (London, Andre Deutsch, 1977).

44. Alan Gilbert and Peter Ward, "Community Action by the Urban Poor: Democratic Involvement, Community Self-Help or a Means of Social Control," *World Development* (August 1984), 12(8):769–92.

45. See, for example, Aban B. Mehta, *The Domestic Servant Class* (Bombay, Popular Books, 1960); and J. Cock, *Maids and Madams: A Study in the Politics of Exploitation* (Johannesberg, Raven Press, 1980), and Ximena Bunster and Elsa M. Chaney, *Sellers and Servants* (New York, Praeger, 1985).

46. The differences between rates for casual and regular workers even performing the same tasks has already been noted—Mazumdar, *The Urban Labour Markets*; Remy, "Formal and Informal Sectors." See also the example of cigarette rollers in Banerjee, "Survival of the Poor," and prostitutes in Phongpaichit, *Rural Women of Thailand*; on casual rates of pay for employment within small workshops, see, for example, *All-India Handicraft Board: Structure of Employment and Wages and Earnings of Handicraft Workers in India* (New Delhi, Government Printer, 1967); P. Marris and A. Somerset, *African Businessmen; A Study of Entrepreneurship and Development in Kenya* (London, Routledge, Kegan Paul, 1971); Gerard Salem, "De la Calabasse a la Production en Serie; Les Reseaux Commerciaux Laobe au Senegal et en France," in Frederick Cooper, ed., *Struggle for the City: Migrant Labour, Capital and the State in Urban Africa* (Beverly Hills, Calif., Sage, 1983), pp. 195–246 (in this case production was based on "apprentices" who were not paid at all); on the general low returns to work for primitive labor market activities, see, for example, J. Keyes, *Manila Scavengers: The Struggle for Survival* (Quezon City, Philippines, Institute of Philippine Culture, 1974); Gbanite, *Third World Urbanization*.

47. See Hake, *African Metropolis*.

48. World Bank Staff Paper No. 223, p. 40; see also Gulati, *Profiles in Female Poverty*.

49. Arizpe, "Women in the Informal Sector," p. 27.

50. See Dipak Mazumdar, *Urban Labour Markets: Malaysia and Bombay* (Washington, D.C., The World Bank 1979).

51. See, for example, the discussion of labor market supply from the "industrial reserve army" in Suzanne Paine, *Exporting Workers: The Turkish Case* (Cambridge, England, Cambridge University Press, 1974); for the similar role of farming populations, see Michael Burawoy, "The Functions and Reproduction of Migrant Labour: Comparative Material from Southern Africa and the US," *American Journal of Sociology* (1981), 81(5):1050–85; on the combination of urban casual labor and "subsistence" activities producing a "reproduction of the working class," see chapter 3, "Unequal Exchange and the Urban Informal Sector," in Portes and Walton, *Labor, Class*, pp. 87–91.

52. Naipaul, *India*.

53. See, for example, the remarks in Marris and Somerset, *African Business-men*, p. 113.

54. For an examination of the fear engendered by slums, see J. Mau, "The Threatening Masses: Myth or Reality," in F. M. Andic and T. C. Mathew, eds., *The Caribbean in Transition* (San Juan, University of Puerto Rico, 1965), pp. 258–70; see also remarks concerning the fear of the slums of Mexico City in William Chislett, "The Macrocephalic Monster in the Smog," *Financial Times* (November 7, 1979), p. 23; fear of revolution or urban upheaval is also discussed in Henry Bienen, "Urbanization and Third World Stability," *World Development* (July 1984), 12(7):661–92.

55. Marcio Moreira Alves, *A Grain of Mustard Seed: The Awakening of the Brazilian Revolution* (New York, Doubleday, 1973), p. 175.

56. For a discussion of "counter-revolution as a way of life" and the "institutionalisation of fear," see George Black, *Garrison Guatemala* (London, Zed Press, 1984); see also the comment concerning the middle-class administrator's dream of "beautiful and orderly cities" in Bienen, "Urbanization," p. 681.

57. See, for example, Frank Bonilla, "Rio's Favelas: The Rural Slum Within the City," in Mangin, ed., *Peasants in Cities*, where the author notes "for the urban Brazilian, the *favela* is the most powerful argument in favor of agrarian reform," p. 83; a survey of several country experiments in controlling rural-urban migration is found in A. S. Oberai, *State Policies and Internal Migration: Studies in Market and Planned Economies* (London, Croom Helm, 1983).

58. This was in fact advocated by the ILO report on Colombia; see Seers, "New Approaches."

59. The bulldozer against squatter settlements does not come only in police or army colors—"settlement planning" also requires "squaring up of lots," "upgrading," and may require "great upheaval"; see Alan Turner, ed., *The Cities of the Poor: Settlement Planning in Developing Countries* (London, Croom Helm, 1980), especially p. 255. See also on the change of Indian government policy from "redevelopment" to "improvement" of slum housing, D. B. Gupta, *Urban Housing in India* (Washington, The World Bank, 1985).

60. *Power, Production, and the Established Worker*, Jeffrey Harrod, (New York, Columbia University Press, forthcoming.

61. See comments in Keyes, *Manila Scavengers*; see, for example, Filomina C. Steady, "Urban Malnutrition in West Africa: A Consequence of Abnormal Urbanization and Underdevelopment," in Safa, *Towards a Political Economy*, pp. 84–101.

62. On identity crisis of uprooted or socially traumatized populations, see, for example, Erik H. Erikson, "Identity and Uprootedness in our Time," in Erik H. Erikson, *Insight and Responsibility* (New York, Norton, 1964), pp. 81–109; Taufik Abdullah, "Identity Maintenance and Identity Crisis in Minangkabau," in Hans Mol, ed., *Identity and Religion: International Cross Cultural Approaches* (Beverly Hills, Sage, 1978), pp. 151–67.

63. A. L. Epstein, *Ethos and Identity: Three Studies in Ethnicity* (London, Tavistock, 1978).

64. Sonia Cuales, "Attitudes of Women Workers in Electronics Industry," *Caribsch Forum* (1981), no. 2.

65. Cock, *Maids and Madams*, p. 123.

66. Oscar Lewis, "*La Vida: A Puerto Rican Family in the Culture of Poverty—San Juan and New York* (New York, Random House, 1966).

67. See, for example, the discussions in Jocano, Slums as a Way of Life; Manuel Castells, "Squatters and Politics in Latin America', in Safa, Towards a Political Economy, pp. 250–80; Bienen, "Urbanization."

68. For a concise description of millennialist movements, see Yonina Talmon, "Millennarism," Encyclopedia of Social Sciences, vol. 10 (New York, Macmillan, 1968), pp. 349–62; for a sociological examination of the concept of millennialism, see G. Allan, "A Theory of Millennialism: The Irvingite Movement as an Illustration," The British Journal of Sociology, 25(3):296–333.

69. See, for example, Max Assimeg, "Crisis Identity and Integration in African Religion," in Mol, Identity and Religion, pp. 97–119.

70. Maria Isaura Pereira de Queiroz, "Brazilian Messianic Movements: A Help or a Hindrance to Participation," Bulletin of the International Institute for Labor Studies (June 1970), no. 7, pp. 93–122.

71. See the reviews of different religions in this respect in D. E. Smith, Religion and Political Development (Boston, Little Brown, 1970); for examples of Islam, see, for example, Abdullah, "Identity Maintenance"; B. T. Grindal, "Islamic Affiliations and Urban Adaptation: The Sisala Migrant in Accra, Ghana," Africa, 43(4):333–46, as quoted in David Drakakis-Smith, Urbanisation Housing and the Development Process (London, Croom Helm, 1981).

72. See, for example, Michael Barkun, Disaster and the Millennium (New Haven, Conn., Yale University Press, 1974), and conclusion in Pereira de Queiroz, "Brazilian Messianic Movements," pp. 120–22.

73. Smith, Religion and Political Development.

74. Michael Dodson, "Priests and Peronism," Latin American Perspectives (Fall 1974), 1(3):65; for a review of popular religious appeal within left-wing movements, see the articles in the special issue on "Religion and the Left," Monthly Review (July-August 1984), 36(3).

75. Smith, Religion and Political Development, p. 167–68.

76. See H. L. Bretton, Rise and Fall of Kwame Nkrumah (London, Pall Mall Press, 1967).

77. See, for example, T. F. Ray, The Politics of the Barrios of Venezuela (Berkeley: University of California Press, 1969), pp. 177–79; A. E. Van Niekerk, Populism and Political Development in Latin America (Rotterdam, 1974), p. 25; Nancy Hollander, "Si Evita Viviera," Latin American Perspectives (Fall 1974), 1(3):44; Dodson, "Priests and Peronism."

78. See R. H. Jackson and C. G. Roseberg, Personal Rule in Black Africa; Prince Autocrat, Prophet, Tyrant (Berkeley, California University Press, 1982).

79. For a discussion of this view, see S. N. Eisenstadt, ed., Max Weber: On Charisma and Institute Building—Selected Papers (Chicago, University of Chicago Press, 1968), pp. 56 and 313.

80. One writer argues also that populism restores to urban migrants "socially holistic former times"; see M. L. Coniff, Urban Politics in Brazil, the Rise of Populism, 1925–1945 (Pittsburgh, University Press of Pittsburgh, 1981).

81. See, for example, the discussion of urban populism and social movements in Manuel Castells, The City and the Grassroots: A Cross-Cultural Theory of Urban Social Movements (London, Arnold, 1983).

82. Hollander, "Si Evita Viviera."

83. For a thorough account and examination of the conservative bias of a populist leader, see K. Post, Arise Ye Starvelings: The Jamaican Labour Rebellion of 1938 and its Aftermath (The Hague, Nijhoff, 1978).

84. See, for example, the figures and arguments for the decrease in income equality as "development" proceeds in Montek S. Ahluwalia, "Inequality, Poverty and Development," *Journal of Development Economics* (December 1976), 3(4):307–41.

85. See Russell King, *Land Reform: A World Survey* (London, Bell, 1977), chapter on Taiwan.

86. For general accounts of the labor situation in Singapore, see "Focus: Singapore '79," *Far Eastern Economic Review* (August 10, 1979), 105(32):35–38; Shee Poon-Kim, "Singapore 1978: Preparation for the 1980s," *Asian Survey* (February 1979), 19(2):124–30.

87. See, for example, Kim Chang Soo, "Marginalisation, Development and the Korean Workers Movement," *AMPO* (1977), 9(3):20–39.

88. William S. Turley, "Urban Transformation in South Vietnam," *Pacific Affairs* (1976–1977), 49(4):607–24.

89. Raymond B. Pratt, "Community Political Organizations and Lower Class Politicization in Two Latin American Cities," *Journal of Development Studies* (1971), 5(4):523–42.

90. See, for example, "After Industrialisation More Cake for the Workers?" (Algeria), *African Business* (March 1979), no. 7, pp. 24–25; "Plan National de Development," *El Moudjahid* (Alger), July 18, 1979.

91. Frank Bovenkerk, "The Rehabilitation of the Rabble: How and Why Marx and Engels Wrongly Depicted the Lumpenproletariat as a Reactionary Force," *The Netherlands Journal of Sociology* (1984), 20(13–14):13–41.

92. As quoted in R. Cohen and D. Michael, "Revolutionary Potential of the African Lumpenproletariat," *Institute of Development Studies Bulletin* (1973), 5:31–42.

93. See L. Dietz, "Political Participation by the Urban Poor in an Authoritarian Context: The Case of Lima, Peru," *Journal of Political and Military Sociology* (1977), 5(1):63–77; as abstracted in *Sociological Abstracts* (1977), 25(5):1344.

94. Wayne A. Cornelius, "Urbanization and Political Demand Making: Political Poor in Latin American Cities," *American Political Science Review* (1974), 68(3):1145; for similar findings, see also Mau, "The Threatening Masses"; J. C. Van Es and William J. Finn, "A Note on the Determinants of Satisfaction Among Urban Migrants in Bogota, Colombia," *Inter-American Economic Affairs* (1973), 27(2):15–28.

95. See, for example, R. Clignet, "Urban Unemployment as a Determinant of Political Unrest: The Case of Douda Cameroon," *Canadian Journal of African Studies* (Summer 1969), 3(2):463–87; Pauline Baker, *Urbanization and Political Change: The Politics of Lagos, 1917–1977* (Berkeley, University of California Press, 1978); Sudhendu Mukherjee, *Under the Shadow of the Metropolis* (Calcutta, Calcutta Metropolitan Development Authority, 1974).

96. See, for example, Hector Bejar, *Peru 1965: Notes on a Guerrilla Experience* (New York, Monthly Review Press, 1970), p. 42.

97. John Geller, *Bayonets in the Streets* (Toronto, Collier-Macmillan, 1974), p. 2.

98. R. Moss, *The War for the Cities* (New York, Coward, McCann Geoghegan, 1972), pp. 138–40.

99. See, for example, the discussion by H. C. F. Mansilla, "On Some Psychological and Cultural Aspects of Latin American Guerrilla Warfare," in Johan Niezing, *Urban Guerrilla*, (Rotterdam, Netherlands, University of Rotterdam Press, 1974) pp. 139–41.

100. See Arthuro C. Porzencanski, *Uruguay's Tupamaros: The Urban Guerrilla* (New York, Praeger, 1973); M. E. Gilio, *The Tupamaros* (London, Secker and Warburg, 1973).

101. Carlos Marighela, *For the Liberation of Brazil* (Harmondsworth, England: Penguin, 1971), and especially the document "A Mini-Manuel of Guerrilla Warfare."

102. This has even extended to a reassessment of the historical reasons for Marx and Engels' low opinion of the "lumpenproletariat"; see Bovenkirk, "Rehabilitation of the Rabble."

103. For a review of these, see Josef Gugler, "Political Responses to Poverty," in A. Gilbert and J. Gugler, *Cities, Poverty, and Development; Urbanization in the Third World* (London, Oxford University Press, 1981), pp. 134–61.

104. *Ibid.*, p. 146.

105. For a discussion of "new social movements" with special reference to social identity, which was earlier identified as one of the elements in primitive labor market workers' consciousness, see T. Evers, "Identity: The Hidden Side of New Social Movements in Latin America' (unpublished paper, Amsterdam, CEDLA, 1983).

106. See Castells, *The City and the Grassroots*, p. 288; Paul Singer, "Neighbourhood Movements in Sao Paulo," in Safa, *Towards a Political Economy*, pp. 283–302.

107. Gilbert and Ward, "Community Action."

108. For a review of the importance of such actions, see Bienen, "Urbanization," pp. 668–70.

109. See, for example, Fred Halliday, "The Peoples Democratic Republic of Yemen: The Cuban 'Path in Arabia,' " and David Weild, "Mozambique—Late Colonialism and Early Problems in Transition," both in G. White, R. Murray, and C. White, eds., *Revolutionary Socialist Development in the Third World* (Brighton, England, Wheatsheaf Books, 1983), and for the use of the "urban mass' concept, see Gugler, "Political Responses."

110. Thomas H. Henriksen, *Revolution and Counterrevolution; Mozambiques War of Independence 1964–1974* (London, Greenwood Press, 1983), p. 81.

111. See Luis Serra, "The Sandanist Mass Organization," in Thomas W. Walker, ed., *Nicaragua in Revolution* (New York, Praeger, 1982), pp. 95–115.

112. See, for example, Homa Katanzian, "The Agrarian Question in Iran," in A. K. Ghose, ed., *Agrarian Reform in Contemporary Developing Countries* (London, Croom Helm, 1983), p. 351.

113. Jonathan Kelly and Herbert S. Klein, *Resolution and the Rebirth of Inequality: A Theory Applied to the National Revolution in Bolivia* (Berkeley, University of California, 1981).

114. Andrew Mack, "The Non-Strategy of Urban Guerrilla Warfare," in Niezing, *Urban Guerrilla*, pp. 22–46.

115. Gugler, "Political Responses," pp. 156–57.

116. Ralph Thaxton, "Mao Zedong, Red Miserables, and the Moral Economy of Peasant Rebellion in Modern China," in R. P. Weller an S. E. Guggenheim, eds., *Power and Protest in the Countryside: Studies or Rural Unrest in Asia, Europe, and Latin America* (Durham, N. C., Duke University Press, 1982), pp. 132–56.

117. *Ibid.*, pp. 153 and 156.

CHAPTER 5

ENTERPRISE
LABOR MARKET
SOCIAL RELATIONS

Once while I was away in Nairobi,
a trade union official came and incited the workers to strike.
About 160 bags of flour were wasted. When I came back, I gave
a rise to the workers who lived around the township. Then I
went to our own country branch, and sacked about ten. The rest
agreed to come back to work. After a while, I sacked the workers
in the town I'd given a rise to, because there were lots of people
wanting to work who were prepared to accept less.[1]

This statement was made by an African employer; it reveals his
complete power to dismiss workers, to fix the level of wages, to
reject unions, and, by implication, to change the pace and conditions of work.

The type of authority and domination of employer over
employees expressed in this statement is at the core of the pattern
of power relations associated with an enterprise labor market—
"enterprise," because the relations are invariably found within a
structured productive organization that is the source of wage
work, and "labor market," because employers' power is shaped
by a market in which individuals are forced to compete to sell
their ability to work.

The essence of these social relations is the individual labor
contract between employer and employed in which the employer
is basically dominant. The negative conditions then are that there

is no effective worker organization or state protective agency that intervenes between buyer and seller of labor to redress the power inequality of the parties in any substantial way. The employer's dominance is manifested by the ability to take alone major decisions about wages and conditions of work, hiring, dismissal, investment, location, products, and other factors associated with the management of an enterprise.

Workers are not, however, in the same position as the casual workers of the primitive labor market, for employers' power is not entirely without restraint. The restraint arises from three factors not apparent in primitive labor market social relations. First, social relations are within a structured enterprise, which means that the work force must have a minimum of skills in order to be efficient and profitable. It is the skill and regularity factor that creates a structured labor market and restrains the employer from using frequent and arbitrary dismissal as a means of disciplining labor. Second, the state may intervene in a number of ways and in varying degrees to condition and restrain employers' power. Third, classes and dominant groups in control of worker organizations and large enterprises and other forms of social relations make decisions and policies that substantially affect the power of employers within the enterprise labor market.

The restraints do not amount to a protection enjoyed by established workers in large corporations, who are often members of powerful worker organizations or in receipt of wide-ranging forms of state intervention on their behalf. The workers of the enterprise labor market have acquired structured, regular, and wage employment and have therefore left the casual work of the primitive labor market or the dominated peasant life of the peasant-lord social relations. But they have not been able to translate the structured wage employment within an enterprise into the collective power protecting them from arbitrary dismissal, increased hours and pace of work, direct or indirect reduction of wages, and lack of health and safety provisions. In short, for several reasons, discussed later in this chapter, they have not acquired sufficient power to redress employers' power or to call up the power of the state or unions to act on their behalf.

Although the workers of the enterprise labor market have

not been able to alter significantly the balance of power between them and the employers, the employers themselves are subject to the power of groups and classes in dominant forms of social relations. The bulk of the employers in the enterprise labor market are the owners or controllers of small enterprises and as such they may be mere agents of transfer of surplus to banks, large corporations, and the state, the controllers of which manipulate capital, labor, and product markets. Thus employers in the enterprise labor market have rarely developed sufficient collective power to determine their own future or alter the direction of the social formation, although they may well see their survival as being based upon the prevention and defeat of attacks against their privileges and power arising from their subordinate workers.

The workers and the employers of the enterprise labor market form of social relations correspond to the "wage slaves" and "capitalists" of the nineteenth century about whom Marx and Engels theorized. At that time the enterprise labor market was a dominant form of social relations, and employers were a class that led the industrialization process. Now, as a subordinate form of social relations, the social composition of both employers and workers has changed, as well as their possible role of maintaining stability or promoting change. Most employers, instead of predominantly emerging from self-employment and founding enterprises with capital accumulated by themselves, are now also inheritors of functioning enterprises, or organize enterprises with state grants or loans or capital transferred from wealth accumulated in peasant-lord relations.[2] Workers, as the weakest and most exploited of the industrial labor force, are disproportionately composed of socially disadvantaged groups as they appear within social relations of production—women, ethnic and racial minorities, migrants, and children. The fruits of their labor accrue in unequal amounts to their immediate employers within enterprise labor market relations and then to workers and dominant groups in other social relations. The subordinate position of enterprise labor market social relations in the hierarchy of forms of social relations is a crucial political and social factor of the transnational world economy of the latter half of the twentieth century.

VARIANTS OF ENTERPRISE
LABOR MARKET RELATIONS

Enterprise labor market social relations are found in almost every country in the world. There are three variants of the basic pattern of power relations of the enterprise labor market associated with, first, workers who work in small-to-medium enterprises in industry and commerce, second, those who work in larger enterprises but have not been able to achieve security of employment or union protection, and third, rural seasonal workers on farm enterprises.

Some of the more vivid examples of the first variant—the small enterprise—was found in Hong Kong in the late 1960s. At that time 80 percent of Hong Kong enterprises employed fewer than fifty persons. The workers were, in the main, refugees from mainland China who were grateful for work and cooperated, according to some officials, with the employers in avoiding state regulation and would not join the existing but ineffective unions. They suffered the extreme work conditions willingly, apparently sharing the entrepreneurs' efforts for competitive struggle for the survival of the enterprise. Hong Kong's phenomenal export-led industrial growth was based upon these social relations.[3] If the workers succumbed willingly to employer domination and the harsh conditions it produced in small enterprises in Hong Kong, this was not the case in another Asian country—South Korea. In the mid 1970s, a worker burned himself to death using a copy of the South Korean labor code as a torch in protest against the authorities' refusal to enforce the provisions of the code. After the protest, newspapers revealed that in Seoul's Peace Market, which was the scene of the demonstration, there were 270,000 workers employed in small textile establishments. Most of these were young women between 12 and 22 who often worked sixteen hours a day and at peak season worked two or three days without sleep, with enterprise owners providing pills and injections to keep them awake.[4] In the mid 1980s in Japan small enterprises, and even some larger nonunionized enterprises, have resorted to employing women on a "part-time" basis; in fact the women work an eight-hour day at wages as much as 50 percent less then for men doing similar work and have no social security benefits or rights.[5] These examples are from Asian countries at differing levels of economic wealth, but as the example from Africa quoted above illustrates, such conditions are found in all regions and countries.

The second type of situation of the enterprise labor market social relations is that of an unprotected worker enclave within a larger enterprise in which there also exists an established worker labor force enjoying the protection provided by trade unions, state-enforced labour law, and/or negotiated corporate arrangements. Examples of this type are most common in all larger enterprises which make distinctions between permanent and temporary employees. The better known examples of this situation are found in Japan, where a selected number of workers in large enterprises have the promise of life-time security of work; in India, where large enterprises have long made a practice of employing a formal category of "temporary" workers; and more recently in the United States and elsewhere in Western Europe, where union-negotiated agreements, such as those in the US auto industry, have provided job security for a limited number of workers. The excluded workers are invariably subjected to the power relations of the enterprise labor market.

In different forms such dualism of social relations within one enterprise has existed in situations other than the more publicized examples given above. This has been especially the case with large companies operating outside large, urban industrial areas and away from large labor markets. Such an example is that of a large shoe company in Switzerland; partly as a result of tradition, this company established very early in its history, a policy of long-term job security for its employees. Such employees were the beneficiaries of a large number of company-derived social welfare provision, including, for example, a basket of clothes for every child born in an employee's immediate family.

The labor force for the plant was originally drawn from the local communities and daily bussed to the plant so that the villages retained their social cohesion. Although there were no external trade unions, an employees' association presided over the organization of the corporate-derived benefits. In the late 1950s this situation began to change as the company expanded its labor force—not by adding more local Swiss citizens but by employing many thousands of migrant Italian workers who had temporary work permits and who were not allowed to bring their families with them. They were housed under collective conditions near the factory. These workers did not receive the benefits of the longer term established Swiss employees; they performed the more dirty, less skilled work and were paid wages substantially below those of Swiss workers engaged in similar tasks in other enterprises. They could be dismissed without restriction and were always under the threat of having their work permits removed if they incurred managerial disapproval. They were unprotected workers in enterprise labor market relations subjected to the overwhelming and, in this case, almost absolute power of the corporate employer.[6]

The third situation in which enterprise labor market social relations exist concerns the landless wage laborer in third-world countries. Transformations in subsistence and peasant-lord relations have resulted in more and more landless laborers prepared to engage in wage-labor agricultural work. Employment patterns and social relations are in transition and vary greatly from country, region, and crop. Thus, for example, some employers, such as those in parts of Indonesia, provide rewards other than wages in order to try and keep a returning and cooperative labor force.[7] If such employment were regular, it is clear that the employer would have dominance, based upon an individual contract of work with no intervening power on behalf of the workers, and the social relations would be those of the enterprise labor market. However, the seasonal nature of agriculture and the growing numbers of landless laborers mean that the workers are more often than not employed on a casual basis and the social relations governing their production are closer to the atomized, irregular, primitive labor market variety.[8]

The discussion of enterprise labor market relations in this chapter concentrates on the first two variants—the small enterprise and the nonestablished worker in the larger enterprise both within the industrial and commercial sectors. Nevertheless, the fact that enterprise social relations exist, and may in the future be more widespread in third-world agricultural production, should not be obscured by the particular emphasis that must be given here.[9]

Enterprise labor market social relations are found in al-

most every social formation in the world. Even in those dominated by central planning and state ownership of the means of
production, there is a lenient attitude to the power of small-
enterprise employers. Thus it was not until seven years after the
1949 victory of the Chinese Communists that the authorities
brought small enterprises within central planning.[10] In Yugoslavia employers with fewer than five workers are officially permitted to escape the restriction on their power arising from the
state industrial sector system of worker's self-management.

Until recently enterprise labor market social relations in
Western Europe and North America were covering a declining
proportion of the labor force. The growth of the parallel economy
and the policies of governments designed to increase employer
power, promote small enterprises, and reduce numbers of unionized workers have, however, created an upward swing in the
numbers of people entering such social relations.

In the third world the development of special zones subject
to different labor laws and out-of-bounds for unions, the disruption of the rural labor structures, and the continuing state policy
of encouragement of small industries in which unions are banned
(as, for example, in Pakistan where enterprises with fewer than
twenty employees may not have unions) are causing the numbers
in this form of social relations to grow. For countries following a
capitalist developmental path the numbers in the enterprise labor
market have always been a high percentage of the total industrial labor force, although, of course, owing to the low level of
industrialization, a relatively low percentage of the *total* labor
force.

Estimations of the numbers of workers in the world found
in the three variants of the enterprise labor market relations can
be made by considering statistics such as the numbers of workers
in the commercial and industrial labor force who are not in
unions, employment in the state sector, civil service, and military
and the numbers of socially disadvantaged workers employed.
These, combined with other statistics, such as the numbers of
small enterprises, help to arrive at an estimated 10 to 15 percent
of the world labor force, exclusive of the socialist countries of
Eastern Europe and China. In the absence of statistics based on
the criteria of social relations, however, such estimations can at
best be approximate.

EMPLOYERS' POWER,
STATE, AND UNIONS

Enterprise labor market social relations of production made their appearance with the development of industrialization and the factory labor system; the origin of this form of social relations is, then, also the origin of what has become known as capitalism. The reasons for the emergence of industrialism and capitalism in the United Kingdom in the eighteenth and nineteenth centuries are unclear—the exact combination of factors that caused the displacement of workers from rural areas, the accumulation of wealth and its transformation into productive capital, and the combination of such capital and labor is in doubt. Any attempt to weigh such factors and investigate their origins would take the discussion deep into the controversies of economic historians and development economists. In contrast, the development of industrialization and its social dynamics is better known because it has been formalized into a model and made the base of modern market-oriented economic theory so well pioneered by the classical economists such as Smith, Ricardo, and Marx. It is sufficient here to consider this classical model of development in relation to the origin of employers' power over labor as it is now manifested in modern enterprise labor market social relations.

The essential lines of the model were that workers were displaced from rural areas and were therefore severed from the ownership or control over their means of making a living, which had been either land or the tools of artisans. They were left only with their ability to labor at any task available as their means of acquiring subsistence. Entrepreneurs or employers were those who combined such available labor with capital—which they owned or over which they had power—to produce goods within a factory system.[11] Under the technological conditions of the time the result was myriads of what would now be called small-to medium-scale enterprises employing between five and one hundred workers. Because each enterprise tended to be individually owned, it also meant that there developed a numerically large capital-owning class.

The industrial centers of the United Kingdom—Birmingham, Manchester, and London—were characterized by this labor-intensive, small-unit industrial production, sometimes known as the "workshop" type of industrial organization.

Theoretically, capital-owning entrepreneurs and labor-selling workers were both set within a framework of competition between individual entrepreneurs and their enterprises in the product market and between individual laborers in the labor market. Neither worker nor employer was assumed or supposed to have control of these markets, which automatically, through the dynamics of competition, respectively fixed the price of the products and the price of labor. The market was supposed to censure the inefficient entrepreneur, by forcing the controlled enterprise out of production because the product prices were too high, or to deny the laborer work if he or she demanded too high wages or failed to work at the pace and intensity demanded. This system never worked in its pure economic and market-based form, and right from the beginning, entrepreneurs and workers came into conflict socially and politically (both in conjunction with and independently of so-called market forces) concerning wages, hours of work, and basic human rights.

The omission of the force of these social and humanitarian demands was not the only factor that made the model inaccurate. More important was that employers soon avoided the confines of the labor market through the development of a pool of unemployed workers that ensured an oversupply of interchangeable labor that kept wages low. At the same time it provided a disciplining instrument for anyone with the power to grant or withhold employment. Logically, the force of the disciplining impact of the refusal to grant work to a laborer increased with the level of misery of the unemployed. Writing of the individual labor contract in 1902, Sidney and Beatrice Webb noted: "There is no freedom of contract. The alternative on one side (the employers) is inconvenience; on the other it is starvation."[12] The importance of such labor-disciplining factors is well known and recognized even in the currently changed situation. Paul A. Samuelson, a leading economist of the neoclassical school, attributed the apparent decline in the discipline of labour, and therefore in productivity, in the 1970s to a weakening of the "hungriness motives."[13]

On the entrepreneurial side, in contrast, the market for

products rarely sanctioned the individual entrepreneur, for many mechanisms were found, including protective collusion and enlargement of enterprises, to offset any market strictures. Even when entrepreneurs failed, closed the enterprise, and declared bankruptcy, they almost never descended to the level of material misery of the workers and never to that of the unemployed—the classic route for a hopelessly bankrupt entrepreneur was to emigrate to the colonies, where even a small amount of capital or talent could purchase a materially comfortable life.[14]

With little censure from the product market and any individual power of a worker destroyed by an engineered oversupply of labor, the employer had virtually absolute power within the enterprise. At the beginning of industrialization in the early 1800s in the United Kingdom, skills were less important to production, and the bulk of workers could be hired or fired at will, for there was a ready supply of interchangeable unskilled labor. The desperate plight of those without work was all that was needed to enforce grueling work rhythms and a sixteen-hour day. The employment of children became widespread as parents tried to make up a subsistence family budget.[15]

Although the conditions of industrial poverty continued, for some part of the population, well into the twentieth century in the now industrialized countries, the absolute power of employers within the enterprise was a relatively short-lived phenomenon. With the decline of absolute employer power, enterprise labor market social relations of production ceased to be a dominant form in the social formations. Instead, the power relations among worker organizations (usually trade unions), the state, and employers, particularly those in control of larger enterprises, gradually began to determine the level of return and the conditions of work for the unionized workers. In effect, worker intervention in the labor market through "combination" into trade unions signaled the beginning of the replacement of the individual contract of labor by the collective contract concluded between organized workers and employers. Likewise, the intervention of the state in attempting to regulate working conditions began to develop the rules and patterns with which any remaining individual contract of labor had to conform.

The growth of unions and the beginnings of state intervention thus transformed nineteenth-century enterprise labor relations, in which employers had absolute power, into the now familiar patterns of bargaining between workers organized into unions and employers. That pattern became the dominant tripartite form of social relations. The discussion of this transformation will be taken up in *Power, Production, and the Established Worker*, for it concerns the origins of the bipartite and tripartite forms of social relations and the established workers. It is, however, important to look here at the process of this transformation because it determined the nature of enterprise labor market relations that continue to exist in a subordinate position.

In this transformation employers' basic power to hire and fire at will and to determine wages was lost through two interconnected developments. It has been noted that employers' power in these respects was based upon the oversupply of labor, which allowed any unsatisfactory or recalcitrant worker to be dismissed and replaced by one of the many who clamored for the position so vacated. It follows that any decline in the substitutability of workers—when it became less easy to replace one worker by *any* other one chosen at random from the unemployed—would weaken employers' power. They would become more hesitant in dismissing a worker who demanded higher wages and, conversely, more inclined to bargain over the demand.

In fact, industry and the factory system developed in a manner that made it more difficult to use unskilled and irregular labor. Machines required at least rudimentary skills and manual dexterity, while the ever-increasing division of labor, in which total production became dependent on each worker's performing a specified task at the required pace, meant that dismissals and replacement of workers became very disruptive to production and profit. Employers' need for skills and regularity of work undermined worker substitutability and constrained their power in all circumstances except where totally industrially unskilled labor was used. Thus the developments of the physical production process began to weaken employers' power, even in the framework of the individual contract of labor. The developments in the production process also assisted the emergence and growth of trades unions and their collective intervention in the labor market. The unions finally destroyed the "pure" or "primitive" function of the labor market, which had already been eroded.[16] When wage rates became determined by the bargaining power of the employers and unions, the absolute power of employers to fix general wage rates came to an end. Smaller employers had to follow the lead established by the bargaining process between unions and industrialists taking place elsewhere. Employers who are not forced to bargain still have a wide wage-fixing power, but it is confined to limits set by the bargaining among worker organizations, employers, or states within dominant forms of social relations.[17]

Perhaps more important to the development of the contemporary version of enterprise labor market relations was the growth of state intervention in fixing conditions of work. The series of acts in the United Kingdom in the nineteenth century, known collectively as the Factory Acts, are among the first examples of such intervention in an industrializing country. They began in 1802 with an act to regulate excesses meted out to child apprentices in cotton mills, and since that time numerous acts have produced a complex and detailed labor legislation similar to that on the statute books throughout the world.[18] The early acts are important because they were passed long before the development of trade unions and worker-based political parties, which at a later date were to be the source and inspiration of so many state legal interventions on behalf of workers.

It was the aristocracy and employers then who instigated the first state intervention in the United Kingdom. Their reasons for this were many and not easy to discover; they were certainly interested in limiting the self-destructive downward pressures on wages and conditions of work resulting from product market competition, some had humanitarian concern,[19] and others had fears of the social consequences of continuing impoverishment of the workers. They also had an interest in regularizing and formalizing employer power over workers and especially over any possible worker organizations.

State intervention stabilized employer power because it brought into existence a body of law that defined and established basic "rights" of employers over workers. The nineteenth-century United Kingdom was not legally well equipped with laws that would uphold the rights of owners of industrial, as opposed to landed, property. Laws such as that of "trespass" clearly arising from the notion of physical invasion of land, were clumsily extended to industrial property. Thus although the existing law of contract might proved the right of an employer to dismiss a worker without giving a reason, if the worker refused to leave the place of work, the employer would have to rely on the law of trespass to secure eviction by agents of the state. The Factory Acts, which established legal provisions concerning the physical conditions of work, such as the amount of space per worker, and put limits on the number of hours of work, also then spawned legislation formalizing the employer's right of dismissing, of making investment decisions, of locating factories, and of taking disciplinary measures. These have all now been incorporated in the concepts of employers' "rights" and "managerial perogatives."

In this way then the state consolidated employers' power. It is significant to note that when interventionist labor laws were drafted for colonies, or were otherwise spread throughout the world from the early examples in Western Europe, restrictions of employers' power were coupled with more overt restrictions on workers' organizations. Varieties of the British colonial provisions that workers' organizations must be "registered" with the state authorities to be legal, or that a certain number of workers is required to form such an organization, and other restrictions on spontaneous growth, appear in labor codes and laws throughout the world. The registration provisions in countries of Latin America, for example, have been identified as one important block to the development of trade unions, especially in smaller enterprises.[20]

Nevertheless, state intervention, especially when it subsequently incorporated demands of unions and associated political parties for general regulation of the conditions of work, gradually reduced the power of employers to the currently prevailing levels within enterprise labor market social relations. Labor legislation has, for example, severely restricted one of the early hallowed rights of employers—the power of dismissal of a worker; in all industrialized countries there are elaborate procedures that employers must follow and many protective tribunals to which individual workers may appeal in the case of "wrongful dismissal." Individual contracts of employment must contain provisions laid down by general legislation for the contractual protection of workers. Although, as will be shown in the next section, under enterprise labor market social relations, employers often circumvent or ignore these provisions, there has been sufficient reduction in employer power to make current enterprise labor market relations distinct from their nineteenth-century version when they constituted the dominant form of social relations.

To some extent the modern variants of the form examined in this chapter can be seen either as attempts by employers, as the basic power holders, to prevent further erosion of their power by circumventing existing restraints or as distinct strategies to restore elements of their power, which has been progressively eroded since the middle of the last century.

THE SMALL ENTERPRISE

The bulk of enterprise labor market workers in the world are found in small enterprises. This section considers the psychological, sociological, and organizational blocks to worker power in small enterprises that support the general proposition that the smaller the enterprise the greater the employer power. The economic exploitation of the enterprise labor market at the level of the social formation is analyzed separately.

Small enterprise in this discussion means any organization that has production as its basic goal, whether it is in the industrial, commercial, service, or agricultural sectors, and that employs fewer than 100 persons. As a general rule, it can be said that the qualities of smallness of an enterprise that sustain employer dominance begin to be lost as total employment in the enterprise moves above approximately 50 people. In fact, for the most part small enterprises referred to in this section would have between 5 and 20 workers employed.[21]

Size of enterprise does not *determine* social relations but merely provides a strong indication of the possible type of social relations that govern the lives of the producers who work within it. This means that there are some important exceptions to the general rule correlating small enterprises with employer dominance. Thus, in some countries and some industries countervailing worker power has been established even in the smallest of enterprises; the engineering industry in the United Kingdom and the transport industry in the United States, for example, have had a tradition of aggressive and efficient unions operating in small companies. In Norway and Sweden, which have a relatively large number of small enterprises, the national unions have been able to include in their membership, and therefore in their national bargaining, the majority of small-enterprise workers. At one period in the recent history of Sudan small enterprise unions proliferated, and this development was one of the causes of moves by subsequent regimes to "consolidate" them into state-approved unions.[22] These are cases of unusual transformation of enterprise labor market social relations.

An even broader reservation to the general rule of employer dominance in small enterprises arises from cultural, religious, and traditional factors. Organizational dynamics are profoundly affected by culture and religion; in any single culture the point at which the size of the enterprise, in terms of numbers employed, begins to offset the qualities of smallness that support employer power will be different. Paternalist employers, for example, may be able to use this ethic and tradition to control much larger enterprises in India and Kenya than in Colombia, Argentina, or other Latin American countries where industrial paternalist tradition is less well entrenched. As with other forms of social relations the precise determination of the pattern and presence of social relations can be made only through extensive study and observation of each particular case. There are, however, some special qualities of smallness within enterprises that at the same time prevent worker organization, assist in circumventing state intervention, support employers' power, and result in enterprise labor market social relations. These qualities may be divided into two groups: first, the social and psychological aspects of small organizations, and second, the administrative problems of the state agencies, unions, and other large organizations that attempt to regulate small productive units.

The social and psychological aspects amount to four

closely interconnected factors—face-to-face relationships between employers and workers, paternalism, work satisfaction, and enterprise loyalty. Face-to-face relationships between employer and employed mean that the person in highest authority in the enterprise has considerable personal contact with the subordinate personnel, in contrast to larger enterprises, where the highest authority may rarely be seen and communication is indirect, being through the intermediaries of the organizational hierarchy.[23] Face-to-face relationships of this kind are one of the social qualities most commonly associated with small enterprises and the characteristic most quoted as being the principal reason for the persistent and stated economic success of small enterprises. It is argued that such relationships reduce social distance between employer, owner, or manager to such an extent that antagonisms and conflicts of interest that potentially exist between them are eliminated.[24] Personnel management advisers interested in the elimination of disputes and conflict, without changing the authority structure within the enterprise, advocate face-to-face contact as a solution to any employer-worker antagonism.[25] Even in large enterprises the emulation of face-to-face contact by using the form, rather than the substance, of such relations is seen as a solution to conflict and restriction on worker organization. Face-to-face relations merge with the "working boss" ethic that is often revered by small entrepreneurs and claimed to be the basis of a labor-"trouble-free" enterprise. It is believed that owners of small enterprises working alongside their employees solve the problems of social conflict based upon envy of the authority, larger incomes, and generally higher status of the employer.[26]

The importance of face-to-face relationships as a basis for a social cohesion within small enterprises has unquestionably been overstated in both popular and academic accounts. In the first place, detailed studies of worker attitudes and opinions have revealed a different picture: a survey of workers in small enterprises in the United Kingdom showed that they were very much aware of the income and class differences between them and their employers.[27] In France, workers in small enterprises believed that worker power based on unionization was definitely desirable, contrary to the small unit "social harmony" thesis, but was not administratively possible within a small enterprise.[28] In Hong Kong an anthropological family study has revealed a wide range of hostile attitudes toward management, owners, and supervisors within both small and medium, but all nonunionized, enterprises in which members of the family had worked.[29]

A more substantial reservation to the importance of face-to-face relations in eliminating social tension, making harmonious relations, and weakening social barriers is that, in many countries, owners and entrepreneurs are of one caste, ethnic group, race, or nationality and workers are of another.[30] One socially distinct group in authority and another in subordination invariably results in the development of mutual disparagement, hate, and racism. So it is that entrepreneurs and the entrepreneurial class of the overseas Chinese in Southeast Asia or East Indians and Lebanese in West Africa, and of different castes in India, have become unpopular or hated, as the expulsion of East Indians from Uganda in 1972 and the pogroms, violent and otherwise, against Chinese small businessmen in Malaysia, Jamaica, and elsewhere have demonstrated. Face-to-face relations in the small enterprise certainly have a role in the prevention of the development of power relations based on formal, impersonal bargaining from different positions of strength. They are therefore a quality of small enterprises that support enterprise labor market relations, but the relatively minor importance has been disguised because they have been publicized as the redeeming feature of small enterprises and of private ownership and as an indication of natural harmony and workplace democracy.

A globally more important psychological and social factor supporting enterprise labor market relations in small enterprises is the ethic of paternalism expressed and practiced by many employers. Paternalism within a productive organization is more usually the description of an attitude of an employer, rather than the actual existence of a social relations in which there are morally enforceable and reciprocal rights and duties between worker and employers similar to those between a parent and child. It is, in fact, a description of an authority structure in which the dominance of the employer is expressed or disguised through a superficial concern for welfare: Kenyan businessmen have "tried to educate them (the workers) to understand the need for discipline, hard work and wage restraint, lectured them about drinking and improvidence and sometimes took a fatherly interest in their personal problems.[31] In Colombia one factory owner claimed "I want my girls to find good husbands and be good mothers when they leave."[32]

Paternalism as a managerial style enables the employer to exercise authority as if of right and encourages the worker to develop psychological, social, or material debts to the employer and the enterprise, all of which promote a resistance to outside intervention and the formation of countervailing worker organizations. When backed up by minor material concessions, paternalism represents an attempt to create small-unit protective corporatism without the expense usually involved and without the ability, as in larger corporations, to pass on the cost to the consumer. For this reason paternalism usually rests at the level of style and of psychological relations and does not in the ultimate redress the power in favor of subordinate workers.[33]

Employers invariably build upon all these characteristics of the small enterprise to sustain and maintain their power. They select out workers who are likely to be "troublemakers" and refuse to hire them or, alternatively, dismiss those who ask for their legal rights. To avoid high labor turnover, especially of skilled workers, some employers try to create a core of regular workers who then acquire, on the personal or informal level, a precarious established status.[34] These are the exceptions rather than the rule, and on a world scale high labor turnover in small enterprises is normal.

Face-to-face relations, working bosses, and paternalism clearly do not, despite publicity to the contrary, create social cohesion within the enterprise. They are, nevertheless, of crucial importance for the maintenance of employer dominance because of their role in the development and intensification of two aspects of worker consciousness. The first is a preference for a personalized work relationship and the second, loyalty to the workplace organization. The preference for personalized work relationships has been found in surveys in several different countries and under very different cultural circumstances.[35] That the small enterprise maximizes the possibility of workers' achieving individual friendship and companionship based at the place of work has also been established. The special qualities of the small enterprise are maximized when there is the highest possible informality of operation and the most consistent face-to-face relationships with authority.

The possibility that social relations in small enterprises may satisfy worker demand for interpersonal work relations is also used to create or reinforce a worker consciousness of loyalty toward the enterprise. Manipulative management actively promotes and encourages the development of such consciousness to offset hostile attitudes for purposes of more effective control. In the United Kingdom a study of small enterprises noted that "managerial control in small firms relies not only on the control of remuneration but also on a significant level of identive power."[36] Likewise, in India, management specialists advise employers that "making the workers feel important so that they develop a sense of loyalty etc., needs only behavioural inputs from small industry management [rather] than any financial inputs."[37]

These factors of consciousness, reinforced and manipulated by managerial practice, often therefore make workers in small enterprises resist the incursions of unions and state. They may see these as an outside force that may disturb established relationships or put their work and security in jeopardy.[38] Under circumstances when the unions or state agencies are large bureaucratic organizations in which the leadership may seek increased power for itself rather than for the workers of the enterprise, then worker consciousness is objectively reinforced and the resistance to outside intervention is particularly intense. The net effect of all the social, psychological, and organizational factors discussed so far is that they impede the development of all types of restrictions of employer power within small enterprises.

There remain to be discussed three aspects of an organizational, rather than an internal social character, of small enterprises that contribute to continued dominance of employers. The first is that small size alone makes it difficult to incorporate small enterprise workers within large national unions even if such workers were themselves willing and enthusiastic about being union members. The second is that the lack of bureaucratic procedures in small enterprises provides a greater possibility of flexible and informal operation and therefore of avoiding regulation and control when such regulation might reduce employer power. And third, small enterprises can use state power and regulation when it might increase rather than reduce employer power.

Throughout the world workers in small enterprises are generally more difficult to organize into unions both from the psychological and administrative aspects.[39] It is more difficult to collect dues, keep open lines of communication, deal with grievances, and make wage claims among a number of widely scattered enterprises employing between five and fifty persons than it is to organize a single plant in a single location with a labor force of thousands. There is also a financial incentive involved. Bringing the workers of a large plant into union membership means that with the result of a single organizing effort the union may suddenly acquire a large increase in its income from membership dues. It also means greater power for the union in an industry if the larger rather than smaller enterprises are organized. As a result, unions are reluctant to put the massive administrative and financial effort into organizing small enterprises, and consequently, unions are less prevalent in small enterprises.

In turn the absence of worker organizations is also a contributing factor to the ease with which smaller enterprises avoid state regulation because unions and other worker organizations often monitor management's application of statutory regulations on conditions of work.[40] An industry in which there are large numbers of enterprises requires a greater number of government enforcing agents, if there is indeed an intention to attempt to force conformity to labor codes. The result is that many governments are content, either through default or through deliberate policy, to concentrate on the larger, more easily policed enterprises. In Japan, special labor laws have been enacted whose purpose is to release specifically *small* enterprise employers from some legal obligations to the employees; in India wholesale disregard of labor laws by small enterprise employers has prompted similar proposals.[41] Such moves represent attempts to legally institutionalize enterprise labor market social relations within small enterprises.

One of the most glaring contemporary examples of the apparent ease with which small enterprise employers are able to ignore, or circumvent, laws governing conditions of work is that of the undeclared or illegal worker in Western Europe and North America. Such workers (often migrants, minority groups, or children under working age) are not registered as enterprise employees and do not therefore pay either income tax on money earned or social security charges. Employers do not pay social security charges for the worker involved and need not conform to minimum wage legislation, statutory holidays, or health and safety provisions. The workers are therefore totally unprotected by labour laws and uninsured against accident and unjust treatment.[42] The bulk of these illegal workers are found in small enterprises where, if governments are in fact attempting to eliminate such work as in France and Belgium, financial accounts are more easily fixed to pay wages informally and the chances of inspection are rarer. The social relations governing illegal or undeclared work—"travail noir," (black work) as it is known in France—are of the enterprise labor market variety.[43]

It should not be concluded, of course, that state regulation and intervention always mitigates employers' power and undermines enterprise labor market relations. It may do so, but equally, according to policies and orientations of groups in control of the state and its agencies, intervention may be in the employers' favor.[44]

All these factors mitigating against the development of a more nearly equal power relationship between employers and employed are enhanced if the workers employed are themselves as individuals, less likely to insist upon their rights, or wish to start unions, or resist employer demands. For this reason a high proportion of socially disadvantaged workers is found in the enterprise labor market.

SOCIALLY DISADVANTAGED WORKERS

The discussion of enterprise labor market social relations within small enterprise has so far concentrated on the psychological and organizational mechanisms used to circumvent and resist potential constraints on employer power that may arise from the intervention of state or worker organizations. There exist, however, some personal and social characteristics of individual workers that provide for employer domination *regardless* of organizational circumstance and, in particular, of enterprise size. These characteristics amount to a person's having the condition of being socially disadvantaged. Social disadvantage may include physical or mental defects, long-term mental or physical diseases, and under certain circumstances the attributes arising from race, ethnicity, nationality, age, and sex.

These individual characteristics are not social disadvantages merely by virtue of their existence—they are made into social stigmata by the larger society and dominant groups or classes. Thus male domination and xenophobia are not natural phenomena, at least as they manifest themselves in social relations of production; they are created, promoted, and maintained, with the result that being female or foreign becomes a social disadvantage. The social disadvantage would be removed or lessened with any change in attitudes toward women and foreignness. Enterprise labor market social relations are established and prevail when employers use these social disadvantages to prevent accumulation of countervailing worker power and as a basis for the development of a more intimidated and docile labor force. The special point to note, in contrast to the previous discussion, is that the socially disadvantaged worker carries with him or her the seeds of a potential subordination rather than such subordination's being developed within an enterprise. This means that groups of socially disadvantaged workers may constitute a pocket, or enclave, of enterprise labor market social relations in situations where other social relations generally prevail, that is, a special group of workers in any enterprise or national labor force over whom employers have greater power.

One of the most studied and publicized examples of the use of foreignness as a social disadvantage to create or restore enterprise labor market relations has been that of the foreign workers in Western Europe.[45] This situation is, however, similar to the case of migrant and foreign labor anywhere in the world, as, for example, the more recent interstate migrations in Africa and the interregional migrations to the Eastern oil-producing countries.[46] In the early 1950s labor-short Western European countries began to take into their national labor force numbers of workers from other countries. The majority of these workers were from the poorer countries or from regions at Western Europe's industrial periphery such as Spain, Southern Italy, Yugoslavia, Turkey, and in the case of France, Algeria and other Arab states of the Mediterranean. The workers suffered a number of restrictions—they were almost all temporary in the sense that they either had to, or wanted to, return to their country of origin; some countries granted work permits tied to one particular employment and workers were prevented from changing employment.[47] In addition to the approximately 47 million foreign workers in Western European countries in 1975, there were also believed to be 11 million "illegal" workers who had no official permits to work and were, then, at the mercy of both employers and of any arbitrary enforcement of the law. In the extreme case of Switzerland it was not until the mid-1960s that foreign workers could even bring their families with them to Switzerland or change their jobs, even though at that time nearly one third of the Swiss labor force was composed of foreign workers.

Enterprise labor market social relations prevail almost everywhere such migrants are found, and indeed they are sometimes used to destroy social relations that had been based upon collective bargaining with powerful unions. In France, in 1975, a French woman novelist wrote autobiographically of a love affair with an Algerian worker working on the production line in the Renault car factory.[48] At the time of her writing, more than 60 percent of the production workers in the factory were migrants. For very different reasons neither existing union officials nor the migrants themselves were interested in cooperating with each other. The unionists were unsure and suspicious of the migrants, if not overtly racist, while the migrants could not see that the unions, which were basically organized to provide permanent advantages and security, could do anything for foreigners destined to be temporarily working in the country. The factory gravitated to having a minority of workers well protected by efficient and militant unionists and a majority, namely, the foreign workers, not being unionized or having only a weak formal relationship with the union. This situation, however, was not, completely stable, for a more militant unionism erupted during the mid-1980s when the company attempted to reduce its work force.

Renault is a large company with both national and foreign workers, but more typical of employer dominance of foreign workers and enterprise labor market relations is the case reported in 1980 of a Danish plastics enterprise employing 81 workers who were mostly from Turkey, Yugoslavia, and Pakistan. A union took up their case because it had come to its notice that the management had, apart from paying wages below national averages and failing to provide safety provisions, made a practice of pressuring workers to sign their own resignation when holidays became due or when the bad conditions led one of them to complain.[49] These examples are not exceptional and can be cited for every Western European country that has migrant labor.

The social disadvantage of being a woman has also been used to establish employer dominance in enterprise labor market relations. As a result of the more general interest in the condition of women there is now a substantial literature demonstrating how employers have used preexisting social attitudes toward women and social demands on women in relation to childbearing and childbearing to keep them as an unorganized part-time labor force.[50] While this has become particularly prevalent in third-world countries where multinationals deliberately exclusively employ young women in their manufacturing subsidiaries,[51] even in rich industrialized countries the process still continues. Giving evidence to a legislative committee in the United States on how the Pittsburgh Plate Glass Company organized resistance to unions, a woman worker explained that all of the company antiunion efforts were concentrated in a section of the plant where there was a greater proportion of women.[52] In fact, the company began to develop the duality of established workers, organized by one of the most powerful unions in the country, alongside one or two departments unorganized and staffed by women, non-members of the union. These departments, in the company strategy, were to be the spearhead for a disaffiliation campaign to render the whole plant nonunion and so reintroduce enterprise labor market relations.

From the standpoint of acquiring any bargaining power, children must also clearly be considered as socially disadvantaged workers, and their appearance in structured industrial work almost always ensures that enterprise labor market social relations prevail. The main locale for employment of children in industrial enterprises (as distinct from work on family farms or shops) is in third-world countries and in small enterprises, construction work and textiles being the industries most concerned. In Morocco, the whole carpet industry was dependent on female child labor between the ages of eight and twelve. A labor contractor system is used in which the entrepreneur passes the responsibility for the supply of child labor to a *"maalema."* The children worked at least a 48-hour week, sometimes for no wages and most look "undernourished and overworked."[53]

The cases of socially disadvantaged labor's being used to ensure employer dominance and maximum control and exploitation are numerous. The increased use of socially disadvantaged labor—particularly migrants and women—has caused a weakening of worker power in many industries as unorganized and "unorganizable" labor displaces unions and union members. Such displacement partially explains the decline in the rate of unionization in the industrialized countries of Western Europe and North America mentioned earlier.

Not until recently did trade unions in general make any serious attempts to organize foreign workers, small enterprises, part-time women workers, and others found in enterprise labor market social relations. Particularly in Europe, unions in general paid only lip service to the need to eradicate the social injustices associated with foreign workers. Union leaders in the Netherlands, for example, accepted the argument that foreign workers were "necessary for the economic growth of the economy"[54] and that the better incomes they received, compared with what they would receive in their country of origin, were sufficient reward for the privations of employer dominance. Organizational dynamics meant that, because foreign workers and others were not permanent or committed citizens or residents, political careers of union leaders could not be built upon their support.

The social stigma that such workers carry can be made the basis of a boundary between workers capable of, and successful in, redressing employer power and those who continue to be dominated. In recent years there have been attempts to institutionalize this distinction through legal separation or through enterprise practice. The duality of unprotected workers and established workers, principally within the same enterprise, but also when special sections of the population are nationally designated as outside protection from unions or law, is the basis of the last type of enterprise labor market situation that needs to be examined in detail.

STRUCTURING LIFETIME INSECURITY

The cases so far mentioned in which workers covered by enterprise labor market relations work alongside established workers with bargaining relations have been principally the result of employers' use of strategies associated with enterprise size or social disadvantage to maintain the duality and prevent the emergence of a unified, worker-based countervailing power. The blocks to transformation of social relations have not, in the case of migrant or women workers in Western Europe or small enterprise workers in India, been those of state prohibition or formalized enterprise practice. There is, however, a large and growing number of workers in the world who are *formally* prevented by the power of the state or of the established workers and employers in an enterprise to form worker organizations or to otherwise improve their conditions of work.

Japan and South Africa present two dramatic examples of the institutionalization of enterprise labor market relations and the development of a formal, structured, and proximate relationship between established worker and unprotected worker. In Japan, since the end of the 1940–1945 war, a large number of workers in the larger enterprises—which employ approximately 30 percent of Japan's work force—enjoy a lifetime security of employment.[55] These workers are integrated into a pattern of relations between unions, staff associations, management, and the state, the result of which is that they secure the benefits of lifetime permanent employment, regular and predictable promotion, substantial pension rights, and enterprise-based social benefits. In contrast, there are usually workers who are described as temporary or subcontract workers who do not have security or pension rights and are often not allowed to use enterprise social facilities.

This dichotomy is maintained by the different degrees of power between the established, permanent staff, who occupy strategic jobs and who, in the ultimate case of a strike, could close the factories, and the subcontract workers, who have more menial jobs with no strategic potential for the exercise of collective power. The relationship between the permanent, established worker and the subcontracted worker within enterprise labor market relations is regulated by agreement between the established workers and management. In the Nippon Steel Company, and in other such companies, because permanent and subcontract workers are racially or ethnically indistinguishable from each other, the practice has developed that the established workers wear silver hats and the subcontract workers, yellow hats—the visual symbols of two forms of social relations of production in the same enterprise.[56] Although this level of institutionalization has not been reached elsewhere, in India, for example, it is now the practice for plant-based unions to bargain with management about the criteria of permanent, temporary, or day workers in full acceptance of the difference in benefits for the two types of workers who are essentially governed by two sets of social relations.

In South Africa, at least until 1979, it was not necessary to wear different hats to distinguish the permanent established workers of the bargaining modes of social relations from the unprotected in the enterprise labor market, for skin color was the basis for laws that instituted and maintained employer power over the black population. Black workers, but not white workers, were prohibited by law from forming unions and redressing employer power.[57]

Other attempts to formally and permanently create employer dominance not restricted to a single special national experience are found in the Free Industrial Zones (FIZ) that were created in many third-world countries during the 1970s. By the early 1980s there were more than 300 FIZs in about 66 countries.[58] The country setting up a FIZ usually provides an economic infrastructure, company tax incentives, and other advantages and invites foreign companies to develop an "export processing capacity" in which goods are exported from mainly imported materials and technology. The majority of FIZs are subject to special national legislation that either prohibits or severely restricts the activities of trade unions. In effect, the state guarantees that unions and bargaining forms of social relations will not be permitted within the FIZ. Foreign companies may, therefore, take advantage of the lower wage rates without fear of union intervention. Such companies are sometimes known as "runaway" companies or industries, for they "run away" from unions, higher labor costs, and state restriction in industrialized countries to the FIZs and elsewhere in poor countries. In Malaysia, for example, a major program for FIZs has been based upon special labor legislation that restricts the scope of collective bargaining and enforcement of minimum wage laws.[59]

This type of legislation, as well as the use of socially disadvantaged labor and small enterprises, means that employers begin to regain absolute power in these zones reminiscent of the power they had in Europe of the nineteenth century. Studies of the Korean Nasan Free Export Zone in mid-1970s, revealed that 88 percent of firms in the zone were guilty of illegal labor practices. Japanese companies in the zone insisted on a three-month initiation period for all new workers employed in small enterprises—who were almost exclusively young females—during which time they received a 20 to 30 percent lower salary and were required to do extra work free. It was also reported that "unscrupulous" methods were used to make workers resign rather than be dismissed, which would technically involve severance pay and transportation costs.[60] Wages in the Zone were one seventh of those in Japan where most companies originated. The FIZs are the most current attempt to establish enterprise labor market relations by force of the state within a social formation where established workers have in one way or another already developed at least some countervailing power.

This enforced duality of social relations within industrial production, whether at the level of the enterprise or of the social formation, is one of the current principal strategies for increasing the proportion of the labor force that is sufficiently weak to be unable to resist increased intensity of work, declining real wages and conditions, and therefore higher levels of extraction for dominant groups and classes.

THE ECONOMIC VALUE
OF EMPLOYERS' POWER

Enterprise labor market relations result in the maximum of employer and managerial control over work and production, which in turn produces some of the lowest labor costs within industrial production. This material fact is at the base of the external relations of the form of social relations.

Economically the products from, and value of, the enterprise labor market form of social relations must always be viewed in relation to those of the dominant forms. Thus the "low" wages in the enterprise labor market essentially mean they are low in relation to those of the established workers in the dominant forms. The control of employers in the enterprise labor market extends over wages, physical conditions of work, fringe benefits, and pace and intensity of work; these differentially affect the ultimate result of relatively cheaper labor cost.

The ability of employers in the enterprise labor market to keep money wages down is one of their weakest areas of power. General wage structures and rates are determined by bargaining between larger enterprises and unions in dominant forms of social relations or controlled and influenced by the state using a variety of macro wage control mechanisms.[61] Within this general framework, however, employers of the enterprise labor market have a limited power to adjust rates in relation to the overall structure. Such power is manifested, for example, by wide wage differences between similar sized enterprises for similar work. It is this limited power that produces the crucial differences in wages between workers in the enterprise labor market and the established workers in the bargaining or corporate forms of social relations.[62]

More important to the maintenance of low labor costs within the enterprise labor market is the power of employers to control the pace, intensity, and conditions of work. Employers may have sufficient power (according to country and sector) to insist on an exhausting pace of work, to pay by amount produced (piecework), to reduce or eliminate rest periods, or paid holidays, and to refuse to provide so-called fringe benefits, such as pay when sick. At the same time social security benefits and payments can be avoided or not paid when due. Finally, of increasing importance, as speed and toxicity of manufacturing processes increase, is that employers can substantially cut costs by not conforming to health and safety standards and procedures that would be demanded by workers with more power. These then are the main ways in which employer power is translated into lower labor costs.

Such lower labor costs do not mean necessarily that the goods or services produced are cheaper or that workers produce more, because these factors are determined by the amount of capital available. With the same capital the lower labor costs of the enterprise labor market will be revealed in substantial differences in the economic cost of the good or service produced. But the second most important economic characteristic of the enterprise labor market relations is that within them productivity per worker is, in general, lower than in dominant forms. The low productivity of the workers is also a source of their weakness. Workers with high productivity have greater power because any alteration of their relationship with their work means greater loss of output—they are more essential to the running of the entire system and are often, although not always, more skilled. The less powerful enterprise labor market workers are, then, generally distinguishable from workers in other forms in industrial production by their lower level of productivity. Even within the same enterprise it is not uncommon to find the low productivity workers, such as cleaners, unskilled operatives, and clerical staff, to be the temporary, unprotected, socially disadvantaged workers and the established workers to be those with higher productivity. A strike, sabotage, go-slow, or general lack of motivation by workers in the high productivity sector produces greater disruption or loss than in the low—a control engineer in a chemical plant refusing to open a valve that no one else can operate competently clearly has more impact than a sweeper refusing to sweep the floor.

Productivity is largely determined by the amount of capital used, and essentially the groups in dominant forms decide the direction and amount of capital investment or technological advance that will improve productivity. The trade-off for dominant groups is between capital cost and technological advance and labor cost. The enterprise labor market tends therefore to be given manufacturing processes in which either capital intensity, that is, the amount of machines that can be used in production, is limited, either by technical problems or by their counterpart, the cost of overcoming them. As a result, the typical industries of the enterprise labor market are the labor-intensive, low-productivity industries, such as textiles, leather, and clothing manufacturing, or the labor-intensive sections of industries, such as electronics assembly. More recently there is a tendency for the enterprise labor market to be left with "dirty," that is, dangerous or unpleasant, work even though productivity may be high.

It is now necessary to examine some of the contemporary commentaries and theorizing on the position of what might roughly be considered as the enterprise labor market within the total economy.

There are two relevant approaches or theories: first, the dual-labor market, or labor market segmentation, theories and, second, the two-sector model of an industrializing or industrialized economy. Essentially both these approaches depart from an observed duality in the structure of contemporary economies.

For the dual labor market theorists the dualism was between a primary and a secondary labor market, or sometimes between an internal labor market of a large organization and an external labor market.[63] In the so-called secondary labor market are trapped the socially disadvantaged workers and others who compete on an individual basis for low-paid, low-productivity, low-status, and unstable jobs. The major point by these theorists was that the duality was structural; that is, through a variety of processes, workers in the secondary labor market could not move into, or compete for, jobs in the primary labor market, which became reserved for established workers, often unionized, in larger enterprises and holding higher wage and high-productivity jobs. Some of the original work on dual labor markets, which subsequently became more generally known as labor market segmentation, emerged from scholars working for the U.S. government and charged with the task of improving the lot of minority groups, who were almost exclusively found in the secondary labor market.[64] After the original work and observations in the early 1970s, other researchers found such segmentation and structural blocks within urban labor markets in the third world and elsewhere.[65]

While labor market segmentation theories were a crucial

and important indicator of the presence of different segments of labor markets, some of which correspond to the forms of social relations of production identified in this study, the theories do not attempt to provide any detail about who in the wider society or social formation benefits from such segmentation or in what proportions such benefits were delivered.

The two-sector economy approach has marxist and non-marxist variants. Writers from within both variants see two basic sectors in contemporary economies, one characterized by large enterprises, structured production, techniques, and monopoly or oligopoly power, the other by smaller enterprises, unstructured production techniques, and a weakness in face of the power of larger enterprises. Conditions of work and wages are worse in the second sector. For many writers concerned with the economies of the third world these two sectors are the so-called formal and informal sector;[66] for Galbraith the two sectors in the U.S. economy are the "planning sector," dominated by large corporations, and the "market" sector composed of small enterprises.[67] This formulation is similar to that of marxist writers who identified a "corporate" or "monopoly" sector within the larger framework of economies designated as "late monopoly capitalist."[68] In both variants the formal, planning, or monopoly sector exploits the other via the mechanism of the exchange of goods between the two sectors. Thus Galbraith notes "the planning system, in the general case, has power over the prices at which it sells to the market system and over the prices at which it buys from the market system. The terms of trade have in consequence a reliable tendency to be in its favor."[69]

Whereas the nonmarxist two-sector theorists easily accept the transfers between the two sectors and can even propose prescriptions in order to improve the conditions of workers in the subordinate sector, marxist writers have had difficulty in accepting transfers between what for them are different sections of a generally exploited working class.[70] The theories identify transfers between sectors but stop short at discussion of the mechanisms of transfers that occur between unprotected workers in the enterprise labor market and established workers in bargaining forms of social relations and their associated employers and capital owners. Detailed discussion of these mechanisms is not possible here, but in order to indicate the place of workers governed by enterprise labor market relations, or in other words, the value of employers' power to other groups in the social formation, it is necessary to look briefly at the mechanisms of transfer of surpluses.

THE TRANSFER OF SURPLUSES

Within industrial production, enterprise labor market workers are at the bottom of the hierarchy of differential extraction. The fruit of their labor is disproportionately distributed in favor of, first, their immediate employers, and then, moving up the hierarchy, to groups in dominant forms of social relations.

The first line of beneficiaries is the employer within the small enterprise locale of the enterprise labor market social relations. Unlike managers and salaried officers in larger enterprises, the employer of the small enterprise usually benefits directly—in terms of greater profits or self-awarded salary—the more wages or the numbers of workers can be reduced or work pace increased. To support the working boss ethic and face-to-face relations, it is sometimes necessary for employers to imply that they are paid only marginally more than their workers, or at least that they get a "just" return for their hard work. This is usually not the case, and the entrepreneur in a small enterprise gets, as a result of ownership or control over capital and authority derived from it, far in excess of the employees: A Japanese study showed that such a small enterprise entrepreneur earned an average of Yen 77,000 per month throughout his whole working life while his highest paid worker reached his peak of Yen 41,000 per month at age thirty.[71]

These remarks refer to the entrepreneur's personal return to work as a producer in a subordinate form; when the entrepreneur transfers profits or pays mortgages and interest, then the transfer is to other producers in the social formation.

These latter transfers are made through indirect and direct mechanisms. The indirect mechanisms arise from the supply and the demand side of the economic functioning of an enterprise, that is, from the suppliers of the inputs such as industrial machinery, finance, or raw materials and through the purchasers of the products produced.

Powerful corporations provide machinery or raw materials at administered prices as a result of their dominant position. When money has to be loaned for such purchases, the enterprises must pay interest on money loaned to the banks. Employers in the enterprise labor market must use their power over workers and production to secure sufficient surpluses to maintain their own privileged position, as well as to pay the prices demanded by the corporations in the dominant forms. Producers in the enterprise labor market then contribute to the better conditions of work, to profits and accumulation of capital in the dominant forms; in short, the cost of the sports ground, plant medical services, longer holidays and security of employment, high executive salaries, and privileges found within the large corporations are partially supported by the workers of the enterprise labor market, who have none of these advantages.

There are two direct types, as opposed to the indirect, of subordination and mechanisms of economic transfer from the enterprise labor market social relations: first, when there is a duality of social relations in one enterprise and, second, when large corporations directly subcontract component manufacture or services to enterprises with different social relations. The first case has been examined in some detail in an early section dealing with the unprotected worker within large enterprises. Essentially the pocket of social relations of the enterprise labor market type reduces the total wages bill of the enterprise, providing greater possibilities for both wage increases, and even sometimes profit sharing, for the permanent staff, as well as greater dividends, profits, and expansion for the enterprise concerned.

The second direct mechanism has a similar effect as the first although the details of the transfer are different. As upward pressures on wages and conditions of work have increased, large organizations have begun to subcontract component manufacture and service production to other enterprises, usually those that have enterprise labor market relations.[72] This is one way in which large unionized corporations may indirectly employ nonunionized labor. For example, in most countries of Western Europe, office-cleaning enterprises have been created that use socially disadvantaged labor. Governments, government-owned corporations, and large companies contract out their cleaning rather than employ similar groups of cleaners who would have to be governed by the rules of employment and often be required to be members of unions. The lower labor costs stemming from socially disadvantaged labor under enterprise labor market relations lower the costs of services and products that emerge from clean offices, but just as important they directly contribute to the superior conditions of work for those who work in them; in 1982, the Swiss-headquartered multinational pharmaceutical corporation Ciba-Geigy dismissed twenty five cleaning women from its payroll. The women were then employed by a local cleaning enterprise who sent them back to Ciba-Geigy as contract cleaners. They had to perform their previous work in one hour less and at 21 percent less pay. In addition they lost holiday bonuses and other privileges accruing to employees of a corporation, which represented a loss of 40 percent of their previous earnings.[73]

All of these mechanisms have been internationalized. Both the product market and the component subcontracting mechanism of extraction for enterprise labor market relations have reached a high level of international coordination. Multinational companies have labor-intensive components manufactured in poor countries, often in the Free Industrial Zones, in which the state guarantees that enterprise labor market social relations will prevail. These are then imported into rich industrialized countries and joined with components manufactured under corporate or tripartite social relations. A similar transfer occurs with consumer products when they are exported from the poor countries where such social relations prevail. For many products, particularly textiles, clothing, plastic fabrication, and electronics, the level of consumption is maintained or increased in industrialized countries partially as a result of social relations in third-world countries that keep labor costs, and therefore prices, lower. The form of social relations under which manufacturing will take place in the third world has then become a central issue in the politics and economics of the transnational economy and in general international relations.

CONTEMPORARY RESURGENCE
OF ENTERPRISE LABOR MARKET
SOCIAL RELATIONS

There has been a resurgence in the numbers of workers covered by enterprise labor market relations in the past fifteen years. There are two fundamental reasons for this. The first is the result of attempts of dominant groups and classes in the industrialized world to undercut the power of established workers and to avoid state-imposed labor regulations and social security costs. The second is the result of continuing industrialization in the third world based on the labor of the unprotected worker in export-oriented industries and in small-scale industries and enterprises.[74]

In the industrialized countries of Western Europe and North America the historic connection between the power of organized labor and the development of the welfare state has meant that much of welfare legislation has been directed at regulating employers' power over labor and providing security for employees in face of dismissal, disablement, and retirement. The power of organized labor is thus manifested not only in the growth of direct labor costs to employers, in the form of wages or an increased proportion of national income going to labor, but also in the growth of indirect labor costs. Indirect labor costs would normally include payments for social security, pension funds, profit-sharing schemes, and in some calculations would also include payments for time not worked, such as holidays, rest periods, absenteeism, bonuses, and so on. The direct/indirect calculation does not include capital expenditure employers must make for health and safety measures demanded by unions or state that would further increase the difference between the cost to the enterprise of employment and the wage received by the worker. Taking the broadest definition of indirect costs, which would include payment for time not worked, indirect labor costs in most industrialized countries are between 20 to 40 percent of total labor cost. Thus, in Western Germany in the late 1970s, only 61 percent of the total wage costs to the enterprise was actually paid for time worked, 17 percent was paid for social security, 13 percent for nonworked time, and 10 percent in other costs; in the

United States, employee benefits went up 20 percent between 1957 and 1967 as a proportion of total labor cost but increased by 33 percent in the 1967–1978 period.[75] Apart from reducing the numbers of workers employed, there is only one way to avoid such indirect labor costs and that is to transfer production toward enterprises that illegally or quasi-legally avoid social security payments, fail to provide the required holidays or rest periods, and avoid other state taxes on employment, in short, transfer production toward the enterprise labor market form of social relations. In Italy, for example, this has resulted in an illegal, submerged economy based on small enterprise or domestic production that in 1980 was estimated to amount to 20 percent of the gross national product. The workers within it are socially and legally unprotected, and it has been described as the "shock absorber" of the Italian economy, helping producers in dominant forms to sustain their level of living without increases in productivity or when demand for their products falls.[76] The "parallel" or "underground" economies have continued to expand in almost all of the industrialized countries.[77]

The increase in direct labor costs does not come principally from an increase in real wages of established workers; it comes more from a decline in the rate of productivity growth in the industrialized countries. This means that output per person working has not increased as it has in the past years, and employers therefore cannot claw back increased wages via increased output per worker. The labor cost component in any goods produced would, under such conditions, have a tendency to rise. The reasons for the decline in the rate of growth of productivity are doubtful and in dispute. Factors involved are a plateauing of technology-based increases in productivity; environmental strain—where further technologically induced increases in productivity produce unacceptable destruction of natural or artificial environments; decrease in the numbers of workers leaving the land (which always inflates national productivity growth, for industrial workers have a much higher productivity); successful demands of organized workers for a slower pace of work; lack of positive workers' motivation; and so on.[78]

One way to make up this relative decline is to try to increase productivity by increasing the pace, intensity, and duration of work with no increase in pay. This is difficult when unions, corporate agreements, or effective state laws prevent it. As a result there is a transfer of production toward enterprise labor market social relations where employer power is sufficient to be able to effect such actions. The transfer of production, in terms of both workers and locale, is thus from established workers in large enterprises toward unprotected workers in small enterprises.[79] Because all phases of production cannot technically be so transferred, what production remains in dominant forms and with established workers tend to be capital intensive with high productivity.

Another way to circumvent a decline in labor productivity that also increases the numbers in enterprise labor market relations is to "deskill," that is, apply capital in such a way that skilled workers, usually in dominant forms of social relations, are replaced by a combination of capital and less-skilled workers who are likely to be in the subordinate forms of social relations. This option has become even easier for large corporations as their monopoly power has increased sufficiently for them to easily raise their own capital via increased prices; they have become self-financing and capital abundant. This ease of access to capital has meant that the massive investment needed to replace skilled labor is now feasible. Industrial robots can be hooked to a computer enabling them to sense, adjust, correct, and take decisions; unlike earlier automation, which replaced muscle power and repetitive tasks and therefore tended to replace unskilled labor, the new machines, with their combination of information-processing and mechanical agility, replace skilled labor. This process of deskilling is also therefore a process of transferring production toward unskilled enterprise labor market workers.[80]

The enterprise labor market social relations are even further stabilized if the unskilled workers toward whom production is transferred are also socially disadvantaged workers. This is precisely what happened in the West German and French automobile industries. In the case of France, between 1965 and 1969 the proportion of skilled to unskilled workers in the Renault factory dropped by 10 percent per year and at the same time the numbers of foreign workers increased substantially, so that by the early 1970s Renault had 60 percent foreign workers—most of them unskilled.[81]

The increase in the numbers of unprotected workers in industrial production in the third world is the result of the form or structure that industrial production is taking as it grows. The first aspect is that of the transfer of production from the higher labor costs of Western Europe, North America, and Japan to the lower labor costs, partially based on the lower wages of unprotected workers, in the third world. Mention has already been made of the growth of Free Industrial Zones during the 1970s; production within these zones for export is invariably from enterprises, both large and small, which are not unionized and in which state labor regulation is weak. Thus the policy of "export-oriented" industrial growth or international subcontracting, as it is known, has added workers to the proportion of the world labor force covered by enterprise labor market relations.[82]

However, such workers represent only a small proportion of the total growth of unprotected workers in the third world in the past decade. The largest proportion has come as a result of industrialization's being pursued through small, labor-intensive industries and enterprises. There has been a tendency for new industrial employment to be split between capital-intensive, large-scale industry, such as petrochemicals, plastics, and heavy metals in countries such as Mexico and South Korea, using established workers, and smaller scale, labor-intensive industries—textiles, garments, leather, and plastics fabrication—using unprotected workers. The latter are then an expanding proportion of the industrial labor force where industrialization is a continuing process.

Major international agencies and governments, such as the World Bank and the International Labor Organization, have been actively encouraging such industrial structures through programs promoting "small-scale industries," "artisanal production," and the "informal sector."[83] Thus in the preamble of the first Lomé Convention—essentially a trade and finance agreement between European Common Market countries and certain third-world countries—there appears a clause that commits the signatories in the third world to support the growth of small enterprises. When such initiatives are successful, new workers, and sometimes new entrepreneurs and enterprises, are added to those who, or which, are subject to enterprise labor market social relations.

FREE ENTERPRISE IDEOLOGY
AND SMALL ENTERPRISE EMPLOYER
SOLIDARITY

Unlike other subordinate forms of social relations, the enterprise labor market form is associated with, and assists in support of, a generalized ideology that operates at the level of the social formation and within the transnational world economy. The nature of this ideology, which may be termed the ideology of free enterprise, and its impact on the consciousness of employers within the enterprise labor market are important to the dynamics of transformation of the form and to the development of any class alliances.

The linkage between the enterprise labor market social relations and the ideology of free enterprise is the employer who, within the ideology, is idealized as an "entrepreneur." The image of the employer as promoted by the ideology is that of a rugged individualist who works hard; responds to a competitive challenge; takes risks with his (and it is invariably a male image that is projected) income, wealth, and capital; and seeks material gain within a framework of basic moral integrity referred to as business ethics. Above all he is supposed to have the qualities of leadership and management that are necessary to command an enterprise and manage it efficiently according to the criteria of maximum material output. The entrepreneur and the freedom to pursue individual economic objectives via employment of labor and use of capital are seen as the dynamic of a system that is claimed to produce political and personal freedom, as well as material plenty, at least for those who succeed.[84]

The power of employers over their employees—seen as necessary to compete with other enterprises on a free market— is as hallowed in the ideology as the personal attributes they are individually supposed to possess. Thus all attacks on the power of employers are then loudly decried by the disseminators of the free enterprise ideology; both the state and the unions are castigated for their intervention in the social relations of the enterprise and are consistently cast in the role of harbingers of the destruction of the free enterprise system.[85]

It is undeniable that some of the qualities attributed to the entrepreneur in the free enterprise ideology, particularly those of leadership that can inspire confidence and cohesion within a group created for collective production, are necessary in a variety of situations regardless of the power relations of production. But it is uncertain whether such an entrepreneur existed even when the enterprise labor market was a dominant form of social relations. It is certain, however, that the numbers of entrepreneurs corresponding to the ideology are now extremely rare on a global scale. The social theorist Veblen accurately predicted the decline in numbers of such entrepreneurs by the mid-twentieth century in the United States in face of the rise of the managerial industrialists.[86] Significantly, another important theorist on the subject—Schumpeter—when analyzing the role of the entrepreneur in the United States in the 1930s, had to resort to England of the nineteenth century rather than the contemporary United States for examples of the operation of the entrepreneurial economic system.[87]

So it is that the main proponents and sources of the ideology of free enterprise in contemporary social formations are not only the employers of the enterprise labor market but also the owners, managers, and controllers in dominant corporatist forms of social relations who bear no resemblance at all to the entrepreneur in the ideology. Pronouncements about the virtues of free enterprise, competition, and entrepreneurship are made by managers of large corporations and sympathetic politicians. The ideology is used to support the continued private control of large blocks of capital and accumulation by corporations with turnovers larger than many nation-states and in which prices are administered and management is routinized. People with secure employment and far removed from the harsh reality of the enterprise labor market social relations extol the virtues of risk-taking, innovation, and competition.[88] Employers of the enterprise labor market are then made the repositories of past images of the entrepreneur, even though they have little political power and in many cases merely render services to the managerial class in corporatist forms of social relations. This dissonance between ideologically promoted image and reality of operations is an important factor in the consciousness of employers in the enterprise labor market.

Throughout the world the ideology of free enterprise and the call for personal incentive and initiative are used to promote the extension of the enterprise labor market form of social relations. In the third world, in particular, such extension also implies the development of a group or class of entrepreneurs that might defend a more generalized capitalist path to industrial development. This phenomenon was said to ensure support for sustaining access for foreign investment, enabling extraction of raw materials at low cost and providing for strategic military bases.[89] The creation of such a group or class was inherent in the spate of projects, programs, and international publicity given to the creation of entrepreneurship in the third world during the 1950s and early 1960s.[90] Typical of such programs was the Benteng program in Indonesia, which was designed to create enterprises owned by Indonesian entrepreneurs to match those already in existence in the hands of the Chinese.[91] The general policy was based on the notion of overriding cultural blocks by the creation of an "achieving society" in which entrepreneurship and free enterprise would become the principal mode of development.[92]

In fact these efforts faltered as many of the target countries adopted state-corporatist policies of capital-intensive industrialization based on multinational company investment or they enlarged the sectors of the economies under state control. Still others adopted socialist policies of complete state ownership of industry in which there was little room for free enterprise at all. The new policies promoting enterprise labor market social relations in the third world consist of promoting a capitalist path of industrial development, creating an entrepreneurial class, transferring production, limiting the number and power of established workers, supporting already established large-scale and capital-intensive industries, and attempting to alleviate poverty by creating employment and transferring technology.

Objectively the presence of a widely promoted free enterprise ideology, with its idealization of the entrepreneur and aggressive promotion of practices and values that seemingly serve the small businessman, should promote the solidarity of the employers of the enterprise labor market relations. It might be expected that such solidarity would be class oriented in the sense of small enterprise employers' seeing their interests opposed by groups of workers.

There are some indications that this indeed is the case. When employers form an important part of the class coalition of the petty bourgeoisie, they swell the ranks of conservative political parties and private associations that promote their interests vis-à-vis the state and the workers.[93] The International Chamber of Commerce, a well-organized lobby and coordinating body incorporating small businessmen, is found in almost all countries of the world.[94] The International Rotary Club organization and the Free Masons combine civic and charitable operations with social and political functions in which small businessmen are well represented. In some countries there are specific organizations of small businessmen, such as the association of the Petits et Moyens Enterprises in France.

But in other organizations the contradictions between the corporate sector and the enterprise labor market businesses manifest themselves. In national associations of employers, employers employing five or twenty five workers are placed alongside corporate managers with 100,000 workers, and these latter have the power and finance to control the organizations. The vunerability of the employers in the enterprise labor market to the power of large enterprises makes them ambivalent in a number of crucial areas. While managers of the corporate sector may advocate freedom from state intervention, in contrast, the enterprise labor market employers may seek its assistance in controlling the corporations' use of small enterprises. They may in general lend themselves to antiunion stance, but their face-to-face relations in enterprises without unions make the arguments on union economic power, so much the concern of larger enterprises, removed from their most immediate preoccupations. The threat to their interests may be as much from the banks and corporations of the enterprise corporatist or bipartite forms of social relations as it is from the state or unions. When, in the United States and the United Kingdom in the early 1980s, governments came to power committed to free enterprise, it brought mixed blessings to the small businessman who suffered increased bankruptcies and disruptions as corporate power increased.

They may become either the unwitting or willing instruments of power exercised by dominant groups in the hierarchy of the social formations. Thus, for example, when the mineral asbestos came under attack for health reasons, the dominant world corporations organized the many thousands of small entrepreneurs in the construction industry throughout the world to lobby for continued use of the substance.[95] The numerical strength of the small businessman and his place in the associations, political parties, and local government were then used, through the medium of founding and paying for lobbying associations, to support the interests of the large corporations, which is not to say that there was not some convergence of interests.

In the third-world countries the situation is even less clear. Most third-world countries are multiracial or multiethnic. The predominant characteristic of a small enterprise employer is his racial, religious, and/or ethnic distinction from that of the workers and even the rest of the population.[96] Thus solidarity, action, and demonstration of the employers of the enterprise labor market are indelibly linked to the position of the group within the social formation. Solidarity and class orientation may then be encouraged or destroyed by the overarching condition of ethnicity.

The ambivalence in face of the most powerful corporations, the state, the social relations within the enterprise, and the ethnic distinction mean that small businessmen do not emerge clearly as a class operating within the social formation or within the social relations cohesively seeking class interests. They may join class coalitions under special conditions, and the social relations produce a base of consciousness upon which such political manipulations may be made. They will support conservative policies and free enterprise in principle and therefore form a group that is part of the political support for such policies and slogans, but they have not usually taken the lead in any attack against opposing interests.[97]

TRANSFORMATION AND THE TENDENCY TOWARDS ORGANIZATION

Enterprise labor market social relations may be transformed at the level of the enterprise or at the level of the social formation. Transformation takes place at the level of the enterprise under three circumstances: first, when there occurs an indigenous development of worker organizations that substantially restrains or destroys employers' power; second, when an already established worker organization, external to the enterprise, successfully intervenes in the power relations; and third, when the enterprise is acquired by the state or other enterprise and another form of social relations introduced. Transformation within the social formation takes place when unionization, centrally planned or self-managed socialism, and occasionally, state corporatism is extended throughout the society. In these latter transformations, enterprise labor market social relations invariably continue to exist but cover a drastically reduced part of the total labor force.

To some extent and to different degrees, these transformations are based on the internal dynamics of the enterprise labor market relations. These dynamics result in what might be termed the "iron law of worker organization formation" within industrial and commercial enterprises. In such enterprises people are gathered together in one physical place; made to produce collectively, usually under conditions in which their tasks are specialized and interdependent; and are subjected to an authority structure in which there is a clear and regularly enforced distinction between those with power and those without. Under such conditions there apparently develops a sense of solidarity or social cohesion among those without power, the manifestations of which are the attempts to contain or restrain the power exercised over them.[98] There is both positive and negative evidence for this phenomenon. Positively, apart from the actual organizational developments discussed below, evidence arises from current and historic studies and observations of workers' attitudes, first in relation to the awareness of power, especially when they have migrated from other social relations, and second, the social elevation granted to those who in some way resist authority. The awareness of their position in relation to power was reported about workers in Panama, Latin America, when previously poor subsistence farmers said that before they were employed by a sugar mill they had tried to "live without compromise" but in wage employment they had to make the "daily compromise at the mill."[99] An example of the social prestige attained by resistance comes from Zambia where a workers' song exalts a particular tribe as being the best because its members were "*saini ofu,*" which the reporting writer believes means the worker under colonialism who would "sign off" from work rather than accept the authority of the compound manager.[100] These are but two interesting examples of what is reported in almost all scientific and journalists' accounts of unprotected workers in industrial production.[101]

Whether or not the existence of these attitudes may be disputed, state authorities and employers provide negative evidence for their existence by being convinced of the organizing potential of enterprise labor market workers; not only do employers consistently express their expectation or fear of such organization but also, almost universally, laws have been passed to prevent it or make it difficult, especially in small enterprises.[102]

It is, of course, against the tendency to organize that employers use the whole range of psychological, organizational, and social tactics identified earlier. Transformation takes place when the tendency to organize overcomes the blocks and barriers constructed against it.

Organization of workers within enterprises, that is, against employers' authority, may be of three basic types: informal, ad hoc, and formal. In informal organizations (the term is used here in the technical sense in that there are leaders, structures, and authority regardless of their external form), workers cooperate with each other over time to reduce the pressures of work and defeat attempts to increase intensity of work. The effects of such organizations take the form of deliberately working at a slow pace, actively or passively sabotaging production, increasing material benefits through collectively organized or sanctioned theft, and other basically clandestine operations.[103] Such organizations do not transform social relations, for although the effects of employer power are weakened, the power itself is not contained. Informal organizations of this type, however, form the basis of both ad hoc and formal organizations and must be considered as perhaps the most uncomplicated expression of the iron law of emergence of worker organizations.

Ad hoc organizations are those that are formed spontaneously, often as a result of some unacceptable expression of employer dominance. Thus when a new order is received that shortens rest periods, demands an increased pace, or dismisses a leader of an informal organization, it is possible that workers will immediately protest, strike, or take other action. In some countries these are known as "wildcat" strikes, that is, spontaneous and uncontrolled by formal worker organizations. In Malaysia, for example, such protests have sometimes taken the form of a "hysteria" in which a predominantly women's work force working with microscopes under conditions of employer domination in a Free Industrial Zone, collectively stop work and "shout and scream."[104] Such ad hoc organization likewise does not change social relations.

Formal, as opposed to informal and ad hoc, organizations may emerge spontaneously out of the previous organizational forms or as a result of intervention and encouragement from the outside. The establishment of formal organizations unconnected with any outside supporting power, such as a political party, state agency, or national union, is rare. Nevertheless, attempts to confront employer power openly and in a structured fashion are one of the basic results of the dynamics of the power distribution in enterprise labor market relations. Organizing is, in effect, the struggle between established power in the form of the employer and potential power in the form of worker consciousness. Both sides use tactics in this struggle that range from the subtle psychology of managerial manipulation, as discussed earlier in this chapter, to extreme violence. If formal organizations emerge and transform the social relations without intervention from outside, it is more often the result of the failure of the employer to manipulate the blocks to organization rather than of the strength of the expression of worker solidarity. The important exception to this latter observation is when organization is based not only on a consciousness arising from the power relations of the enterprise labor market, but also on solidarity arising from the social characteristics of disadvantaged workers involved.

The contradiction for the employer in employing socially disadvantaged workers is that whereas at the time of employment their disadvantages may make them more easily manipulable and receptive to the power relations of the enterprise labor market, when circumstances change and time has provided experience in confronting power, the social disadvantage may transform itself into a base for solidarity. Thus consciousness-raising efforts of women's movements have helped in organizing enterprises or preventing attacks on worker organizations in a manner that would have not been possible before the 1960s. Similarly ethnic and minority-group-based organization has occurred and has attacked the position of the enterprise labor market social relations within large enterprises. This has been the case in France with the foreign workers within the auto industry who, although formally linked with external unions, have made policy and demands based on their ethnicity rather than on their position as part of the industrial proletariat of France.

Transformation of the enterprise labor market social relations that arise from external interventions within individual enterprises or groups of enterprises may be assisted or rejected by elements of worker consciousness. The contradictions between the solidarity arising from the position of subordination and the consciousness relating to face-to-face contact with power and from loyalty to the enterprise and fear of ineffective disturbance or power relations are heightened when interventions from outside seek to transform the social relations of the enterprise toward tripartite, bipartite, enterprise, or state corporatist social relations.

Such interventions are made by the state, employers, and unions. When an enterprise or an industry is brought under state ownership, then the social relations of the enterprise are often, although not always, transformed into the direction of enterprise corporatist. Thus the Mexican government's nationalization of the oil industry in the 1930s, the British nationalization of small transport enterprises in the 1940s, and the introduction of worker-employer syndicates in Spain in 1937 changed social relations within these enterprises.

Employers and dominant groups from dominant social relations also transform social relations when they create larger enterprises through expansion or amalgamation. This transformation is inherent in the contradiction, for employers, between the higher efficiency and larger profits that result from large-scale operations and the increased possibility of the emergence of worker organizations as the result of the increased size. As the size of the enterprise increases, the blocks to organization in small enterprises are lost, and workers either organize to change the power relations or outside interventions are more successful.

Unionization of the workers of an enterprise arising from the actions of worker organizations outside the enterprise has been the principal way enterprise labor market social relations are transformed, both historically and currently. In general the organizing efforts of the established union must coincide and use the dynamics of the enterprise labor market social relations, that is, coincide with the attitudes and consciousness of the workers or the weakness of employers.[105] Only when an enterprise is absorbed by another in which a "closed" or "union" shop prevails can workers be made union members without effort and persuasion.

When unionization of nonunionized enterprises begins, it invariably means an extension of tripartite of bipartite forms of social relations rather than the elimination of the enterprise labor market form from the social formation. The difficulties of organizing small enterprises and enclaves of socially disadvantaged workers within large corporations have been detailed in an earlier section of this chapter. Union organizers must deal with the mixed reactions that enterprise labor market workers display concerning worker organizations. On the one hand they have usually cooperated with fellow workers in ad hoc or informal organizations, but on the other hand, they may have developed a loyalty to the enterprise, internalized employers' exhortations about the desired "autonomy" of the enterprise, or feared the loss of face-to-face relationships. In addition union organizers often face the power of employers acting as a class and calling up the resources of opposition resting in the state, local community, or larger enterprises. As a result, efforts to organize the enterprise labor market workers from the outside have had only limited success.

Unionization from the outside is not usually an attack against the presence of enterprise labor market social relations within the hierarchy of forms of social relations in the social formation. If, however, unionization reaches throughout the whole labor force, then enterprise labor market social relations will have been transformed throughout the social formation. This is what has happened most clearly in Sweden. In Sweden 95 percent of the labor force is in unions, even though, in comparison with other European countries, it has a high proportion of small enterprises. In addition, for many years, the union followed a "solidaristic" labor policy designed to prevent extreme wage differentials occurring between sections of industry would de facto restore the economic conditions of the enterprise labor market. This is perhaps the only case in which enterprise labor market social relations have ben transformed by incremental extension of unionization. The reasons for such a high unionization rate are unclear but are sufficiently special to raise doubts about whether the same process can be duplicated in other industrialized countries.[106]

The only other possibility of transformation at the level of the social formation is that of the establishment of revolutionary regimes that have the intention of substituting a form of socialism, that is, eliminating private ownership of enterprises throughout the whole social formation. This raises the question of the role of the enterprise labor market workers in movements and actions that have revolutionary intent. The enterprise labor market workers are theoretically a part of the industrial proletariat. Until recently, in industrialized countries, they were so isolated and their consciousness was so associated with the special circumstances of the small enterprise that they did not have a class consciousness in which their destiny seemed to be associated with workers in corporate or burgaining social relations. Although this may be changing as currently the established workers are showing a more defensive posture, there are still few signs that the unorganized workers of the enterprise labor market are prepared either to launch action themselves or even to join actively in movements spearheaded by workers from other forms.

In third-world countries, especially those in which the industrialization process is rapidly advancing, the situation is different. In the first place the enterprise labor market workers form a larger proportion of the industrial labor force than in the industrialized countries; second, material conditions and employer power are more extreme; third, the established workers are perhaps less absorbed by state corporatism or tripartitism; fourth, the ideology of free enterprise or the capitalist path to development has not assumed such hegemonic proportions as in the already industrialized countries; and finally, the multiethnicity of both the work force and employers is an important intervening factor. Under these conditions the worker of the enterprise labor market may respond to the appeals of populism, religious activism, ethnic appeals, or socialism. In Chile, for example, workers in smaller enterprises joined political parties of the left and instituted forms of self-management in enterprises. But there is even less evidence about the past or potential role of enterprise labor market workers in social movements and revolutionary situations than there is about urban marginals and other subordinate workers. Established workers in large and powerful unions seem to take the lead, such as the chemical and steel workers in Brazil or the railway workers in India, and how enthusiastically they are followed, supported, or opposed by the enterprise labor market worker in the small enterprise and in the "temporary" category in the larger enterprise is rarely discussed or analyzed.

NOTES

1. P. Marris and A. Somerset, *African Businessmen: A Study of Entrepreneurship and Development in Kenya* (London, Routhledge, Kegan Paul, 1971), p. 113. Materials used in writing this chapter are drawn from (1) management, industrial relations, and labor markets academic literature; (2) literature on small enterprises; (3) union newspapers and reports; (4) personal intentional and unintentional participant observation in France, United Kingdom, and United States; (5) specific observations and investigations.

2. To what extent entrepreneurs of small enterprises are "self-made" varies greatly among countries. In the Federal Republic of Germany inherited capital is the most important factor—see B. Biermann, "Structural Factors of Entrepreneurial Recruiting," *Sociale Welt* (1970–71), 21 (221):33–34; in Taiwan and Korea most of the proprietors of small enterprises are self-made—see S. P. S. Ho, *Small-Scale Enterprises in Korea and Taiwan* (Washington, D.C., the World Bank, 1980) p. 81; in India both inherited status and capital are important—see E. Wayne Nafziger, "Class, Caste and Community of South India Industrialists—An Examination of the Horatio Alger Model," *Journal of Development Studies* (January 1975), 6 (2):132–86.

3. As observed by R. W. Cox during a study visit in the late 1960s; see also R. W. Cox, "Industrial Relations and Rapid Industrialization: Some Far Eastern Cases," *Bulletin of International Institute for Labor Studies* (1972), no. 10, pp. 5–47.

4. Kim Chang Soo, "Marginalisation, Development and Korea's Workers Movement," *AMPO* (1977), 9 (3):20.

5. R.-P. Paringaux, "Japon: Mi-temps a journee pleine," Le Monde (7–8 April 1985), p. 6.

6. The plant was visited for three days by the author in the early 1960s. The report was published in Footwear News (New York, Fairchild Publications) circa September 1964. This information was of interest in the United States' footwear industry, for it was lobbying for import restrictions against shoes made with "cheap labor," of which the Swiss and European companies' use of "underpaid" foreign labor was claimed to be one example; another company case with some similar features was the electronics firm Pye Ltd., operating in Cambridgeshire; see Tony Lawson, "Paternalism and Labour Market Segmentation Theory," in Frank Wilkinson, ed., The Dynamics of Labour Market Segmentation (London, Academic Press, 1981), pp. 47–66.

7. See, for example, B. White and Makali, "Wage Labour and Wage Relations in Rural Java: Some Preliminary Notes from the Agro-Economic Survey" (The Hague, mimeo, Institute of Social Studies, 1979).

8. See, for example, Nicholas VAn Hear, "By-Day Boys and Dariga Men," Review of African Political Economy (Cecember 1984), 31, pp. 44–57.

9. The development of enterprise labor market relations in third-world agriculture is discussed in chapter 3, and the consideration of landless labor's being governed by a distinct set of power relations is found in chapter 1.

10. See John Gardener, "Conflict, Control and Cleavage in the Chinese People's Republic," in Richard Scase, ed., Industrial Society: Class, Cleavage and Control (London, George Allen and Unwin 1974), pp. 191-202.

11. For a general exposition of the classical model and in particular the role of the entrepreneur in making "combinations" of labor and capital, see J. Schumpeter, The Theory of Economic Development (New York, Harper and Row, 1961, first published 1934), especially p. 132.

12. Sidney and Beatrice Webb, Problems of Modern Industry (London, Longmans, Green, 1902), p. 86.

13. As quoted in William Bowen, "Better Prospects for our Ailing Productivity," Fortune (December 3, 1979), p. 80.

14. See Eric Hobsbawm, Industry and Empire (Harmondsworth, England, Penguin), and see also the remarks of Webb (2), Problems, pp. 86–88.

15. For a description of the inhumane conditions produced by nineteenth-century enterprise labor market relations, see, for example, Brian Inglis, Poverty and the Industrial Revolution (Harmondsworth, England, Penguin, 1971), pp. 271–85.

16. This is not to accept that the labor market ever functioned in the way believed by classical economists (or still accepted by many now). For an argument that labor markets, even before current "segmentation," never functioned in the classical way, see Francois Michon, "Dualism and the French Labour Market: Business Strategy, Non-Standard and Secondary Jobs," in Wilkinson, Dynamics, p. 98.

An account of the early Factory Acts is found in J. L. and Barbara Hammond, The Town Labourer 1760–1832 (London, Longmans Green, 1920), pp. 148-55.

17. This issue is taken up in a later section; for an account of the typical restraints on employer power with regard to wages, see, for example, Lisa R. Peattie, "What Is To Be Done with the 'Informal Sector': A Case Study of Shoe Manufacturers in Colombia," in Helen I. Safa, ed., Towards a Political Economy of Urbanisation in Third World Countries (Dehli, Oxford University Press, 1982), pp. 208–32.

18. An account of the early Factory Acts is found in J. L. and Barbara Ham-

mond, *The Town Labourer 1760–1832* (London, Longmans Green, 1920), pp. 148–55.

19. On the motives behind the Factory Acts and especially the thesis that they were prudent attempts to limit competition in labor costs in order to preserve the useful working life of workers, see Karl Marx, *Das Kapital*, vol. 1, chapter 10, "The Greed for Surplus–Labor Manufacturer and Boyard."

20. See, for example, Louis Wolf Goodman, "Legal Controls on Union Activity in Latin American," in Stanley M. Davies and Louis Wolf Goodman, eds., *Workers and Managers in Latin America* (Lexington, Mass., Heath, 1972), pp. 233–34. Government intervention in Malaysia is also cited as an important reason, among others, for low organization rates, see Hing A. Yun "Work Orientation: A Case Study of Factory Workers in Peninsular Malaysia," *Journal of Contemporary Asia* (1985) 15(3):267–86.

21. There are a number of criteria for the definition of small enterprises, or small-scale industries, as they are often called in the third world. These include the amount of capital or assets, the sales or turnover figures, and the quantity of output. Thus references to small business or enterprise in the general literature may or may not be defined by numbers employed, which is the criteria on used in this book. For some discussions of the definition of small enterprises, see, for example, J-P. Nioche and M. Didier, *Deux Etudes sur la Dimension des Entreprises Industrielles* (Paris, Institut National de la Statistique et des Etudes Economiques, 1969), p. 140; Mark Granovetter, "Small Is Bountiful: Labor Markets and Establishment Size," *American Sociology Review* (June 1984), 49(3):323–34.

22. See A. H. El Jack and C. Leggett. *Industrial Relations and the Political Process in the Sudan* (Geneva, International Institute for Labour Studies, 1980).

23. This has been called "simple" versus "structural" control of labor; see Richard Edwards, *Contested Terrain* (New York, Basic Books, 1979).

24. This is made explicit or implicit in most of the managerial literature about small enterprises. It was particularly important in the social philosophy expressed by E. F. Schumacher, *Small Is Beautiful: A Study of Economics as if People Mattered* (London, Blond and Briggs, 1973). See also Geoffrey K. Ingham, *Size of Industrial Organisation and Worker Behaviour,* (Cambridge, England, Cambridge University Press, 1970), p. 105; Edwards, *ContestedTerrain.*

25. See, for example, Pierre de Lannurien, *Cent Ans de Retard* (Paris, L'Express-Denoel, 1969), p. 244; A. W. Baker, *Personnel Management in Small Plants* (Columbus, Ohio, Ohio State University, 1955), p. 147; and Roy Hill, "How Some Firms are Managing Without Unions," *International Management* (June 1979), p. 54.

26. See, for example, Joan Henderson and Bert Johnson, "Labour Relations and the Smaller Firm," *Personnel Management* (London) (December 1974) 6(12):28–31. For general reviews see Peter Kilby, "The Role of Alien Entrepreneurs in Economic Development: An Entrepreneurial Problem," in Papers and Proceedings of 95th Annual Meeting of American Economic Association," *American Economic Review* (May 1983), pp. 107–11; Yuan-Li Wu, "Chinese Entrepreneurs in Southeast Asia," in *ibid.*, pp. 112–17; William Glade, "The Levantines in Latin America," in *ibid.*, pp. 118–22; see also, on regional distinctiveness of entrepreneurs, Zafar Altaf, *Pakistan Entrepreneurs: Their Development, Characteristics and Attitudes* (London: Croom Helm, 1983). Likewise, "more frictions" between employers and management were reported in family-owned small-scale textile clothing enterprises than in larger enterprises; see *Social and Labour Practices of Multinational Enterprises in Textiles, Clothing and Footwear Industries* (Geneva: International Labor Office, 1984), p. 154.

27. James Curran and John Stanworth, "Worker Involvement and Social Relations in the Small Firm," *The Sociological Review* (Keele) (May 1979), 27(2):317–42. Owners also exercise stricter control than it generally apperars; see Robert Goffee and Richard Scase, "Proprietorial Control in Family Firms: Some Functions of 'Quasi-Organic' Management Systems," *Journal of Mangement Studies* (1985), 22(1):53–68.

28. Claire Beauville, "Dans le miroir des sondages," *Aujourd'hui* (Cofnederation Français Démocratique de Travaileurs) (May–June 1980), no 43, p. 14–26.

29. Janet W. Salaff, *Working Daughters of Hong Kong* (New York: Cambridge University Press, 1981). It should be noted that "at home" structured and unstructured interviews and participant observation are more revealing of basic worker attitudes than survey or "at work" investigations.

30. See, for example, on the predominatly high caste composition of entrepreneurs in India, Nafziger, "Class, Caste, and Community."

31. Marris and Somerset, *African Businessmen*, p. 112.

32. O. Gomez, "Women in Wage Labour and Workers Organizations: A Case Study in Colombia" (The Hague, Institute of Social Studies, unpublished dissertation, 1980).

33. Paternalism as a strategy of labor control, although not within small enterprises, is discussed in J. Crisp, *The Story of an African Working Class: Ghanaian Miners' Struggles, 1870–1980* (London, Zed Books, 1984); likewise Lawson, "Paternalism," where paternalism is defined as Weber's "traditional" authority category held by employers; that paternalism may block growth of enterprise size, as entrepreneurs prefer it, see comments in Shanti S. Tangri, "Family Structure and Industrial Entrepreneurship in Urban India: The Evolution of a Field Study," in Safa, *Towards a Political Economy*, pp. 188–207.

34. See, for example, Allen R. Cohen, *Tradition, Change and Conflict in Indian Family Business*, (The Hague, Mouton, 1974), p. 230; One factory in which this author worked made ice cream in the summer season and christmas decorations during the winter. A "permanent" core of three men was retained throughout the year as supervisors over the 40 seasonal women who worked packing ice cream in the summer and as handicraft workers for the Christmas decorations in the winter (1958).

35. See, for example, Oguz Ari, "Commitment and Integration of the Industrial Labor Force in Two Turkish Cities," in Marie R. Haug and Jaques Dofny, eds., *Work and Technology* (Berkeley, Sage, 1977), pp. 98–131; Margaret Peil, *The Ghanaian Factory Worker: Industrial Man in Africa* (Cambridge, England, Cambridge University Press, 1972), p. 219, and Ingham, *Size of Industrial Organization*, p. 118.

36. Ingham, *ibid.*, p. 117.

37. T. Venkateswara Rao and S. N. Chattopashyay, "A Study of the Perceptions of Organizational Climate by the Employees of Small Industries," *Indian Journal of Industrial Relations* (New Delhi) (July 1974), 10 (1):64–65.

38. See, for example, Ari, "Commitment and Integration."

39. See, for example, Beauville, "Dans le miroir," pp. 16–17. Employers are generally convinced that remaining small reduces the possibility of unionization. See, for example, Peattie, "What Is To Be Done"; S. Brusco and C. Sabel, "Artisan Production and Economic Growth," in Wilkinson, *Dynamics*, p. 102.

40. This is a widely reported characteristic of small enterprises; see, for example, Peattie, *ibid.* Brusco and Sabel *ibid.*; Paola Villa, "Labour Market Segmentation and the Construction Industry in Italy," in Wilkinson, *ibid.*, p. 143; and the

observation on lack of enforcement made in Martha R. Lowenstern, *Profile of Labor Conditions: Mexico* (U.S. Department of Labor, Bureau of International Affairs, 1979), p. 2.

41. U.C.N. Vharyulu, "Industrial Legislation and Small Industry Workers," *Khadigramodyoq* (September 1975), pp. 543–47.

42. The author, in participant observation of *travail noir* with a French demolition contractor (one of the most dangerous types of work), was told before he started removing tiles from the roof of a four-story building "You understand, if you have an accident it is at your expense" (1978).

43. Anon, "Dossier: Le Travail Noir en Europe et aux U.S.A.," *Intersocial* (June 1980), no. 61, pp. 3–16. R. Grazia, *Clandestine Employment: The Situation in the Industrialised Market Economy Countries* (Geneva, International Labor Office, 1984).

44. See, for example, Goodman, "Legal Controls"; Sivanthiram Alagandram, "Labour Relations in Malaysia: The State, Foreign Capital, Unions and the Young Women Workers in Export Oriented Industries" (unpublished master's thesis, The Hague, Institute of Social Studies, 1981); Salaff, *Working Daughters*.

45. See, for example, Suzanne Paine, *Exporting Workers: The Turkish Case* (Cambridge, England, Cambridge University Press, 1974), and S. Castles and G. Kosack, *Immigrant Workers and Class Structure in Western Europe* (London, Oxford University Press, 1977).

46. See, for example, Janet Abu-Lughod, "Urbanization and Social Change in the Arab World," in John Walton, ed., *Capital and Labour in the Urbanized World* (London, Sage, 1985), pp. 126–45.

47. For a description of typical permit legislation, see Paine, *Exporting Workers*, pp. 69–70.

48. Claire Etcherelli, *Elise ou La Vraie Vie* (Paris, Editions Denoel, 1967).

49. "A Modern Slavery Institution in Denmark," *Fagbladet* (Denmark) (10 April, 1980).

50. See, for example, the detailed account of the manipulations of employers in factories with predominantly female labor force as found in O. Gomez, "Women in Wage Labour"; on the political structure that supports the subordinate position of women in social relations of production, see, for example, Jane Kenrick, "Politics and the Construction of Women as Second Class Workers," in Wilkinson *Dynamics*, pp. 167–91.

51. See, for example, "Changing Role of South East Asian Women," special issue of *South East Asia Journal and Pacific Research* (1980), 9 (5–6); A. Fuentes and B. Ehrenreich, *Women in the Global Factory* (Boston, South End Press, 1983).

52. "Congress Learns of Pittsburgh Plate Glass Anti-Union Tactics," *International Teamster* (April 1980), 77(4):5.

53. *Child Labour in Morocco's Carpet Industry* (London, Anti-Slavery Society, 1978); in Calcutta 30 percent of children less than 15 years of age work regularly; see Nirmala Banerjee, "Survival of the Poor," in Safa, *Towards a Political Economy*.

54. Adriana J. Marshall-Goldschwartz, *The Import of Labour: The Case of the Netherlands* (Rotterdam, University Press, 1973), p. 65.

55. This pattern of social relations is fully discussed in J. Harrod, *Power, Production and the Established Worker*. (New York, Columbia University Press, forthcoming 1988).

56. Robert C. Wood, "Japan's Multitier Wage System," *Forbes* (August 18, 1980), pp. 53–58. This author writes:

The difference between Nippon Steel employees in silver helmets and the men in yellow is based on something that has divided upper and lower classes in every country for thousands of years: power. As a group, regular employees of Nippon Steel could easily shut down the Kimitsu works. Sub-contract workers—while not always completely powerless—can cause much less trouble (p. 53).

57. See, for example, Robin Smith, "Industrial Relations Policies and Political Change: The EEC Code for South African Subsidiaries," British Journal of Industrial Relations (March 1980), 18(1):99–114.

58. "Free Trade Zones: A Backgrounder," Impact (Manila) (October 1979), 14(10):340–45 (the zones are called under a variety of names according to the writer and the region).

59. Alagandram, "Labour Relations in Malaysia."

60. Antonia B. Quizon, "FTZs—A Critical Assessment," Impact (Manila) (October 1979), 14(10):348; Augustine Barque, "Problems et Politiques Migrataires au Japon" Revue Tiers Monde (Jan-March 1977), 28(69): (77–9) (for statistics and conditions in South Korean FTZ, pp. 94–95); Charles Ford, Wages, Hours and Working Conditions in Asian Free Trade Zones (Bruxelles, International Textile, Garment, and Leather Workers Federation, 1983).

61. The exact mechanism through which this works is complex. The relationship between union-negotiated wage rates and other rates is well established for the statistically rich industrialized countries; see, for example, Guy Routh, Occupation and Pay in Great Britain 1906–1960 (Cambridge, England Cambridge University Press, 1965), pp. 147–54; and P. Kumar, "Differentials in Wage Rates of Unskilled Labour", Industrial Relations and Labour Relations Review (October 1972), 26(1):643–44. In third-world countries there remain some uncertainties about the exact nature of the relationship; see, for example, on the connection between negotiated, skilled rates and unnegotiated, unskilled rates, T. V. S. Ramamohan and Sarthi Acharya, "Wage Policies in Small-Scale Firms and Their Implications for Industrial Relations," Indian Journal of Industrial Relations (New Dehli) (July 1976), 12(1): especially p. 74; for a discussion and empirical study, see R. Mohan, The Determinants of Labor Earnings in Developing Metropoli; Estimates from Bogata and Cali (Washington, D. C., The World Bank, 1981); and Christopher J. Heady, The Determination of Industrial Wages in Less Developed Countries (Ann Arbor, Mich., University Microfilms, 1976).

62. This means, of course, that labor market influences have been countered or "blocked off" or that the classical view of labor market wage determination is faulty. For a critique of the classical viewpoint, see Albert Rees and George P. Schultz, Workers and Wages in an Urban Market (Chicago, University of Chicago Press, 1970), pp. 3–13; see also, on employers' ability to vary wage rates, D. Robinson, "External and Internal Labour Markets," in D. Robinson, ed., Local Labour Markets and Wage Structures (London, Gower Press, 1970), pp. 64–65; on wage differentials between small and large enterprises in manufacturing, average weekly wages "rise almost monotonically with establishment size," Granovetter, "Small Is Bountiful," p. 331; but in Colombia "large enterprises earn only slightly more," Mohan, Determinants of Labor Earnings, p. 101; among the many accounts of wage and condition differences between small and large enterprises, see Peattie, "What Is To Be Done"; Dorothy Remy, "Formal and Informal Sectors of Nigeria Economy: An Analytical Framework with Empirical Contents" in Safa, Towards a Political Economy, pp. 233–46; Brusco and Sabel, "Artisan Production," pp. 101–3.

63. The most important writers and innovators in the dual labor market thesis are P. Dorringer and M. Piore, Internal Labor Market and Manpower Analysis (Lexington Mass, Heath, 1971); D. M. Gordon, Theories of Poverty and Underemployment;

Orthodox, Radical and Dual Labor Market Perspective (Lexington, Mass, Health, 1972); David Gordon, Richard Edwards, and Michael Reich, Segmented Work, Divided Workers: Historical Transformation of Labor in the United States (New York, Cambridge University Press, 1982); a review of segmentation and duality is found in Paul Ryan, "Segmentation, Duality and the Internal Labour Market," in Wilkinson Dynamics, pp. 3–20.

64. See Michael J. Priore, "Labor Market Segmentation: To What Paradigm Does It Belong?" American Economic Review (Papers and Proceedings of 95th Annual Meeting of American Economic Association, 1982) (May 1983), pp. 249–53.

65. See, for example, M. Lipton, Labor and Poverty (Washington, D. C., World Bank, 1983) J. Gugler, "Employment in the City," in A. Gilbert and J. Gugler, Cities, Poverty and Development; Urbanisation in the Third World (London, Oxford University Press, 1981); Subbiah Kannappan, Employment Problems and Urban Labor in Developing Nations (Ann Arbor, Mich., University of Michigan, 1983).

66. See, for example, Peattie, "What Is To Be Done." The informal sector concept is also discussed in chapter 4, Primitive Labor Market Social Relations.

67. John Kenneth Galbraith, Economics of the Public Purpose (London, Andre Deutsch, 1973).

68. See, for example, Claus Offe, Industry and Inequality: The Achievement Principle in Work and Social Status (London, Arnold, 1976).

69. Galbraith, Economics, pp. 252–53.

70. For a discussion of the application of the theory of unequal exchange to transfers between a high-and low-wage sector, see V. M. Dandekar, "Bourgeois Politics of the Working Class," Economic and Political Weekly (January 12, 1980), pp. 75–83. For a writer within a marxist framework who sees capitalism resorting to different sectors to correct inbalances, see Christian Palloix, L'Internationalisation du Capital (Paris, Maspero, 1975), especially p. 103; feminist writers frequently argue that the "working class" are also the beneficiaries of women's domestic labor–see, for example, the concluding remark in N. J. Sokoloff, Between Money and Love: The Dialectics of Women's Home and Market Work (New York, Praeger, 1981), p. 202.

71. Susumu Watanabe, "Entrepreneurship in Small Enterprises in Japanese Manufacturing," International Labor Review (December 1970), 102(6):531–76; see also, for example, comments on the conspicuous consumption of entrepreneurs in Tangri, "Family Structure," in Safa, Towards a Political Economy.

72. For specific reasons and the strategies of this arrangement, see, for example, Edward B. Roberts, "New Ventures for Corporate Growth," Harvard Business Review (July-August, 1980), 58(4).

73. Report in Gewerkschaft (Journal of the Swiss Textile Chemical and Paper Union) (April 1983), no. 8, p. 28. On cleaners as enterprise labor market workers within corporatist organizations, see also Ian Beardwell, David Miles, and Elizabeth Worman, The Twilight Army: A Study of Civil Service Cleaners (London, Low Pay Unit and Civil Service Union, 1981).

74. Cox, "Industrial Relations," pp. 277–80.

75. Figures for Western Germany are found in Intersocial (October 1978), no. 42, p. 32, and for the United States in Chamber of Commerce of the United States; Employee Benefits 1978, pp. 30 and 31; for comparative statistics, see Robert A. Hart, The Economics of Non-Wage Labour Costs (London, George Allen and Unwin, 1984).

76. Michel Boyer, "L'Economie Italienne entre le 'miracle' et le masque," Le Monde (June 3, 1980), pp. 1 and 44; anon, "Italie: Le boom de l'economie immergee," Intersocial (June 1980), no. 61, pp. 5–7.

77. See, for example, Grazia, *Clandestine Employment*; for the argument that the development of the underground economy is slowing and will be reduced, see Moises Ikonicoff, "Economie Souterraine, Accumulation et Tiers Monde," *Revue Tier-Monde* (April-June 1984), 25(98):318–37.

78. The reasons for this decline in productivity growth are discussed in Bowen, "Better Prospects," pp. 68–86; Otto Eckstein, "Economic Choices for the 1980s," *Challenge* (1980), 23(2):15–27; "Decline in Productivity Growth After 1973: A Further Look at Explanatory Factors," in *United Nations Economic Survey of Europe in 1982* (New York, United Nations, 1983), pp. 36–52.

79. This shows up in studies indicating an increase in the numbers of small enterprises; see, for example, Granovetter, "Small Is Bountiful"; Paola Villa, "Labour Market Segmentation and the Construction Industry in Italy," in Wilkinson, *Dynamics*, pp. 133–44, and in labor market restructuring see, for example, Sam Rosenberg, "Reagan Social Policy and Labour Force Restructuring," *Cambridge Journal of Economics*, (June 1983), 7(2):179–96.

80. This process was identified as a long-term trend by Harry Braverman, *Labor and Monopoly Capital: The Degradation of Work in the Twentieth Century* (New York, Monthly Review Press, 1974); on the continued creation of low-wage, unskilled jobs, see Saskia Sassen-Koob, "The New Labor Demand in Global Cities," in M. P. Smith, *Cities in Transformation; Class Capital and the State* (Beverly Hills, Sage, 1984), pp. 139–71.

81. Previously "skilled" workers are then forced to take "unskilled" jobs; see, for example, B. Harrison, "Education and Unemployment in the Urban Ghetto," *American Economic Review* (December 1972), 62(5):796–812.

82. See this chapter; see also, for example, C. Berthomieu and A. Hanaut, "Can International Subcontracting Promote Industrialization?" *International Labor Review* (May-June 1980), 119(3).

83. See, for example, IBRD: *Financing the Development of Small Scale Industries*, Bank Staff Working Paper No. 191, (November 1974); Ho, *Small-Scale Enterprises*; R. Bromley, ed., *Planning For Small Enterprises in Third World Cities* (Oxford, Pergamon, 1985). Some of the results of these policies can be seen in N. Lee, "Business Concentration in LDCs," in C. H. Kirkpatrick, N. Lee, and F. I. Nixson, *Industrial Structure and Policy in Less Developed Countries* (London, George Allen and Unwin, 1984), pp. 47–85.

84. See for example the model of the "achiever" in D. C. McClelland, *The Achieving Society* (New York, Random House, 1956), and see also J. Zahn, "Les Problemes des Moyennes Enterprises familiales dans l'economie de l'avenir," *Revue de la Societe d'Etudes et Expansion* (Liege) (1974), 64(217):611–31; for a view of the entrepreneur as the key to freedom and plenty, see, for example W. Miller, *Men in Business—Essays on the Historical Role of the Entrepreneur* (New York), Harper and Row, 1962).

85. See, for example, the press responses to trade unionism as quoted in J. Harrod, *Trade Union Foreign Policy* (London, Macmillan, 1972), p. 28.

86. Thorstein Veblen, *The Theory of Business Entrepreises* (New York, Scribner, 1910).

87. J. Schumpeter, *Theory of Economic Development*, p. 130.

88. See the contrasts made between operations of small and large business organizations in *Conglomerate Mergers—Their Effects on Small Business and Local Communities*, Report of the Committee on Small Business, House of Representatives, 96th Congress, Second Session (Washington, U.S. Government Printing Office, 1980); see also Francis X. Sutton, et al., *The American Business Creed* (Cam-

bridge, Mass., Harvard University Press, 1956). That "corporate spokesmen" regularly equate large corporations with a "corner grocer" or "friendly neighborhood news vendor" is noted in John Kenneth Galbraith, "The Social Consensus and the Conservative Onslaught", *Millennium* (Spring 1982) 11(4): p. 7.

89. See the arguments made by President Dwight D. Eisenhower when proposing the establishment of a risk capital organization—the International Finance Corporation. *Department of State Bulletin* (1954), vol. 30.

90. Discussion of this point is found in Jeffrey Harrod, "Development Studies: From Change to Stabilisation," in R. Apthorpe and A. Krahl, eds., *Development Studies: Critique and Renewal* (Leiden, Brill, 1986) examples of the international promotion of entrepreneurship are *Technical Expert Meeting on Development and Entrepreneurial Resources in Africa*, (Geneva, International Labor Office, 1966); P. Medhora, "Enterpreneurship in India," *Political Science Quarterly* (Lancaster, Pa.) (December 1965), 80(4):558–80; Lim E. Aldaba and G. Javillonar, "Achievement Motivation in Filipino Entrepreneurship," *International Social Science Journal* (UNESCO) (1968), 20(3):397–411. For a critique of the value to economic development of certain types of "entrepreneurs," see P. C. Garlick, *African Traders and Economic Development in Ghana* (Oxford, Clarendon Press, 1971).

91. A. M. Siregar, "Indonesian Entrepreneurs," *Asian Survey* (Berkeley, Calif.) (May 1969), 9(5):345.

92. McClelland, *The Achieving Society.*

93. See chapters 6, Self-Employment Social Relations.

94. See, for example, the account of local chambers of commerce in small towns in Nepal in D. Seddon, ed., *Peasants and Workers in Nepal* (Warminster, England, Aris and Phillips, 1979), pp. 207–11.

95. J. Harrod and V. Thorpe. *Asbestos: Politics and Economics of a Lethal Product* (Geneva: International Chemical and Energy Unions, 1985), pp. 42–55.

96. See note 30, above.

97. See R. W. Cox, *Production, Power, and World Order: Social Forces in the Making of History* (New York, Columbia University Press, 1987), where this question is discussed in terms of capital factions.

98. Organization in industrial enterprises is postulated as inevitable in Frank Tannenbaum, *The True Society* (London, Jonathan Cape, 1965).

99. Stephan Gudeman, *The Demise of a Rural Economy: From Subsistence to Capitalism in a Latin American Village* (London, Routledge, Kegan Paul 1978), p. 179. See also Curran and Stanworth, "Worker Involvement."

100. A. L. Epstein, *Ethos and Identity: Three Studies in Ethnicity* (London, Tavistock, 1978), p. 115.

101. Participant observation and see also, for example, Sheila Cunnison, "Participation in Local Union Organization: School Meals Staff: A Case Study," in Eva Gamarnikow, David Morgan, June Purvis, and Daphne Taylorson, *Gender Class and Work* (London, Heinemann, 1983), pp. 77–95; Van Hear, "By-Day Boys." For the argument that current analysis of politics and class ignore the consciousness of both employer and worker in small enterprises see Chris Gerry, "The Working Class and Small Enterprise in the UK Recession" in Nanneke Redclift and Enzo Mingione eds., *Beyond Employment: Household, Gender and Subsistence* (London, Blackwell, 1985) pp. 288–316.

102. Participant observation and see also, for example, accounts in Peattie, "What Is To Be Done"; Salaff, *Working Daughters;* C. K. Dalaya, *Economic Activities of Voluntary Women's Organization (Mahila Mandals) in the City of Bombay*, (Ramnarain Rui College, Department of Economics, 1982).

103. Participant observation; and see also, for example, reports in Michael Burawoy, "The Hidden Abode of Underdevelopment: Labor Process and the State in Zambia," *Politics and Society* (1982), 11(2):123–66; Salaff, *Working Daughters;* Crisp, *Story of an African Working Class.*

104. "Malaysian Malady: When the Spirit Hits, a Scapegoat Suffers," *Wall Street Journal* (March 7, 1980), p. 1.

105. An interesting example of the unionization process is found in Nilima Acharji, *Trade Union Leadership Profile* (New Dehli, Ambika Publications, 1980).

106. See W. v.d. Geest and J. Harrod, *The Political Economy of the Swedish Model* (The Hague, Institute of Social Studies, unpublished paper, 1983).

Part 3

Self-Employed and Housewives

The introductions to parts 1 and 2 of this book have dealt with the problems of disaggregating the unprotected workers from the blanket notions and concepts that have encompassed them. This is much less necessary in the case of the self-employed and housewives, for they have not generally suffered from the submergence into such concepts as mass, peasants, or working class. Each of them has, however, been subjected to confusing definitions and exclusions.

The self-employed are the subject of some confusion as the result of imprecise definitions, and this has meant that, as an occupational category, self-employment has included the itinerant, casual own-account worker, as well as the owner and entrepreneur of a large enterprise. Also, the inclusion of the self-employed within the marxist petty commodity mode of social relations of production has prevented any serious examination of their precise social relations and the consciousness arising from them. These problems are corrected by precise definitions based on power relations criteria and on the approach that recognizes the distinctiveness of the pattern of power relations that surround their production.

In the case of housewives it was not that they were included in any misleading designation such as peasant or informal sector worker but rather that they were excluded from them all. The production of household services within the household was discounted as production by both marxist and nonmarxist commentators and therefore the social relations of production could not exist. In this book housewives are seen as subordinate workers within a distinct form of social relations of production even though many of them are also at the same time in other forms of social relations.

The reason for including housewives and self-employed in the same part of the book is partly for convenience and partly because housewives and self-employed have some similarities that they do not share with other unprotected workers. First, neither are in a labor market in that they do not sell their ability to work to purchasers of labor. When they do they either transform their social relations, as when a self-employed person decides to sell all his/her production to one purchaser and become a disguised outworker, or they enter other social relations, as when a housewife also takes wage employment. Second, the pace of their work and the nature and quality of their production are not directly and immediately supervised. There are no employers, foremen, labor buyers, or labor contractors watching the movements they make and controlling their output. They therefore retain some ability to control their own labor. Third, they are both often associated with a family, however that may be culturally defined. The bulk of people within self-employment social relations are in nonwaged family labor, and the housewife produces in the context of a family for family consumption. Thus the nature of the relations within the family, within the household, substantially affect any treatment of an individual and return for effort.

These similarities do not spill over into any similarity in actions taken by housewives and self-employed in the social formation. There is a traditional suspicion that workers with a minimal control over their own production will have conservative responses to social movements. The self-employed support of a class coalition opposing socialism or liberal reform and the instances of conservative behavior by women household workers might seem to reinforce that suspicion. But, as will be discussed later, such orientations are not entirely proven and it cannot easily be said that the two forms of social relations produce a uniformly conservative consciousness.

Even if this were the case, any possible similarities are destroyed by two overriding factors. First, the predominant household worker is a woman and the predominant head of a self-employed household is male. Second, women household workers, unlike the self-employed, are nearly always in other forms of social relations at the same time. The mixture of consciousness produced by household social relations (and its supporting ideology of patriarchy) and the consciousness derived from being a worker at the same time in other social relations is sufficient in itself to override any social similarities arising from the mere structure of the work of self-employed and housewives.

CHAPTER 6

SELF-EMPLOYMENT SOCIAL RELATIONS

In Ghana a goldsmith puffs at his blowpipe, forming by heat and lung power a golden trinket for a customer who waits impatiently. His lungs bear the strain of blowing and his eyes suffer from the heat of the forge, but for him this is an occupational hazard that must be borne if he is to satisfy his customer and continue to live by his trade.[1] A vast distance from him in culture, space, and time, an independent French farmer attaches his milking machine to his cows and reflects upon recent complaints made by the cheese wholesaler about the quality of his cheese made from the milk produced. The farmer knows his basic decision must now be whether to sell the milk unconverted and get less income or to increase the amount of work done by himself and family in order to produce better cheese. What unites these apparently disparate individuals is the way they must sell to and please their customers. This relationship is part of their common form of social relations of production, named here as self-employment.

Four large occupational groups are covered by the self-employment form of social relations of production. First, there are independent, usually land-owning, small farmers who sell their products on a market; second, there are shopkeepers, traders, and merchants; third, artisans; and fourth, independent suppliers of personal services.

As a result of this range the occupations self-employment social relations cover individuals at great extremes of social status, working conditions, and income levels. Conditions of work and life-styles may vary from the physical drudgery of a Djakarta thrishaw driver to the prestige and wealth of a successful shopkeeper, from the tedium of a ma-and-pa grocery store in the United States to the supposed excitement of a private detective in Italy and from the fine skills of an African goldsmith to the heavy physical work of the French independent farmer. The following description and analysis of self-employment social relations has as one of its tasks to demonstrate the fundamental power dynamics governing all those who work in these occupations and professions.

The self-employed are distinguishable from other producers principally in that they do not directly sell their ability to work to others, nor do they buy directly the labor of other workers. In marxist terms, they have entered exchange relations, in that they produce for a market, but have not entered capitalist relations, for they neither directly sell nor buy labor power.

The self-employed have either emerged from a transformation of subsistence or peasant-lord relations, as, for example, in the case where a subsistence farmer manages to produce a meaningful surplus for sale in the market, or they have migrated from other social relations but have not acquired the position of wage worker or employer within enterprise labor market relations. The self-employed may, of course, be individual migrants from almost any form of social relations.

The essential condition for self-employment is the development or presence of a market for the goods and services produced by the individuals. The term *market* is used here in the sense of an outlet for production fully or partially controlled in one way or another by a variety of individuals and organizations. Thus the power relations governing the production of the self-employed are between the self-employed producer and four types of individuals or organizations: first, those who control the market for the product or service; second, those who control the supply and price of any necessary inputs to production; third, employers in enterprises or other self-employed operators when they compete or cooperate to control markets or supplies; and fourth, the regulatory agencies of the state. In short the self-employed struggle with, or against, as the case may be, buyers, suppliers, competitors, and regulators.

To take an example of an independent retailer of fruit and vegetables in the United Kingdom; what determines the conditions of work and income for him and his family workers are such factors as the prices fixed by suppliers of produce, who may be farmers or wholesalers; what range of produce the local supermarket sells; how stringent the hygiene laws enforced by the state inspectorate are; and how forceful and diligent the tax inspectors are. Changes in any of these relations will directly affect such a greengrocer. If hygiene regulations are strictly enforced, he may have to raise more capital for equipment or space—such as cold rooms or air conditioning; he may have to remove profitable items from stock because a local supermarket decides to sell them cheaper; he may have the "mark-up"—the sale price over the supplier's price—squeezed by an increase in supplier's price or a decline in quality resulting in greater wastage; his chances of tax evasion may be reduced by a new tax inspector or a new policy of the government. If there exists a powerful association of independent greengrocers, some of these factors may be controlled to his advantage through pressure and lobbying. Otherwise, he may be able to find other suppliers with lower prices or to bribe the hygiene inspector; if all of these fail, or are not possible, he must alter his operation and income in accordance with the dictates of his suppliers, buyers, or regulators.

It may be stated then, at least at a high level of generality, that income, and often status, of any particular group of self-employed will be determined by its success in controlling markets, in other words, the success in developing sufficient power to control the supply, demand, and therefore the price and conditions of sale, for goods or service. The so-called liberal professions—lawyers, doctors, architects—have been so successful at restricting entry to their professions that their powerful organizations have assumed almost total control over entry and negotiate with the state for enforcement of fees. As a result they are among the highest paid persons in the world labor force and have successfully transformed their social relations from that of self-employment to that of bipartite bargaining relations with the state. Similar attempts by other self-employed have not been so successful. Self-employed farmers in third-world countries have usually not been able to control supply and prices for agricultural goods they produce, and they, like some small shopkeepers, are among the poorest people in the world.

From what has been said so far it is clear that the definition of a self-employed person within self-employment social relations differs substantially from the general use of the term *self-employment*, which in any case, is subject to a number of definitions.[2]

It is necessary to avoid all possible confusion by separating the definition used here, which is associated *exclusively* with a set of social relations, from those used more loosely. Self-employment is used in this book only to describe a person or household independently engaged in a productive activity who, or which, has an established and continuing relationship with those who comprise, control, or regulate markets for products and services or returns from the sales of such products and services and/or who control supplies necessary for production.[3] The "stable" or established element of this definition excludes those casual and irregular workers, such as occasional street vendors, shoecleaners, and car minders, who are often, however, described as self-employed. The "independent" character of production would exclude those persons who are superficially self-employed but are in fact linked, in an indirect manner, to one supplier or purchaser and who in effect become indirect employees. Vendors working on commission from one supplier, for example, may be considered as "disguised wage workers" or "out workers."[4] They are not self-employed according to the definition used here, but neither are casual workers of the primitive labor market or unorganized workers of the enterprise labor market. Finally, the "market" provision of the definition means also that women workers producing household services can also be excluded from self-employment social relations, for they do not produce their services for sale to buyers in a market. Moreover, owners of businesses and entrepreneurs are not included as self-employed, although that is often the case in national statistics. Such entrepreneurs are employers within enterprise labor market social relations discussed in the last chapter.

There are some universal and noticeable characteristics associated with self-employment regardless of definition. Usually self-employed people do not employ and are not employed; they sell the fruits of their labor rather than their ability to work; they have direct contact with the purchaser of their product or service; they are independent in the sense that they have no immediate supervision or direction over the way they work, the pace of their work, and the type and style of goods and services produced; and they often dispose of some form of capital, whether it be tools, stocks, shops, workshops, or the human capital of skill and experience.

Two of the principal characteristics—the absence of any employment relationships and an independent status—require a more careful examination, for it may be difficult to determine in practice what is employment and independence. A person in self-employment relations does not employ other workers on a regular basis and is not himself employed on a regular basis, since to do so, would transform the social relations. Thus when a self-employed producer employs someone else, the social relations are transformed into the employer-employee relationship of the enterprise labor market. The power relations between the self-employed, who has become an employer, and the controllers of the market for the product or service may not change, but there is now the additional relationship of power between the employer and employed, which changes the composition of the total pattern.

There are, however, a number of types of quasi-employment that do not necessarily create distinguishable employers and employees and do not therefore destroy self-employment relations. This is especially true of the case of family labor. A household producing goods or services for sale or exchange and using only family labor may well be within self-employment relations. Although allocation of asks and division of labor take place and even though such divisions and allocations may involve injustices and exploitation within the household, they do not constitute an employment relationship such as that which exists between workers who sell their ability to work to an employer in the enterprise labor market. What governs production, return, and to some extent distribution are the power relations of self-employment. Shopkeepers, artisans, and independent farmers almost always and everywhere in the world use family labor; such a collective effort may alter the nature and quantity of the product or service and therefore alter income, but the crucial power relations governing production and income remain those between the producing self-employed family and the controllers of markets or supplies.

There are also other cases where labor is "employed" but self-employment relations are not transformed. Irregular, seasonal, or casual employment, either by, or of, self-employed workers, would be such a case; it is the practice in India for some landowning peasant families producing for a market to hire out labor at certain times and hire it in at others.[5] This practice does not undermine the household's dependency on the farm income, which in turn is derived from the market for its produce. Nevertheless, such a case would certainly be on the margins between self-employment relations and enterprise labor market social relations.

When a self-employed producer is dependent upon one supplier or customer (either as a person or organization) to such an extent that control over production is lost to that person, then independence is lost and self-employment relations are destroyed. Thus, when an artisan producing goods for customers in a market starts to sell his/her whole production to one customer, then, despite an appearance of self-employment, the power relations have shifted from indirect, between the self-employed and the controllers of the market, to direct, with a single customer. What in this situation determines income, pace, and conditions of work, is the relationship of power between the producer and his/her single dominant customer or supplier, who is then in the power position of an employer—the self-employed producer is in "disguised" employment of the enterprise labor market. This situation is particularly prevalent in the case of the "apparent" self-employed farmer. Often land, tools, and livestock are legally all owned by the farmer's family, which produces and sells on the market. However, the farm may become so heavily indebted that surpluses and production rhythms are subordinated to the moneylender as the supplier of the input—credit—or to a single merchant who controls access to the market. A landowning, surplus-producing, superficially independent, and self-employed farming household may in fact be a dominated peasant household in the peasant-lord form.[6]

Individuals, then, move in and out of self-employment as they fail and become employed, or opt to become employing entrepreneurs, or as they in other ways acquire or lose control over their production. Although such personal fluidity is probably greater than in other social relations, entry into the self-employment form is not instantly available to all those who desire it. Usually the entrant has to have some capital and skills, although self-employment may be passed from generation to generation; children who inherit farms, shops, and artisanal workshops are provided, by inheritance, with the possibility of working within self-employment relations.

In the case of those who provide personal and professional services, such capital may have to be combined with skills— such as those of a barber or scribe. These skills are also the result of a capital expenditure in the form of periods of training, education, or apprenticeship during which the person is not earning sufficient for his/her own subsistence and must be maintained by transfers from elsewhere.

The self-employment form of social relations is found in almost every social formation. By use of a variety of statistical indicators, it has been estimated that at least 7 to 10 percent of the world labor force is covered by such social relations. The form appears in all social formations in which private economic power exists. Even in central planning or communally dominated social formations, self-employment has been permitted—the independent farmers of Poland are one such example; in 1981, the government of the People's Republic of China announced the approved return of self-employed street vendors after nearly twenty-five years during which time they had been totally banned.

ORIGIN OF SELF-EMPLOYMENT: MARKETS

Historically the two preconditions for self-employment were the development of a certain level of specialization in skills and crafts and a number of individuals, productive units, or organizations who, or which, could serve as separate purchasers of goods and services.

The first self-employed occupations developed were those providing personal services, for inasmuch as their customers were individuals there existed a natural market that was not dependent upon the creation of organizational structures such as farms, courts, or monasteries. Haircutters, medical men and women, midwives, scribes, and prostitutes have always tended to be self-employed. They were the precursors of what are now known as the liberal professionals. More important, however, to the development of observable, and sometimes institutionalized, self-employment relations were the artisans whose manner of distributing their production has been associated with markets. The nature and definition of a market are crucial to the power relations of self-employment, and it is necessary to comment briefly on the notion of the market and to distinguish its use here as a framework for a struggle for power over production, rather than as an economic power-balancing mechanism, which is at the essence of its conventional meaning.

For a brief moment in time, and in different places, there may have existed a market for the products of self-employed artisans in the sense that it is used in some modern economics, namely, that through the dynamics of competition based upon many purchasers and many sellers, prices were automatically fixed for the goods and services traded. During such periods the social relations of the self-employed would have, indeed, been between the individual producer and the market, or to use the term of Adam Smith, between the individual craftsman and the "invisible hand" that governed markets—invisible because it was the total of interactions of a multiplicity of buyers and sellers. Such a situation is short-lived, if it existed at all, and would perhaps not even have been historically significant if it had not been fossilized in an ideology of "free enterprise" that justifies or disguises the power of dominant groups and classes who are, in effect, the brains and arms that control the "hand."

It has been demonstrated by anthropological studies and some economic studies that economic and productive factors never entirely dominate the nature and behavior of any single society or set of producers within it;[7] further, whenever there was a risk that the "invisible hand" might have started to pull the strings of productive puppets, both buyers and sellers attempted to develop structures, processes, and organizations that successfully controlled production, prices, quality, and, inevitably, the conditions of work and return to the self-employed; in short, to ensure that the market worked mainly for them rather than against them. As already discussed in the chapter on the enterprise labor market, such actions destroyed any self-regulation and produced power relations between different groups concerned with the control or domination of the market. For this reason the essential power relations of the self-employed are not between the individual producer and the individual customer but between the individual producer and the group or entity that controls different aspects of the market. For the self-employed the market is, then, nothing more than an arena providing boundaries for the power struggle over their production.

The historical development of the occupational groupings of the self-employed started with the suppliers of personal services and artisans producing items for personal decoration, utensils for cooking, and other tools and implements associated with food, clothing, and housing. Traveling traders of these goods emerged later and hastened the process of specialization as they widened the market for artisanal goods.

The greatest historical impetus to the emergence of large numbers of self-employed, of workshop-based artisans, fixed traders, and stable professionals, was the creation of another large and crucial group of self-employed—the independent farming families. The breakup of feudalism often resulted in a large number of productive units—the farm household producing for the market. Although this process was uneven—in France the position of the independent farming family was established by the revolution of 1789, but in China it took two hundred years fort the same pattern to develop gradually—by the end of the nineteenth century a large proportion of world production and employment was taken up by self-employed, that is, by landowning and market-producing, farming families. Self-employment was at that time a dominant form of social relations. The emergence of self-employed farmers gave sustenance to an accelerated development of artisans and traders supplying the increased number of units and consumers, and of the professionals for the regulation of land exchange, inheritance, disputes, and so on.[8]

Self-employed artisans were originally found at the village level and were almost part of a cooperative production system in which the prices were fixed socially rather than by the markets. Soon, however, they began to concentrate in market towns, which in turn provided a base for professionals and the emergence of the centralized store and shopkeeper in addition to the itinerant trader.

The extension of skills among the population was an essential condition of the industrial revolution in the United Kingdom in the eighteenth century and for the development of industry elsewhere. The skills of large numbers of shoemakers, blacksmiths, carpenters, leather workers, coppersmiths, wheelwrights, and others were the skill foundation of the development of large-scale manufacturing. The latter meant that the artisans were pushed to further specialization under the principles of division of labor and were brought together in the factory system as "wage slaves" rather than independent producers. Not only were their skills needed, but also, in order to extract the greatest surplus, the dominant class at that time—the entrepreneurs of the enterprise labor market—had to make sure that the pace of work was maintained for as long periods as possible. They knew then, as is well known now, that there is a tendency for workers who directly control their work to reduce their pace and output once basic material needs have been secured.

In the marxist analysis self-employment was a precapitalist form of production, in that the ability to work is not bought or sold and was to have disappeared under the onslaught of the capitalist mode of production and the concentration and centralization of capital. Although this has clearly not happened, it is equally clear that self-employment has ceased to be a dominant form of social relations and has persisted only as a subordinant form—subordinated but not eliminated. As a result there have been continuing fluctuations in the number of artisans, farmers, retailers, and professionals. In the industrialized countries, artisans have been reduced in numbers, amalgamation of farms has virtually eliminated the family farms, and large-scale retailing has displaced shopkeepers; in the United States in the 1930s, 25 percent of the population was estimated as self-employed, whereas it was less than 10 percent in 1965.[9] In third-world countries there has been an expansion of self-employment in the urban areas coupled with a reduction in the numbers of self-employed. How these various self-employed occupations have fared is considered in detail below.

THE POWER STRUGGLE: SUPPLIERS, BUYERS, AND THE STATE

The self-employed must manipulate relations with suppliers, buyers, competitors, and the state (in its role of regulation of production and of taxation) to maximize their return as more income, less work, or generally better working conditions. In addition, they must be on their guard against generalized attempts, arising from policies and actions of the powerful in dominant forms, to gain control over their production or elminate them entirely.

There are some typical tactics and strategies pursued by the self-employed, their opposers, or their allies derived from the common objectives of acquiring power within the market. Suppliers of materials needed for production may attempt to maximize their own power and return by limiting the number of suppliers and maximizing the number of self-employed customers; buyers seek to force competition among self-employed producers to gain a lower price; competitors other than the self-employed, such as larger enterprises, may seek to drive the self-employed from the market; and the state may devise complicated schemes to regulate and control production in the public interest or to secure higher taxation. To all of these, self-employed producers—individual or household—must respond by confrontation, by making alliances, or by trading one predator off against another. Out of these battles and tactics emerge the organizations and well-known practices associated with groups of self-employed and their attempts to control entry to the trade or profession, to weaken suppliers, and manipuled customers.

Control of the numbers of people acquiring a skill necessary to enter self-employment has a long history. The craft guilds of fifteenth-century England operated to restrict entry to a craft, and one of their main activities was to found and organize schools and apprenticeship systems.[10] Control of medical schools and law schools by the already qualified doctors and lawyers has been so successful that they have virtually escaped the insecurity of self-employment while retaining many of the advantages. If skills are freely purchased or available, then, in order to control supply, the self-employed must resort to practices that prevent people who already have acquired the skills or capital from entering the occupation, and this is usually difficult without state assistance.

An example of control of the supplies of material goods, rather than skills, is found among the self-employed farmers of Europe in the last century when they created consumer cooperatives in order to buy from suppliers in bulk and then distribute themselves, through the cooperative, the necessary inputs to production, such as fertilizers, seeds, and implements. In this case individual farmers united to deal in strength with suppliers of inputs, that is, as one large buyer able to affect prices. In contrast, in the third world, and especially after the introduction of new high-yield seeds of the Green Revolution, seed and fertilizer merchants, as suppliers of the most essential inputs to production, have been able to weaken self-employed farmers' control over their production to the point of acquiring the dominance of a "lord" in peasant-lord relations.[11]

The self-employed seek also to control customers. In this they are rarely successful unless they can enlist the power of the state. Thus self-employed electricians in Switzerland have been able to secure state legislation—on the prima facie grounds of safety—that allows customers to resort only to state-authorized electricians. Attempts by self-employed to control suppliers and customers are not necessarily separate operations and often extend backward and forward from production at the same time and may also be combined with attempts to restrict entry to the trade and secure state help in controlling customers.

When these attempts to control suppliers and purchasers fail, or are not made, self-employed producers may find themselves under the domination of one customer or supplier and see their social relations change. This is particularly the case with self-employed who supply intermediate goods—that is, their clients are enterprise rather than individuals. Any concentration of such enterprises reduces their customers until they become indirect employees of a single large customer. This has been the process affecting garage mechanics servicing commercial vehicles in Western Europe, as the original 1930s pattern of "one-truck" enterprises has been replaced by transport enterprises with huge fleets and their own service departments. The success or failure of the self-employed and their predators depends to some extent on the nature of the product or service produced, but such market factors are always emphasized or mitigated by the institutions and the tactics the self-employed use within their power relationships.

Perhaps the key relationship common to all the occupations and suboccupations within self-employment social relations is that with the state, as represented by its regulating and taxing agencies and personnel. The state appears to the self-employed to be in an ambivalent position: on the one hand it may be benefactor and ally in the power struggle of the market, but on the other it may be the most potent threat and even the instrument for the complete destruction of self-employment relations.

The state is important for the self-employed as a regulator of both products and people. In regulating products the state legal and administrative apparatus adds conditions to a principle superficially held dear by most self-employed, that is, the principle of "caveat-emptor" or "let the buyer beware." Without any reservations this rule would make the buyer take the responsibility for the quality and price of goods and services on the principle that he or she must not be foolish enough to purchase poor quality goods at high prices. Almost all national legislations have, however, placed restraints on this basic legal principle in the form of safety standards, labeling rules, laws of professional negligence, standardization, and so on. Such regulations are drawn up to apply to all producers, whether they are large or small enterprises or self-employed. The further the regulations are extended the greater the conformity of production and the less possibility the self-employed have in adjusting the quality and nature of their production in order to manipulate suppliers and buyers. In these cases the state appears to be in alliance with the buyers or suppliers against the self-employed and has, on occasions, eliminated completely some self-employed occupations; the independent ice-cream makers of Europe, for example, were eliminated by quality control set to modern factory standards. Only very occasionally is the state regulation of products to the benefit of self-employed, as with the regulation descriptions such as "hand-made," which encourages artisanal production.

As a regulator of people, the state has had more of a beneficial impact on the self-employed, especially the professionals and highly skilled producers. In almost all countries the state has supported through legislation monopolies established by professionals. Groups of self-employed have also been protected by licensing and state-wide qualification laws that restrict entry to the occupation. Conversely, in regulating conditions of work for people, the state has often eliminated self-employed producing households in which family labor is involved in conditions that are not considered standard. In general, such rules on conditions of work have proved to act against the self-employed. In Melbourne, Australia, at the turn of the century, state regulation on the size of workshops eliminated the Chinese family-based artisan furniture maker.[12]

Even when state regulation has directly assisted self-employed occupations, it may not dissipate a general hostility of the self-employed toward the state as a result of the tax-collecting role it invariably plays. The direct nature of production and sale, the absence of supervision, and the individual way in which production may be organized means that the self-employed are notoriously difficult to tax. The opportunities they have to understate their turnover and earnings are greater than in any other productive activity. In order to tax effectively, therefore, the state must often monitor production and control transactions, and this is usually seen as an affront by the self-employed against their freedom to organize their own production. The incursive procedures the state must adopt in order to tax runs in the face of the psychological value of autonomy and freedom that causes many persons to migrate to self-employment. In addition to the general unpopularity of paying tax, the payment of social security contributions is similarly viewed by the self-employed, whose irregular production and unstructured work schedules mean that they must pay for benefits that are difficult to realize. The internecine war between self-employed and the tax inspector is a topic of universal conversation among such producers; in France in 1976 the leader of a self-employed organization was jailed for avowing that there would be no respite from tax-inspector harassment until an inspector was killed during the exercise of his duty.[13]

It is only on rare occasions that groups of self-employed have been able to reverse the flow between themselves and the state and to acquire direct financial benefit from the state. One example would be the price supports, grants, and other payments made to independent farmers of Western Europe, beginning during the 1950s, which had the effect of encouraging the decline in numbers of such farms through amalgamation but nevertheless of supporting those that remained. This was achieved only through intensive political action by the farmers. The increasing role of the state is one of the factors that encourage self-employed to take political and organizational rather than economic action in their defensive moves.

It now remains to consider the various forms of collective actions self-employed adopt in the power struggle of the market. it should be noted first that any general categorization of self-employed as being part of an "unorganized" section of the labor force is erroneous. In fact, the self-employed have, in many cases, developed efficient organizations for their protection; an example, containing all the elements so far discussed and relating to the self-employed, is that of the organization of some stall holders in India. Approximately thirty people were established as "patriwallah" in the precincts of a shopping center, but the police demanded bribes or took food from the stalls. The stall holders formed a union, collected dues, and printed posters, and in a political move to gain popular support, inaugurated "Shastri Market" in honor of the then Indian Prime Minister Shastri.[14] In Equador, in 1962, four new shoe factories using plastic injection molding machines were introduced that would have the effect of displacing 15,000 persons in artisanal shoe production. Vigorous action and organization by the artisans was able to postpone the opening of these factories and force discussion about the future of the industry with the government, despite the shoemakers' having the economic disadvantage of producing shoes at a higher cost than those made of plastic.[15]

The tendency toward organization for the protection of

income and working conditions is a characteristic of self-employment relations similar to more well-known and structured relations of trade union and employer. Self-employed organizations have, however, a greater variety of forms and purposes and are only infrequently studied because they do not influence general wage rates or other economic conditions at the national level.

Self-employed organizations may be informal or formal and are based upon the use of economic or political instruments, given that the latter term is used restrictively to indicate the pressure applied through lobbying on governments. Informal organizations operate without any clear structure, officers, or management in much the same way as informal organizations of primitive labor market workers discussed earlier. They are usually based upon a need for protection against new or different actions by opponents such as the police in the above example. Informal organizations are often illegal, especially when they are based upon violent or other illegal means of preventing competition or for securing relief from extortionate suppliers or state agencies; otherwise they appear as a complex of understandings, agreements, or short-term reactions developed to offset some new event in short-term reactions developed to offset some new event in self-employment relations that threatens to upset the balanced incursion into self-employment.

Formal organizations operate both in the economic sphere, as in the case of groupings of bulk purchasers, or politically as pressure groups or within ideological or class-based movements. An example of the first type found in most countries is the "trade association," which groups self-employed for bulk-buying purposes. These operate particularly in food, clothing, and hardware sectors. More important are the organizations of self-employed for purposes of political lobbying and for controlling the entry to an occupation, such as professional associations. The FNSEA— the French National Federation of Independent Farmers—has had an international impact as the result of the successful pressure on French governments to keep up the price of food within the European Economic Community.

The range of action such organizations take is very wide but certainly includes strikes, boycotts, demonstrations, and political lobbying. Strikes are, however, difficult to sustain among the self-employed, mainly because ceasing work means a direct and immediate loss of income, and in trade, where regularity of service is important, it may even mean a future loss of income as regular customers are lost. For this reason the self-employed more often resort to direct action taken by one occupational grouping or they support political movements perceived to hold policies that would solve some of more immediate problems. The political role of self-employed is also a question of consciousness and is discussed in more detail below.

ECONOMIC EXTRACTION
AND SURVIVAL: AN OVERVIEW

Self-employment relations are used in three different ways in the wider society: first, through general economic extraction, as in the case with other subordinate social relations; second, as a repository of political allies for dominant groups in the social formation; and, third, as a haven in which social dissidents, ethnic minorities, and those who wish to escape the structures of other work situations may find refuge. The political role of self-employed and the social relations as a refuge are discussed under the heading of consciousness and politics. In this section the mechanisms of economic transfers and the material position and survival conditions for the various self-employed occupational groupings are examined.

In reality, and certainly in the perception of most self-employed, the powerful groups and coalitions in the social formation are either hostile to, or are ambivalent about, the continued existence of the self-employed. The fundamental basis for such ambivalence is that, in comparison with other social relations, extraction from the self-employment relations is a difficult operation. The power struggle of the self-employed within the market is, at a different level, also a struggle to prevent the extraction of surpluses. The peasant renders surplus to the landlord, the casual worker of the primitive labor market occasionally supplies cheap labor, the workers of the enterprise labor market supply goods, and the house-wife, cheap and nonwage services. The social relations of the latter workers are stabilized around a continued surrender of surpluses to those who are dominant within the social relations and thence to the producers in the dominant forms in the social formation.

In contrast, if social relations can be seen as precipitating a system of labor control, then the self-employed are the only subordinate group that has partially escaped from the rigors of such control.[16] Such lack of control makes difficulty of extraction of surpluses the fundamental political-economic characteristic of self-employment social relations. Theoretically, part of production could be extracted from the self-employed by using mechanisms similar to those associated with the small enterprise discussed earlier, namely, through subcontracting between enterprises and the self-employed, through taxation, through interest on capital needed for production, through suppliers, through unequal exchange of goods with market dominators, and so on.[17] However, in the case of the self-employed each point of potential extraction is, in effect, an attack on the existence of self-employment and is resisted in the ways already discussed. Furthermore, the residual power of the self-employed to control their pace of work, quality, and income means that all the standard and structured methods of extraction—especially taxes—are difficult to apply to production and work schedules that retain at least the potential to be unstructured.

This is not to say that there are no transfers from the self-employed to producers in dominant forms but rather that extraction is more difficult, less automatic, and therefore less secure and predictable. The state authorities as a taxing agent, the large enterprise as a consumer of skills,[18] an the small enterprise producing similar goods, respectively, view the self-employed as tax evaders, skill hoarders, or wily competitors. Self-employed are tolerated economically because their numbers are not sufficient to make them an economic threat and because some useful goods and services are extracted—especially at the margins where enterprises find it difficult to operate. The distributive trades, for example, need too much attention to detail, too many outlets, and too much flexibility to be easily and totally incorporated within the framework of large organizations; as a consequence they are frequently left in the hands of the self-employed or the "private sector," as it is called in centrally planned economies.

This function at the periphery of the mainstream of economic life, plus the social refuge function, are set by those in power against the general difficulty of extraction from the self-employed. Together such trade-offs help produce the ambivalence toward the self-employed—on the one hand they are not easily integrated into a smoothly functioning hierarchy of transfers, extraction, accumulation, or redistribution, but on the other hand they do have a less tangible social and material usefulness. How the different occupational groups have fared both in the internal struggle of the market and in face of a sometimes hostile or ambivalent authority in the social formation may now be considered in brief and general terms.

SELF-EMPLOYED FARMERS

Independent farming families are the most numerous and important occupational groupings of the self-employed. The difference between self-employed farmers and cultivators covered by other social relations has been extensively discussed within the framework of peasant-lord and subsistence social relations.[19] To recapitulate, the self-employed farming family is distinguished from other cultivators (and cultivating families) in that the land is owned or controlled over a long-term basis, unlike the peasant in peasant-lord relations. There are also significant sales on the market, unlike subsistence social relations. The other almost universal necessity for self-employed farming is the use of large amounts of family labor. Thus the basic picture is of a farming household, usually headed by a male, working family-owned or family-controlled land and selling a proportion of total production on a market. In power terms the family still has some control over its production and has not become subordinated to money-lenders through indebtedness or to the merchants who buy the crops; in short, it has been sufficiently successful in the power struggle of the market to maintain self-employment social relations although, in the majority of cases, not sufficiently successful to avoid a grueling level of self-imposed exploitation.

As in the case of other self-employed, farming families may make decisions about what proportion of production they use for personal subsistence, what proportion they sell on the market, and whether they forgo rest for work, or whether they use labor for "accumulation," that is, initially nonproductive additions to their "capital."[20] Because most such farmers within third-world countries do not have sufficient land to support the family, it is generally the case that the combined subsistence and market proportions of production must be secured by applying more and more labor, even though the increase in output is very small. The action of farming families means that the behavior of the family is clearly that of the self-employed, who often count their own labor at zero cost, rather than an enterprise in which labor input is a major part of costs.[21] It is this factor of family labor use that raises the level of exploitation in the sense that it is not always clear to an outsider that the extra work done is worth the extra production.

The mechanism of transfer from self-employed farmers to dominant groups is through taxation and pricing of the proportion of goods sold on the market, and in the case of Western European and Japanese farmers in the middle of the twentieth century, through unfavorable exchanges between agricultural and industrial goods. The partial control over production means that for the state the universal characteristic of the independent farmer is the difficulty of extracting taxes. Devices for tax collection are extremely diiverse. In France, peasants were ordered by law to take their pigs to a central slaughterhouse for slaughter and then bring them back to the farm in order that the state could extract a tax per kilo on meat essentially produced for subsistence needs. In Uganda at one time tax evaders were publicly roped together. The difficulty of tax collection has also meant that the function has been subcontracted to a local person who could make precise assessments of output; this was the case with the Zamindar in colonial India.[22]

The result is that extraction is frequently secured by pricing of the goods on the market. Throughout the world, governments have tended to be the price-fixing authority.[23] Where independent farmers have some power—usually in association with enterprise farms—the price fixing represents a battle of the market and involves bargaining. In other cases especially in third-world countries it is only the individual wiles of the farmer that defeat the state pricing authority.

When farming families are persuaded, or are able, to buy substantial inputs for their farming activities, then another method of extraction occurs. The prices of seeds and chemicals needed for increased rice production have recently become a typical way of extracting from farmers in the third world. In Western Europe the beginnings of mechanization meant that family farms, many for the first time in their history, entered into debt to secure tractors and other implements. The interest on the loans and the price of the industrial goods was a principal mechanism of extraction in Western Europe after 1940.[24]

The success or failure of the self-employed farmers and their current situation differs greatly according to the level of industrial development and wealth. Independent family farms in Western Europe and Japan have suffered their most precipitous decline in numbers since 1950. They have now become the residue of a dominant agricultural form of social relations of the eighteenth and nineteenth century. They were forced out of existence by the development of large-scale, high-energy, and capital-intensive agriculture. This meant that smaller farms had to be amalgamated. States, backed by large farmers and industrialists interested in cheaper food and more industrial sales, offered schemes and incentives for such amalgamations. Small farms on marginal land were then squeezed out by competing prices from the large-scale farms. In the Netherlands the number of farms declined by 75 percent between 1950 and 1970 while the larger farms of twenty to fifty hectares increased by 100 percent.[25]

From the very beginning of this process independent farmers formed defensive associations and exerted all possible political pressure. In France small farmers were a major support for the Gaullist Party from 1958 onward while Bavarian farmers in The Federal Republic of Germany provided the substantial support for the conservative wing of the Christian Democrats and both parties acquired substantial political power. As a result of this action most governments continued their efforts to reduce the numbers of self-employed farmers but at the same time made major concessions to those that would remain. These included security of tenure, fixed rents, and other legal protection (which made farmers de facto owners of the land they rented), grants, cheap loans for machinery, and support prices and subsidies. The result has been that the remaining European and Japanese independent family farmers have a material level of living comparable with the industrial sector. But increasingly the return to their labor is the subject of national bargaining over the prices of agricultural produce and, in the case of Western Europe, of bargaining at the international level within the European Economic Community. The result of this is that the organizations of small farmers are among the most powerful of all self-employed groups and social relations therefore move toward a bipartite pattern of power bargaining between associations of farmers and the state over agricultural prices, on which income depends.

Almost all social formations in the third-world countries have a proportion of the agricultural labor force covered by self-employed social relations. In India it has been estimated that approximately 30 percent of farming households may be considered as self-employed according to the definition used in this book.[26] Also in India, as well as elsewhere, such independent farmers tend to be materially better off than tenant farmers and agricultural laborers, although that does not mean they can be designated as "rich" peasants as in the Leninist categories.[27] In general, they have nowhere been successful in resisting the market price mechanism of extraction. Their numbers fluctuate increasingly as the result of government policies in relation to agriculture and land reform.

All land reform policies, other than those based upon collectivization, would, if successfully implemented, have a tendency to create self-employed social relations out of peasant-lord social relations. Distributing land and giving ownership to tenants has the objective of creating land owning, market-producing farming households. As already noted in the chapter on peasant-lord social relations, such reforms have rarely been completely carried out, usually because of the reluctance of reformers to face the power of landlords or because reforms are reversed when self-employed farmers revert, via indebtedness and merchant domination, to peasants. When reforms have been effected by revolutionary regimes, the immediate problem has been that of extracting from the self-employed farming households so created. Peasant households free from the necessity to pass upward of 50 percent of their total production to dominant landlords in the new situation of self-employment have the ability to reduce the level of work performed or consume or invest more. Production falls, and to restore it to previous levels via taxation threats is even more difficult than taxing a landlord after extraction has been made. Enthusiasm by revolutionary and reformist regimes alike for self-employment social relations has tended to be short-lived as the problems of extraction, even for desirable goals such as social infrastructure, become manifest.[28]

Self-employed farming families in the third world are declining under the impact of collectivizing land reforms, large-scale agriculture, and the development of enterprise farms employing wage labor.[29] Like most self-employed then, those that remain are often in a precarious position with the threat of becoming peasants or landless laborers,[30] of being absorbed by agribusiness,[31] or of moving to become entrepreneurs in a rural enterprise labor market. The consciousness arising from such insecurity, combined with a promise, inherent in the social relations, of independence, makes self-employed farmers a volatile but key political group in rural reform and revolutionary movements.

ARTISANS

The universal situation of a manufacturing or service artisan is similar to that provided by the example of the African goldsmith cited earlier. Essentially he/she operates alone or with family labor from a small workshop, which may be integrated within the family residence. He is usually highly skilled and derived from parents the skill he passes on through instruction to off-spring. In this way generations of self-employed within the same craft and from the same family are established. Capital used is often minimal, extending only to the workshop and tools,[32] although in some of the more modern trades such as printing, it can be considerable. Manufacturing artisans are engaged in transforming malleable materials—wood, leather, iron metal, clay, glass, fibers—into utilitarian or decorative items. Service artisans are associated with servicing things. Those supplying personal services are categorized as professional or quasi-professional and will be discussed in that section. Service artisans maintain and service capital invested in shelter and transport and are clustered in contemporary conditions around the construction and transport industries. They include "jobbing" carpenters, plasterers, plumbers, bricklayers, mechanics, and, in earlier times, shoesmiths for horses and wheelwrights for carts.

The method of extraction from artisans is principally through the relative pricing of the goods they produce. The supplies of materials for production and capital are not quantitatively important enough for the prices of these to be a major mechanism for removing surpluses as in the case of a small enterprise. The price for the goods or services produced must bear a relation to the general price structure of the economy but also to possible substitutes and goods manufactured by capital-intensive and mass methods—all of which are controlled by groups in dominant forms. In general, the downward pressures on the price of artisanal goods means that artisans do not acquire high material levels of living although the conditions of work may be more favorable than in the industrial circumstances.[33] In many cases manufacturing artisans must work long hours with dangerous substances on monotonous tasks. In a similar position, the service artisan has often had greater success in preventing entrants to the trade than the manufacturing artisan.

Artisans have usually not been able to form national associations with any power. Their organizations tend to be local and more specifically related to the immediate power struggle of the market and aimed more at buyers than suppliers. They are tolerated by those in power and have a reasonable level of return for their work. But they are increasingly regulated by the state and pressured toward surrendering the partial freedom they have over their production.

Social security laws, taxation, and labor laws tend to make life more difficult than easier for both service and manufacturing artisans.[34] The wide range of industrial goods available means that they are constantly being chased from a manufacturing niche by mass-produced goods or even by imports of cheaper artisanal goods from other countries. They suffer from "technological" elimination as when labor-saving innovations are made. Sometimes the innovation is directed specifically at self-employed artisans; prefabricated building components and reinforced concrete, for example, eliminated many of the highly skilled, highly paid self-employed bricklayers. In recent years the numbers of artisans in industrialized countries have increased as a result of taking to artisanal production as an alternative to unemployment.[35] Economic forecasts, however, predict only a slight increase in the numbers and level of such production up to the year 2000.[36]

The situation is somewhat different in social formations of the third world. There artisanal production plays its role as a preindustrial form of production. However, unlike the industrial growth as experienced in the history of the now industrialized countries, self-employed artisans have not been part of a dominant form of social relations. This was because either large-scale capital-intensive industry was introduced in the country or the goods from large-scale, capital-intensive production from elsewhere were imported. In the process of establishing British colonies, for example, factory-produced goods plus British sea power and military might were instrumental in forcing the end of artisanal production of textiles and similar goods. This was the case of artisanal cotton textile production in Bengal and elsewhere in India in the nineteenth century.

Nevertheless, because the range of industrial goods produced is narrower or cannot be imported at reasonable prices, artisanal production provides a substantial proportion of total national income and occupies a sizable section of the labor force. Artisans' return is almost always lower than that of employed workers with equivalent skills, and it is, therefore, fairly easy for large enterprises to attract skilled artisans to wage employment.

The artisan in third-world countries has recently been made the center of attention as efforts have been made to restore small-scale, labor-intensive industrial production. However, most of the programs advocated by international agencies and governments have been intended not to sustain self-employment relations, but rather to convert the self-employed artisan into an employing entrepreneur.[37]

SHOPKEEPERS, TRADERS, AND MERCHANTS

The universal image of shopkeeping is that of a shop into which is packed a stock of goods suited to the needs of customers and behind or above which lives the shopkeeping family. Most of the family help in the shop at one time or another, and family labor is always an important part of the operation. Their business causes members of the family to be perennially occupied with markups, suppliers, customers, spoilage, stocks, theft, opening hours, and, increasingly, competition from large-scale retailing operations. Traveling traders are basically itinerant shopkeepers and are currently found predominantly in third-world countries. They hawk their wares from "pitches," territories, or designated spaces in fixed marketplaces. Traders emerge from casual work into self-employment social relations when they secure a degree of regularity and permanence.[38] Merchants are buyers and sellers of bulk merchandise operating from an office, stock-room, or truck. They rely on superior knowledge and transport to enable them to buy from one person and sell to another without either seller or buyer's being able to deal directly with each other.

The markup, that is, the difference between the purchase price of the goods and the price at which they sell, is the main indicator of the level of income from work. Returns from, and working conditions in, these occupations have declined considerably over the past thirty years.

For the shopkeeper—and this term is used here to cover trader and merchant as well—the result has been a triple deterioration of security of livelihood and return to work.[38] First, the shopkeeper may be eliminated completely as larger retailing enterprises sell the same range of goods more cheaply and conveniently. In Switzerland between 1970 and 1975, 4,000 out of 15,000 small grocery stores closed.[39] The shopkeeper may also be eliminated by a change in the social formation in which state control is extended to the distributive trades.

The second cause of difficulty for shopkeepers and traders is the decrease in the numbers of suppliers through concentration of enterprises and decline of artisans: they then have less opportunity to secure goods cheaply from different suppliers. Thirdly, price competition from larger operations squeezes markups from the prices side. There are also other aspects of large-scale competition cutting into "traditional" economics of shopkeeping— large-scale operations often specialize in "fast-turn" items for which there is a constant demand and which used to be the staple of small retail units. Now the latter are forced into "slower turn" items, which means longer time on the shelf with greater spoilage and loss of interest on the capital tied up in goods waiting for sale.

Like the self-employed farmer the shopkeeping family tends to fall back on what is viewed as infinitely extendable family labor and increases the number of hours open, the amount of time spent on tedious minor transformations of stock and packaging, and other labor-intensive applications to retailing.

Moreover, shopkeepers are often from minority groups and have also suffered both as minority groups and as shopkeepers in the racial discrimination, violence, and nationalism of the past half-century.

Some shopkeepers in third-world countries have also been eliminated by competition from urban shopping centers but much less so than in industrialized countries. In rural areas they have retained their importance and status and are still able to command high returns. Further, merchants, as has been noted in the chapter on peasant-lord social relations, through a monopoly of transport or knowledge of markets have sometimes secured sufficient dominance over self-employed farmers to leave self-employment relations and become part of dominant groups within peasant-lord relations.

Shopkeepers have not then in general been noticeably successful in the power struggle of the market. Organizations against suppliers and competitors have not been significantly successful. It is perhaps for this reason that shopkeepers and traders have been noticeably politically active in order to try to secure a generalized state protection—this aspect is discussed in the next section.

In summary, it can be said that the numbers of shopkeepers, traders, and merchants are declining and those that remain are under increasing material pressure. Nevertheless, the conditions of, and return to work, still make the occupation attractive in comparison with wage or casual labor, and most social formations continue to find a use for self-employment relations within distribution. This means a continued persistence of self-employment relations in these trades.

PERSONAL SERVICE SUPPLIERS

The independent suppliers of personal services include occupations such as haircutters, footcare specialists, prostitutes, masseurs, clotheswashers, fortune-tellers, witch doctors, midwives, and so forth. All of these occupations may be found in social relations other than self-employment, and the services can be performed by waged workers in the enterprise labor market or corporatist social relations. There is, however, a large proportion of each occupation that operates independently and in self-employment social relations.[40] Other personal service suppliers are known as liberal professions, such as doctors, dentists, and lawyers.

Entry into the occupations of personal service, unlike that into the liberal professions, is sufficiently easy for there to be an actual, or threatened, oversupply of suitable operators, which creates a downward pressure on prices that can be charged for the service. Organizations of such independents then tend to be based on the acquisition and retention of a regular set of customers, for the struggle of the marketplace is not against the suppliers or the state as much as against new entrants and other "poachers" of established customers. Such organizations are often remnants of those associated with casual work, which have become more established when the social relations change to self-employment through regularity of work.[41] Thus the typical Western European and North American pimp/prostitute relationship is one to protect a market, for the pimp is supposed to prevent other competing prostitutes from poaching on the territory.[42] The gang wars, murders, and ill treatment this system produces in relation to prostitution occur also in other personal service "professions" where competition for customers is fierce, especially in the urban areas of the third world. As such organizations develop, those in power within them seek to change the social relations to those of the enterprise labor market by making themselves the "employer." Thus personal service suppliers have usually been unable to control the market and, in general, are in a weak position. They are, however, a permanent feature of all societies, although often operating illegally or underground.

The acquisition of professional status is one way for the

self-employed to transform social relations in their favor. But professional status is a status acquired from power, principally the power to control entry, to surround the profession with a protective myth providing status and an established social power. Thus there are many self-employed who aspire to liberal professional status but have not been able to secure a monopoly of the market sufficient to insist on professional bargaining with the state. These are usually an intermediate group of highly skilled persons who do not offer a service associated with individual needs. Thus self-employed engineers, chemists, and management specialists supplying services, usually to organizations, must still, although highly paid, exist with the insecurity and remain essentially subordinate to their more powerful customers.

The liberal professions themselves, although protected by successful dominant organizations, may still on occasion suffer from a reduction in numbers as a result of shifts in power that affect more typically subordinate self-employed. Thus, for example, more and more doctors work for hospitals and medical organizations as these latter have increased their power within modern capital-intensive medicine. Between 1968 and 1973, hospital-based physicians in the United States increased by 22 percent while office-based physicians, (that is, self-employed) recorded a much smaller increase. The conclusion was that self-employed physicians were gradually declining.[43] Such declines will not, however, affect the power of the liberal professions in other social relations.[44] They will continue to exercise their accumulated social power until direct attacks are made against them by the state, as sometimes occurs in revolutionary regimes.

CONSCIOUSNESS: ESCAPISM, INSECURITY, AND RESENTMENT

Any discussion of the consciousness of the self-employed that aspires to any level of generality is made difficult by the multiplicity of the occupational groups and their material and social position in different social formations. Nevertheless, the social relations of self-employed are universal and elements of a universal consciousness are apparent. It is on these aspect that the discussion must concentrate, even though they may have varying degrees of relevance to the different occupational groups.

In the case of the self-employed there must be added to the nature of the social relations two other sources for the development of consciousness. First, is the importance of the type of person and groups attracted to self-employed and, second, is the current social status of the self-employed in general.

There are basically four types of persons and reasons for entering or staying within self-employment: first are those who are attracted by a belief that their return to work will be improved. This is a general reason for people migrating between different social relations and is not especially relevant to consciousness. Second are ethnic or religious minority groups who seek escape from various forms of discrimination. Third are what might be called conscious social dissidents who wish to escape from what they believe to be an unacceptable or socially or politically abhorrent society of which regular and structured work is symbolic. Fourth are the unconscious social dissidents, that is, those who find the authoritarian structures of other work in other social relations psychologically hard to bear. These latter three categories mean that the self-employed are often from minority groups or are social, religious or political dissidents.

The most obvious example of the prevalence of minority groups within self-employment social relations is that of shopkeepers, who, almost everywhere in the world, are drawn from minority groups. The minority Chinese, Jewish, Syrian, and Indian groups in Europe, Africa, and Asia frequently dominate the retail trade. In Egypt, for example, Christian Copts own shops and are tailors although the population is predominantly Muslim. In a detailed and extensive survey of a Malaysian village in 1965 it was shown that *all* the resident Chinese and Indians were in commerce and *all* the Malays worked on the land.[45]

There are several reasons for minority groups' being overly concentrated within self-employment. Sometimes it is that the minority group, as a collectivity, has acquired sufficient economic power to provide others from the same minority with the capital necessary to enter self-employment.[46] Family patterns and cultures are also relevant—those in which service to the family is considered important produce large amounts of family labor, whereas when children leave the household to seek work elsewhere at an early age, the continuity of available labor is broken. In Jamaica the female-headed, loose, extended family of the African-descended black Jamaicans provides the labor for industry and plantations while the male-headed, close, nuclear family of the Chinese minority groups owns the stores.

These factors are of considerable importance, but in almost every case it can also be shown that such minority groups have also found it difficult to secure employment elsewhere. In state service and in large corporations overt discrimination may prevent minority group employment. Further, in the work of the factory, construction site, and farm enterprise, minority groups have often been subjected to social harassment from fellow workers. Thus the relative social isolation of self-employment represents the possibility of earning a living, of escaping individual discrimination, and at the same time, maintaining desired cultural, linguistic, or religious practices of the minority group. It has been through self-employment that in some countries minority groups have flourished and prospered despite a generalized ethnic or racial hostility. Any collective cohesion based on religion or ethnicity is then cemented by social relations and reinforces the hold of the minority group on the trade.

Such prosperity and escape from discrimination, however, also result in a high visibility of the minority groups, as, for example, the apparent suppliers of food in agricultural markets and in shops—the basic points of contact with material goods and basic needs in any society in which there is exchange for money. As a result, and apart from any general racial or religious hostility, such self-employed are often erroneously perceived as the major source of economic power contributing to the lack of needed goods for the population. They are also the targets for the feelings of relative deprivation, for in many cases the self-employed are the only people with greater wealth with which the population comes in contact outside of an employment or master-servant relationship. Thus, when society is disturbed, minority groups in control of trade or other self-employed occupations become the targets for social wrath, as the lootings, violence, and harassment of the Chinese merchants and shopkeepers in Jamaica in the 1960s and in Malaysia in 1969 and of Indian businesses in Uganda in 1973 and Kenya in 1982 are prime examples. The expropriation of Jewish-held businesses and shops was a step in the process leading to the subsequent mass slaughter of the Jewish people of Europe between 1942 and 1945; in Poland, in 1938, 70 percent of all shopkeepers and traders were Jewish, the majority of whom did not survive the extermination camps and ghettos.[47]

Minority groups in self-employment are under a triple threat: that of economic elimination, as described earlier; of racially inspired discrimination and harassment; and of social violence in case of widespread social turbulence. The minority group psychosis, as an input into the consciousness of the self-employed, must always be a point of departure for the consideration of any specific situation and case.

The second type of minority person to be considered is the conscious social dissident—"conscious" because the dissent and opposition to society is made extant in general terms and the refusal to conform sufficiently for acceptance into regular employment is deliberate. In Western Europe and North America of the 1960s and 1970s it was to self-employment that the "new marginals" resorted—hippies and others earned money by artisanal production, by keeping market stalls, by subsistence farming, and by trading.

The third type of person can be designated as an unconscious social dissident—"unconscious" because the escape into self-employment arises from a personal inability to sustain the regulated and authoritarian procedures of structured employment. For such a person this does not constitute a general condemnation of regular work—it is merely that it does not suit a person who strives to be his or her own boss. Yet the escape into self-employment represents social dissent in the sense that is is really a rejection of what is the basic standard of the wider society—that of structured work forms. Such sentiments are expressed in the United Kingdom when it is noted that self-employed occupations are "better than nine-to-five," the latter being a popular expression for regulated office work—in France the equivalent expression is "auto-bulot-auto-dodo" (car-work-car-sleep). These types of entrants are often ex-industrial workers and their aspiration for self-employment is both an escape and a perception of upward mobility.[48]

The social dissident type of entrant reinforces the value of individualism that is apparent as a major value of the self-employed. The residue of individual control over production, the isolation and apparent self-sufficiency of the family production unit, the lack of direct supervision, the ownership of land, and the self-perception of difference of superiority contribute to the promotion and adherence to all aspects of independence and individualism. This is particularly noticeable in the self-employed's role in opposing political movements based on socialist or collectivist policies.

The position of social dissidents and minority groups within self-employment relations may be an important factor for the stability of the wider society. If all social dissidents were forced, by virtue of lack of opportunity, to remain in other social relations, it may be that their dissidence would manifest itself in greater disturbance, radicalism, or activism within those relations. In this way then self-employment social relations can be considered as supplying a niche where social dissidence and malaise can be relieved of an immediate target such as an employer or landlord and therefore as a contribution to greater social stability.

This "safety valve" function of self-employment is not necessarily a natural or accidental self-selection. The presence of the self-employed is integrated into a dominant ideology, as well as a promoted mechanism of operation of capitalist social formations and others that accept a plurality of centers of power.[49] Thus, despite the general ambivalence and hostility toward self-employment relations found among dominant groups, in practice, in theory, and in ideology, self-employment is within "free enterprise," which in turn is part of the ideology instrumental in the maintenance of the configuration of the whole social formation. The broader ideology, therefore, reinforces and encourages the self-employed adherence to individualism.

The second special aspect of inputs into the consciousness of the self-employed is their relations with groups in proximate forms of social relations, many of which are their customers. In particular, their relationship with the organized workers of bargaining social relations, the workers of the enterprise labor market, and the employers in all other social relations is problematic.

The self-employed are economically and socially peripheral to all these groups. In industrialized countries the self-employed usually consider themselves as having left the "working
class," having "bettered themselves," or as holding a higher status. They expect to have a social prestige above that of workers
in other social relations. Yet the power and material advancement
of the unionized workers have often overtaken that of the self-
employed—neither in income nor in power (as manifested by
seeing their image or representatives in the highest reaches of
power) can the self-employed match the unionized workers or
the workers in corporatist social relations. The self-employed
perceived status does not match the actual status. Such "status
incongruency," as sociologists call it, is considered to be a major
input into the world view of the self-employed and a particular
goad to action to try and restore equilibrium by increasing their
own status, or, more often, decreasing that of others. The situation
is somewhat different in third-world countries, where many self-
employed aspire to regular wage work, which is perceived as
having a higher status.

Only when self-employment is seen as an upwardly mobile activity, and not as an alternative to unemployment and
poverty, does status incongruity appear. Perhaps a more important relationship is between the self-employed and the employers
of the enterprise labor market. Whereas the self-employed often
see themselves as small-business people, it is not possible for
them, in the ultimate, to acquire the social prestige of an employer, because they cannot dispense the "reward" or "gift" of
employment. They may belong to associations of small businessmen and entrepreneurs and be statistically counted among them,
but they invariably remain peripheral—they are in essence only
marginal members of the class coalition designated as the petit
bourgeoisie.[50]

In these cases, despite notions of difference and high prestige of having escaped from material disadvantage and the "lower
orders," the self-employed know from experience that those who
control the state, or large enterprises, or land reform programs
will, when they feel it necessary, eliminate large number of self-
employed. The social relations rarely result in a lifetime of stable,
secure income; the incessant struggle of the market on the four

fronts—buyers, suppliers, competitors, and the state—serves as a constant reminder of the vulnerable situation. Self-employment seems to the practitioners to be under attack from all sides from predatory competitors, greedy suppliers, state regulators, land reform, big business, trade unions, collectivist political movements, urban planners, tax inspectors, labor inspectors, consumer organizations, and all those who might upset the delicate power balance of the market that enables the self-employed to survive.

The struggle of the market produces both insecurity and aggressivity—insecurity because of the need to calculate a strategy for survival and advancement and aggressivity because of the need to put the strategy into action. Insecurity and a latent aggressivity produced by the struggle of the market manifest themselves in direct and indirect action in the wider society. The self-employed insecurity is magnified by the degree to which there are alternatives open to them if they were forced out of their chosen activity. Psychologically these alternatives are meager: it is difficult for a personality who has become his or her own boss, who has become a land owner instead of a peasant, or has acquired the security of a liberal professional to "descend" to factory, office, or dominated agricultural labor. Self-employment is a way of life with its own individual value system—a threat to it is a threat to a way of life for which many would rather perish than give it up. Such a consciousness extracts from the self-employed extremes of self-sacrifice and exploitation in order to cling to the status; in China independent farmers burned themselves with their farms when the threat of collectivization appeared with the victory of the policies of the first Communist government in 1949.

In summary, it may be said that the basic condition of the self-employed is that of being peripheral and therefore isolated and the basic element of consciousness is insecurity. They are peripheral economically and subservient to the interests of dominant groups, tolerated without enthusiasm, and when a minority group, apparently disliked or hated by customers with whom they have daily contact. They may voice the adherence to values of individualism, free enterprise, and private landownership, but they are more often than not rejected by employers and large landowners except to be used as pawns in the bigger battles. As social marginals they may view the wider society with a jaundiced eye—a view reciprocated by the socially established, and this makes them doubly isolated. Their value of individualism and their lack of shared work experience prevent the resort to psychological solace in solidarity with workers in other social relations; on the other hand their diversity of occupation and dislike of collective operations prevent the comfort of solidarity between themselves. They strive not to be identified with workers and renting peasants and so become peripheral to all of them. They become the "uneasy stratum," as they have been called,[51] fretful with anxiety, fearful of all change, approving of no other groups and of no other social action, and hostile to and resentful of all those who do not exaggerate belief in values and political ideas that they perceive would lessen their insecurity by cementing self-employment social relations more firmly in the social formation.

ACTION AND POLITICS

Translating such a consciousness into social action takes three forms: first, the slender and rare possibility of collective direct action of all self-employed groups; second, direct action by single occupational groups of self-employed; and third, the creation, or more often, support, of broader political movements.

The multiplicity of occupations, the variety of individual struggles of the market, and the value of individualism make any action based on a collective consciousness very difficult to establish. A rare case occurred in Belgium in 1972 when doctors, shopkeepers, and other self-employed joined together to make a "Common Front of Independents" and declared the city a "dead town" through a series of one-day strikes against "bureaucratic tax pollution."[52] Only under extreme conditions can such beginnings of a collective consciousness be translated into political action. This was seemingly the situation in Poland after 1949 when under the new Communist regime the self-employed formed an Individual Trade and Services Association that included shopkeepers, artisans, and very small employing entrepreneurs and that negotiated with the government in order to keep a private sector alive. The association signed agreements and was involved with the government concerning matters affecting shopkeepers and artisans.[53]

Solidarity of a single occupational group of the self-employed, especially if reinforced by ethnicity or gender, also provides some examples of contemporary concerted and structured actions. The Self-Employed Women's Association in India has created a "union" of women working at a variety of tasks designated as self-employed.[54] Although many of the women are within self-employment social relations and the organization has moved against suppliers of credit and materials, much of the membership is, in fact, disguised wage workers within a "home working system" that provides the organization with employer targets similar to a union in the enterprise labor market. In this case gender is a key factor in securing at least a temporary unity across social relations.

Direct and immediate action by a single occupational group of self-employed is more frequently observed. Self-employed may feel a need for a reduction in their personal insecurity, but equally the importance of the preservation of the social formation is usually recognized. This means that action is taken only after a period of pent-up agitation. This essential contradiction—insecurity within stability—is also the social psychological source for the self-employed support of radical and extreme political groups. The power struggle of the market is part of the social relations, part of the necessary tasks of daily action, unlike the organization and activities of workers in other social relations, where the power struggle is part of an ultimate transformation of conditions. Self-employment organizations created in the context of the struggle for power in the market are rarely political, with the notable exception of the organizations of liberal professionals. Political action is taken more through larger organizations operating at a more general level.

Thus direct action is usually specifically targeted at solving an immediate problem—such as the violent demonstrations of independent farmers in Europe in support of higher agricultural prices and the equally violent demonstrations by traders in the third world against the urban redevelopment programs that displace or disrupt trade.

The violence of the occasional occupation-specific direct action is matched by the surrogate violence extant in the indirect support by the self-employed of the more radical and extreme movements and parties of the right. In these cases self-employed appear in a coalition with the employers of the enterprise labor market (and some of their upwardly mobile workers) that is directly or indirectly supported by dominant groups. In such political manifestations the self-employed are part of the petit bourgeoisie coalition. They swell the ranks of radical anticollectivitist, antistate parties or movements. They are used in this respect as political pawns by those in power to increase support for policies that serve private power and continued relative freedom of corporatist enterprises vis-a-vis the state. Self-employed shopkeepers and others have supported right-wing radical movements such as Nazism in Germany of the 1930s and McCarthyism in the United States in the 1950s.[55] The bazaar merchants of Iran supported the radical Muslim movement in Iran in 1980 in the expectation that the return to the fundamental values of religion would prevent further erosion of their position by large retail enterprises introduced by the existing regime's use of the revenues from oil to create a "modern," urban, mass society. It was the self-employed owner-drivers of trucks who, through an externally supported strike, spearheaded the contrived overthrow of the democratically elected marxist government of Salvador Allende in Chile in 1974. In contrast, and most likely reflecting the immediate direct action of the self-employed, it was the strike against higher petrol prices of self-employed taxi-drivers in Addis Ababa that set off the wave of strikes and social unrest that precipitated the downfall of the Ethiopian emperor by a marxist military group.[56]

The role of self-employed farmers in peasant movements and revolutions is not clear.[57] Superficially they may be expected to support the status quo and oppose reformist or revolutionary movements, and indeed, the little evidence that exists shows that they are reluctant to support movements, and indeed, the little evidence that exists shows that they are reluctant to support movements whose objective is to acquire what they have already—ownership of land. But disturbances in the power relations may well bring forward their wrath and social action; such was the case of a revolt of Burmese farmers against the British colonial power because of the latter's failure to control market fluctuations.[58]

That the self-employed exist uneasily in political and ideological coalitions is evidenced when there have been political movements or parties that express more precisely the consciousness of the self-employed. When this is the case then the radicalism expressed is closer to a general antiregulatory nihilism than the anticollectivist orientation of the radical right. The targets are all that is large in size and include, for example, large enterprises. The political objectives therefore depart from the ideology of free enterprise and industrial pluralism.

In the early 1950s in France a political movement was founded that became known as the Poujade movement after the name of its leader. Poujade openly proclaimed the base of his movement and part to be the shopkeepers, traders, and artisans, pronouncing them to be the "backbone of the nation."[59] The main position of the party was anti-big business and antigovernment. The movement was geared toward a stratum that was becoming increasingly peripheral yet that remained an integral part of a social formation, whose dominant ideology was supposed to give power and prestige as rewards for individualism, enterprise, and incentive rather than what appeared to be increasing elimination and harassment.

This movement and others like it, however, were at a particular stage of development of industrial societies where the infrastructure of communication, urbanism, and private car ownership permitted the development of distributive and manufacturing forms that displaced those traditionally performed by the self-employed. At the same time the development of power of the corporations in the dominant forms of social relations began to politically exclude the self-employed. Such self-employed political movements at the level of the social formation are expressions of desperation and defeat rather than of consolidation. They can be expected whenever there is a massive dislocation of artisans and traders resulting from power shifts and struggles taking place elsewhere.

Political movements and expressions of collective consciousness then, are rarely moves toward transformation. Self-employment as a form of social relations of production will seemingly endure, regardless of the composition and ideology of the social formation. The insecurity and consciousness it produces will continue to make the self-employed have a political importance disproportionate to their numbers and to make their social and political action the least predictable of subordinate workers in a subordinate form of social relations of production.

NOTES

1. Adapted from Camara Laye, *The African Child* (London, Collins-Fontana, 1959), p. 31. Because of the definitional problem the precise descriptions and analysis of the power relations, attitudes, working conditions, and consciousness of the self-employed are in short supply. The sources for this chapter include most of those mentioned in the appendix, including unstructured interviews with artisans in Jamaica, Mexico, Philippines, and US; intentional participant observation with self-employed farmers in France; and unintentional participant observation as family labor for self-employed shopkeepers and as self-employed researcher and writer.

2. For an earlier discussion that distinguished casual own-account workers from the self-employed, see chapter 4. The mixture of criteria used to distinguish self-employed workers leads even the most respected authorities into confusion, as is evident from the statement of Talcott Parsons relating to the liberal professions:

Professional men are neither 'capitalists' nor 'workers,' nor are they typically governmental administrators or 'bureaucrats.' They are certainly not peasant proprietors or members of small urban proprietory groups. "Professions," in *International Encyclopedia of the Social Sciences* (New York, Macmillan) 1968, 12:536–46.

Official British classifications, for example, define self-employment as those employments that require the use of capital, which means that shopkeepers would be self-employed but a window cleaner would not. For various official use of criteria, see also Feliciano Tamas de Resende, "Aspectors do Seguro Social dos Traballiadores Autonomes," *Estudios Sociais e Corporativos* (Lisbon) (October-December, 1970), 5(20):79–155 (in this document distinction is made between an "autonomous" and an "independent" worker); and note the problems with self-employed definitions encountered by G. Routh, *Occupation and Pay in Britain*, (Cambridge, England, Cambridge University Press, 1965), p. 155, fn. 3. For problems of categorization and definition associated with a traditional marxist approach see, for example, D. Seddon, ed., *Peasants and Workers in Nepal* (Warminster, England, Aris and Phillips, 1979), pp. 190–91.

3. A discussion of definitions using some of these criteria is found in R. Bromley and C. Gerry, eds., *Casual Work and Poverty in Third World Cities* (New York, Wiley, 1979). These authors use the notion of "true" self-employment, which means a person who is dependent on markets and suppliers but not on employers. This is one of the few definitions that come near to the one associated in the book with self-employment social relations.

4. See *ibid.*, pp. 23–24.

5. See, for example, Dulip S. Swamy, "Differentiation of Peasantry in India," *Economic and Political Weekly* (December 11, 1976), p. 1934.

6. See chapter 3, Peasant-Lord Social Relations.

7. See, for example, Edwin R. Dean, "Social Determinants of Price in Several African Markets," *Economic Development and Cultural Change*, 2(3):part 1, 239–56.

8. See Barrington-Moore, Jr., *Social Origins of Dictatorship and Democracy: Lord and Peasant in the Making of the Modern World* (London, Allen Lane, 1967), pp. 416–21.

9. H. Braverman, *Labor and Monopoly Capital: The Degradation of Work in the Twentieth Century* (New York, Monthly Review Press, 1974), p. 53.

10. See, for example, William Foster, *A Short History of the Worshipful Company of Coopers of London* (Cambridge, England, Cambridge University Press, 1944).

11. See chapter 4, Peasant-Lord Social Relations.

12. C. Y. Choi, "Occupational Choice Among Chinese in Melbourne," *Race* (January 1970) 11(3):303–11.

13. *Le Monde* July 19, 1976.

14. Madhu Sarin, "Urban Planning, Petty Trading and Squatter Settlements in Chandigarh, India," in Bromley and Gerry, *Casual Work*, pp. 133–61. For further information on the organization of self-employed in India, see David Mandelbaum, *Society in India*, vol. 2 (Berkeley, University of California Press, 1970), especially pages 325–665.

15. Anthony Bottomley, "Fate of the Artisans in Developing Economies," *Social and Economic Studies* (June 1965), 14(2):194.

16. See, for example, such statements as: "in addition, however, lower productivity among self employed may be due in part to less discipline on the part of the worker when there is no employer relationship involved, and surely also to the absence of the division-of-labour inherent in the firm." J. Encarnacion, *Income Distribution in the Philippines: The Employed and Self-Employed* (Geneva, International Labor Office, 1974), p. 22.

17. See chapter 5, Enterprise Labor Market Social Relations.

18. Artisanal production is considered by some theorists as restricting industrial growth by starving employers of skilled labor; see Kenneth J. King, "Kenya's Informal Machine-Makers, A Study of Small Scale Industry in Kenya's Emergent Artisan Society," *World Development* (April-May 1974), 2(4,5):26.; for a contrasting view, see S. Brusco and C. Sabel, "Artisan Production and Economic Growth," in Frank Wilkinson, ed., *The Dynamics of Labor Market Segmentation* (New York, Academic Press, 1982), pp. 99–113.

19. See introduction to part 1 and chapter 3, Peasant-Lord Social Relations.

20. ". . . the partial character of control over the results of one's own labour exposes peasant agriculture to constant ups and downs.," Teodor Shanin, "The Nature and Change of Peasant Economies," *Sociologia Ruralis* (1973), 13(2):141–72.

21. ". . . when rest forms the main alternative to labour within his farm, a peasant tends to approach his own labour as of no cost and use it even when the small amount of the additional output achieved makes the labour input incredibly cheap." Shanin, ibid., p. 146.

22. See D. Warriner, Land Reform in Principle and Practice (Oxford, Clarendon Press, 1969).

23. For accounts of surplus extraction when commercial crops are involved, see, for example, S. M. Essang, The Distribution of Earnings in the Cocoa Economy of Western Nigeria (Ann Arbor, Mich., University Microfilms International, 1970); Sara S. Berry, "Work, Migration and Class in Western Nigeria: A Reinterpretation," in Frederick Cooper, ed., Struggle for the City: Migrant Labor, Capital, and the State in Urban Africa (Beverly Hills, Calif., Sage, 1983), pp. 247–73.

24. See Daniel Faucher, "Sociological Aspects of Agricultural Labour in France," Sociologie Rurale (April-September 1964) 13-14; and Bernard Lambert, Les Paysans dans la Lutte des Classes (Paris, Seuil, 1970); see also Ouchi Tsufomu, "Agricultural Depression and Japanese Villages," Developing Economies (December 1967) 5(4):597–627; Constantin Hadjimchalis, The Geographical Transfer of Value: A Comparative Analysis of Regional Development in Southern Europe (Ann Arbor, Mich., University Microfilms International, 1980), pp. 282–310.

25. See Agricultural Policy Reports: Agricultural Policy in the Netherlands (Paris, OECD, 1973).

26. Swamy, "Differentiation of Peasantry." For a quantitative and analytical review of self-employed farmers in the third world, see Eric Clayton, Agriculture, Poverty and Freedom in Developing Countries (London, Macmillan, 1983).

27. See, for example, the data in K. L. Lamba, "Measure of Economic Justice to Agricultural Labour Households," Indian Labour Journal (Delhi) (October, 1970) 11(10):1525–34; C. Mukherjee and A. V. Jose, Report of a Survey of Rural Households in the Hat Xai Fong District in Vientiane Province of the Lao People's Democratic Republic (Bangkok, International Labor Organization Asian Employment Program, 1982); Masuo and Ioshihiro, "Paddy Farming and Social Structures in a Malay Village," Developing Economies (December 1967), 5(4):469, 470, and 480.

28. More contemporary land reforms are, however, experimenting with a mix of social relations of production in agriculture, including retaining market-producing, self-employed farmers; see, for example, Peter Peek, "Agrarian Reform and Rural Development in Nicaragua, 1979-1981," in A. K. Ghose, ed., Agrarian Reform in Contemporary Developing Countries (London, Croom Helm, 1983), pp. 273–302. Sometimes state policy creates self-employed farming households unintentionally, see, for example, David Goodman, Bernardo Sorj and John Wilkinson, "Agro-industry, state policy and rural social structures: Recent Analysis of Proletarianisation in Brazilian Agriculture" in B. Muslow and H. Finch, eds. Proletarianisation in the Third World (London, Croom Helm, 1984) pp. 189–215.

29. See A. K. Ghose, "Agrarian Reform in Developing Countries: Issues of Theory and Problems of Practice," in Ghose, ibid., pp. 3–28; so serious is the decline in self-employed farmers in some areas that policies of "repeasantisation," that is, restoration of market-producing independent farmers, are being advocated; see, for example K. N. Raj and Michael Tharakan, "Agrarian Reform in Kerala and Its Impact on the Rural Economy—A Preliminary Assessment," in Ghose, ibid., pp. 31–123; see also the policies advocated by Clayton, Agriculture, Poverty.

30. For the attitudes of previously independent subsistence/market farmers on taking wage labor, see, for example, Stephan Gudman, The Demise of a Rural

Economy: From Subsistence to Capitalism in a Latin American Village (London, Routledge, Kogan, Paul, 1978), p. 179.

31. A "small landowner" who grows cane for a new sugar mill reported that it was like "being hired for wages on your own land"; Andrew Turton, "Limits of Ideological Domination and the Formation of Social Consciousness," in A. Turton and S. Tanabe, *History of Peasant Consciousness in South East Asia* (Osaka, National Museum of Ethnology, 1984), p. 34.

32. The low level of economies of scale, capital use, and the preparedness of self-employed to take a lower income were reasons cited for the survival of "traditional" self-employed in modern Japan; see Henry Rosovsky and Kazushi Ohkawa, "The Indigenous Components in the Modern Japanese Economy," *Economic Development and Cultural Change* (April, 1961), 8(3): 476–501; for descriptions of artisans in the third world, see chapter 4, "Rural Artisans," in Seddon, *Peasants and Workers;* for a classification of small manufacturing including artisans as a separate category, see Brusco and Sabel, "Artisan Production."

33. For the generally low returns to the broadly defined self-employed who are within self-employment social relations, see, for example, E. L. McFarland, "Employment Growth in Services: Mexico 1950-1969" (unpublished thesis, Columbia University, New York, 1974).

34. For example, "if you are self-employed or nonemployed you are not covered by EEC social security regulations and you and your dependents will have to pay for all treatment received.," *Essential Information for Holders of United Kingdom Passports Who Intend To Travel Overseas* (London, Her Majesty's Stationery Office, 1974), p. 6.

35. Under certain circumstances employers in the enterprise labor market and elsewhere encourage "self-employment" as a means of cutting indirect labor costs; see, for example, Roger Moore, "Aspects of Segmentation in the United Kingdom Building Industry Labor Market," in Wilkinson, *Dynamics,* pp. 151–63.

36. See *Interfutures* (Paris, OECD, 1979).

37. See chapter 5, Enterprise Labor Market Social Relations.

38. See, for example, Lea Jellinex, "The Life of a Jakarta Street Trader," in J. Abu-Lughod and R. Hay, *Third World Urbanization* (New York, Methuen, 1977), pp. 244–56; for the dual self-employment and primitive labor market social relations of African women food sellers, see J. May, *African Women in Urban Employment: Factors Influencing Their Employment in Zimbabwe* (Gwelo, Africa, Mambo Press, 1979), p. 48.

39. See Frank Bechhofer and Brian Elliot, "An Approach to a Study of Small Shopkeepers and the Class Structure," *Archives Européenes de Sociologie* (1968)9(2):189. for similar figures for the United Kingdom, see Ross L. Davies, *Retail and Commercial Planning* (New York, Croom Helm, 1984).

40. For an application of the multiple social relations of production approach to the occupation of prostitution and an assessment of the types found in self-employment, see Thanh-Dam Truong, *Virtue Order, Health and Money: Towards a Comprehensive Perspective on Female Prostitution in Asia* (The Hague, Institute of Social Studies Advisory Service, 1985).

41. See chapter 4, "Primitive Labor Market Social Relations."

42. See, for example, the accounts in Barbara Sherman Heyl, *The Madam as Entrepreneur: Career Management in House Prostitution* (New Jersey, Transaction Books, 1979).

43. Harry Schwartz, "Physician Unionization and the Failure of American

Medicare," in American Federation of Physicians and Dentists: *Doctors' Unions and Collective Bargaining* (Berkeley, University of California, 1974), p. 11.

44. This aspect is discussed in such sources as T. J. Johnson, *Professions and Power* (London, Macmillan, 1972), P. C. Lloyd, *The New Elites of Tropical Africa* (Oxford, Oxford University Press, 1966).

45. Masuo and Ioshihiro, "Paddy Farming."

46. See, for example, A. Gordon Darroch and Wilfred G. Marston, "Patterns of Urban Ethnicity," in Noel Iverson, *Urbanism and Urbanization: Views Aspects and Dimensions* (Leiden, Brill, 1984) pp. 127–59. See also the discussion of "alien" entrepreneurs in chapter 5, Enterprise Labor Market Social Relations.

47. Bronislaw Misztal, "The Petit Bourgeoisie in Socialist Society," in Frank Bechhofer and Brian Elliot, *The Petit Bourgeoisie: Comparative Studies of an Uneasy Stratum* (London, Macmillan, 1981), p. 93.

48. See, for example, reports in Berry, "Work, Migration and Class

49. Bechofer and Elliot, *Petit Bourgeoisie*, p. 189.; this is made explicit also in the "industrial-pluralist" school of thinkers; see Ralf Dahrendorf, *Class and Class Conflict in Industrial Society* (Stanford, Calif., Stanford University Press, 1959).

50. Particularly useful sources in this respect are Bechhofer and Elliot, *Petit Bourgeoisie*, which provides a good review of the literature and explanation of concepts, and Misztal, "The Petit Bourgeoisie," p. 41, in Bechhofer and Elliot, *ibid.*

51. Bechhofer and Elliot, *ibid.*

52. See Guy Spitaels, "Independent Workers: In Search of a Collective Consciousness," *Cahiers Internationaux Sociologie* (1965), 39:110–11; and John V. Craven, "A Strike of Self-Employed Professionals: Belgian Doctors in 1964," *Industrial and Labor Relations Review* (October 1967), 21(1):18–30.

53. Misztal, "The Petit Bourgeoisie," pp. 94–95.

54. See the reports "The Bank That Takes 20 Cents" (report on the operation of the Self-Employed Women's Association Bank), *Euromoney* (December 1983), pp. 46–47; "We, the Self-Employed (report on activities of the Self-Employed Women's Association), *Free Labor World* (1984), no. 1, pp. 20–21.

55. Bechhofer and Elliot, *Petit Bourgeoisie*, p. 193, quoting Martin Trow, "Small Businessmen, Political Tolerance and Support for McCarthy," in L. Coser, ed., *Political Sociology* (New York, Harper and Row, 1967); G. Rush, "Status Inconsistency and Right Wing Extremism," *American Sociology* (1957), 32:86–92.

56. See Bogdan Szajkowski, *The Establishment of Marxist Regimes* (London, Butterworths, 1982), p. 118.

57. See the discussion in chapter 3, Peasant-Lord Social Relations.

58. Michael Adas, "Bandits, Monks and Pretender Kings: Patterns of Peasant Resistance and Protest in Colonial Burma: 1826-1941," in R P. Weller and S. E. Guggenheim, eds., *Power and Protest in the Countryside: Studies of Rural Unrest in Asia, Europe and Latin America* (Durham, N.C., Duke University Press, 1982), pp. 75–105.

59. Stanley Hoffman, *Le Movement Poujade* (Paris, Seuil, 1956).

CHAPTER 7

HOUSEHOLD
SOCIAL RELATIONS

Throughout the world women
may be seen in street markets, supermarkets, and shops and
shopping centers, holding children, carrying shopping baskets,
or pushing supermarket carts, as they inspect, select, and discuss
the food and other items they buy for their children and husbands, and others, who comprise their household. Shopping, as
one of the major services women provide for the household, is
exceptional inasmuch as it is public, for most of the household
work is done in the seclusion of the house, apartment, room,
shanty, or hut. It is there that housewives work to provide the
full range of services for the household, including childrearing,
food preparation, repairing, cleaning, and management of the
household budget with money they earn or is passed to them
from the wages of other members of the family.

The social relations surrounding the production of these
services are designated as household social relations, for the
services (and sometimes goods) are produced within the framework of a household, are intended for consumption by its members, and are not for sale on the market.[1]

The household form of social relations is essentially characterized by a dominant-subordinate relationship within the
household in which the preponderant power is derived and supported from the outside. The wider society grants certain individuals economic power and reinforces subordination of others

through various ideologies and rationalities, particularly those relating to the place and role of women in the household and society.

It is always necessary to distinguish the use of the word "household" to designate a pattern of power relations surrounding production of goods and services within the household for consumption by the household, from the use of the word to describe the production in the household of goods or services for direct external sale or exchange. The latter refers to a collective production unit with the possibility of being within different social relations, such as are found within the farming households of subsistence, peasant-lord, and self-employment social relations. The distinction between the two will be further discussed in the context of the history of the development of the household form of social relations as described in this chapter. More recently household production has also been used to describe the modern "putting out" system in which a wage worker works "at home" to produce goods or services collected by an external enterprise. Here again, despite the name, the social relations of such a worker are not those of the household form but more likely are employee-employer relations found in the enterprise labor market.

Household social relations such as those that surround the production of such household services have the following characteristics or preconditions.[2] First, there must be a social unit that can be described as a household. This is essentially a relatively small group of people—almost always fewer than twenty—and is normally, but not always, a family, however that may be culturally defined. Second, there must have occurred a specialization of tasks within the household, which has separated into one category the household service tasks of childcare, cooking, cleaning, nursing, clothes repairing and making, sometimes psychic support and care, budgeting activities, and many more. Third, these tasks have been assigned low status in the hierarchy of production in the wider society and no money wage is attached to those who perform them and who receive basic subsistence in the form of food, clothing, and housing. Fourth, the person who performs household tasks is usually and in different ways subordinated to the person or persons who are at the head of the household.[3] Fifth, and finally, the power relations within the household, through which tasks have been allotted and status determined, have been substantially derived from external ideology, tradition, finance, and influence from associated patterns of social relations of production.

Household social relations are subordinate to all other dominant forms of social relations and, to a substantial extent, other subordinate forms as well, There is no special association with one or other form such as, for example, enterprise labor market relations have with the corporate or bargaining patterns. The production associated with household social relations benefits almost all the producers in the wider society. This is a special feature, among several others, that distinguishes household social relations from the others discussed in this book.

The characteristics have so far been stated without reference to gender; this is to avoid the confusion of household social relations both with housework and with the general position of women in the wider society. Elements of housework can be performed within a variety of forms of social relations, such as when it is done by paid servants, commercial cleaners, professional nurses, and so on. There is no natural or biological reason why any single sex or race should have been allocated household service tasks, and indeed, some societies have not done so. It is theoretically possible to envisage a single-sex household—a group of men or women living together—in which household social relations of production exist and one or other individual is in a subordinate position and performs household service work. In practice, however, and almost exclusively throughout the world, it has been women who have been rendered subordinate within the household and allocated the production of household services.[4] The bulk of the discussion of the household social relations will then be concerned both with the production of household services and with subordinated women and how,and to a lesser extent why, they are joined to produce the typical example of the household social relations.

The most specialized, and therefore the purest example, of household relations surrounds the full-time housewife, producing within a nuclear family household, whose husband, the head of the household, is a wage or salary earner. Conventionally, then, household social relations as described above are based upon a sexual division of labor in which males earn a wage from work outside the household and females are engaged exclusively in nonwage work within the household. In the context of the whole world labor force only a very small proportion of women are in such a position, and they are found mainly in industrialized countries and among the rich strata of poor countries. Full-time housewives represent approximately 40 percent of the total female labor force in industrialized countries—countries differ widely in this respect with, in 1984, approximately 60 percent of Dutch women of working age working as full-time housewives but only 20 percent of Swedish women doing the same. Only approximately 2 percent of the total world labor force can be considered to be in such a pure example of household relations.

Household social relations are, however, far more prevalent than the numbers of full-time housewives would imply because the vast majority of women combine the production of nonwage household services with wage labor outside the household. This situation has been aptly named the "double-shift," that is, the one shift on nonwage work of producing services within and for the household in the time not taken up by the second shift of wage work producing goods and services outside the household.[5] Although the name "double-shift" has industrial connotations indicating a split work day within factory production, by analogy the notion can easily be extended to the situation of other women who do not necessarily have the double-shift of industrial wage work and nonwage housework. This is particularly the case of women within social relations surrounding agricultural production. Within a peasant-lord household in the third world, women always have the double shift of work in the fields to produce agricultural goods for sale and work to produce household services. In Denmark the wives of self-employed farmers spend twenty to thirty hours per week on farm work, as well as producing household services. In Yugoslavia in 1969 only 30 percent of farmers' wives were full-time housewives; the rest did both farm work and housework.[6] In Turkey the economic input into farm work and housework is recognized by a "brideprice" in which the family from which the woman worker and bride leaves is compensated for the loss of the two types of labor.[7] Women's labor is equally a major component of family labor within self-employment relations. Casual women workers of the primitive labor market extend their household-acquired skills of cooking to produce cooked food for market sales but maintain child care and other services at the same time.[8] Full-time housewives are the only women within the household form of social relations who are within one form of social relations; wage-working, market-producing, "double-shift" women workers are covered by two forms of social relations simultaneously.

There are, of course, other cases in which producers are in two forms of social relations at the same time—the civil servant who works at weekends or in the evenings as self-employed or the independent farming household in India that hires in labor at a certain time and releases members of the household for wage work at other times would be such examples. But in these latter cases the person involved invariably has dominant social relations from which his or her consciousness and working conditions are basically derived. In the case of women working both within and outside the household the situation is very different. The production of household services never becomes a "spare-time" activity or "moonlighting," as wage jobs performed in evenings after "normal" work is over are sometimes called. The production of household services is invariably a lifetime constant for women, and it is only rarely (although currently increasing in industrialized countries) that social relations surrounding work outside the household assume a psychological, social, or material force greater than those arising from household production. It is for this reason that women wage workers present themselves as a special case when compared with the range of male workers within different social relations and why there has been much intellectual and activist discussion about how women can be classified within conventional categories of class, status group or production relations.

The duality of wage labor and household labor of women workers is then the principal reason why household social relations are more important than the small proportion of full-time housewives within the world labor force would indicate. The full-time housewife represents, however, an extreme of a pattern of power relations surrounding production, and all other variations are more complex and sophisticated variations of this extreme. The discussion that follows takes as its benchmark, for heuristic reasons, the power relations surrounding the production of household services by a full-time housewife, in the full recognition that such a circumstance is usually outside the experience of double-shift and rural women workers who make up the bulk of women household workers.

ORIGINS: BIOLOGY, ALLOCATION, AND IDEOLOGY

The origins of household social relations are found within the process in which household tasks were separated from others, were assigned low status, and were consequently allocated to subordinate workers. Because these latter are, almost everywhere, women, the origin of the pattern of relations is also associated with the general subordination of women, the creation of a family household with dominant male heads, and the emergence of the concept of "women's work" used to describe household tasks.

While it is not possible here to consider the ancient and complex origin of the almost universal, generalized subordination of women, it is important to note that the development of patriarchy most likely preceded household social relations and that the original objective of patriarchy was not only for the express purpose of exploiting women's ability to work. Thus household social relations emerge as a result rather than the cause of the development of patriarchy. It must be recognized, however, that there is little agreement on the principal cause of the origin of male domination of females; one theory argues that by nature women are subservient to man,[9] another that it was the males' preparedness to use superior force and social monopoly of arms that subordinated women,[10] another that women were steered toward a domestic role in order to provide them (and procreation) protection when their numbers in the population declined,[11] another that the emergence of private property precipitated the male-dominated nuclear family,[12] and another that the independent development of the male desire for assured paternity meant that a woman had to be confined, that is, not allowed sexual and social contact with other males, and power then had to be developed to secure such female isolation and confinement.[13]

Regardless of the veracity or exclusiveness of these theories, the origins of patriarchy have bequeathed some of the beliefs and perceptions that are crucial to the current household social relations. The most important of these is the notion of the inseparability of childbearing and childrearing. In collective production based upon the tribe or community, women's childbearing role has often been given a high value; she has the sole power of creating future workers and members of the community, and the worship of women and of fertility consequently has ancient origins.[14] In circumstances where children contributed to the collectivity and not to individual or private production, women were found in a very different position from those in which the work potential of the children contributed to a privatized or household production unit.[15] In the latter situation the male demand for paternity and the eventual production from offspring are joined, for paternity not only meant assured self-reproduction from the male side but also, given the confinement of women needed to achieve it, meant the exclusive appropriation by the male-headed production unit of the work of both the mother and the children. Thus women were required to reproduce for a specified male and their children to serve the specified male-headed family.

Such a development does not necessarily subordinate women in the production of goods and services, although in destroying their freedom of choice of sexual partners, of general mobility, and of the disposition of their children, it laid the power foundations for such an eventuality. The childbearing of women then is not itself the origin of male domination, but the forced confinement to secure paternity and the exclusive service of reproduction to a single household resulted in a crucial ideological and practical factor in household power relations—the forced and artificial merger of childbearing and childrearing functions. Apart from the period of lactation there is no biological imperative that children should be reared exclusively by women, and in many societies (including, increasingly, modern industrial societies) this has not been the case.[16] But the promoted belief, accepted by many women, that women by nature should be childrearers meant that the *biological* function of childbearing was merged with the *social and work* function of childrearing.[17] The latter, but not of course, the former, could easily be performed by men. It is then a short step to extend childrearing to husband care, restriction to the household and household tasks, and above all, the notion that "women's work" was the production of household services regardless of what other productive activities she performed either inside or outside the household.[18]

The emergence of household social relations incorporating, as it does, male domination can be traced through various stages, particularly in the process of industrialization.

The first of these stages could be considered as subsistence agriculture, in which the whole household is engaged in a production it consumes itself. This form of social relations has been discussed in some detail in chapter 2 of this book, where a rough criterion of subsistence was used, namely, that the production from at least 80 percent of total time worked by the members of the household would be for immediate consumption. Under these conditions the division of labor within the household is indistinct—cleaning and childrearing merge with work in the fields for males and females, food preparation is part of a continuum that begins with animal husbandry and cultivation. The household is the physical center for a collective production of all the needs for existence. The mixing of tasks means that interpersonal relations have an element of interdependency at the level of basic existence, and any differences in what males and females produce cannot easily become the source of dominant-subordinate relations.[19] Also all members of the household are then governed by the same social relations.

This is not to say that division of labor does not exist or that the authority structure has elements of male domination, but that what exists of these are only the beginnings of household social relations that are subject to intensification and refinements during the next stage.

The next stage can be seen as the cultivating household within peasant-lord or self-employment social relations, that is, where there is a surplus of production extracted as rent, debt service, taxes or market sales. At this point childrearing and household services begin to become ancillary to the basic economic survival of the household, which is the production of a surplus for delivery elsewhere. Men's work becomes more concentrated on production for delivery external to the household and women become partially specialized in household services tasks and more subjected to a society-wide male-dominated authority structure in which ideology and religion encourage or sanction a subordinate and exploited position for women.[20] The emergence of this situation is connected with the attempt to ensure a continuation of the household nature of production incorporating male heads of household regardless of what form the family took, such as nuclear with a single male head or extended with male power sharing. Household social relations begin to emerge more clearly as women perform productive tasks connected with external delivery from the household and are also expected to occupy themselves more or less exclusively with the internal services—the double shift then begins to emerge.

This situation continued within capitalist industrialization through the "putting-out" system in seventeenth-century Western Europe. All members of the family—which was under strong economic pressure to assume the patriarchal-monogamous form with a single male head with one wife[21]—worked at weaving looms and other industrial tasks with materials "put-out" by owners of capital. Women worked at production for delivery to the capitalists, as well as at childbearing, childrearing, and household services.[22]

The development of the factory system destroyed the household as a unit of collective production as men, women, and children were removed from the household to work under rigid supervision in factories. The possibility then arose for different members of the household to work within different social relations, as for example, when women were employed on a casual basis as domestic help within the primitive labor market relations and men as wage labor within an enterprise labor market. Household services became an additional burden that women were forced to bear. The purest form of household social relations appeared, especially among women with constant pregnancies and large families, which made it more difficult for them to be engaged in wage labor and therefore to work the double shift. The converging pattern of childbearing, childrearing, and household services as the essential work of women thus became endemic within industrialized societies.[23]

The next stage of the emergence of household social relations came, not from the mass of working class families within the nineteenth-century enterprise labor market, but from the higher income groups; these accepted as an ideal the nuclear family based upon an internal and external male authority structure in which the wife was to occupy herself exclusively with housework and children and perform no other productive activities.[24] The "nonworking" wife became a mark of prestige, of wealth—a social indicator to distinguish the bourgeois or aspiring bourgeois from the working class. The male in salaried and professional labor and the women in full-time nonwage household service production brought into existence then the clearest of the household social relations with all its currently conventional sexual division of labor and subordination of women. At a later date the nonworking wife spread to the lower income groups, and the full-time housewife was found within all social classes and groups.[25] This latter development was not always and necessarily a coerced one; women faced with the choice between wage factory labor combined with continued household labor may well find elimination of the wage labor "shift" and concentration exclusively on household work to be a desirable development.[26] The emergence of the "family wage" for male wage earners and the often militant support for male workers' efforts to maintain it were an integral part of the whole process of the emergence of the full-time housewife.[27]

At the same time that these structural changes were taking place, ideological developments had been occurring. The most important of these was the social devaluation of child care and household tasks. Household work—especially cooking, repairing, and child care—are highly skilled tasks requiring a range of knowledge, dexterity, and sensibility far beyond what would be required for a male "skilled" industrial worker whose skill, anyway, would normally be highly concentrated in one function or area of knowledge. Women, as girl-children, have a lengthy apprenticeship under tutelage of their mothers in the skills, knowledge, and perception needed to organize and service a household. Yet housework was ascribed a low social value and purported to be the most menial and unskilled of work subject to no social or extra material rewards if it was performed efficiently. The devaluation of the work of women in household was part of the ideology supporting the subordination of the people—women—who were normally to perform it.[28]

The final and perhaps current stage of development of

household social relations is their increasing appearance primarily as governing the nonwage work of women parallel to other social relations governing the wage work—the double shift. Three trends in capital-rich industrialized countries and the rich strata of third-world countries have assisted this development, which is technically expressed as an increasing rate of participation of women in the work force. First, housework has been partially automated—the availability of household capital has meant the introduction of labor-saving machinery—especially washing machines, refrigerators, floor polishers, food processors, and sometimes minicomputers—have reduced the physical effort for those who perform housework.[29]

Secondly, technology has been applied to produce instant foods and disposable linen and babies nappies and has been coupled with the promotion of a "speedup" in housework through "quick" cooking lessons and ergonomically planned kitchens.[30] Finally, education and development in birth control techniques have substantially reduced birth rates and family size in industrialized countries. The result is that a woman in such countries, with a planned two-children family and labor-saving devices has potentially less physical input into household work and higher productivity than her grandmother or greatgrandmother, who has six or more children and little household capital, did. For full-time housewives, time available has not necessarily increased as a result of these trends, because household capital has brought with it new tasks associated with modern urban living—collection and delivery of children from and to distant schools and so forth.[31] It has, however, meant that double-shift women workers can spend less time and physical effort both per day and over a lifetime on housework, leaving more room for energy and time to spend in wage work. Capitalization or modernization of housework then was part of the institutionalization of "women's work" by making it physically possible for women to continue to be responsible for household tasks despite full-time work elsewhere.

In poorer countries where household capital is not widely available and birth control education is lacking, women continue, as in nineteenth-century Europe, to work the double shift between frequent pregnancies and abortions and to perform household tasks with very little mechanization.[32] In the centrally planned countries of Eastern Europe an egalitarian ideology in respect of male and female work has resulted in the appearance of women in professions and occupations that in the capitalist countries have been a male preserve. Thus, in the Soviet Union, most women are in wage work and, for example, most physicians are women. Although this may have had important effects on women's consciousness, it has not destroyed household social relations—it is still the woman who is expected to supply household services.[33] In the Peoples' Republic of China public policy has fluctuated concerning the place of women in the home. In the 1950s women were urged to return to home, and an attempt was made to revalue housework. But it was done in the context of dependency and service to the husband. In the 1970s, however, there was public discussion of "sharing housework."[34] Household social relations exist then in all social formations.

In addition to the universal appearance of household social relations, the various stages of their development also all exist in the last quarter of the twentieth century—the Haitian woman working her subsistence vegetable plot, the Philippines peasant woman struggling with pregnancies and rice growing, the Mexican slum-dwelling woman selling her cooked food in the street, the data-processing wife of an U.S. truck driver, the working engineer and flat-cleaning wife of a Soviet civil servant, and the full-time housewife of a physician in West Germany are all within household social relations, and all, with the exception of the last, are in other social relations at the same time. Further development and transformations of the household form will then depend upon the dynamics within the relations and the relationship and contradictions with the social formation, which must now be discussed.

POWER IN THE HOUSEHOLD: SOCIAL AND PERSONAL

The power relations surrounding the production of household services are such that the manner, level, and appropriation of the production are governed by male household heads and the work is performed by females. At a basic minimum a woman producing household services and childbearing receives housing, clothing and food; she is thus paid in kind for the work she does, making her a paid but nonwage worker.[35] In many countries, religions, and legal systems, this relationship is based upon a labor contract, commonly known as a legal marriage. The marriage-labor contract has understood or explicit terms that specify that the wife will bear and rear children of one man and provide services for the household.[36] In many countries performance of these services is legally enforceable, making the contract dissolvable by divorce if the wife should refuse to comply. The husband under such a contract has the duty to "provide," that is, supply the basic needs at least, for wife and children. This is also legally enforceable, although the stringency of enforcement varies from country to country, particularly affected as it is by religion.[37]

Such a contract, however, only formalizes an existing social situation in which the dominance over the production of women in the household is sufficiently established and structured to be independent of legal and state enforcement. However, these basic power relations produce a variety of conditions and return for work performed by women as household service producers. Thus the amount of money or material consumption acquired above basic needs, the intensity of work demanded, and the range of services produced depend on a number of factors external and internal to the household. These are, first, the general level of wealth and development of the social formation; second, the strength of the general social enforcement of the subordination of women within the household; third, the social relations that govern the work and production of the head of the household; and fourth, the interpersonal relations within the household.

It may seem superfluous to note that the material consumption of housewives, as with all other workers, is to some extent determined by the level of wealth and development of the social formation. In the case of women in household relations the relationship between national wealth and their material consumption is not the same as for the rest of the population. This is particularly the case of women in the poorest countries. The lack of medical facilities, the lack of work for males, and the squeeze on peasant income are coupled with the constant and unvarying work of women of childbearing and childrearing, which means that poverty falls disproportionately upon women. Thus the hardest working and poorest in a poor population are most often women.

There is more variety in the importance of the second factor, that of strength of social enforcement or acceptance of the ideology of male domination and especially that aspect of it which designates women's place as the home and women's work as household services. Wherever household relations exist there is always a social element of patriarchy that to some degree or other is used within the household to support continuation of the relations.

The importance of this element in household relations depends on the level of social pressure exerted to support patriarchy and the level of its acceptance (or internationalization) by women. In Japan, middle-class women have been referred to as "Kanaai," which literally translated means "inside the house." Resistance to this notion in Japan has been very weak until recently.[38] In Morocco the practice for urban wives is still to be subjected to "severe seclusion," and it is considered socially "shameful" for women to take wage work.[39] In many regions of Switzerland it was until recently compulsory for schoolgirls, but not for schoolboys, to take cookery lessons. Other aspects being equal, therefore, the stronger the generalized social belief and mechanisms of enforcement of women's work, the harder it is for women to resist, within the household, the demands made of them, excessive as they might be.

Another aspect of social attitudes supporting male domination is the socially determined structure of finance for households. When males are paid "a family wage" in return for their work, this means that women houseworkers are ultimately financially dependent upon the male and upon his perception of the needs of the household. Wives of cultivators whose husbands go to market are likewise dependent upon sums paid first to the male. In the United Kingdom some husbands pass over their pay packets unopened, others merely deduct money for their personal needs as determined by them, but most, at least in the 1970s, still pass out a regular fixed sum with which the wife must make do.[40] In Japan, however, urban housewives control 80 percent of the family budget, giving back lunch and cigarette money to their husbands.[41] The result of the personal battles about the amount of money received by the women for both household and personal needs determines their material level of living above basic needs but does not, of course, alter the financial power inherent in the notion of a sole "wage earner."[42] The impact of the double shift on this situation is discussed later in this chapter.

Conditions of work for the household worker also vary substantially according to the social relations that cover the male household heads' wage work. This is not only because some sets of social relations are associated with higher incomes—a worker within the larger enterprises with corporatist relations invariably has a higher income than the person in the small enterprise of enterprise labor market relations—but also because of the integration of the woman household worker with the work of the male external worker. Thus a wife whose husband is in the enterprise corporatist relations may find that there is an employer's attempt to integrate her into a corporate "package" of a family, or couple, for the service of the corporation. At one time in the United States large companies insisted on interviewing wives when husbands applied for positions. In any case, if her husband is in the higher reaches of the corporate hierarchy she will be expected to cater for dinner parties, accompany the husband on social occasions, and entertain visiting executives. In contrast, housewives whose husbands suffer the exigencies of the enterprise labor market must be ready to adjust family life and financial patterns and take on more wage work themselves in the event of the layoff or dismissal of their husbands.[43] The wife of a self-employed shopkeeper forms part of family labor and will be expected to "mind the shop," as well as perform her household duties.[44] A renting cultivator's wife will have to work, at the minimum, at peak seasons, in the fields. The level of the husband's income sets limits to the amount of equipment the household can potentially purchase, given that the woman is not earning on the double shift and thus is not able to pay for labor-saving devices herself.

Finally, interpersonal relations within the household make differences in conditions of work experienced by household workers. Thus housewives with husbands within the same income levels and the same social relations may nevertheless experience great differences in the amounts of free time and of labor-saving capital and personal finance they have. In industrialized countries, differences in the levels of cooperation, collaboration, and role playing within the household will determine how much of the household service tasks the males may perform or how much they agree to dispense upon capital equipment.[45] The husband who insists and enforces rigidly the notions of women's work and women's place and who unilaterally determines how much she needs for running the house clearly forces more work for less income. It is this factor that is an important precipitator of attempts to redress male power within the household.

So far only the basis and nature of male power have been considered within the household, but the dynamics and power relations are produced by the resistance of women as the workers subordinate to this power. Until recently there was little attempt to make such a resistance through a collective consciousness and action outside the household. Inside the household there are two important aspects of attempts to resist the structure of male domination. The first is at the level of individual psychology, and the second was the attempt to secure financial and personal independence through the right to perform wage work outside the house.

The nature and form of the individual psychological attempts of women household workers to redress the material, social, and psychological domination of males that they may experience within the household are determined by personal, religious, and cultural backgrounds, which make universal generalizations almost impossible. In Europe and North America popular literature, folklore, and verbal expressions are full of accounts and indications of the psychological strategies used by women to secure more money, different household policies, and more nearly equal division of household work.

One example of such a strategy is that of *"marianismo"* found in Latin America. Marianismo is the female counterpart of machismo; machismo provides the image of an aggressive, supermasculine, dominant male, and marianismo that of a humble, superfeminine, faithful woman.[46] The female duty is then to exhibit humility and endurance and, above all, serve and be obedient to husbands. Such devoted service is sometimes used by women to create a material and psychological dependency in men that provides a weak lever against male social and economic power; thus one researcher reports that these male-promoted ideals were referred to by working-class women as "useful strategies to 'manage' their husbands without rebellion against authority."[47] In a very different location and within the Muslim religion women have been observed to redress their lack of formal power through the manipulation of information passed by networks of women and to raise the fear of "sorcery" or blackmail in men.[48]

The second limited attempt to redress male authority in the household has been the acquisition of wage work outside the household. From the standpoint of the internal power relations wage work for women has three important effects: first, it destroys any confinement of women to the household and any notion that women should be exclusively engaged on household tasks; second, it provides the potential of redressing the financial dependency and sometimes isolation arising from the conditions of full-time housework. It has these effects only in situations in which men and society contrive to keep women within the household and out of wage work. This was particularly the case of middle-class women in Western Europe at the turn of the century, and it spread to wives of skilled and white-collar workers by the 1920s and 1930s. It is also the case of women entering the urban-industrial sector in poor countries, as noted earlier.

Wage work for women became a slogan and a demand within a general feminist attempt to achieve greater equality for women. Inasmuch as the feminists who demanded it saw confinement of women to the household and household tasks as one of the principal mechanisms of the oppression of women in general, then the demand for wage work was seen as more than a mere limited attempt to reduce inequality within the household; it was seen as a transformational attempt, whose effect would liberate women and destroy household social relations. If this is understood it comes as no surprise that the demand of women of the professional and wealthier groups could, in Europe of 1914, be put in such sweeping terms that in a future society "we (women) shall have our share of honoured and socially useful toil. We demand nothing more than this and will take nothing less. This is our women's right."[49]

There can be no doubt that power relations within the

household are affected by wage work of women, but the alteration of the configuration of power was not substantial enough to transform social relations and certainly not strong enough to override the general male structure of domination. On the contrary it was absorbed into the pattern of the double shift, which had in any case been the lot of most working class women since the beginning of industrialization, and produced the duality of social relations now experienced by most women in the world. Nevertheless, in the absence of a revaluation of housework or of independent economic reward for housework, the right and practice for women to have wage work can be seen as a step or precondition to a transformation in which, even within the existing family structure, an equality of male and female partnership is recognized.

HOUSEHOLD WORK AND THE SOCIAL FORMATION: NUMEROUS BENEFICIARIES

At every traditional celebration of a marriage-labor contract there is an invisible reveler who has as great a reason as anyone to celebrate a productive union. This symbolic third party is the user or purchaser of labor in other sets of social relations who will benefit from the production of the future housewife and mother. Given that labor is used universally, its production and servicing means that the labor of women in childbearing, childrearing, and household services is universally appropriated throughout the social formation. These services are either technically or humanly difficult to supply or prohibitively costly in comparison with the nonwage work supplied by women—household social relations then become a supportive base for all other forms of social relations, supplying an essential service for which there can be no substitution.

Despite this crucial position, household services production has been consistently downplayed or ignored; in calculation of national production figures, for example, the production of housewives has been excluded in both socialist and capitalist countries.[50] Thus the reproduction of the labor force and its maintenance have almost universally been assigned a low economic value and remain nonwage. That this is the case is testimony to the strength of the ideology of male domination and the tenacity of household social relations.

Economic theory of the work of women has until very recently been eclipsed by the overarching ideology degrading housework and discounting biological reproduction as work or production. In marxist economics the belief that only industrial workers could create surplus value for the capitalist tended to confine the notion of production to industrial wage workers only and therefore excluded women household services production. In market economic theory the production of women was also discounted, for it did not enter the market and was not exchanged, while labor was considered as a naturally occurring resource.[51] marxist economics, with its emphasis on the labor theory of value, upon reproduction of the capitalist system and of labor power, has the potential, once freed of the restrictive notion of surplus value, to analyze the role of women both as essential reproducers of labor power in the form of children and of producers of surplus value when entering wage work.[52] The reproductive and productive spheres of women's work have thus become major concepts within current marxist analysis.[53] However, in most of such analysis, production is still confined to wage work, meaning that household service work is amalgamated with childbearing as part of the total reproductive sphere in a manner similar to the ideological fusing of childbearing and childrearing mentioned earlier. A disaggregating approach to the total productive—using the word in its nonmarxist sense—work of women, is needed, and that begins in this book with the production that occurs within different forms of social relations.

Household social relations as a subordinate form within any social formation covers two types of production that are partially or wholly appropriated by producers within other social relations.[54] These are the biological reproduction of childbearing and the social production of childrearing and household services.

It is a truism, of course, that women's biological childbearing is essential for the survival of any society. Given that bearing a child entails "work" in the form of expenditure of energy, sacrifice, and consumption of health and physique, then it is not given high status or adequate reward anywhere in the world. If it were possible to measure the energy consumed in pregnancy and childbirth, it would become abundantly clear that any similar effort in other social relations would be more substantially rewarded. The analogies between work and childbearing break down, however, mainly because of the impossibility, until very recently and then with only a small proportion of the world's women, of biologically avoiding or refusing such "work." But even this is not as absolute as it may seem—there have been recorded incidents of "birth" strikes in which women who were required to bear more slaves deliberately aborted or resorted to infanticide rather than produce more children for their masters.[55] Furthermore, women's reproductive function has been manipulated to produce more laborers when conditions of development and accumulation demanded it and vice versa; "family policy," consisting of financial incentives paid to usually male-dominated families for women to bear more children, as in France after 1950, or social pressures to have fewer children, as in China after 1955 and India currently, are indications of the economic influence of women's work in childbearing. That childbearing is set within household social relations means that this work is performed within a framework of both generalized and particular male authority structure, which in turn results in its being a major transfer of women's nonwage work to other producers.

In childrearing, women, again as subordinate workers within subordinate social relations, provide a service at the lowest possible labor cost, often for nothing more than their basic needs or less. Within any economic community the cost of the unproductive years of a child, that is, the period when he or she consumes but does not produce, is disproportionately borne by the family and particularly the women within the family when they both care for and sometimes completely provide for their children. The process or economic transfer is vividly illustrated in the cases when adult or near-adult laborers migrate from the location of their upbringing to another country or region where employers purchase the labor without having to pay (via a "family" wage, social security, schooling, and other social infrastructure charges) any of the cost of upbringing. In the case of Botswana women left on the land when their men had already migrated to work in South Africa not only care for the children but also work in the fields to provide food, clothing, and shelter for them.[56] This production of adult laborers by women also occurs in rural-town labor migration, which is one reason why labor in countries with a large population within peasant-lord social relations can supply to the world cheap labor, cheaper that is, than when the cost of reproduction is borne by women and families who have an above-subsistence level of consumption and a life expectancy above that of an exploited farmer. It has been argued that this function of women in third-world countries is the principal economic reason for their continued subordination.[57]

Even in situations where a "family" wage is received, the child care services of women represent a large service production at low economic cost to the wider society. The insistence that childbearing and childrearing are the necessary and essential work of women has been used to oppose the building of nurseries and child care centers where the service could be produced within different social relations.

Finally, housework that includes cleaning, repair, cooking, and budgeting represents a maintenance of both capital, in the form of housing, and labor in those members of the family, including the houseworker herself, who supply wage labor elsewhere. The household woman worker supplies a service not only at low economic cost but also one that improves the efficiency of workers being maintained. During the campaign to revalue household work in China in the 1950s it was argued that one important part of housework was to protect the man from domestic worries in order that he could conserve all his energy for work.[58] Economic estimates have been made of the proportion of any country's total national product constituted by household service production, and these range from one third to one half of total national product.[59] The income received for it by women cannot, of course, be estimated, for no wages are involved. It represents a massive output for low material reward, and household social relations are a mechanism for harnessing and delivering the results of women's labor to the rest of the social formation.

One other important economic function household relations play is that of a reserve of labor. The financial structure of social formations in which heads of households are paid a "family" wage means that it is possible to withdraw women from full-time household work into wage labor when needed and push them back into the household when they are no longer needed.[60] This process accounts for the fluctuations experienced in the numbers of women in the wage work force at different times. Furthermore, the withdrawal of such labor from wage work does not usually cost the employer as much as an equivalent male worker. The cost is borne by the members of the household in the form of lowered consumption and harder work for the women, for they are expected, through extended service and goods production, to make up the lost wage.

The psychological and ideological functions of household social relations within the social formation are less distinct than the economic aspects. The most important and more easily observable of these is the type of worker the woman becomes when entering wage labor. As wage workers women initially appear less resistant to employer domination, meaning that they sustain a greater pace of production and make fewer demands for better wages and working conditions and sometimes oppose others who make such demands. This is partly due to the general ideology of male domination and female subordination, which makes being female a social disadvantage used by employers to sustain a greater degree of labor control. But it is also a transfer of a consciousness of subordination from household social relations to that of the factory or office.[61]

Likewise, patriarchial domination within the family household may be so severe that the worst of employer domination may seem desirable in comparison; this was identified as one factor in why rural young women in Malaysia tolerated authoritarian and exploitative working conditions in the garment and textile industries of the Penang Free Industrial Zone.[62] The isolation some housewives experience also makes the social contact at work a desirable factor and therefore a psychological compensation for low wages and poor working conditions. All of these factors mean that women are found in disproportionately large numbers within the ranks of the workers covered by enterprise labor market relations—the social relations in which, currently, employer domination is the greatest. These are also the factors that have made feminist revolutionaries argue that the subordination of women and the use of women in wage labor was a deliberate attempt to break the militancy of the working class.[63]

There is a deeper and even less distinct role that the domination of women within household social relations may play, that is, as a compensation to males for the domination they may also experience within the social relations that govern their work. A male wage or salaried worker may find it difficult to psychologically accept authoritarian action taken against him at his place of work; the frustration and anger he then feels may be released by equally repressive and authoritarian and sometimes violent action taken against others over whom he may have power, namely, the subordinated woman household worker. The subordination of women within household social relations then appears as a psychological safety valve, or earthing point, for the psychological burdens borne by males who work in particularly stressful occupations within an industrialized society.[64] In this way the position of women in the household is integrated into the total power configuration of the social formation.

These are some of the social-psychological factors that provide the nonmaterial support for the continuance of household social relations and cause such a fierce resistance to transforming them and to the demands made by women for equality and emancipation in general.[65]

TRANSFORMATION: WOMEN'S CONSCIOUSNESS

Household social relations may be transformed either by the destruction of the household as a basic social unit and its replacement by another social structure in which child care and household services would be performed under different social relations or by the continuation of the household as a social unit but with internal relations transformed to eliminate the woman subordinate worker producing household services. It would be replaced by a joint production by members of the household of those household tasks and child care that cannot be contracted out to other social relations. Such transformations require, however, the destruction of the wider structure of the subordination of women

because household social relations are sustained by the acceptance by many women of the tenets of an ideology that state that
it is they who should rear children and perform household services under conditions of male authority.

In no social relations other than those of the household
are the subordinate workers subjected to a society-wide ideology
that seeks to define the place, role, and position of the worker;
the nature of the work performed; and the conditions under
which it is to take place. The consciousness of women arising
from the domination within the household is then only part of
the overall consciousness produced by the much broader and
more pervasive ideology incorporating the general subordination
of women.

Any attempt at transformation of household social relations is, therefore, faced with the task of dismantling the ideology
and reducing the level of its acceptance and internalization as a
truth by women household workers. In this, women's movements
are faced by a phalanx of accrued social power (including the
world's major religions) opposed to the transformation of household social relations and the disappearance of the "traditional"
or religious functions ascribed to women. As already noted, even
in the postrevolutionary situations in the Soviet Union, China,
Algeria, and Cuba, where there is a nominal adherence to an
ideology of total sexual equality, household social relations have
persisted and the ideology of egalitarianism has not been able to
overcome the material and ideological forces that give women a
less than equal place within the household.

In any serious attempt at transformation, activists and
movements are not assisted by the internal dynamics oft he
household and the consciousness emerging from them. Although
there are reports of women communalizing household services
work and childrearing,[66] such solidarity is strongly mitigated by
the eventual return to the individualized power relations that
exist within the household. Such fragmentation of subordinated
workers, within the same social relations and producing the same
goods and services, provides a formidable barrier against the
development of collective consciousness strong enough to transform social relations. There are, however, some contradictions
and dynamics between the household form of social relations

and the social formation that may eventually be the base for broader attempts to eliminate subordination of women within the household.

The most important of these is the need or demand by dominant groups that women perform wage work, as well as household work. Although, as discussed earlier in this chapter, the mere acquisition of wage work did not destroy household social relations, under modern conditions it produced material and consciousness aspects of importance for continuing change. Once the wage work of women moved beyond that of unskilled and menial factory, mine, and mill and domestic labor and became concentrated on clerical, administrative, and services, it became necessary for women to be afforded the opportunity for higher educational standards. At the same time the movement for entry to higher education and professions was spearheaded in Western Europe and North America at the turn of the century by the confined wives and daughters of professional men. Women began to appear in the professions and in white-collar work, although husbands of these women may still have been unskilled manual workers. The existence of women practicing the professions exposed the myth of female inferiority while white-collar wage work brought education, some financial independence, and the end to the isolation of the household. The contradiction between the existence of skilled or professional women workers and the ideology of subordination—that women's work was, if not exclusively, household services and was always menial and inferior to that of men's—laid part of the base for current feminist movements.

Linked to this contradiction are many of the policy positions of feminist movements that have obvious intent to transform household social relations. The earlier fervent belief that wage work would in the short term transform women's place in the household has already been mentioned. Likewise, the proposition that wages should be paid for housework would certainly, if it came into effect, transform household social relations by revaluing housework and providing financial independence for women without resorting to the double shift. In Argentina of the 1930s the towns were swollen by a mass of women migrating alone from the rural areas, where male but not female labor was needed in ranching. Eva Peron, the popular leader and wife of General Peron, the president of the military regime, had as her constituency this mass of urban poor women, and one of her proposals for them was that a wage should be paid for housework.[67] A similar demand has been made by feminists at one time calling themselves the Wages for Housework Campaign.[68] These demands have played their role in a general educational manner instead of having made any substantial real progress toward achieving wages for housework.

More important have been the efforts of feminist groups and movements led by the better educated professional and intellectual women to raise the consciousness of women in general through the examination and reexamination of the condition of women and their roles as defined by tradition and culture. These groups comprise the mainstream of the feminist movements of the last quarter of the twentieth century. With a financial power stemming from their base in the richest countries, they have been able to raise questions about, and provide information on, the condition of women throughout the world, as the explosion of literature on the subject testifies.[69] Among these and other groups also, experiments with family forms have been made, principally in the direction of communes. Although most of these latter have not persisted, the more mundane experiments in work sharing in the household have had a more enduring effect. These groups have been able to secure legislation such as long-term paternity leave and leave of absence for males, allowing the potential for males to take up child care. Thus, there exists already an alternative model of household service production in which there is a male-female joint work and child care sharing, as well as joint finance and property and subcontracting of many household service tasks.[70] These are isolated cases but serve as an indication of the introduction of new sets of social relations. It is not inconceivable that such practices may be easier to institute in societies in which family forms are not traditionally nuclear and in which female power within the household is not so constrained as in the main location of these experiments, which is Western Europe and North America.[71]

The modern feminists have also demonstrated that traditional theories of revolution are not sufficient to eliminate household social relations and that any proposal for revolutionary transformation or society that does not attack more fundamentally the material and ideological forces sustaining household social relations will, from the standpoint of subordinated women and general social justice, fail.

Although models of transformed household social relations exist and consciousness has changed in the industrialized countries and within some groups in poorer countries, these can be seen only as the very beginning of a process aimed at transformation. For the bulk of women in the world labor force, household social relations persist, and as rural-urban migration continues, the numbers within household social relations continue to grow.

NOTES

1. The literature on the general condition of women throughout the world has expanded enormously during the last two decades, and some of it served as materials for this chapter. However, there are fewer studies aimed directly at analyzing the internal relations of the household. Anthropological studies (for example, those appearing in a special issue of *Antropologiska Studier*(1981) no. 30–31, "Women: on work and household systems") and novels and autobiographical accounts were therefore of some importance. For nonparticipant observations and investigations in this area, see appendix.

2. For a review of the concept of a "household," see Prudence Woodford-Berger, "Women in Houses: The Organisation of Residence and Work in Rural Ghana," *Antropologiska Studier*(1981) no. 30–31, pp. 1–31. See also Kathie Friedman "Households as Income-Pooling Units" in Joan Smith, Immanuel Wallerstein, Hans-Dieter Evers eds., *Household and the World Economy* (Beverly Hills, Sage, 1984) pp. 37–55.

3. This applies even when authority over the tasks within the household rests with those who perform them. See, for example, Gunilla Bjeren, "Female and Male in a Swedish Forest Region: Old Roles Under New Conditions," *Antropologiska Studier*(1981) no. 30–31, pp. 57–58.

4. For a notable exception to this general statement, see "Mary Searle-Chatterjee, "Reversible Sex Role: The Case of Benares Sweepers," in *Women in Development*, vol. 2 (London, Pergamon Press, 1982).

5. See, for example, C. S. Pincus, *Double Duties: An ACtion Plan for the Working Wife* (New York, Chatham Square Press, 1978).

6. For precise accounts of women's rural work in the third world but where their "reproductive role" is generally assumed rather than analyzed, see Lourdes Beneria, ed., *Women and Development: The Sexual Division of Labor in Rural Societies* (New York, Praeger, 1982); for Denmark, see Henrik Morkeberg, "Working Conditions of Women Married to Self-Employed Farmers," *Sociologica Ruralis* (1978), 18(2/3):91–216; and for detailed accounts of the total divisions of rural women's time, see T. Scarlett Epstein and Rosemary A. Watts, eds., *The Endless Day: Some Case Material on Asian Rural Women* (Oxford, Pergamon, 1981).

7. See Deniz Kandiyoti, "Turkey's Women," *Signs* (Autumn 1977), 3(1):57–74. The economic importance of the dual work of women is often recognized in customary law and tradition; see, for example, Ann Stoler, "Class Structure and Female Autonomy in Rural Java," *Signs* (Autumn 1977), 3(1):74–92.

8. See, for example, Lourdes Arizpe, "Women in the Informal Labour Sector—Mexico City," *Signs* (Autumn 1977), 3(1):30–35, and C. K. Dabaya, *Economic Activities of Voluntary Womens Organisations in the City of Bombay* (Bombay, Ramnarain Ruia College, 1982).

9. See, for example, Shulamith Firestone, *The Dialectic of Sex: The Case for the Feminist Revolution* (London, Jonathan Cape, 1971).

10. See, for example, Maria Mies, *The Origins of the Sexual Division of Labour* (The Hague, Institute of Social Studies, occasional paper, 1979).

11. Marcia Guttentag and Paul F. Secord, *Too Many Women: The Sex Ratio Question* (Beverly Hills, Sage, 1983).

12. The most well-known example of this view is that of Frederich Engels, *The Origin of the Family, Private Property and the State* (first published 1884) (New York, Pathfinder Press, 1972), and see the introductory discussion in this edition by Evelyn Reed.

13. See, for example, Eva Figes, *Patriarchial Attitudes* (New York, Panther Books, 1972), especially pp. 37–48.

14. The displacement of women from positions of glorification and the thesis that all religions originally had a white goddess is ably argued by Robert Graves, *The White Goddess* (London, Faber and Faber, 1981).

15. See, for example, B. Malinowski, *The Sexual Life of Savages in North Western Melanesia* (New York, Routledge, 1932).

16. See Nancy Chodorow, *The Reproduction of Mothering: Psychoanalysis and the Sociology of Gender* (Berkeley, University of California Press, 1978).

17. Among the many discourses on this point, see, for example, Z. Ferge, "Relation Between Paid and Unpaid Work of Women, a Source of Inequality; with Special Reference to Hungary," *Labor and Society* (April 1976), 1(2):42. The connection has been made for some time "ignorant et asservie la femme a jusqu' ici subi de la force dans les fait relatifs a la reproduction," August Fabre, *Le Feminisme, ses origines et son avenir* (Nimes, no publisher, 1897), p. 71.

18. Feminist descriptions of the repressive nature of housework and husband care are found in Lee Comer, *Wedlocked Women* (Leeds, England, Feminist Books, 1974), and Kate Millet, *Sexual Politics* (London, Sphere Books, 1971), pp. 98–108; see also Diana Leonard Barker and Sheila Allen, eds., *Dependence and Exploitation in Work and Marriage* (New York, Longmans, 1976). For a plea to reconsider the "onerous housework" thesis, see Joseph J. Valadez and Remi Clignet, "Household

as an Ordeal: Culture of Standard Versus Standardization of Culture," *American Journal of Sociology* (January 1984), 89(4):812–35.

19. See, for example, the discussion of the constrains on male power and on the "corporate" nature in peasant and farming production in S. C. Rogers, "Female Forms of Power and the Might of Male Dominance: A Model of Female/Male Interaction in Peasant Societies," *The American Ethnologist* (1975), no. 2, pp. 727–56; Ester Boserup, *Women and Their Role in Peasant Societies* (London, University of London, Centre of International Area Studies, 1974); Eva Skold Westerland, "Women's Work and Modernisation in Gorsko Selo, a Yugoslav village," *Antropologiska Studier*(1981) no. 30–31, pp. 37–55; Martine Segalen, *Love and Power in the Peasant Family of Rural France in the Nineteenth Century* (Oxford, Basil Blackwell, 1983); the argument that sex discrimination is not at the base of the plight of rural women is found in Sjafri Mangkuprawira, "Married Women's Work Pattern in Rural Java," in Epstein and Watts, *Endless Day*, pp. 85–107.

20. See, for example, Nadia H. Youssef, "Women and Agricultural Production in Muslim Societies," *Studies in Comparative International Development* (1977), 12(1):41–58; Shrimati Asha Dhar, "Rural Women of India," *Kurukshetra* (March 1978), 26(2):4–6.

21. See Felicity Edholm, "The Unnatural Family," in (collectively edited), *The Changing Experience of Women* (Oxford, Martin Robertson, 1982), pp. 166–77.

22. See Hans Medich, "The Proto-industrial Family Economy: The Structural Function of Household and Family During the Transition from Peasant Society to Industrial Capitalism," *Social History* (October 1976), no. 3, pp. 291–315.

23. For different views concerning allocation of work in the household and the causes of the current patterns in industrialized societies, see Michael Geerken and Walter Gove, *At Home and at Work: The Family's Allocation of Labor* (Beverly Hills, Calif., Sage, 1983), and Catherin Hall and and Susan Himmelweit, "Development of Family and Work in Capitalist Society" in *The Changing Experience of Women* (Milton Keynes, England, Open University Press, 1983).

24. See, for example, R. O'Day, "Women in the Household; a Historical Analysis, 1500–1850," in *The Changing Experience of Women*, pp. 1–56.

25. See Jane Lewis, *Women in England 1870-1950: Sexual Divisions and Social Change* (Sussex, England, Wheatsheaf, 1984), especially pp. 149–56. This development occurred unevenly among different countries, but the hegemonic position of the United Kingdom throughout the formative period makes its history illustrative of general international trends.

26. See, for example, the survey findings in A. Oakley, *Sociology of Housework* (London, Martin Robertson, 1974), and the discussion in Valadez and Clignet, "Household as Ordeal."

27. See, for example, Jane L. Papart, "Class and Gender on the Copperbelt: Women in Northern Rhodesian Mining Communities 1926-1964" (unpublished paper, 1985).

28. For discussion on this important development, see Mary Moore, *The Defeat of Women*, (London, Macmillan, 1935), B. Ehrenreich and D. English, "The Manufacture of Housework," *Socialist Revolution* (October/December 1975) 5(26); Susan Strasser, "The Business of Housekeeping: The Ideology of the Household at the Turn of the Twentieth Century," *Insurgent Sociology* (1978), 8(2,3); B. Rogers, *The Domestication of Women* (New York, Tavistock Publications, 1980).

29. See, for example, Christine E. Bose and Philip L. Bereano, "Household Technologies: Burden or Blessing," in Jan Zimmermand, *The Technological Woman:*

Interfacing with Tomorrow (New York, Praeger, 1983), pp. 83–93 and Philip Bereano, Christine Bose and Erik Arnold, "Kitchen Technology and the Liberation of Women from Housework" in Wendy Faulkner and Erik Arnold eds., Smothered by Invention: Technology in Women's Lives (London, Pluto Press, 1985) pp. 162–81.

30. See, for example, E. Gundrey, Jobs for Mothers (London, Hodder and Stoughton, 1967), p. 59.

31. Bose and Bereano, "Household Technologies."

32. See, for example, D. F. Bryceson, "Proletarianization of Women in Tanzania," Review of African Political Economy (London) (January-April 1980), 17:4–7; Peter Peek, Family Composition and Married Female Employment: The Case of Chile, Population and Employment Working Paper no. 13 (Geneva, International Labor Office, 1975).

33. See Ferge, "Relation Between Paid and Unpaid Work," and Bernice Flatzer Rosenthal, "The Role and Status of Women in the Soviet Union: 1912 to the Present" in Ruby Rohrlich-Leavitt, ed., Women Cross Culturally: Change and Challenge (The Hague, Mouton, 1975), pp. 429–55.

34. Delia Davin, Women Work: Women and the Party in Revolutionary China (Oxford, Clarendon Press, 1976); and see, for example, Joan M. McCrea, "The Social Economic Role of Women in the People's Republic of China," Women's Studies International Forum (1983), 6(1):57–72.

35. Terminology is sometimes confusing. Many writers use the term unpaid, which means not paid in money. Others, recognizing the confusion of paid/unpaid, use unwage. For a discussion of the various definitions see Joan Smith "Nonwage Labour and Subsistence' in Smith, Wallerstein and Evers "Households and the World-Economy" pp. 64–89.

36. This is the case across a wide range of religions, cultures, and customs; see, for example, Madelain Farah, Marriage and Sexuality in Islam: A Translation of al-Ghazali's Book on the Etiquette of Marriage from the Ihya (Salt Lake City, University of Utah Press, 1984).

37. For an example of the lack of enforcement of basically protective laws for women, see C. Smart, The Ties That Bind: Law, Marriage and the Reproduction of Patriarchal Relations (London, Routledge, Kegan, Paul, 1984).

38. Ezra F. Vogel, Japan's New Middle Class (Los Angeles, University of California Press, 1963), p. 193; Michael Berger, "Japanese Women—Old Images and New Realities, The Japan Interpreter (Spring 1976), 11(1):56–57; D. Robins-Mowry, The Hidden Sun: Women of Modern Japan (Boulder, Colorado, Westview Press, 1983).

39. Vanessa Maher, "Kin, Clients and Accomplices: Relationships Among Women in Morocco," in Diana Barker and Sheila Allen, eds., Sexual Divisions and Society: Process and Change (London, Tavistock, 1976), pp. 52–75.

40. Oakley, Sociology of Housework.

41. Robins-Mowry, The Hidden Sun.

42. See, for example, Kristina Bohman, "Houses, House-Work and Kinship: Aspects of the Female Sphere in a Colombian City," Antropologiska Studier(1981) no. 30–31, pp. 115–41.

43. See chapter 5, Enterprise Labor Market Social Relations.

44. See chapter 6, Self-Employment Social Relations.

45. Oakley, Sociology of Housework, p. 131; M. Mitterauer and R. Sieder, Patriarchy to Partnership from the Middle Ages to the Present (Oxford, Basil Blackwell, 1982).

46. See Elise Boulding and M. Wallace, *Black Macho and the Myth of Super-woman* (London, John Calder, 1979).

47. K. Bohman, "La Mujer Proletaria en un Barrio de Medellin" (Research Paper, Medellin, 1977), as quoted in Ofelia Gomez, "Women Wage Labour and Worker's Organisation: A Case-Study in Colombia (The Hague Institute of Social Studies, unpublished master's thesis, 1980), p. 95.

48. Eva Evers Rosander, "Female and Male Spheres of Activity in Soza, Ceuta: A Case Study," *Antropologiska Studier*(1981) no. 30–31, pp. 87–101; see also Papart, "Class and Gender." Significantly internal conflicts within households arising from a changed economic position of women led to charges of witchcraft and a nation-wide "witch hunt" in Benin, West Africa see, Georg Elwert "Conflicts Inside and Outside the Household: A West African Case Study" in Smith, Wallerstein and Evers eds., *Households and the World-Economy*, pp. 272–296.

49. Olive Schreiner, *Woman and Labour* (London, Fisher Unwin, 1911), p. 68.

50. For a review of the economic reasons and purported theory behind such exclusions, see M. Mertens, "La Valeur Economique du Travail Menager," in *La Femme dans Notre Society, Documents CEPESS* (1965), 4(2):100–6.

51. *Ibid*.

52. See Susan Himmelweit and Simon Mahun, "Domestic Labour and Capital," *Cambridge Journal of Economics* (1977), 1(1):15–31; Jean Gardiner, "Women's Domestic Labour," *New Left Review* (1975), no. 89, pp. 47–58.

53. See, for example, L. Beneira, "Reproduction, Production and the Sexual Division of Labour," *Cambridge Journal of Economics* (September 1979), 3(3):203–225; N. J. Sokoloff, *Between Money and Love: The Dialectics of Women's Home and Market Work* (New York, Praeger, 1981).

54. Sokoloff, *ibid*.

55. See, for example, Rhoda Reddock, "Women and Slavery in the Caribbean: A Feminist Perspective," *Latin American Perspectives* (Winter 1985), 12(1):63–80.

56. Michael Burawoy, "The Functions and Reproduction of Migrant Labor: Comparative Material from Southern Africa and the United States," *American Journal of Sociology* (1981), 81(5):1050–85.

57. Beneria, *Women and Development*.

58. Davin, *Women Work*.

59. See A. H. Amsden, ed., *The Economics of Women and Work* (Harmondsworth, England, Penguin, 1980).

60. L. J. Waite, "Working Wives 1940-60," *American Sociology Review* (February 1976), 41(1):65–80; for an eloquent description of the male fear of women's entry into the professions, see Schreiner, *Women and Labour*, pp. 242–43. See, for example, M. Gavron, *The Captive Wife*, (London, Routledge and McClean, 1966); Shelia Cunnison, "Participation in Local Union Organisation: School Meals Staff: A Case Study," in Eva Gamarnikow, David Margan, June Purvis, and Daphne Taylorson, eds., *Gender, Class and Work* (London, Heinemann, 1983), pp. 94–95; for a less clear case study of the union attitudes of women, see John Heritage, "Feminisation and Unionisation: A Case Study from Banking," in Gamarnikow et al., *ibid*, pp. 131–48.

61. See, for example, Gomez, "Women Wage Labor"; Papart, "Class and Gender."

62. Sivananthiram Alagandram, "Labour Relations in Malaysia: The State, Foreign Capital, Unions and the Young Women Workers in the Export Oriented

Industries" (The Hague Institute of Social Studies, unpublished masters thesis, 1981).

63. Alexandra Kollontai, *La Femme Nouvelle et la classe ouvriere* (Paris-Bruxelles, Les Cahiers de L'Eglantine, no. 13, 1932).

64. See, for example, the remarks made by M. A. Vanderreyd, "Le Travail professional de la Femme," in *La Femme dans Notre Societé,* Documents - CEPESS (1965), 4(2):2. For the view that all societies are hierarchical and each rank needs a lower order for its psychological sustenance, see Humphrey Knipe and George Maclay, *The Dominant Man: The Pecking Order in Human Society* (London, Fontana, 1973).

65. See, for example, the discussion in A. Dworkin, *Right-Wing Women: The Politics of Domesticated Females* (London, The Women's Press, 1983).

66. See Bohman, "Houses, House-Work and Kinship."

67. Nancy Hollander, "The Peronist Movement Reconsidered" (unpublished paper, 1979).

68. In Marxist terms, wages for housework meant that women would become productive workers and then acquire the revolutionary potential of all productive workers; see, M. Dala Costa, "Women and the Subversion of the Community," in *Power of Women and the Subversion of the Community* (Bristol, England, Falling Wall Press, 1972), and Selma James, *Women, the Union and Work, or . . . What Is Not To Be Done* (Pittsburgh, Know, 1974); for contending views on the nature of "wages for housework" strategies, see Silvia Federici, "Wages Against Housework," in E. Mallos, ed., *The Politics of Housework* (London, Allison & Busby, 1980), pp. 253–61, and Joan Laudes, "Wages for Housework—Political and Theoretical Considerations," in Mallos—*ibid.,* pp. 262–75; also "Myra Marx Ferree, "Satisfaction with Housework: The Social Context," in Sarah Fenstermaker Berk, ed., *Women and Household Labor* (Beverly Hills, Calif., Sage, 1980).

69. See, for example, Sheila Rowbotham, *Woman's Consciousness and Man's World* (Harmondsworth, England, Penguin, 1973), and for a review of the early period of the movement, see Barbara Deckward, *The Women's Movement: Political, Socio-economic and Psychological Issues* (New York, Harper and Row, 1975).

70. See Mitterauer and Sieder, *Patriarchy to Partnership;* and Susan Harding, "Family Reform Movements: Recent Feminism and Its Opposition," *Feminist Studies* (Spring 1981), 7(1):57–75.

71. See, for example, accounts in L. Gulati, *Profiles of Female Poverty: A Study of Five Poor Working Women in Kerala* (Oxford, Pergamon Press, 1982) and J. Massiah, *Women as Heads of Households in the Caribbean: Family Structure and Feminine Status* (Paris UNESCO, 1983).

AFTERWORD

There can be no traditional conclusion to this book, which has presented six forms of social relations of production, described the power relations of the dominant and subordinate groups within the forms, and discussed the consciousness and paths of transformation produced by such power relations. The objective, as explained in the introductory chapter, was to demonstrate the viability of a new approach and thereby change, however slightly, the way of seeing things, particularly the ways of perceiving categories of workers, classes, social conditions, politics, economic policy and the processes of change. If such an objective has even been partially achieved, then it goes without saying that prescriptions for social amelioration, change, or revolution will also change, derived as they are from a particular way of viewing the world. Of course, the approach would not have been presented if it were not thought that there were possibilities that such changes in vision, prescription, and perhaps strategies, would be positive and ultimately beneficial to the victims of unbalanced social and economic power.[1]

The manner of presentation of the material was purposefully not designed to satisfy the furious demand for short-term prognosis or the incessant search for a single cause. This is even more important to remember in the context of a global examination of unprotected workers, for a global analysis tends to raise the expectations of a global single cause and perhaps even a global prescription commensurate with the identified global cause. The approach presented here, although analyzing social relations horizontally across the world labor force, rather than vertically by nation-state, nevertheless still respects the autonomy of local variants. Thus, if it is true that those people uprooted from the land, thrown out of work, or born with a destiny to be part of a labor surplus respond to the appeals of millennialism and other forms of religious fundamentalism, then dire predictions can be made (given the rapid expansion of primitive labor market social relations) about the inevitable arrival of repressive, fundamentalist and antimodernist regimes. But such a view would be mechanistic, for it is also possible that the leadership of a social movement would respond to such a consciousness, born of the primitive labor market social relations, and weave into its secular prescriptions some vision of a poor person's heaven.[2] The result thus might just as equally be a modernizing socialist regime as an antimodernist fundamentalist one.

The political economy of international change begins with the consciousness and dynamics of power relations in production, of forms of social relations, but its route takes it through the teeming diversity of culture, religion, history and tradition. It is these that translate into forms of social action the chafing of the peasant under the domination of moneylender, landlord, or merchant; the anomie and bitterness of workers at the extremes of employer domination in the enterprise labor market; the frustration of being rejected that is felt by primitive labor market workers; the querulous insecurity of some occupations of the self-employed; and the emerging sense of injustice felt by the woman household worker. It is the elements of local diversity that will also interpret and provide instruments for the power of landlords trying to recapture lost social prestige in peasant-lord relations; of emerging rural employers in enterprise labor market farm enterprises; of embattled privileged minorities, fearful of, among other things, losing their labor-surplus life-style provided by primitive labor market workers; of overenthusiastic tax inspectors harassing self-employed; and of heads of households no longer confident of the continuing servitude of their women workers in household social relations. How all of this is fitted into, or fits into, strategies for reformist change, for stabilizing the status quo, or for revolution is then what makes politics and change at both the national and international levels. The analysis incorporated in the multiple social relations or production approach provides the fundamental themes, and the local circumstances provide the variations; the study of both is essential for any meaningful and fruitful social and political analysis.

In the last quarter of the twentieth century the number of unprotected workers is, for reasons given in the various chapters, increasing as a proportion of the world labor force. This development makes even more important an urgent reassessment of old approaches and movement toward a genuine openness to new approaches. Unprotected workers and the different social relations of production associated with them have for so long been excluded from economic, social and policy analysis and if included often only in misleading and blanket categories. Any approach should be welcome which can integrate or accommodate into policy and strategies the different dynamics, power groups, and consciousness emerging from different patterns of power relations. In general, as noted in the opening chapter, in policy planning, in devising strategies for political and social change, and in investigating the nature of human societies any social scientist or general observer of the human condition who ignores, or fails to analyze rigorously, the variety of patterns of power relations in production is likely to produce at best uneven and at worst self-defeating results.

NOTES

1. For a discussion of the various uses of the approach, see chapter 1.
2. As did Mao Zedong and his collaborators in the Red Army. See Ralph Thaxton, "Mao Zedong, Red Miserables and the Moral Economy of Peasant Rebellion in Modern China," in R. P. Weller and S. E. Guggenheim, eds., Power and Protest in the Countryside: Studies of Rural Unrest in Asia, Europe and Latin America (Durham, N.C., Duke University Press, 1982) pp. 132–56.

APPENDIX: REFERENCES
AND SOURCES

REFERENCES

In the writing of this book many hundreds of articles and books have been examined. In addition more than 7,000 clippings from the world's managerial, labor, and popular press have been consulted. Many of these were of little worth, but even those that were valuable were too numerous to be individually cited. To reduce citations the "for example" formula has been adopted; when this is used, it means that the reference cited provides a clear example of the general phenomenon under discussion. The reference selected may not necessarily be the best of those reviewed; it may be the more accessible, or the one that provides a review of the literature, or the one that is most clearly written, or simply the one closest at hand.

For this reason there is no general bibliography. Such a bibliography would be misleading on two grounds: first, it might indicate that somehow the book was based exclusively upon those references cited, which is not the case, as explained below, and second, it would perhaps give more importance to the "for example" citations than is deserved.

The notes are presented by chapter and all shortened references are from within the chapter, meaning that whenever a reference is shortened, it has been presented in full earlier in that chapter's notes. An index of authors is provided, through which a full reference may be traced.

WRITTEN SOURCES

The basic sources of this book have been the so-called secondary sources, that is, the reports and analysis of primary or field research done by other social scientists. Such references to reports and analysis have been gathered over a span of almost twenty years. While it is nearly always possible to replace the citations of earlier reports and articles with later ones in many cases both the earlier and later have been presented. The objective of this latter procedure is to indicate the unchanging nature, at least in the medium term, of the phenomena discussed or that for many years social analysts have been troubled with the same analytical problem.

BOOKS AND ARTICLES

Books often try to demonstrate an approach or a thesis and are, within a framework of study which itself attempts to present an innovative approach, of less utility than articles which are often more descriptive or analytical in orientation.

The bulk of references are to articles within social science journals identified by both computorized and manual search techniques. The difficulty with these sources is that conventional key words and catalogue sections follow disaggregation and subject divisions different from those of this study. Indirect search methods have then had to be adopted and important evidence for the subjects discussed in this book have often been found in material considered as marginal to some of the more standard analysis.

JOURNALS AND NEWSPAPERS

Of particular importance as source material was open access in a private library to the journals and newspapers of trade unions from over fifty countries, and similarly with management literature from the main capital exporting and trading nations. The reportage of labor conditions and power relations throughout the world from these two sources—the labor and managerial press—surpassed in detail the information found in the academic sphere.

UNWRITTEN SOURCES

The unwritten sources for this study have comprised interviews, intentional and unintentional participant observation, and nonparticipant observation.

INTERVIEWS

(a) *Structured* In the course of the work more than 50 structured interviews were concluded, principally with individuals from third-world countries who were involved with labor questions arising from professional experience in trade unions, state agencies, or universities and institutes.

(b) *Unstructured* As a faculty member, first, at the International Institute for Labor Studies in Geneva and then at the Institute of Social Studies, The Hague (Labor and Development Program), the author had numerous discussions at seminars, lectures, and informal conversations about the subject of this book, with people involved in labor from the third world.

INTENTIONAL PARTICIPANT OBSERVATION

Participant observation in anthropology means that the researcher actually participates in the social task or process upon which he/she will write and report. Intentional participant observation means that either the participation itself was for the purposes of observation or that within participation, although for some other purposes, observation was consciously pursued. Unintentional participation means that observation was not the objective, nor was it consciously considered at the time of participation. It is then "life-experience" used as observation at a later date.

In the preparation of this volume the author had three opportunities to engage in intentional participant observation: (1) as a foreign demolition worker within the illegal, black, or parallel economy (enterprise labor market social relations); (2) Working with self-employed dairy farmers in the French Alps (self-employment social relations—family or casual labor); (3) self-employed liberal professional (self-employment–household).

UNINTENTIONAL PARTICIPANT OBSERVATION

Before I began to consciously collect material for this study in 1972 a variety of work situations have produced memory tests for the reality of the reportage and social science analysis that were later examined. Some of these were: invoice typist (two years, enterprise labor market), greengrocer's assistant (one year, part-time self-employed), compulsory military service (two years enterprise labor market—enterprise corporatist variety), bus conductor (fifteen months, tripartite), unemployed migrant (approaching primitive labor market), journalist (two years, enterprise labor market), university lecturer (six years, enterprise corporatist).

NONPARTICIPANT OBSERVATIONS AND INVESTIGATIONS

Training in the investigatory techniques of critical social science and investigatory journalism has meant that I have rarely forgone the opportunity to interview people and seek the basis of their life conditions and consciousness. This is especially the case in third-world countries, where, with the exception of being a faculty member, I had no work experience. Writing an earlier book on Jamaica and the trade unions there brought me for the first time to the slums of a third-world city—Kingston—to observe and discuss with people there, and likewise, subsequently in Mexico, Belize, Guatemala, Egypt, and the Philippines, and also in rural areas, although with fewer interviews.

As an economic journalist past reports and investigations proved useful, as, for example, the reportage on the large European company and employment of foreign workers cited in chapter 5. Thus a year's continuous reporting on shoe retailing in the greater Los Angeles area yielded material on the problems and attitudes relating to ethnicity, supermarkets, concealed stock, and political attitudes of self-employed shopkeepers. Likewise, as an assistant editor of a small newspaper for a managerial suburb in another urban area of the United States, a vantage point was secured in the early 1960s to observe the growing emergence of a male managerial class and the frustration of their educated women worker housewives and the local political parties' use of the consciousness of them both.

It would be incomplete not to mention under the heading of observations the family social experience that provides the background to all intellectual work. In my case it was of my father's perigrinations through work situations ranging from a truck driver, salesman, and a night shift auto worker to a ceremonial position with a City of London Guild founded in the fifteenth century (enterprise labor market-tripartite-enterprise corporatist); of my mother's almost fifty years on the "double shift" (household-enterprise labor market); and of many other aunts, uncles, and grandparents whose experiences have been typical, although individual, of unprotected workers in industrialized capitalist countries. These must always be the existential inputs into any writing about work and social relations of production.

AUTHOR INDEX

SUBJECT INDEX